Nationalism and Moderr

In light of its remarkable resurgence in the last two decades, how do we explain the continuing power of nationalism today? Why do so many people remain attached to their nations? Are nations and nationalism recent phenomena, or can we trace their roots far back in history?

These are some of the questions addressed in Anthony Smith's thought-provoking analysis of recent approaches and theories of nations and nationalism. In the first part of his survey, Smith explores the varieties of 'modernism', the current orthodoxy in the field, concentrating on the work of such seminal figures as Gellner, Nairn, Giddens, Breuilly, Anderson and Hobsbawm. In the second part he presents the critics of modernism and their alternatives, from the primordialisms of van den Berghe and Geertz to the ethno-symbolic approaches of Armstrong and Smith, as well as the contributions of, among others, Seton-Watson, Greenfeld, Horowitz, Connor, Reynolds and Brass. The survey concludes with a brief analysis of some 'postmodern' approaches to issues of contemporary national identity, gender and nation, civic and ethnic nationalisms, as well as supranationalism and globalisation.

The first comprehensive theoretical survey of the subject of nationalism for nearly thirty years, *Nationalism and Modernism* provides a concise and balanced guide to its often confusing debates, revealing a rich and complex field rent by deep disagreements and rival paradigms. This work places nationalism firmly within the arena of current political and cultural thought and paves the way to more systematic and focused progress in this rapidly expanding field.

Anthony D. Smith is Professor of Ethnicity and Nationalism in the European Institute at the London School of Economics. His previous publications include *Theories of Nationalism* (1971, 1983), *The Ethnic Origins of Nations* (1986), *National Identity* (1991) and *Nations and Nationalism in a Global Era* (1995).

Nationalism and Modernism

A critical survey of recent theories of nations and nationalism

Anthony D. Smith

London and New York

First published 1998
by Routledge
11 New Fetter Lane, London EC4P 4EE

Simultaneously published in the USA and Canada
by Routledge
29 West 35th Street, New York, NY 10001

Typeset in Baskerville by Routledge
Printed and bound in Great Britain by TJ International,
Padstow, Cornwall

British Library Cataloguing in Publication Data
A catalogue record for this book is available from the British Library

Library of Congress Cataloging in Publication Data
Smith, Anthony D.
Nationalism and modernism: a critical survey of recent theories of nations
and nationalism / Anthony D. Smith
p. cm.
Includes bibliographical references and index.
1. Nationalism. I. Title.
JC311.N5388 1998
320.54'01–dc21   98-18648
                                                                                      CIP

0–415–06340–X (hbk)
0–415–06341–8 (pbk)

For my research students

from whom I have learnt so much

Contents

Preface

When Benjamin West was working on his celebrated painting of *The Death of General Wolfe* in 1770, he was visited by Archbishop Drummond and Sir Joshua Reynolds, who warned West not to paint Wolfe's death scene, unless he were to 'adopt the classic costume of antiquity, as much more becoming the inherent greatness of . . . [the] subject than the modern garb of war'. Whereupon West, we are told, replied that

> the event intended to be commemorated took place on the 13th September 1758 [actually 1759] in a region of the world unknown to the Greeks and Romans, and at a period of time when no such nations, nor heroes in their costume, any longer existed. The subject I have to represent is the conquest of a great province of America by the British troops. . . . If, instead of the facts of the transaction, I represent classical fictions, how shall I be understood by posterity!
>
> (John Galt, *The Life, Studies, and Works of Benjamin West, Esquire*, London, 1820: 2, 46–50, cited in Abrams 1986: 14)

Nationalism, in West's understanding, is not the exclusive property of the ancients, nor is heroic self-sacrifice for one's country. It is as much a phenomenon of the modern world as of the ancient. When the painting was finished, Reynolds, we are told, relented, and predicted that West's painting would 'occasion a revolution in the art'. He hardly realised that West was, in fact, one of the very first to portray a revolution in the style and content of politics, proclaiming an upheaval in society that has continued to our day.

Of course, we are privileged with the hindsight of that posterity to which Benjamin West, and the new age of which he was a child, had begun to appeal. We can see, as he could not, that he was painting an early icon of one of the great pillars, and forces, of modernity. Yet, when we look at his painting, it seems as old-fashioned as it is revolutionary. For, beneath the modern dress and the accessories of modern warfare, West has composed a *pietà*, a religious image of the dying hero as Christ. His painting, like that of *Marat Assassiné* by David, looks back to a Christian past, even as it looks forward to the modern age of secular nationalism. Perhaps, West is telling us, heroic self-sacrifice for king and country is as much ancient as it is modern, and that the nationalism which was already evident, and was to flourish so widely in the next two centuries, is merely a recent version of something far older?

This issue of the modernity or antiquity of nations has become central to the study of nationalism over the last few decades. The recent upsurge of ethnic nationalism in many parts of the world has only made more acute questions about the origins, nature and consequences of nationalism. The last ten years have witnessed a phenomenal growth in the practice and the study of nationalism. Since the unravelling of the Soviet Union, some twenty new states have been created, claiming to represent 'nations' which had been suppressed within empires or federations. In the former Soviet Union, Yugoslavia, Czechoslovakia and Ethiopia, we have witnessed both peaceful and violent examples of national secession, and in several more states there remains the distinct possibility of further successful partitions and secessions. Elsewhere, a score or more movements of ethnic protest have generated more or less hidden, and more or less hopeless, insurgencies and wars, and it is not difficult to find many other instances of uneasy coexistence of ethnic communities in both old and new states around the globe. In the last decade, not only has ethnic nationalism shown no signs of abating, it has flourished more widely and powerfully than at any period since the Second World War.

Such a remarkable resurgence has spurred an equally unprecedented increase in the number of investigations into the phenomena of ethnicity, nations and nationalism. Of course, there had been a considerable spate of studies of these phenomena in the 1950s and 1960s, the era of decolonisation in Africa and Asia. But well into the 1980s, scholarly attention had been devoted to other kinds of ideology and social movement, and in particular the varieties of Marxism and communism. The nation had received little attention apart from its combination (as junior partner) with the state – in the 'nation-state' – and nationalism had attracted much less interest than 'class', 'race' or 'gender'. All this changed after the fall of the Berlin Wall and the break-up of the Soviet Union. Since 1990, there has been a veritable flood of publications on ethnicity and nationalism – case-studies, reports, monographs, textbooks and latterly readers – or on sub-fields within this huge terrain. Indeed, even as I was writing my conclusions, several new books appeared, including Adrian Hastings' *The Construction of Nationhood* (1997), Craig Calhoun's *Nationalism* (1997), Sian Jones' *The Archaeology of Ethnicity* (1997), Lyn Spillman's *Nation and Commemoration* (1997), Michael Ignatieff's *The Warrior's Honour* (1998), as well as the new *Ethnicity Reader* by Montserrat Guibernau and John Rex (1997), not to mention several edited collections of essays on nations and nationalism. It has indeed become quite impossible to keep abreast of the tide of publications in the field.

Yet for all this scholarly activity, the *theory* of nations and nationalism has been much less well served. There was, it is true, a renewed interest in theory construction and in general perspectives in the later 1970s and early 1980s, but, as I hope to show, recent years have seen a turning away from attempts to provide overall theoretical accounts of nations and nationalism. Compared to the 1950s and 1960s – the period to which I devoted attention in my first overview of theories of nationalism – there has been a marked increase in the number of general approaches and theories. But, given the very few examples of general approaches and theories in that early period, the production of original theories and approaches still remains relatively modest compared to the veritable outpouring of other kinds of study in the field.

The present book aims to provide a critical survey of recent *explanatory* theories and approaches to nations and nationalism. It therefore constitutes a sequel to my first book, *Theories of Nationalism*, which was originally published in 1971. Though there have been some reviews of more recent theories in article form, there has been no recent comprehensive book-length attempt to provide a theoretical survey of the field, with the partial exception of Paul James' thought-provoking *Nation Formation* (1996) and the shorter evaluations of some theories of nationalism in Thomas Eriksen's equally stimulating *Ethnicity and Nationalism* (1993). Although the first chapter of the present work is devoted to summarising the position in the 1960s by way of necessary context and background, I have concentrated on perspectives, models and theories produced *after 1970* – from Elie Kedourie's second major work (*Nationalism in Asia and Africa*, 1971) and the reformulation by Ernest Gellner of his theory in *Nations and Nationalism* (1983), right up to Eric Hobsbawm's *Nations and Nationalism since 1780* (1990) and the second volume of Michael Mann's *The Sources of Social Power* (1993), as well as some of the 'postmodern' analyses of the last decade. In particular, I aim to examine in some detail the varieties of what remains the dominant orthodoxy in the field, namely the 'modernist' approach to nations and nationalism, while giving due weight to the many criticisms of modernism and to the main theoretical alternatives in the field.

I make no claim to be impartial as between the various approaches and paradigms. While I hope to have indicated both the strengths and the weaknesses in each approach or theory, as a partisan in the theoretical debate, I make no pretence to a value-free stance *vis-à-vis* the various theories and perspectives that I explore. This would in any case be out of the question in a field so riddled with deep disagreements and schisms. Instead, I have sought to give students new to the field some feel for the debates and intersecting monologues with which they are confronted, and to provide some kind of map by which to orient themselves in what must appear to be a particularly confusing intellectual terrain. Throughout, I have tried to bring out the insights, and problems, of each major approach, and some of the reasons behind particular formulations and objections.

The last chapter proved to be particularly problematic. In one sense it may seem out of place, since I argue that, with the possible exception of the 'gender-nation' theorists, recent postmodern and postmodernist approaches have eschewed grand theory and large-scale narratives. However, not to have included some analysis of the most recent general scholarly trends in the field, would have left students with a decidely incomplete, and therefore one-sided overview of the contemporary field. On the other hand, to have given each of these trends their proper attention would have doubled the length of the book, or required another volume. In the end, I compromised by focusing on four major trends, briefly describing their contributions, with special emphasis on their theoretical relevance or lack of it to an overall understanding of nations and nationalism.

A book of this scope required some clear parameters, if it was not to become unwieldy. I have confined myself, for the most part, to analysis of perspectives and theories of *nations and nationalism*, concentrating on books in the first place, and using articles only where they seemed to provide more succinct and accessible statements of the theory. The one exception to this focus was the need to introduce, in Part II, sections on *ethnicity*, because for primordialists, perennialists and ethno-symbolists, ethnic identity and community is a major point of reference and a vital building-block for theories of nations and nationalism. I have excluded, as far as possible, separate analysis of other major sources of cleavage and identity – racial, gender, class and religious – except where these sources are invoked by the theories of nationalism themselves; not because I thought them unimportant or irrelevant, but because to have treated them in any depth *in their own right* would have muddied the primary focus of the book and greatly extended its scope and length. In this respect, it was necessary, in the interests of clarity of focus and purpose, to hew close to the chosen path. Similarly, I have omitted the many important and fascinating normative debates which have developed over the last decade in political science and international relations, over the compatibility or otherwise of liberal democracy with mainly civic forms of nationalism. Once again, limitations of space and the desire to focus on explanatory theories precluded consideration of these debates.

I am all too conscious of the many other omissions, to some of which I allude all too briefly in the text or notes. The relationships between nationalism and such developing fields as migration, diasporas, post-colonialism, neo-fascism, genocide, ethnic cleansing, minority rights and multiculturalism – all much-discussed topics today – I have had to leave on one side. My reasons, apart from considerations of space, are twofold. First, I felt that serious examination of the contribution of these topics would have deflected attention from the book's main purpose, the description and evaluation of explanatory theories of nations and nationalism. Second, while analyses of these issues are vital and immensely valuable in their own right, it is by no means clear that they can further the task of explaining the origins, development and nature of nations and nationalism, or that they seek to do so. It seemed therefore advisable to exclude them from this theoretical survey.

I am also aware of failing to give due space to all the theories considered here, and of having done less than justice to the views of some authors. Once again, I have had to be selective and concentrate on the main representatives of each major approach in the field. If this has meant that I have treated cursorily, or overlooked some contributions – which is inevitable in a field that is expanding so fast – then I hope the authors concerned will accept my apologies for these omissions and for any errors, for which I take full responsibility.

The book is written primarily for students new to the field. I owe a great debt to my students, who in both good and difficult times have worked with me through many of the issues explored in this book, in our many absorbing and fruitful discussions in our Workshop on Ethnicity and Nationalism, in the master's course on Nationalism and in the conferences and seminars organised by The Association for the Study of Ethnicity and Nationalism at the London School of Economics. To them I dedicate this book, in the hope that we may continue to search for answers to the many questions raised by the fundamental issues of nations and nationalism.

Anthony D. Smith
London School of Economics
November 1997

Introduction
The modernist paradigm

A single red line traverses the history of the modern world from the fall of the Bastille to the fall of the Berlin Wall. Emerging fitfully in sixteenth- and seventeenth-century England and Holland, it rises bright and clear in late eighteenth-century France and America. Dividing and redividing lands and peoples, it stretches the length of Central and Latin America, pushes across southern, central, eastern, then northern Europe into Russia, India and the Far East, and then winds its way in many guises into the Middle East, Africa and Australasia. In its wake come protest and terror, war and revolution, the inclusion of some, the exclusion of many. At last, the red line becomes blurred, fragmented, faded, as the world moves on.

The name of the red line is nationalism, and its story is the central thread binding, and dividing, the peoples of the modern world. Though its forms are many, it is all one red line. The story of its progress is one of emergence and decline, the rise and fall of nations and nationalism. Historians may differ over the exact moment of nationalism's birth, but social scientists are clear: nationalism is a modern movement and ideology, which emerged in the latter half of the eighteenth century in Western Europe and America, and which, after its apogee in two world wars, is now beginning to decline and give way to global forces which transcend the boundaries of nation-states.

The rise and decline of nationalism?

At the outset, nationalism was an inclusive and liberating force. It broke down the various localisms of region, dialect, custom and clan, and helped to create large and powerful nation-states, with centralised markets and systems of administration, taxation and education. Its appeal was popular and democratic. It attacked feudal practices and oppressive imperial tyrannies and proclaimed the sovereignty of the people and the right of all peoples to determine their own destinies, in states of their own, if that was what they desired. Throughout the nineteenth and well into the twentieth centuries, nationalism was found wherever native elites fought to overthrow foreign imperial and colonial administrations, so much so that for a time it seemed indistinguishable from popular democracy. But already by the mid- to late nineteenth century, imperial and colonial rulers had found ways to siphon off the force of nationalism from its democratic base; the 'official nationalisms' of Tsarist Russia, Ottoman Turkey and Meiji Japan revealed the malleability of national sentiments, traditions and myths and the contortions of that single red line (Anderson 1991, ch.6).

Worse was to come. The large-scale mass-democratic nationalisms of the earlier nineteenth century were later joined by a host of small-scale mini-nationalisms led by intellectuals who appealed to language and cultural differences. Their successes after Versailles transformed the map of Europe, but more significantly presaged a world of self-aware and assertive ethnic nations. And these again were shadowed, ominously, by nationalisms that appealed to 'race' – to cranium, blood and genes – and to violence and the cult of brutality, the cradle of fascism. In the convulsions that followed, first in Europe, then across the world, the rampant red line of nationalism blended with the darker forces of fascism, racism and anti-Semitism, to produce the horrors of the Holocaust and Hiroshima.

In the revulsion which this has engendered in Europe, at least, there arose a desire among many to put an end to internecine conflicts and build a supranational continent free of national lines of division. The old faith in the unity and superiority of the nation and its state was shaken, and the new generations in the West, accustomed to travel, migrants and the mixing of cultures, no longer felt the full force of ancient national memories, traditions and boundaries. Of course, in other parts of the world, the red lines of nationalism still mark the violent antagonisms of ethnic cleavages, which threaten to dissolve the fragile unities of new territorial states. But even in Asia, Africa and Latin America, the earlier faith in the mass civic nation has been eroded by the economic and political realities of a very unequal international division of labour, the power of transnational forces, and ethnic cleavages within. In this respect, the advanced industrial societies only hold up a mirror to the future of the planet, when nations and nationalism will be revealed as transient forces which are fast becoming obsolete in a world of vast transnational markets, power blocs, global consumerism and mass communications (Horsman and Marshall 1994).

The rise and decline of modernism?

Alongside this gradual dissolution of the bonds of the nation in the minds and hearts of many of its members, there has been a parallel evolution in the scholarship and theory of nationalism. The idea that nations are real entities, grounded in history and social life, that they are homogeneous and united, that they represent the major social and political actors in the modern world – all this no longer seems as true as it did thirty and even twenty years ago.[1]

In the mid-twentieth century, right up indeed until the late 1960s and early 1970s, an optimistic and realist view of nations and nationalism prevailed. Whatever their other differences, scholars and theorists of nationalism seemed to agree on the psychological power and sociological reality of nations and nation-states. They spoke of the need to 'build' nations through such techniques as communications, urbanisation, mass education and political participation, in much the same way as one might speak of building machines or edifices through the application of design and technical devices to matter. It was a question of institutionalisation, of getting the necessary norms embodied in appropriate institutions, so as to create good copies of the Western model of the civic participant nation. This became a technical question of appropriate recipes for national development, of securing balanced and diversified economic growth, open channels of communication and expression, well organised and responsive publics, and mature and flexible elites. This was the way to replicate the successful model of the Western nation-state in the ex-colonies of Africa and Asia.[2]

In the late 1980s and 1990s, such optimism seems touchingly naive. Not only have the early democratic dreams of African and Asian states not been realised; the developed countries of the West too have experienced the rumblings of ethnic discontent and fragmentation, and in the East the demise of the last great European multinational empire has encouraged the unravelling of the cosmopolitan dream of fraternity into its ethno-national components. The great tides of immigration and the massive increase in communications and information technology have brought into question the earlier beliefs in a single civic nation with a homogeneous national identity which could be used as a model for 'healthy' national development. As a result, the old models have been discarded along with much of the paradigm of nationalism in which they were embedded. Moving beyond the older paradigm, new ideas, methods and approaches, hardly amounting to an alternative paradigm, yet corrosive of the established orthodoxies, have called into question the very idea of the unitary nation, revealing its fictive bases in the narratives of its purveyors. The deconstruction of the nation foreshadows the demise of the theory of nationalism.[3]

The paradigm of nationalism which was so widely accepted till recently is that of *classical modernism*. This is the conception that nations and nationalism are intrinsic to the nature of the modern world and to the revolution of modernity. It achieved its canonical formulation in the 1960s, above all in the model of 'nation-building'. This model had a wide appeal in the social sciences in the wake of the vast movement of decolonisation in Africa and Asia, and it had considerable influence on policy-makers in the West. But the model of nation-building, although the best known and most obvious, was by no means the only, let alone the most subtle or convincing, version of the modernist paradigm of nations and nationalism. In its wake there emerged a variety of other, more comprehensive and sophisticated models and theories, all of which nevertheless accepted the basic premises of classical modernism. It was not until the 1970s and 1980s that there emerged a series of critiques which have called into question the basic assumptions of that paradigm, and with it the model of nation-building; critiques which on the one hand have revealed the nation as an invented, imagined and hybrid category, and on the other hand as modern versions of far older and more basic social and cultural communities. As we shall see, the story of the rise and decline of nations and their nationalisms in the modern world is mirrored in the recital of the rise and decline of the dominant paradigm of nations and nationalism, together with all its associated theories and models.

The last thirty years have seen an efflorescence of historical, comparative and case-studies of nationalism, which have built on but also moved beyond the earlier historical studies of nationalist ideology.[4] Though the *theory* of nations and nationalism has been less well served, there have also been several important new approaches to and models of 'nationalism-in-general'. Together, they have challenged earlier organic and 'essentialist' assumptions of the nation, and have refined and extended the basic paradigm of modernism beyond its classical formulation in the 'nation-building' model of the 1960s. These approaches and theories possess a number of features which the majority of scholars and theorists in the last three decades took for granted, including:

1   a sense of the power and unpredictability of nationalism, the idea that the ideology and movement of nationalism was one of the dominant forces in the modern world and that because it took many forms, it was not possible to predict where and when it could erupt;
2   on the other side, a sense of the problematic nature of the concept of the nation, the difficulty in pinning it down and providing clearcut definitions, but also a feeling that established historical nations were sociological communities of great resonance and power;
3   a belief in the historical specificity of nations and nationalism, that these were phenomena peculiar to a particular period of history, the modern epoch, and that only when that epoch drew to a close would nations pass away;
4   a growing emphasis on the socially created quality of all collective identities, including cultural identities, and hence an understanding of the nation as a cultural construct, forged and engineered by various elites to meet certain needs or cater to specific interests;
5   and therefore a commitment to sociological explanations which derive nations and nationalism from the social conditions and political processes of modernity, with a concomitant methodology of sociological modernism and presentism seeking data drawn mainly from the recent and contemporary worlds.[5]

Of course, not all the theorists to be discussed here share all of these assumptions, even among self-styled modernists. But there is sufficient convergence among many theorists to mark off the dominant paradigm of modernism from its critics. What these characteristics, taken together, suggest is a strong belief in the rise and decline of a powerful, but historically specific and problematic phenomenon, whose era of dominance was rooted in the revolutions of modernity and which is now gradually coming to its close. And in its wake, shadowing reality, we can trace the rise and gradual decline of its intellectual reflection, the dominant paradigm of the modern nation, classical modernism.

Aims and plan

This book is largely about the rise and portended decline of this dominant paradigm of nations and nationalism. Its purpose is fourfold. In the first place, it aims to examine the key assumptions of classical modernism and describe its rich varieties and developments through an analysis of the approaches and theories of some of its leading exponents. Second, it offers an internal critique of these approaches and theories on their own terms, and evaluates the strengths and limitations of the paradigm which they all share. Third, it explores and assesses some of the alternatives proposed by the main critics of classical modernism. A few of these critics have turned their backs entirely on the dominant paradigm, but most have accepted some of its premises while rejecting others and supplementing them with ideas drawn from a perennialist paradigm. Finally, there is an attempt to review some of the new developments in the field, draw up a balance-sheet of where we stand today in terms of theories of nationalism, and give some indications of fruitful lines of enquiry and progress in the field.

The book is divided into two parts, the first devoted to the varieties and problems of the modernist paradigm, the second to its critics and the alternatives they propose.

Part I examines the classical paradigm and its varieties. The first chapter briefly describes the rise of classical modernism as it shook off the assumptions and limitations of older ideas of the organic nation, and then sets out the main features of the classical paradigm in its heyday in the 1960s.

Subsequent chapters analyse the main varieties of the paradigm in the 1970s and 1980s. These include:

- the sociocultural version associated with the later views of Ernest Gellner, which links nations and nationalism to the needs of generating a 'high culture' for modernisation and industrial development;
- the socioeconomic models of Tom Nairn and Michael Hechter, which derive nationalism from the rational workings of the world economy and the social and economic interests of individuals;
- the more political versions of theorists like Charles Tilly, Anthony Giddens, Michael Mann and John Breuilly, which look at the relationship of nationalism to the sources of power, notably war, elites and the modern state;
- and the ideological versions of Elie Kedourie, and more recently Bruce Kapferer and Mark Juergensmeyer, which tend to see nationalism as a belief system, a form of religion surrogate or secular religion, and to link its emergence and power to changes in the sphere of ideas and beliefs.

The concluding chapter of the first part continues the theme of the development of classical modernism, as it were, beyond itself. The main theories in question, those of Eric Hobsbawm and Benedict Anderson, can be regarded both as Marxian varieties of classical modernism, but also as moving beyond some of the assumptions of that paradigm. Their respective formulations of the 'invented traditions' and the 'imagined community' of the nation have provided the seedbed for more radical 'postmodernist' developments in which the idea of national identity is treated as inherently problematic and broken down into its component narratives.

Part II explores the various critiques of classical modernism and its later developments. These range from moderate 'internal' to radical 'external' critiques. Among the latter, the most prominent are those that stress the 'primordial' quality of nations and nationalism, including the sociobiological versions represented by Pierre van den Berghe which have experienced a recent revival, and the cultural primordialism associated with Clifford Geertz, which has been criticised by 'instrumentalists' like Paul Brass. Less radical departures from modernist orthodoxies are represented by those like Walker Connor, Donald Horowitz and Joshua Fishman, who emphasise the psychological and kinship components of ethnicity and ethno-nationalism. Another group of critics is represented by those like John Armstrong and Steven Grosby, who cast doubt on the intrinsic modernity of nations and thereby revive the debate about the 'perennial' presence of nations.

The second chapter of Part II continues this discussion of pre-modern nations by considering the work of historians like Hugh Seton-Watson, Doron Mendels, Adrian Hastings and Susan Reynolds, who have re-examined the evidence for nationality and nationalism in pre-modern epochs, and thereby seek to decouple (some) nations from 'modernisation'. It then examines the work of John Hutchinson, John Armstrong and myself, who stress the cultural and 'ethno-symbolic' nature of ethnicity and nationalism. Whether they adhere to a more phenomenological approach and Barthian emphasis on the use of symbols and myths in maintaining ethnic boundaries, or to a more structural and ethno-historical approach to the formation of nations, they are critical of what they see as the modernist failure to grasp the recurring nature of ethno-symbolic ties and to ground their understanding of modern nations in the *longue durée* and in earlier ethnic myths, memories, symbols and traditions.

The final chapter of Part II provides a brief critical sketch of some of the many recent developments in the field, including analyses of the fragmentation and increasingly hybrid nature of national identity and the uses of 'situational' ethnicity; feminist accounts of gendered national projects, female national symbolism and the relations between gender and ethnicity; debates about the civic or ethnic nature of nationalism and its relations with liberal democracy; and the discussions about the demise of the nation-state in an era of both 'supranationalism' and globalisation processes. These developments are assessed less for their intrinsic merits than for their theoretical contributions to an overall understanding of nations and nationalism, and from this standpoint they are found to be limited and partial extensions or revisions of modernism.

A brief conclusion spells out the main theoretical problems and suggests that, while no unified theory is likely in such a complex and divided field, significant progress has been made in a number of directions, with the result that our understanding of these elusive and protean phenomena has been greatly enriched and deepened. We can envisage, at least, combinations of elements from the main paradigms in the field, which in turn may generate some fruitful historical and comparative research programmes for the elucidation of the most vexed issues in the field.

1 The rise of classical modernism

Three main issues have dominated the theory of nations and nationalism.

The first is ethical and philosophical. It concerns the role of the nation in human affairs. Should we regard the nation as an end in itself, an absolute value which is incommensurable with all other values? Or should we understand the nation and national identity as a means to other ends and values, a proximate value, and therefore bound to time, place and context, and especially to the conditions of a modern epoch?

The second is anthropological and political. It concerns the social definition of the nation. What kind of community is the nation and what is the relationship of the individual to that community? Is the nation fundamentally ethno-cultural in character, a community of (real or fictive) descent whose members are bound together from birth by kinship ties, common history and shared language? Or is it largely a social and political community based on common territory and residence, on citizenship rights and common laws, in relation to which individuals are free to choose whether they wish to belong?

The third is historical and sociological. It concerns the place of the nation in the history of humanity. Should we regard the nation as an immemorial and evolving community, rooted in a long history of shared ties and culture? Or are nations to be treated as recent social constructs or cultural artefacts, at once bounded and malleable, typical products of a certain stage of history and the special conditions of a modern epoch, and hence destined to pass away when that stage has been surpassed and its conditions no longer apply?

These three issues and the debates they have engendered recur continually in discussions of nations and nationalism. As we would expect, they often overlap and intertwine, and it is not unknown for theorists to take up clearcut positions on one issue, only to 'cross over' to the unexpected 'side' in one or other of the debates, to hold for example that nations are recurrent and immemorial yet means to other ends, or that they are social and political communities but constitute absolute values. Moreover, the third and last debate conflates two separate issues: the issue of the antiquity or modernity of the nation in history, and the question of its evolved or socially constructed nature. As we shall see, this conflation of issues makes it difficult to adhere to any simple characterisation of theorists or classification of approaches and theories in the field. Nevertheless, there is enough consistency among analysts and theories to propose a general classificatory scheme based in particular on the third of the above three issues. Such a classification reveals the main lines of debate in the field in recent decades, though it can serve only as an approximation to understanding of the logic at work behind particular approaches and theories.

The roots of classical modernism

Early forerunners

The earliest scholars of nationalism were in fact happy to conflate these issues, mingling an evolutionary account of the development of nations with a degree of voluntarism, and a prescription for political activism with a sense of the long-term ethno-cultural roots of nations. Michelet, for example, viewed the nation as the best defence for individual liberty in the era of fraternity. The French Revolution had ushered in a Rousseauan religion of patriotism, of 'Man fraternising in the presence of God', with France, 'the common child of nations', surrounded by sympathetic countries like Italy, Poland and Ireland, whose nationalisms belonged to Mazzini's Young Europe movement. At the same time, he shared the naturalist assumption of Sieyes and others for whom nations existed outside the social and legal bond, in nature.[1]

For Lord Acton, on the other hand, the central question is ethical: the extent to which the (French) theory of national unity 'makes the nation a source of despotism and revolution', whereas the libertarian (English) theory of nationality harks back to the Glorious Revolution of 1688 and regards the nation 'as the bulwark of self-government, and the foremost limit to the excessive power of the State'. For Acton, the continental idealist view of

> nationality does not aim at either liberty or prosperity, both of which it sacrifices to the imperative necessity of making the nation the mould and measure of the State. Its course will be marked with material as well as moral ruin, in order that a new invention may prevail over the works of God and the interests of mankind.
>
> (Acton 1948: 166–95)

Acton's conservative analysis nevertheless vindicates multinational empires, like the Habsburg, on the ground that, unlike the national state, it can 'satisfy different races'. His general commitment to diversity is not unlike that of Moser and Herder; and his belief in liberty he shares with John Stuart Mill who argued for the right of national self-determination and collective voluntarism.[2]

Perhaps the most influential of these early analyses was that contained in a lecture of 1882 by Ernest Renan, which he delivered to counter the militarist nationalism of Heinrich Treitschke. Renan combines a sense of ethno-cultural formation in Europe over the *longue durée* with a belief in the active political commitment of members of the nation. Renan starts with a contrast that is to have a long history: between the fusion of 'races' in the nations of Western Europe, and the retention of ethnic distinctiveness in Eastern Europe. In France, by the tenth century, the idea of any difference in race between Gallic and Frankish populations had disappeared; what counts today are the shared experiences and common memories (and forgettings) of the members, which makes the nation

> a soul, a spiritual principle. . . . A nation is a great solidarity, created by the sentiment of the sacrifices which have been made and of those which one is disposed to make in the future. It presupposes a past; but it resumes itself in the present by a tangible fact: the consent, the clearly expressed desire to continue life in common. The existence of a nation is a plebiscite of every day, as the existence of the individual is a perpetual affirmation of life.
>
> (Renan 1882, cited in Kohn 1955: 135–40)

In these early commentaries on the principle of nationality, written with specific political developments in mind, there is no attempt to fashion a general theory applicable to all cases, or to resolve the antinomies of each issue in a coherent and systematic manner. This was left to the next generation. By the late nineteenth century, when the concept of 'nation' was often used interchangeably with that of 'race', more comprehensive and reductionist schemes emerged. The racist schema of biological struggle for mastery of organic racial nations was only one, albeit the most striking and influential. Even the Marxists were not immune, despite their official instrumentalist attitude to nationalism. In judging nationalisms by their revolutionary uses, Marx and Engels had also been swayed by their German Romantic and Hegelian inheritance, with its stress on the importance of language and political history for creating nation-states and their animus against small, history-less, as well as backward, nations. Their followers took over this contempt for the 'unhistorical nations', thereby allowing to the concept of the nation a certain historical and sociological independence, and blurring the insistence on the dependance of nationality on the growth of capitalism and its bourgeois ruling classes.[3]

We can see this ambivalence on all the major issues – ethical, anthropological and historical – in the work of the Austro-Marxists like Otto Bauer. On the one hand, Bauer traces the long evolution of European nationalities from their ethnic foundations and class formations into 'communities of character'; on the other hand, he and his associates believed it was possible to influence the course of national (and international) evolution by active political intervention which would separate the principle of cultural nationality from territorial location and political rights. In this conception, the principle of nationality is both an absolute and a proximate value, both an evolved ethno-cultural community and a class-constructed social category. By organising nations within a wider multinational state, it would be possible both to preserve their unique historical character and also ensure that they contributed to wider societal integration and the realisation of social freedom and abundance.[4]

Even among the nationalists themselves, we find the same permutations and inconsistencies. Some, it is true, followed the principles of German Romanticism to their conclusion and became full-blooded organicists, believing in the seamless, immemorial and even biological character of nations. Others were less consistent, believing with Mazzini that, though geography, history, ethnic descent, language and religion might determine much of the character and situation of the nation, political action and the mobilisation of the people were essential if the nation was to be 'reawakened' and recalled to its sacred mission. From an early period, these dilemmas of evolution and intervention, of 'structure' and 'agency', were as acute for nationalists as they were for communists.[5]

Intellectual foundations

It is during this period, at the turn of the twentieth century, that we can discern the intellectual foundations of the classical modernist paradigm of nationalism. Broadly speaking, there were four major streams of influence: Marxism, crowd psychology, Weberian and Durkheimian. I shall deal briefly with the contribution of each to the formulation of a coherent modernist approach to the understanding of nations and nationalism.

1 It is important to stress at the outset that none of these traditions were concerned more than peripherally with the analysis of nations or nationalism. In the case of the Marxist tradition, this might be ascribed to the early period in which the founding fathers wrote; though in the world of 1848, nationalism was already a powerful, if limited, force in Europe. This lack of concern must rather be attributed to the conscious decision on the part of both the founders and their followers, in reacting against German idealism, to relegate environmental and cultural influences to the background, and concentrate on the explication of the role of economic and class factors in the evolution of humanity. This in turn meant that, in relation to the explanatory role attributed to class conflict and to the contradictions in the mode of production in the successive stages of historical development, ethnic and national principles and phenomena had to be accorded a secondary or even derivative role, becoming at most catalysts or contributory (or complicating) rather than major causal factors. There was also a crucial ethical consideration. Given the inbuilt propensity of human evolution to self-transcendence through stages of political revolution, and given the fundamental role of class conflict in generating revolution, there was no place for any other factor, especially one that might impede or divert from the 'movement of history', except insofar as it might contribute to hastening that movement in specific instances. It was in these circumstances that Marxists identified particular nationalist movements in strategic terms, judging their 'progressive' or 'regressive' character in relation to a given revolutionary situation. It was from this perspective that Marx and Engels passed favourable judgments on Polish and Irish nationalism, as they were

likely to weaken Tsarist feudal absolutism and British capitalism respectively and hasten the next stage of historical evolution; whereas nationalist movements among the 'backward' small nations of the western and southern Slavs could only evoke their contempt or disapproval, as they were judged likely to divert the bourgeoisie or proletariat from their historic task in the evolution of Europe (Cummins 1980; Connor 1984).

Neither Marx nor Engels, Lenin nor Stalin, Luxemburg nor Kautsky, endeavoured to present a theory or model of nations and nationalism *per se*, not only because these phenomena were viewed with suspicion, if not outright hostility, even by those who conceded their political significance, but because the 'science' with which they were concerned was intimately linked to a specific worldview and political strategy that sought to reduce all phenomena, at the explanatory level at least, to their economic basis, deriving cultural and political identities and movements from the class alignments thrown up by a specific stage in the development of the mode of production. It was in this context that the 'formalism' associated with Marxist analysis became prominent: the idea that nations provided the forms and vessels, while class formations and their ideologies provided the content and ends to which the next stage of history aspired. This type of reductive reasoning has left a strong imprint on some latterday approaches to the study of nationalism, even where the theorists no longer accept the worldview and strategy in which it was embedded, and even when they eschew the cruder forms of economic reductionism and ideological formalism found in some of Marx's followers.[6]

Equally important for the legacy of the early Marxist tradition has been its historical and global emphasis, and its Eurocentric bias. For Marx, Engels, Lenin and their followers, nations and nationalism were intrinsic to the development of the modern capitalist era. They were to be understood as manifestations both of European capitalism's need for ever larger territorial markets and trading blocs, and of the growing distance between the modern capitalist state and bourgeois civil society and the levelling of all intermediate bodies between state and citizen characteristic of advanced absolutism. Of course, these themes were not confined to Marxists, and they remained relatively undeveloped in the early Marxist corpus. But it is fair to say that with the rediscovery of the early Marx's writings and their debt to Hegel and the Left Hegelians, they assumed a new importance at the very moment when a significant number of scholars were increasingly turning their attention to the theory of nationalism. Similarly, the current interest in the concept of 'globalisation' which can in part be traced to Marxist concerns with the development of late capitalism, has been increasingly linked to the role of nation-states and nationalism in advanced industrial society and as such reasserts the Western and modernist bias characteristic of the Marxist tradition (Davis 1967; Avineri 1968; Nairn 1977).

2   The influence of the second tradition of crowd psychology and Freud's later social psychological work has been more pervasive but also more limited. It

would be difficult to point to particular theorists of national identity and nationalism who have made explicit use of the crowd psychology of Le Bon or the herd instinct of Trotter, or even of the analyses of Simmel, Mead, Adorno and the later theories of Freud – despite the work of Leonard Doob or Morton Grodzins. On the other hand, many of their insights have permeated the thinking of recent scholars of nationalism. Perhaps the most obvious case is that of Kedourie's portrait of the social psychology of restless, alienated youth resentful of parental traditions and the humiliations of authority. But we can also discern the influence of an earlier crowd psychology in some of the functionalist analyses of mass-mobilising nationalism as a 'political religion' in the work of David Apter, Lucian Pye and Leonard Binder, and of crowd behaviour in social movements in the work of Neil Smelser. There is also a measure of influence exerted by the later Freud, as well as Mead and Simmel, in recent theories that emphasise the role of significant Others in the formation of national identities and the oppositional framework of inclusion and exclusion in nationalism [7]

What these approaches have in common is a belief in the dislocating nature of modernity, its disorientation of the individual and its capacity for disrupting the stability of traditional sources of support. It is in these respects that the influence of certain kinds of earlier social psychology contributed to the overall picture of nations and nationalism presented by classical modernism. More generally, social psychological assumptions drawn from a variety of sources can be found in the most unexpected places – among social anthropologists and sociologists as well as historians and political scientists – but these are not confined to those who adhere to the modernist framework (see Brown 1994).

3   The third major influence derives from the work of Max Weber. Strongly imbued with the prevailing tide of German nationalism, Weber never managed to produce the study of the rise of the nation state which he intended to write; yet his writings contain a number of themes that were to become central both to classical modernism and its subsequent development. These included the importance of political memories, the role of intellectuals in preserving the 'irreplaceable culture values' of a nation, and the importance of nation-states in the rise of the special character of the modern West. But what has most marked out the Weberian path of analysis is its emphasis on the role of political action, both generally in the formation of ethnic groups and specifically in the evolution of modern European nations. Weber cannot himself be categorised as a modernist, although when he writes about nations and nationalism, he has in mind mostly contemporary European examples; yet his influence has helped to legitimise the more political versions of the modernist paradigm (see Weber 1948: 171–9, 448, note 6; A. D. Smith 1983b; Guibernau 1996: ch. 1)

Insofar as Weber's huge corpus of writings touches on issues of ethnic identity and nationalism, it ranges far and wide in time and place. This is especially true of his analysis of ethnic groups which, for Weber, are a species of *Stände* (status group) based on the belief in common descent. Again, Weber emphasises the importance of political action and political memories: 'All history', he writes, 'shows how easily political action can give rise to the belief in blood relationship, unless gross differences of anthropological type impede it'. Examples are provided by the Swiss and the Alsatians. Of the latter, Weber writes:

> This sense of community came into being by virtue of common political and, indirectly, social experiences which are highly valued by the masses as symbols of the destruction of feudalism, and the story of these events takes the place of the heroic legends of primitive peoples.
>
> (Weber 1968: I/2, 396)

Whatever Weber's intentions, the political bias in his writings has inspired a number of latterday theorists of nation-states to emphasise the political dimensions of nationalism and especially the role of the modern Western state. In this, they receive strong support from Weber's well known definition of the nation:

> A nation is a community of sentiment which would adequately manifest itself in a state of its own; hence, a nation is a community which normally tends to produce a state of its own.
>
> (Weber 1948: 176)

This quest for statehood is what distinguishes nations from other communities of solidarity, just as it is political, and especially military, action that is required to turn an ethnic group into a nation. For Weber the modern state is a rational type of association, the apogee of occidental rationalism and one of the main agencies of rationalisation in history, whereas the nation is a particular type of community and prestige group. In the modern world, both need each other: the state requires the legitimation and popular direction accorded by the nation, while the nation needs the state to protect its unique culture values against those of other communities (*ibid.*: 176; see Beetham 1974)

Indirectly, then, the elements of Weber's writings on nations and nationalism that have had greatest influence have served to support the different versions of political modernism which stress the role of power, and especially state power, in the definition of the nation and the explanation of nationalism. Latterday theorists have generally accepted the picture of occidental rationalism (if not rationalisation) that forms the background of the Weberian approach to modern politics, extending it globally and revealing its many implications for international relations and the impact of the state on civil society.[8]

4   The final source of influence on the classical modernist paradigm is probably the most important: the legacy of the Durkheimian emphasis on

community. Again, despite the fervour of his French nationalism, Durkheim
wrote little on nations or nationalism until some polemical, occasional pieces
during the First World War; it never figures as a theme in itself in his major
works. Yet, in a sense, the idea of the nation as a moral community with its
conscience collective is the guiding thread of his entire work, and it is made
explicit in his analysis of religion and ritual in his last major book, *The
Elementary Forms of the Religious Life* (Durkheim 1915; Mitchell 1931; see A. D.
Smith 1983b; Guibernau 1996: ch. 1).

Much of what Durkheim has to say which bears on ethnicity and nationalism has a timeless quality about it. This is especially true of his analysis of
religion as the core of moral community and his consequent belief that 'there
is something eternal in religion', whatever the changes in its symbolism,
because all societies feel the need to reaffirm and renew themselves periodi-
cally through collective rites and ceremonies. In this respect, he claims, there
is no difference between Christian or Jewish festivals, and

> a reunion of citizens commemorating the promulgation of a new moral
> or legal system or some great event in the national life,
>
> (Durkheim 1915: 427)

as occurred, most memorably, during the French Revolution when

> under the influence of the general enthusiasm, things purely laical in
> character were transformed by public opinion into sacred things: these
> were the Fatherland, Liberty, Reason. A religion tended to become
> established which had its dogmas, symbols, altars and feasts.
>
> (*ibid.*: 214)

While such an analysis could serve, and was indeed used, to define the role
of mass-mobilising nationalism in the new states of Africa and Asia, it was
another aspect of Durkheim's theories that proved most influential for classical modernism. This was his analysis of the transition from 'mechanical' to
'organic' solidarity. Whereas in ethnic or tribal societies, argued Durkheim,

> mechanical causes and impulsive forces, such as affinity of blood,
> attachment to the same soil, ancestral worship, community of habits,
> etc.
>
> (Durkheim 1964: 278)

bring men together, in modern, industrial societies these forces decline,
along with tradition and the influence of the *conscience collective*, and their
place is taken by the division of labour and its complementarity of roles.
Population growth, increased interaction and competition, and urbanisation
and social mobility, have all eroded tradition and the links with grandpar-
ents. This is exactly what has happened in the advanced industrial societies

of the West. Yet elements of the earlier 'mechanical' type of solidarity remain even in the most modern societies, above all, the cohesion and self-renewal required by every society and the sense of social dependance and individual belonging engendered by professional groups and collective rituals. Here Durkheim foreshadows the theme of ethnic revival which has become an important element in some modernist theories of nationalism (Durkheim 1964; Nisbet 1965; Giddens 1971).

For classical modernists, then, Durkheim provided the framework for inserting nations and nationalism into the evolutionary logic of structural differentiation and modernisation to be found primarily in the West. What the classical modernists understood Durkheim to be saying was that modern societies required a new principle of cohesion and reintegration, after all the dislocations and strains of modernisation, and this was to be found in the idea of the nation and the mobilising power of nationalism. Yet, as we shall see, classical modernism introduced a quite different conception of the nation which amounted to a sharp break in the continuity envisaged by Durkheim's analysis.

Historians and social scientists

If the pre-1914 sociological and social psychological traditions provided the framework for the paradigm of classical modernism, the immediate impetus to its construction and much of its historical content was provided by the labours of sociologically inclined historians from the 1920s. The object of their detailed investigations was the rise and course of the nationalist ideology and its varieties; the hallmark of their studies was a sustained attempt at dispassionate analysis of the ideology. In this they were not entirely successful. The Western and European bias of their enquiries is evident in the work of the major historians of nationalism, Carlton Hayes, Hans Kohn, Frederick Hertz, Alfred Cobban, E. H. Carr, Louis Snyder and Boyd Shafer. There was also a tendency to treat nationalism as an ethical issue and the nation as an ambivalent means to nobler ends. The result was frequently to blur moral judgment with historical analysis, which was understandable, given the horrors of Nazism and the Second World War, and the general disposition to regard fascism as the logical denouement of a chauvinistic nationalism. Perhaps the best known example is Hans Kohn's influential distinction between 'Western' and 'Eastern' nationalisms – east and west of the Rhine: in the West, in England, France, America and Holland, a rational, voluntaristic version of nationalism emerged, whereas in the East, in Germany, Italy, Eastern Europe and Asia, an organic, determinist variety found fertile soil. But there are other examples: Carlton Hayes' distinctions between 'humanitarian', 'liberal', 'traditional' and 'Jacobin' (and later 'economic' and 'integral') varieties of nationalist ideology, the stages of national self-determination in the analyses of Alfred Cobban, and the early chronological typology of nationalisms espoused by Louis Snyder carry similar moralistic overtones (Hayes 1931; Snyder 1954; Kohn 1967a; Cobban 1969).[9]

Two aspects of these early historical analyses have been particularly important for the growth of classical modernism. The first is an increasing recourse to socio-logical factors, if not explanations. Again, the most obvious case is that of Hans Kohn. The pivot of his typology of Eastern and Western nationalisms is sociolog-ical: the presence or absence of a strong bourgeoisie at the moment when the ideology of nationalism was diffused to the particular area or state. States and areas with strong bourgeoisies tended to opt for a rationalist and voluntaristic version of the ideology of nationalism, which required everyone to choose a nation of belonging but did not prescribe a particular nation; whereas states and areas with weak bourgeoisies tended to spawn shrill, authoritarian nationalisms led by tiny intelligentsias who opted for organic nationalisms which prescribed the nation of belonging for each individual from birth. E. H. Carr, too, had recourse to sociological factors in delineating the successive stages of European nation-alism: at first monarchical, dynastic and mercantilist, then from the late eighteenth century popular and democratic and free trading (under the financial aegis of London), and finally (from the 1890s to 1940s) the growing economic nationalism of fully socialised mass nations proliferating across Europe and plunging the conti-nent into total war (Carr 1945; Kohn 1955; Kohn 1967a, 329–31).

The second aspect is the provision of detailed evidence for the modernity and European origins of national*ism*, the ideology and movement. This is not to say that all the historians agreed on a 'date of birth' for nationalism. Kohn placed it in the English Revolution, Cobban opted for the late eighteenth century following the Partitions of Poland and the American Revolution, while Kedourie placed it in 1807, the date of Fichte's *Addresses to the German Nation*. But most accepted the French Revolution as the event and period of nationalism's first full blown manifestation, and thereby tied it firmly to the civic and democratic movements of that period in Europe. They also concentrated on charting the evolution of nationalism, the ideology and movement, within modern Europe. If they chose to look further afield, they tended to derive the later nationalisms of India, Japan, China and Indonesia, or of the Arab and African peoples, from this or that version of European nationalism, imbibed by native intellectuals in the metropolis or at home. Such analyses served to reinforce the conviction that nationalism was a manifestation of a particular *Zeitgeist*, and tied to a specifically modern and European time and place. Chronological modernism was *ipso facto* Eurocentric: the ideology that sprang to life fully fledged in the French Revolutionary Wars was fundamentally European in character as well as loca-tion. This was to have profound implications for the paradigm of classical modernism and the theory of nationalism.[10]

The historians in question were mainly historians of ideas and political history, and of European ideas and political history at that. It was only in the 1950s, with the acceleration of the process of decolonisation and the rise of the new states in Africa and Asia, that their work began to be supplemented and then to some extent overtaken by a spate of political science and sociological analyses of Third World anti-colonial nationalisms. It was only in the late 1950s that the traditional predominance of historians in the study of nationalism came to an end, and the field was opened up to scholars from a variety of disciplines. This was also the moment when the classical paradigm of modernism took shape (see A. D. Smith 1992c).

The classical modernist paradigm of nationalism

The 1960s, the era of Western liberalisation following economic expansion and accelerated decolonisation in Asia and Africa, also saw the widespread adoption of the model and ideal of 'nation-building'. It was a perspective well attuned to the optimistic, heady temper of the decade, and it marks the classical expression of what I have termed the modernist paradigm of nationalism.

Anti-perennialism

Essentially, classical modernism, and especially the model of nation-building, was a reaction to the often tacit ideas and principles of an older generation of scholars of nationalism, many of whom had accepted the main premises of the nationalist ideologies around them, even where they distanced themselves from their more extreme manifestations. This was evident in their language, which often equated the idea of 'race' with the concept of the nation, which saw in national characteristics the underlying principles of history, and which tended to judge international events and relations in terms of national actors and over-riding national interests. Behind these views stood a perspective that viewed nations as the basic communities of history, at once ancient and immemorial, and that regarded national sentiments and consciousness as fundamental elements of historical phenomena and their main explanatory principles. We may term this the 'perennialist' perspective. Many a popular history in Britain, France, Germany and other countries accepted the spirit of this perspective and retold the story of the nation in terms of its rude beginnings, early migrations, golden ages of saints and heroes, its vicissitudes and servitudes, its decline and rebirth, and its glorious future. More serious historians were content to recount the activities of national leaders and aristocracies in antiquity and the medieval era, thereby demonstrating the centrality and durability of the idea and manifestations of the nation in history.[11]

All this was challenged and dismissed by the rising tide of modernism. For these scholars, the propositions on which perennialism was based were either unverifiable or erroneous. They contended that:

1   nations were in no sense ancient or immemorial. This was an assumption unwarranted by any documentary evidence and as such an act of faith in the antiquity of a modern cultural collectivity;
2   nations were in no sense givens, let alone existing in nature or in the first time. Any such assertion was again an act of faith unsupported by any historical or sociological evidence;

3   many nations were in fact relatively recent, both in Europe and latterly in
    Africa and Asia, and this alone disproved the immemorial or primordial
    character of nations;
4   we could not, and should not, read the elements of modern nations and
    nationalism back into earlier, pre-modern collectivities and sentiments; this
    kind of 'retrospective nationalism' only served to distort our understanding
    of the quite different identities, communities and relations of the ancient
    and medieval worlds;
5   nations were not the product of natural, or deep rooted, historical forces,
    but rather of recent historical developments and of the rational, planned
    activity made possible and necessary by the conditions of the modern era.

This was a decidedly anti-historicist and rationalist critique. It viewed with suspicion all genetic explanations and substituted a functionalist analysis of the place
of nations in history and the role of nationalism in the modern world. It was also
markedly optimistic in tone and activist in spirit, arguing that nationalism
created nations and that the activities of national elites served to promote the
needs of social and political development. Hence the model of nation-building,
at once structural and interventionist, with state elites assigned the key role of
constructing the edifice of the nation-to-be along rational, civic lines.

The activist, interventionist character of classical modernism accounts for the
way in which it construes the older perennialism. Generally speaking, it tends to
treat the nation as not only perennial but also 'primordial' in character. Classical
modernism was bitterly opposed to what it saw as the naturalism and essentialism inherent in the older perspectives, the belief that nations are elements of
nature, existing before time, and that we possess a nationality in the same way as
we have eyes and speech, a view that it regarded as responsible for the extremist
emotions and mass following of nationalism. It therefore regarded any idea that
any particular nation or nations in general might have deep historical 'roots' as
part of the naturalistic and genetic fallacy.[12]

It was equally opposed to the non-rational and passive character of perennialism. If nations are 'essences' and elements of nature, and if individuals belong
to this or that nation from birth and are stamped with its being throughout their
existence, then nationalism of whatever hue is simply the non-rational expression of the nation and individuals are passive exemplars of its essence.
Nationalism can never on this view be a rational strategy employed by individuals for their individual or collective interests, nor an expression of deliberate
choice and judgment. Such a view conflicted sharply with the activist and autoemancipatory spirit of the postwar epoch.

Nation-building

In contrast, the main tenets of the modernist paradigm, and especially of its
classical nation-building model, stressed the political nature of nations and the

active role of citizens and leaders in their construction. Broadly speaking, the theorists of nation-building contended that:

1   nations were essentially territorial political communities. They were sovereign, limited and cohesive communities of legally equal citizens, and they were conjoined with modern states to form what we call unitary 'nation-states';
2   nations constituted the primary political bond and the chief loyalty of their members. Other ties – of gender, region, family, class and religion – had to be subordinated to the overriding allegiance of the citizen to his or her nation-state, and this was desirable because it gave form and substance to the ideals of democratic civic participation;
3   nations were the main political actors in the international arena. They were real sociological communities disposing of the political weight of the world's populations and the sole legitimating and coordinating principle of inter-state relations and activity;
4   nations were the constructs of their citizens, and notably of their leaders and elites, and were built up through a variety of processes and institutions. The key to the success of nations was balanced and comprehensive institutionalisation of roles, expectations and values, and the creation of an infrastructure of social communications – transport, bureaucracy, language, education, the media, political parties, etc.;
5   nations were the sole framework, vehicle and beneficiary of social and political development, the only instrument for assuring the needs of all citizens in the production and distribution of resources and the only means of assuring sustainable development. This was because only national loyalty and nationalist ideology could mobilise the masses for the commitment, dedication and self-sacrifice required by modernisation with all its strains and dislocations.

For their examples, the theorists of nation-building had no need to look further than the contemporary processes of decolonisation in Asia and Africa. There they could witness the efforts of nationalist leaders to 'build' nations by creating effective institutions which would express the norms of a civic nation, aggregate the interests of its citizens and enable them to translate their needs and ideals into effective policies. These so-called 'state-nations' (territorial states attempting to create cohesive nations out of heterogeneous ethnic populations) testified to the importance of 'nation-building', revealing the limitations of territorial sovereignty and pointing the way forward through the mobilisation and participation of an active citizenry (see Deutsch and Foltz 1963).[13]

The theorists who subscribed to the classical modernist paradigm, and especially to the model of nation-building – notably Deutsch, Foltz, Lerner, Eisenstadt, Apter, Almond, Pye, Bendix and Binder – differed over the particular elements which were crucial for modernisation and nation-building. Some stressed the role of social mobilisation and social communication, others of mobility and empathy, still others of interest aggregation, political religion and systems of mass mobilisation. But each subscribed to the idea, and ideal, of the nation as a mass participant political culture and as a popular civic-territorial community, into which, as Bendix's work in particular demonstrated, ever wider strata of the territorial population were drawn through processes of employment, mass education and citizenship. This emphasis on civic participation was indicative of the modernism of their outlook. For it was only in a 'modern', i.e. both recent and industrial-bureaucratic, era that a high level of political participation by the masses was possible; and so it was only in the modern era that nations could flourish and become the sole political actors and units of government. The modern era was the first era in which self-government of the people could be conceived and achieved (see Bendix 1996).[14]

Equally important, this was the first era in which self-government was essential. It was necessary because the nation was the ideal agent and framework for social development, and the modern era was the first era in which sustained social development could take place. This in turn implied that nations, and nation-building, were functional for social development. In a non-developmental era, there was no need, no room, for nations. On the contrary: traditional religions acted as barriers to the formation of both nations and the desire for social change and development. With the erosion of traditional religions and the rise of nations, national self-government was the only way to harness the social and political resources necessary for social development. Hence the first aim of nation-building must be to secure the independence necessary for citizens to participate in political decisions and govern themselves. Without independence, as Engels had realised long before, there could be no sustained economic development, because there could be no real commitment and self-sacrifice demanded of those who were not masters of their own destinies (Davis 1967).

Modernism and perennialism

Behind this immediate model stood the larger paradigm of classical modernism. Broadly speaking, it contended that:

1   nations were wholly modern – modern in the sense of being recent, i.e. since the French Revolution, and in the sense that the components of the nation were novel, i.e. part of the new age of modernity, and so modern by definition;

2   nations were the product of modernity, i.e. their elements were not only recent and novel, but also could only emerge, and had to emerge, through processes of 'modernisation', the rise of modern conditions and modernising policies;

3   nations were therefore not deeply rooted in history, but were inevitable consequences of the revolutions that constituted modernity and as such tied to their features and conditions, with the result that, once these features and

conditions were transformed, nations would gradually wither away or be superseded;

4   nationalism likewise was embedded in modernity, or more accurately, in the processes of modernisation and the transition to a modern order, so that when these processes were completed, nationalism too would wane and disappear;

5   nations and nationalisms were social constructs and cultural creations of modernity, designed for an age of revolutions and mass mobilisation, and central to the attempts to control these processes of rapid social change.

In its pure form, the paradigm of classical modernism can be regarded as the polar opposite to the older perennialist assumptions and ideas which regarded nations as more or less persistent and recurrent phenomena of all epochs and continents. Modernism objected to the assumptions of naturalism and immemorialism held by the older generation of scholars on political as well as intellectual grounds. They regarded both fallacies as pernicious influences on the public mind, and in varying degrees responsible for the catalogue of wars and atrocities that had engulfed Europe and the world in the twentieth century. They systematically opposed the assumptions which underlay perennialist accounts of the role of nations in history, and sought to demystify national identity and counteract the claims of nationalism by revealing its inherent absurdity as well as its historical shallowness.

If we follow through the assumptions and claims of perennialists and modernists, we discover a series of recurrent dichotomies, which can be summarised as follows:

1   For the perennialists, the nation is a politicised ethno-cultural community, a community of common ancestry that stakes a claim to political recognition on that basis. For the modernists the nation is a territorialised political community, a civic community of legally equal citizens in a particular territory;

2   For perennialists, the nation is persistent and immemorial, with a history stretching back centuries, if not millennia. For modernists, the nation is both recent and novel, a product of wholly modern and recent conditions, and therefore unknown in pre-modern eras;

3   For perennialists, the nation is 'rooted' in place and time; it is embedded in a historic homeland. For modernists, the nation is a creation. It is consciously and deliberately 'built' by its members, or segments thereof.

4   For perennialists, the nation is a popular or demotic community, a community of 'the people' and mirroring their needs and aspirations. For modernists, it is consciously constructed by elites, who seek to influence the emotions of the masses to achieve their goals.

5   For perennialists, belonging to a nation means possessing certain qualities. It is a state of being. For modernists, it means possessing certain resources. It is a capacity for doing.

6   For perennialists, nations are seamless wholes, with a single will and character. For modernists, nations are typically riven and divided into a number of (regional, class, gender, religious, etc.) social groups, each with their own interests and needs.

7   For perennialists, the underlying principles of the nation are those of ancestral ties and authentic culture. For modernists, the principles of national solidarity are to be found in social communication and citizenship.

These dichotomies can be summarised as follows:

Attributes of the nation according to perennialists and modernists

Perennialism	**Modernism**
The nation as	
Cultural community	Political community
Immemorial	Modern
Rooted	Created
Organic	Mechanical
Seamless	Divided
Quality	Resource
Popular	Elite-construct
Ancestrally-based	Communication-based

These are, of course, ideal-type dichotomies. Not all the scholars who hold in general terms to the perennialist and modernist paradigms would subscribe to all the elements of 'their' paradigm, as listed above. I have deliberately magnified the differences, to bring out some of the antagonistic underlying assumptions which can, and have, been made about nations and nationalism. In fact, a number of theorists have evolved permutations which cross the lines of these paradigms, combining elements from both paradigms in often unexpected ways.

One should add that nationalists themselves, perhaps not unexpectedly, have wanted to have things both ways: seeing the nation as organic and rooted in history and territory, but at the same time as created and engineered by nationalist elites. This is not just opportunism. Nationalism is itself an activist, autoemancipatory programme for the oppressed; at the same time the nation which they seek to 'reawaken' is often seen as part of nature and subject to the laws of evolution like any other organism.

There is a further and critical point. The above inventory of polar types conflates perennialism with the more radical positions of 'primordialism'. Not all perennialists would regard themselves as primordialists or accept primordialist assumptions. Many would refuse to see the nation as organic, seamless and ancestral. Instead they would simply argue from what they saw as the historical record, and regard nations as recurrent and/or persistent phenomena of all epochs and continents, but in no way part of the 'natural order'. This is a distinction to which we shall return in Part II.

From a logical standpoint, however, these dichotomies underlie many of the positions adopted by theorists of nationalism. As such, they demand clearcut choices between the polar types, or a conscious decision to combine elements of each type. In each case, the logic of these paradigms and their dichotomies requires the theorist to clarify the arguments and produce the evidence that has led him or her to adopt a particular standpoint in the debates about nations and nationalism.

The modernist paradigm, and its nation-building model, became the standard orthodoxy by the 1960s, at a time when functionalism was dominant and when even its critics stressed the role of classes, elites and leaders in the processes of modernisation and nation-building. Scholars as different in their theoretical persuasions as Elie Kedourie, J. H. Kautsky, S. N. Eisenstadt, W. C. Smith, Peter Worsley and Ernest Gellner all adhered to the modernist paradigm, and stressed the role of active participation, elite choice and social mobilisation in the building of modern nations, factors which Karl Deutsch and the communications theorists had popularised. Whatever their other theoretical and ideological differences, they all agreed that the age of nation-states was recent and modern, that modern conditions provided fertile soil for the formation of nations and that nationalism was one of the more successful ideologies of modernisation.[15]

In the following chapters I propose to examine in more detail the main varieties of classical modernism – sociocultural, economic, political and ideological – as they were developed during the 1970s and 1980s. In these different versions, classical modernism reached the limits of its explanatory power and heuristic utility, and ultimately exhausted its possibilities, paving the way for critical movements which carried with them the potential for its dissolution.

Part I
Varieties of modernism

2 The culture of industrialism

Perhaps the most original and radical statement of classical modernism was that of Ernest Gellner in the seventh chapter of *Thought and Change* (1964). In that chapter, Gellner outlined a new theory of nationalism that focused on the effects of processes of uneven global modernisation. Likening modernisation to a great tidal wave that sweeps over the world from its West European heartlands, hitting successive areas at different times and rates, Gellner traced the rise of nationalism to the new role of linguistic culture in the modern world. Traditional role relationships in villages and small towns had been shattered by the effects of uneven development, many villagers had been uprooted and driven towards the great, sprawling cities, and their lifestyles and beliefs had been largely destroyed. Dislocated and disoriented in the anonymous city, the new impoverished proletariat of uprooted peasants no longer possessed anything on which to rebuild communities and stave off anarchy except language and culture. In the new urban setting, language and culture replaced the village and tribal structures of role relationships as the cement of society. Hence the growing importance of a critical and ambitious intelligentsia, the producers and purveyors of these linguistic cultures. But it was also incumbent on everyone to become literate as well as numerate, to be a 'clerk' so as to become a citizen and 'an acceptable specimen of humanity'. That in turn required a new kind of schooling, mass, public, standardised schooling, supervised and funded by the state. The size of the education system was directly related to the scale of nations.

But there was another side to uneven development. Not only did the tidal wave erode traditional role structures, it also generated social conflicts in the swollen cities. Conflicts between the waves of newcomers and the urban old-timers, between the urban employed in the city centres and the underemployed proletariat in their shanty-towns on the edge of the cities. Such conflicts were usually social – class conflicts between the propertied and educated and the destitute and illiterate masses. But in some cases social conflict became ethnic antagonism. This happened when the newcomers, the uprooted proletariat, were visibly different, had entirely different belief systems and customs, or spoke unintelligible languages. In such cases the urban old-timers resorted to cultural exclusion and ethnic job reservation. In these circumstances, the intelligentsias on both sides of the cultural divide were able to turn ethnic conflicts into nationalist movements demanding secession from the existing political unit in which both groups had, usually long ago, been incorporated (Gellner 1964: ch. 7).

For Gellner, therefore, nations do not create nationalism. Rather, nationalist movements define and create nations. Indeed,

> Nationalism is not the awakening of nations to self-consciousness: it invents nations where they do not exist – but it does need some pre-existing differentiating marks to work on, even if, as indicated, these are purely negative.
>
> *(ibid.:* 168)

Nationalism is the yearning for, and acceptance of, the norm of the nation, which Gellner at this stage defined as a large, co-cultural, unmediated, anonymous society. Men become nationalists, Gellner concluded, out of 'genuine, objective, practical necessity, however obscurely recognised', because 'it is the need for growth that generates nationalism, not vice-versa'. In this way, nationalism ensures that the world is divided into a system of locks, and acts as a safeguard against a new imperial tyranny *(ibid.:* 160, 168).

The first version of his theory suffered from a number of omissions and problems, and Gellner felt it necessary to address these in a new, fuller formulation. They included:

1 the problems presented by ascribing a unifying role to language, including the recognition that language sometimes failed to fulfil that role, for example, in Spanish Latin America or the Arabic states;
2 the unassimilability of certain cultural groups by and in the 'transition', that is, the failure of modernisation to integrate various groups, notably those based on pigmentation and scriptural religion;
3 the prolongation of the processes of modernisation and the failure of the concept of proletarianism to account for the conflicts in its later stages, as well as the doubtful causal relationship between industrialisation and the rise of nationalism;
4 the importance of divisions within the intelligentsia, and their impact on the very different paths to modernity taken by various nations;
5 the problem of how modernity and its literate cultures are sustained, and the need to find an institutional base for its maintenance rather than merely a social group;
6 the problem of accounting for the absence of nations and nationalism in pre-modern societies, in contrast to their well nigh universal presence in modern, industrial societies.

To deal with these problems, Gellner reformulated his basic modernist theory, first in an article of 1973, and then in a full presentation in *Nations and Nationalism* (Gellner 1973, 1983).[1]

'Nation' and 'nationalism'

The hinge of the new version was the role of mass public education systems in sustaining 'high' cultures in modern, industrial societies. Whereas the earlier version had emphasised the role of language and linguistic culture as the new social cement, the later formulation highlighted the way in which modern growth-oriented societies required a certain kind of literate culture which could only be forged and sustained by 'exo-socialisation', a new kind of public, standardised education unlike any to be found in pre-modern societies.

The logical starting-point of Gellner's second version is his definition of the concept of the nation. Neither 'will' nor 'culture' by themselves can provide useful definitions. The reason is the same: they both bring in far too rich a catch. While nations may be communities that *will* themselves to persist, in a kind of daily, continuous, self-affirming plebiscite, as Renan claimed, so do many other social groups: clubs, conspiracies, teams, parties, as well as pre-modern religious, political or private groups that knew nothing of nationalism. Similarly, to define nations in terms of shared culture, when there are and have been so many varied and rich cultural differences in the world, will not help us: cultural differences only sometimes coincided with the boundaries of political units, and the fact that they are increasingly doing so only reveals the very special conditions that bring culture and politics together in the modern age (Gellner 1983: ch. 5).

Put another way, of the perhaps 8,000 language groups in the world, only a small proportion (about 200) have constituted themselves as nations with their own states, with a somewhat larger proportion (perhaps 600) of others striving to attain their own states, making some 800 in all. With only one tenth of potential cultures striving to become 'nations', we can hardly use shared culture alone to define the concept (*ibid.*: 43–50).

This is why it is necessary to define the concept of the nation in terms of the age of nationalism. Only then, under the peculiar conditions of the age, can we define nations as the product of both *will* and *culture*.

But what then is nationalism? For Gellner, it is a political principle, 'which holds that the political and national unit should be congruent'. It is a theory of political legitimacy,

> which requires that ethnic boundaries should not cut across political ones, and in particular, that ethnic boundaries within a given state . . . should not separate the power-holders from the rest.
>
> (*ibid.*: 1)

National sentiment is the feeling of anger or of satisfaction aroused by the violation or fulfilment of this principle, while nationalist movements are ones actuated by this sentiment.

Agroliterate and industrial societies

The central proposition of Gellner's overall theory – that nations and nationalism are logically contingent, but sociologically necessary in modern industrial
societies – is based on his analysis of the transition from agrarian – or agroliterate – societies to modern, industrial ones. For Gellner, there have been three
main stages in history: the pre-agrarian, the agrarian and the industrial. Each
of these resembles a plateau of human civilisations, with steep, step-like transi-
tions from one stage to the next. In the first, the hunter-gatherer stage, there
was no polity or state, hence no possibility of nations and nationalisms, given
Gellner's definition of nationalism. The second stage saw a variety of types of
society, most (but not all) of which had states of their own. Here there is a
possibility for nations and nationalism to emerge, though it is in fact never
realised. It is only in the third, industrial, stage, that the state has become
inescapable; every society has, or aspires to, a state of its own, but that is only
part of the reason why nationalism becomes so universal an aspiration in
modern society (Gellner 1987: ch. 2).

Why are there no nations and nationalisms in agroliterate societies? These are
societies distinguished, not only by the emergence of the state, but by the transmission of elite literacy. But they are also highly stratified societies. This means
that power and culture are united according to status. At the apex of these societies are a series of small, but powerful, elites, arranged in horizontal strata,
including the military, bureaucratic, priestly and aristocratic castes, who use
culture – their culture – to separate themselves from the rest of society. The mass
of the population in each state consists of agricultural producers, and they too
are separated, but this time into vertical communities, each with its own folk
culture and customs. These small communities of peasants are turned inwards
by economic necessity, and their local cultures are almost invisible. The members
of each such community relate to each other through *contextual* communication.
As a result, culture tends to be either horizontal as social caste, or vertical,
defining small local communities.

So in stratified agroliterate societies, there is neither the possibility nor the
desire to create a single, homogeneous culture for all the members of a given
polity, and hence no possibility of nations or nationalism. Indeed, the only
stratum that might have an interest in such cultural imperialism, the clerisy, is
either indifferent to seeing its norms and rituals extended throughout society (like
the Brahmins) or has neither the resources nor the practical possibility of doing
so (as with the Islamic *ulema*) – since most people must look after the sheep, goats
and camels! For the other elites, the gulf between themselves (and their lifestyles)
and the rest of the population (and their folk cultures) must be maintained, and
even fortified by theories of 'blood' and hallowed descent (Gellner 1983: ch. 2).

The contrast with industrial societies is striking. They *do* require a homogeneous culture uniting all the members of a state, since in such societies, everyone
is mobile, everyone must be a clerk, communication must be context-free and
power-holding must be impersonal:

In an age of universalised clerisy and Mamluk-dom, the relationship of culture and polity changes radically. A high culture pervades the whole of society, defines it, and needs to be sustained by the polity. *That* is the secret of nationalism.

(*ibid.*: 18)

The central ideas of modern society are those of endless cognitive and economic growth, of ceaseless discovery and innovation. Just as everything has to be analysed into its constituent parts before causal relationships can be explored, so all persons and activities in modern society are to be treated as equal, commensurable units so that they can then be conjoined in mass societies, or nations. Modern, industrial societies are by their nature fluid, mobile, constantly changing; their mode of production too depends on an ever changing division of labour, in which individuals must meet and communicate with large numbers of people they never knew before, and must be able to move from one activity to another. This is why, unlike hierarchical and stable pre-modern societies, modern societies are necessarily egalitarian, in their ideals, if not always in practice (*ibid.*: ch. 3, esp. 24–9).

Work in pre-modern society was essentially manual. In modern society, it is mainly semantic. It is a society with a high degree of specialised labour, but the work is strictly standardised and its precondition is a degree of literacy on the part of every member. This means that everyone must have a common *generic* education followed by specialist training for and on the job. The generic education in basic numeracy and literacy enables everyone to be in a position to become specialists; without that generic education in semantic labour, they could not be so trained. This type of education is relatively novel. Unlike the minimal, contextual education given to children in pre-modern societies, usually by the family and village school, education in a modern society is a public affair and of far greater importance to the operation of society. Public, mass education systems, or 'exo-socialisation', provide a rigorous training in the uses of precise, explicit messages and context-free meanings in a standard written language and script (Gellner 1973; Gellner 1983: ch. 3).

Unlike its predecessors, the modern education system is a large, complex system – a public, standardised, academy-supervised and diploma-conferring institution for the inculcation of the skills, techniques and values of modernity. Only a large and complex system could educate great numbers of people to be 'clerks', and only clerks can be useful citizens of a modern state. This means that the size of the mass public education system sets the lower limit for the scale of nations. It also means that mass education alone can endow its citizens with self-respect and a sense of identity:

Modern man is not loyal to a monarch or a land or a faith, whatever he may say, but to a culture.

(Gellner 1983: 36)

Size is crucial in another, political, respect. Only the modern state is large and competent enough to sustain and supervise a system of public, mass education, which is required to train everyone to participate in the literate 'high' culture of an industrial society. The public, mass education system binds state and culture together. In the past, the links between state and culture were thin, loose and fortuitous. Today, the necessity of exo-socialisation means that these links are unavoidable; and that is the reason why we live in an age of nationalism.[2]

From 'low' to 'high' cultures

The transition from an agroliterate to an industrial society is marked by the replacement of 'low' by 'high' cultures. Gellner defines a nation as a society with a high culture, that is, a specially cultivated, standardised, education-based, literate culture. These he calls 'garden' cultures, to distinguish them from the 'wild', spontaneous and undirected cultures found normally in agroliterate societies, which require no conscious design, surveillance or special nutrition. Cultivated or garden cultures, on the other hand, are rich and complex. They are sustained by specialised personnel and to survive, must be nourished by specialised institutions of learning with numerous, dedicated, full-time professionals (*ibid.*: 50–2).

Now, many of the low, 'wild' cultures fail to make it into the industrial era. There are simply too many of them for the number of viable states which can populate the world. So they generally bow out without a struggle and fail to engender a nationalism; while those with prospects of success fight it out among themselves for the available state-space. That is why, in its own terms, nationalism is weak; only a small proportion of potential linguistic candidates stake a claim to becoming nations, and most remain determined 'slumberers'. On the other hand, those that do engender nationalisms and attain to states of their own are much stronger than before. They are pervasive and universal within the boundaries of 'their' state; everyone must share in the same, standardised, literate culture.

What then is the relationship between the 'low' and the 'high' cultures? For Gellner, cultures in the sense of systems of norms and communications have always been important, but they were often overlapping, subtly grouped and intertwined. In general, in pre-modern societies they were confined to elites; indeed, they were used by elites to identify and differentiate themselves from the masses. That is the main reason for the impossibility of nations and nationalism before the onset of modernity. Today, however, cultures are pervasive and homogeneous: and when

> general social conditions make for standardised, homogeneous, centrally sustained high cultures, pervading entire populations and not just elite minorities, a situation arises in which well-defined educationally sanctioned and unified cultures constitute very nearly the only kind of unit with which

men willingly and often ardently identify. The cultures now seem to be the natural repositories of political legitimacy.

(*ibid.*: 55)

These new, pervasive high cultures are so important for the smooth running of industrial society that they must be constantly sustained and controlled by each state. That is why the modern, industrial world resembles a series of structurally similar giant aquaria or 'breathing chambers', which sport superficial, if unduly emphasised cultural differences. The water and the atmosphere in these tanks are specially serviced to breed the new species of industrial person; the name of the specialised plant providing this service is a national educational and communications system (*ibid.*: 51–2).

What happens, typically, is that the successful new high culture of the state is imposed on the population of that state, and uses whatever of the old 'wild' cultures that it requires. This is the main role of nationalism. Nations have not existed from eternity, only to be awakened by the call of the nationalists. But cultures *have* always existed, and nationalism uses their raw materials:

> Nations as a natural, God-given way of classifying men, as an inherent though long-delayed political destiny, are a myth; nationalism, which sometimes takes pre-existing cultures and turns them into nations, sometimes invents them, and often obliterates pre-existing cultures: *that* is a reality, for better or worse, and in general an inescapable one.
>
> (*ibid.*: 48–9)

Contrary to its folk idiom and romantic self-image, nationalism

> is, essentially, the general imposition of a high culture on society, where previously low cultures had taken up the lives of the majority, and in some cases the totality, of the population. It means the generalised diffusion of a school-mediated, academy-supervised idiom, codified for the requirements of reasonably precise bureaucratic and technological communication. It is the establishment of an anonymous, impersonal society, with mutually substitutable, atomised individuals, held together above all by a shared culture of this kind. . . . That is what *really* happens.
>
> (*ibid.*: 57)

Further light is thrown on the relationship between the old 'low' and the modern 'high' cultures when Gellner vigorously separates the principle of nationalism ('nationalism-in-general') from the particular manifestations of nationalism ('specific nationalism'). Against those who would argue that nationalism is sociologically, as well as logically, contingent, Gellner claims that it has deep roots in the modern condition and will not easily be denied. As he explains:

It is nationalism which engenders nations, and not the other way round. Admittedly, nationalism uses the pre-existing, historically inherited proliferation of cultures or cultural wealth, though it uses them very selectively, and it most often transforms them radically. Dead languages can be revived, traditions invented, quite fictitious pristine purities restored. But this culturally creative, fanciful, positively inventive aspect of nationalist ardour ought not to allow anyone to conclude, erroneously, that nationalism is a contingent, artificial, ideological invention. . . . The cultural shreds and patches used by nationalism are often arbitrary historical inventions. Any old shred and patch would have served as well. But in no way does it follow that the principle of nationalism, as opposed to the avatars it happens to pick up for its incarnations, is itself in the least contingent and accidental.

Nationalism is not what it seems, and above all it is not what it seems to itself. The cultures it claims to defend and revive are often its own inventions, or are modified out of all recognition.

(*ibid*.: 55–6)

Gellner concedes that nationalism may not be so far from the truth when the people are ruled by officials of an alien, high culture, and they must first be liberated. But the new culture imposed on them after liberation bears only a remote resemblance to their own local folk cultures; rather,

it revives or invents a local high (literate, specialist-transmitted) culture of its own, though admittedly one that will have some links with the earlier folk styles and dialects.

(*ibid*.: 57)

How do most people acquire the new high culture? In the scenario presented by Gellner, the folk or Ruritanians became conscious of their own local culture and tried to turn it into a literate, standardised 'high' culture. This was not the result of any material calculations or manipulation by an intelligentsia. The exigencies of the labour market and bureaucracy taught the Ruritanians the difference between dealing with sympathetic co-nationals and hostile aliens. This experience taught them to love (or hate) their own culture, and the culture in which they are *taught* to communicate becomes the core of their new identity.[3]

Here we encounter the first of the two principles of fission in industrial societies: that of barriers to communication. There is a second principle, which Gellner terms the inhibitors of 'social entropy'. These are culture traits that resist dispersion throughout the population of an industrial society, even after many decades. This means that it becomes impossible to assimilate individuals who possess the entropy-resistant trait, for example, those with genetic traits like pigmentation or with deeply engrained religious-cultural habits which 'frequently have a limpet-like persistence' – especially peoples with a scriptural religion and a special script, sustained by specialised personnel. In the later phases of industrialisation when inequalities are reduced and communication becomes easier, such groups cannot be assimilated even by a mobile, fluid society. They stand on the other side of the great 'moral chasms' which open up between groups with counter-entropic traits and the host society, creating the possibility of new nationalisms and nations (*ibid.*: ch. 6, esp. 70–3).[4]

Nationalism and industrialism

In many ways, this later version of Gellner's theory presents a much fuller and more elaborate picture of the causes of nationalism and its links with modernity than the earlier formulation. For one thing, it explains why there is no room for nations and nationalism in the pre-modern world. For another, it distinguishes earlier and later phases of industrialisation, and suggests why the later phases may give rise to movements of ethnic secession. And it also presents a new typology of nationalisms in terms of the relationship between cultural diversity, access to education and power-holding. Above all, in the distinction between 'low' and 'high' cultures, it grapples with the ambivalence of nationalism, its backward-looking as well as modernist impulses, and spells out the nature of the cultural transition that must be traversed at the threshold of modernity.

There are also important differences between the two versions. The earlier version had highlighted the role of language as the medium of instruction, and the cement of a modern society. In the later version, language, though still present, becomes secondary to the role of mass public education systems in the creation of citizens and in sustaining the high culture of an industrial society. Similarly, the earlier formulation had emphasised the role of the critical intelligentsia as one of the two 'prongs' of nationalism, the other being the proletariat. In the later version, little attention is given to the peculiar contribution of the intelligentsia, who are replaced by the state and its control and surveillance of the mass education system. This is part of a wider move away from agents of modernisation (classes, professional strata, etc.) to structures of modernity. Not only have individuals and their choices become irrelevant, group actors and their strategies have become at best the products of the interplay of 'structure' and 'culture', their movements preordained in the drama of the transition from 'low' to 'high' cultures. This is as true of the 'proletariat', which had figured prominently in Gellner's earlier version, as of the intelligentsia. Their earlier secessionist role is replaced by the unevenness of the processes of development, which in and by themselves ensure that there can be no modern empires, and that national units are the norm of industrial society. It is only the unassimilability of certain groups defined by pigmentation or ancient religious cultures that defies the determinism of industrialism.[5]

The original core of Gellner's theory, however, remains intact. If anything, it is more pronounced in the later version. Nations, argues Gellner, are functional for industrial society. They are indispensable in the modern world because industrial growth requires both widespread fluidity and patterned homogeneity, individual mobility combined with cultural standardisation. This can only be achieved by creating a uniform body of competent, substitutable citizens, and this in turn requires a large-scale public mass education system funded and controlled by the state. It was only with the onset of modernity that these conditions could be realised, and they explain why the modern era is *ipso facto* an age of nationalism.

This remains a powerful and relevant thesis, which seeks a deep and underlying cause for the impregnability of nations and the recurrence, and proliferation, of nationalisms in the modern world. But it is not without its problems. We might start by asking, with some historians, whether there is indeed such a phenomenon as 'nationalism-in-general', as opposed to the specific varieties, or even instances, of nationalist movement. Gellner counters this objection by elaborating his own typology of nationalisms, and by delineating a general or pure (ideal) type to which particular instances more or less approximate. Of course, this still leaves open the question of whether a particular instance, or even a whole group of instances, should properly be subsumed under the general concept. But the very fact that the participants and their opponents generally do subsume their activities under an overall concept of 'nationalism', testifies to its analytical necessity and utility.

More important is the problem of causation. One might well concede that nationalism is, in some sense, functional for modern, industrial society (on a variety of grounds), but this in no way explains the origins and spread of nationalism. This is not just a question of the logic of explanation. It is borne out by empirical observation of cases where the movement of nationalism quite clearly antedated the arrival of industrialism. In Serbia, Finland, Ireland, Mexico, West Africa and Japan, to take a few cases at random, there was no significant industrial development, or even its beginnings, at the time of the emergence of nationalism. In Denmark and Australia too, where development occurred through the modernisation of agriculture rather than through industrialisation, nationalist movements emerged in the mid-nineteenth and mid-twentieth centuries respectively. In the most striking case – Japan – the Meiji rulers sought to inculcate nationalist values and myths in order to modernise a country emerging from semi-feudal isolation. Even in the West – in France and Germany – nationalism became a powerful force before the onset of industrialism, though it coincided with the first movements towards modernisation.[6]

In Gellner's theory, it is the logic of industrial social organisation that determines the movement from 'low' to 'high' culture and the rise of nations. There is even the suggestion that nations and nationalism are the outward appearances of much deeper structural changes, and can be reduced to those changes. This impression arises out of Gellner's polemic against the self-image of nationalism. It is not nations that constitute the underlying reality waiting to be 'awakened' by nationalist Prince Charmings; it is the cultural homogeneity required by *modern* industrial social organisation that becomes visible as nations and nationalism. Nations and nationalists are, on this view, devoid of independent activity and volition; rather they constitute the *form* of industrialism, the way in which its workings become manifest in the phenomenal world.

This raises a further question. Given the plurality of routes taken by different countries as they move from a 'traditional' community to a more 'modern' type of society, given the varying interests and needs of elites and classes in each society, given the many guises in which nations appear, is it plausible to assume that in their actions, societies and their sub-groups all follow the same 'logic of the transition', and that the transition itself is, with a few minor variations, the selfsame road to be trodden by one and all? Gellner would argue that it was quite possible to accommodate the many variations of process and style, so long as the end-point of the transition, the goal of modernity with all its require-ments, was retained. In his view, the choices open to individuals and groups alike are severely restricted by the parameters of modernisation. Whatever variations elites may execute, the dance remains essentially the same.

It would take us too far from the subject to enter the debate about the charac-teristics of modernity and the validity and utility of the concept of modernisation. Suffice it to say that:

1 there is both lack of clarity, and considerable dispute, about the concept of modernisation and its relationship with industrialisation or development;
2 there is no agreement on the validity or utility of the underlying distinction between 'tradition' and 'modernity' and their alleged concomitants;
3 there are many instances where 'traditional' and 'modern' elements coexist and indeed intertwine;
4 there is a clear danger of ethnocentrism in most of the meanings associated with the concepts of modernity and modernisation.

Gellner's own usage is ambiguous. On the one hand, the concept of modernisa-tion seems to refer to economic growth or industrialisation; on the other hand, it has wider connotations, referring to everything that accompanies industrialisa-tion (its trappings and anticipations), notably westernisation. In its narrower usage, as we briefly saw, it is difficult to uphold a close link between nationalism and industrialism or development. Nationalisms emerge in all kinds of socioeco-nomic settings and social systems. In its wider usage, given the sheer regional and cultural variety of the concomitants of development, the concept of modernisa-tion breaks down into a series of trajectories and processes, which vary historically from state to state and between ethnic communities. The attempt to impose a single, abstract 'pure type' of modernity (and modernisation) on the rich variety of historical processes, so as to illuminate the underlying logic of the contrast and transition between a state of 'tradition' and one of 'modernity', exaggerates the historical gulf between them and denies important continuities and coexistences between elements of both. To this we shall shortly return.[7]

Nationalism and 'high cultures'

The main new concept employed by Gellner in his second formulation is that of 'high culture', that is, a literate, public culture inculcated through a mass, stan-dardised and academy-supervised education system, serviced by cultural specialists. It is essentially a preserve of cultivated urban personnel, and so may be likened to a tamed 'garden' culture. For Gellner national identity is simply the identification of citizens with a public, urban high culture, and the nation is the expression of that high culture in the social and political spheres. Nationalism in turn can be conceived of as the aspiration to obtain and retain such a high culture and make it congruent with a state.

There are a number of problems here. The first is the relationship of high cultures with states, and more generally politics. Is it the case that all 'high' cultures are embodiments of power, whether of powerful elites, powerful states or powerful peoples? Is the achievement of a high culture for a particular population also an act of empowerment, whereby the population enters, as it were, into the political kingdom and becomes a 'subject' of history? Such an implication seems to follow from Gellner's assumption that you need a high culture to 'swim in the sea of industria' and that cultures that fail to become literate, specialist-serviced, education-nourished 'high' cultures are doomed in a modern, industrial era. How then do 'low' cultures among small and powerless peoples, some of them even deprived of elites, convert themselves into 'high' cultures? What are the mechanisms which ensure success for such a metamorphosis? Gellner cites the view of Plamenatz that culturally well equipped peoples can adapt their cultures to the needs of a modern, industrial society much more easily than those that lack this cultural infrastructure. But this only sharpens the problem of accounting for the 'submerged peoples' and the way in which their savage 'low' cultures have managed to become literate, sophisticated, education-nourished and serviced by specialists (Plamenatz 1976; Gellner 1983: 99–100)

The problem is magnified for Gellner whenever he emphasises the discontinuities between the older 'low' and the modern 'high' cultures, whenever he highlights the modern roots of the latter, and the ways in which they answer to modern needs. It is difficult indeed to see how and why anyone should have wanted to turn the pre-modern Finnish or Czech, Kurdish or Ewe 'low' cultures into modern, literate 'high' cultures, rather than adopting the nearest high culture of the dominant ethnic population in the state. Of course, this is just what happened with increasing frequency at the level of the individual. But equally, at the collective level, the reverse process, the modernisation of low into high cultures, has become just as prevalent and of course far more explosive.[8]

There is a further problem. Gellner frequently underlines the invented, even artificial, nature of so much of the high culture of modernity, manufactured by intelligentsias and purveyed to thousands of schoolchildren through standardised textbooks and courses. His point is that we identify with the public *taught* culture in modern society, not with our culture of origin or of family.

Even if we concede the empirical point, the question of loyalty remains: why should anyone ardently identify with an official, school culture? We know from seventy years of communism how ineffective even two generations of mass indoctrination can be. Are we to believe that within a single generation peasants become French patriots simply because they have been processed through a common educational curriculum and school system, and because of this are prepared to die en masse for the *patrie en danger*? Is the sacrifice for the fatherland really a defence of an educationally sustained high culture? The problem becomes even more acute in authoritarian states – especially for non-dominant ethnic communities – as we have been so often reminded in recent years.[9]

It is perfectly true that modern citizens invest a great deal of time and effort in their education. But that of itself cannot explain the often intense commitment and passion for the nation which characterises so many people in all parts of the world. Public education is certainly strongly bound up with personal advancement, but the links between individual career paths and loyalty, let alone self-sacrifice for the nation, are far from clear. Even investment in their linguistic education by an intelligentsia cannot fully explain the ardour of their nationalism.

Nationalism and public education

In Gellner's second theory the mass, public system of education is given the fundamental task of instilling ardent loyalty to the nation in its citizens and sustaining the high cultures necessary for industrial societies. That was very much the role assigned to the new standardised system of mass education in the French Third Republic. In an effort to train and inspire a large number of fervent citizens after the great defeat in the Franco-Prussian War and the loss of Alsace and Lorraine, the republican leaders devised a universal system of mass public education based on a standardised curriculum, especially in 'national' subjects like literature, geography, history and physical education. In history, for example, the standard textbook by Lavisse was circulated for all French schoolchildren at various grades, and its message of French grandeur and territorial integrity became an important element in French national consciousness for succeeding generations. There were similar attempts to forge a national consciousness through mass public education in newly independent national states such as Japan, Turkey and Nigeria.[10]

There is little doubt that the leaders of new states (and some older ones) have taken the civic role of public education very seriously. But those that have done so with the greatest fervour are in most cases the leaders of nationalist regimes. These public, mass education systems and their values are the product, not the cause, of the nationalist movement once it has come to power. If we retrace the genesis and course of these nationalisms, we find that the first nationalists in each designated population, those that proposed the category and championed the cause of the nation-to-be, are not – cannot be – the product of the national mass, public education system which at that point in time had not come into being. In fact, they are more likely to be products of a traditional village education or of some other system of public education – usually of a colonial or imperial variety – within 'their' territories, or of both. In addition, they may have had some access to the education system (or its products) of another, usually distant national state through travel, reading or the mass media. Partly through a desire to imitate and compete with such systems, the first nationalists on coming to power make it their business to establish and maintain a mass public education system of their own which will reflect and express their system of national values (see Argyle 1976; A. D. Smith 1983a: ch. 6).

The same argument can also be applied to the mass of the adherents of these early nationalists, whom Miroslav Hroch has described as the patriotic agitators of phase B of the nationalist movement. They too will have been educated either in the family and village school, or in the gymnasia and public schools of the imperial or colonial power, or in both. In other words, the nationalist movement predates both the new high culture which it helps to create and the new public, mass education system which it establishes in the territory after independence. It follows that the ardour and passionate self-sacrifice of the nationalist movement cannot be explained in terms of exo-socialisation, the national mass education system, and an attachment to high culture. Rather, all these are products of nationalism and its programme of national regeneration (Hroch 1985, 1993).

But should we accept the nationalist belief in the efficacy of mass public education in fashioning a new national citizenry? Was it only the communist experiment in mass indoctrination that failed? Several Western public, mass education systems have, by their own reckonings, proved incapable of inculcating the relevant civic values, skills and loyalties in many of their 'products', which would suggest that even when they attach great importance to mass public education, their expectations are often disappointed. Mass civic education frequently failed to attain the national and political goals for which it was framed, and which nationalist theorists from Rousseau and Fichte to Gökalp and Ben-Zion Dinur expected it to achieve.[11]

Part of the problem with Gellner's account of the role of mass public education systems is that it assumes that there is only one 'genuine' version of nationalism, the German Romantic doctrine of organic nations, whose prime goal was to achieve cultural homogeneity in the designated population by 'educating the national will'. But, though influential in Eastern Europe and parts of Asia, this is by no means the only kind of nationalism, and even in these cases it has proved a singular failure in its own terms. In cases where the attempt was made to apply its premises to states with more than one minority ethnic community, it only succeeded in exacerbating ethnic tensions and highlighting the 'plural' nature of the state, as in the former Yugoslavia, the former Czechoslovakia, Iraq, Iran and India. Most states are in fact plural, so the drive for cultural homogeneity has rarely been able to attain its goal in liberal or democratic states. Even where enforced population transfers and genocide have been practised by authoritarian or totalitarian regimes, significant minorities often remain. Other models of nationalism have set greater store by territorial and political unity than cultural homogeneity – in the West as well as Africa, Latin America, Australasia and parts of Asia. While it would be simplistic to claim that these are 'civic' rather than 'ethnic' nationalisms (many instances are both in varying degrees), it is clear that the ethnic component has often been modified by other political traditions.[12]

In fact, in liberal and democratic states, the aim of a national mass education system has been not so much to homogenise the population as to unify them around certain shared values, symbols, myths and memories, allowing minorities among them to retain their own symbols, memories, myths and values, and seeking to accommodate or incorporate them within the broad public culture and its national mythology. The increasingly vociferous claims of these ethnic and religious minorities and the distaste in liberal societies for cultural repression, has not led to the abandonment of national loyalties or civic education. Instead, attempts have been made within the mass education system by the most advanced industrial societies to cater for a variety of ethno-religious cultures either tacitly or more overtly through the ideal of 'multiculturalism', using the resulting cultural diversity to enhance the quality of a more composite 'national identity'.[13]

Nationalism and historical continuity

Returning to the fundamental process in Gellner's theory, the transition from a low to a high culture, two questions arise. The first concerns the 'understanding co-national'. For Gellner, people do not embrace high cultures because they realise the 'needs of industrialism' or because they calculate its benefits. Rather, the circumstances of modernisation dislocated the Ruritanian peasants, and forced them to migrate to Megalomania in search of work and to come up against an often hostile bureaucracy. So it was the processes of modernisation that engendered an attachment to the new high culture. In these circumstances, the uprooted peasants soon learnt

> the difference between dealing with a co-national, one understanding and sympathising with their culture, and someone hostile to it.

Gellner continues:

> This very concrete experience taught them to be aware of their culture, and to love it (or, indeed, to wish to be rid of it) without any conscious calculation of advantages and prospects of social mobility.
>
> (Gellner 1983: 61)

Here, the culture they are taught to be aware of appears to be their indigenous 'low' culture, not the cultivated 'garden' variety associated with industrialism. The co-national, too, appears to be a member of this same low culture, who understands and sympathises with 'our' rural wild culture. This in turn suggests that the nation and nationalism pre-exist the transition to industrialism, that the particular new high culture has not yet been created, at least, not by understanding co-nationals, and that the actual distance between low and high cultures may not be as great as the theory assumes. Above all, the low culture (no doubt duly updated and streamlined) provides the ground both of affinity between Ruritanian peasants and understanding co-nationals, and of hostility between them and the bureaucrats who do not share the low culture.

There is, in fact, plenty of evidence that it is these low cultures which inspire such ardent loyalties. Thus the culture of the Czech-speaking peasants was not that of the earlier Bohemian aristocracy, nor was the Finnish culture continuous with that of the Swedish-speaking upper class minority. The links between Ukrainian peasant culture and that of Kievan Rus many centuries earlier are equally obscure, as are those between Slovak peasants and their shadowy heroic ancestors over a millennium earlier. In all these cases, it is the 'low' culture of the peasants that has triumphed and become institutionalised as the new high culture of these East European national states.[14]

This is one variation of the Gellnerian model. The other is where a new mass high culture is a modernised version of an older elite high culture, as in France and Poland, Japan and Ethiopia. Here we may wonder whether it is the needs of industrialism that explain and underlie the new high culture, or whether the shape and content of that culture is not better explained and derived from the old elite high culture of a dominant *ethnie*. That such pre-modern elite high cultures are modernised, their concepts developed, their vocabularies extended and their forms streamlined, is not in question. The point at issue is how far the modern, mass public culture of the national state is a modern version of the pre-modern elite high culture of the dominant *ethnie*, or how far it simply uses 'materials' from that culture for its own quite different, and novel, purposes (see Fishman *et al.* 1968, 1972; Edwards 1985).

As we saw, Gellner returns several times to this question. Each time he suggests a range of scenarios: some degree of continuity with the old low or high culture; obliteration of the pre-modern culture; interested selection from its themes and motifs; radical transformation of its elements; indeed, the invention of pre-modern cultures and the almost random use of some of its cultural materials – as he puts it: 'any old shred or patch would have served as well'. This is all part of the repertoire of nationalism and its cavalier use of the past.

The 'uses of history' model has its attractions. Historical precedents may be useful for nationalist rhetoric, as well as nationalist reformers who want to push through painful new measures to strengthen the nation. Historical *exempla virtutis* may also serve the purposes of nationalist moralists, teaching the heroic virtues of 'our ancestors'. The past can undoubtedly be put to good use and serve as a quarry of cultural materials for didactic illustration. In each case, the 'national past' serves the preoccupations, needs and interests of present-day leaders and followers, as is evident in the many territorial claims made by nationalists everywhere. In this Gellner subscribes to the modernist view of the past being shaped by present needs and circumstances (see Gellner 1997, ch. 15).[15]

But can 'the past' be ransacked in this way? Is it composed only of *exempla virtutis*, moral tableaux worthy of emulation? And can nationalists make use of ethno-history in such instrumental ways? That they have tried to do so, sometimes successfully, is not in dispute. Tilak made use of several themes and events of the Marathi and Hindu Indian pasts, including the warrior cult of Shivaji, the worship of the dread goddess Kali, and the advice of Lord Krishna to Arjuna in the *Bhagavad-Gita*. But, once unleashed, the emotions generated by such interpretations of the heroic past have deep and lasting consequences that bind instigators and followers into a framework and tradition not of their own making, as the recent troubled history of India demonstrates. They become subject to the continuities of tradition handed down by successive generations of a community, and by the understandings and emotions crystallised in those traditions in which they have been socialised. In other words, nationalists can sometimes use the 'ethnic past' for their own ends, but not in the long run: they soon find themselves locked in to its framework and sequences, and the assumptions that underlie the interpretations of successive generations.[16]

This is not to say that there is just one 'ethnic past' for each community, or that the understandings of successive generations of that community do not change. On the contrary: as groups and strata within the community are emancipated, new interpretations of the past are generated and, after a time, become part of a more complex overall image and understanding of 'our ethnic pasts'. At the same time, existing continuities and previous interpretations limit the possibilities of radical change.

Even in the case of the major revolutions, there is often a gradual return to some of the older collective interpretations and values after the violent stage of the revolution has run its course. Our understandings of past cultures set limits to the degree to which they can be transformed; the richer and better documented that past and those cultures, and the greater our knowledge and understanding of them, the more complex and more difficult will be the task of transforming those cultures and our interpretations of the past (see Brass 1991: chs 1–2). There is always therefore a complex interplay between the needs and interests of modern generations and elites, the patterns and continuities of older cultures, and the mediating interpretations of 'our' ethnic pasts. This raises a further question, which Gellner's theory does not take seriously: the modern desire to *authenticate* the past, to select from all that has gone before that which is distinctive, unique and 'truly ours', and thereby to mark out a unique shared destiny. In other words, the process of selection from communal traditions and their interpretations cannot be simply reduced to the interests and needs of particular elites and current generations. Such insistence on the shaping present blocks our understanding of the interplay between current and past generations and their respective concerns and achievements.[17]

It also omits the role of nationalism in relating the different generations, past, present and future, and their respective needs and achievements. As a collective salvation drama, nationalism specifies what shall count towards collective purification and regeneration. Briefly, everything that is popular, authentic and emancipatory contributes to the renaissance of the nation, while all that is sectional, cosmopolitan and oppressive must retard its rebirth. For nationalism, the supreme value is collective autonomy. But autonomy requires collective unity and a distinctive identity.

The 'we' cannot be truly self-regulating and inwardly free unless all its members are united and share a distinctive history and culture. Hence the foundation of collective autonomy must always be sought in the unity and distinctiveness of the community; and its distinctiveness or individuality in turn is gauged by the quantity and quality of elements that are peculiarly 'its own', which belong to, and are attributes of, that community and no other. True freedom consists in being 'true to oneself' conceived of as a unique and incommensurable collective cultural identity. The main task of the nationalist is to discover and discern that which is truly 'oneself' and to purge the collective self of any trace of 'the other'. Hence, the rediscovery, authentication and correct interpretation of a unique ethnic past becomes the focus of nationalist labours. Of these three, the process of 'authentication' or sifting elements of the corrupting other from those of the pure and genuine self, is pivotal: and as a rough guide, that which is 'of the people' is pure and genuine. Like Levin, who discovered in the simplicity and purity of the Russian peasant the secret of virtue, so nationalists discover the authentic nation in the life and values of the common people (see Thaden 1964).

For Gellner, of course, this is all part of the deception and self-deception of nationalism. But this is to miss the point. The nationalists may in reality practice urban modernity while extolling the agrarian life and its folkways, but their model of the nation and their inspiration for its regeneration is derived from their belief in the ideal of national authenticity and its embodiment in 'the people'. If we fail to grasp this, we are debarred from explaining the messianic ardour of nationalism, its ability time and again to confound the formal rationality of advanced industrial societies as well as the traditional routines of agrarian ones, and with chameleon-like adaptability provide new interpretations and emendations of received national images and narratives, as is occurring in contemporary Russia and Eastern Europe. It is this flexibility, coupled with its ardent belief in the people as touchstone of national authenticity, that enables nationalism to 'correct itself' and alter official or received versions of the national past and national destiny, while remaining true to its basic goals of collective authenticity, unity and autonomy (see Hutchinson 1987: ch. 1).

Hence nationalism's recurrent appeal to ethno-history, to an authentic past of the people, is no mere posturing or cavalier gesture, nor is it just popular rhetoric disguising the pain behind its true intentions. Rather, the *narodnik* element is essential to the project of modernisation. In this respect, one can see nationalism as a bridge between the distinctive heritage of the ethnic past and its 'irreplaceable culture values', and the necessity for each community to live as one nation among many in the increasingly bureaucratised world of industrial capitalism. In doing so, nationalism acts like a prism through which are preserved, albeit in changed forms, some of the continuities with the past amid the transformations of modernity.

Nationalism and the ethnic past

The problem of national historical continuity is closely bound up with the vexed question of the relationship of ethnicity and nationalism.

For many theorists, the adjectives 'ethnic' and 'national' are interchangeable, and they make little distinction between ethnic groups and nations. For others, ethnicity signifies a cleavage within a nation, usually within a national state; like regionalism, it is regarded as a 'sub-national' phenomenon. Gellner generally avoids the term itself, assimilating the adjective 'ethnic' to 'national' in speaking of boundaries, or using it interchangeably with 'culture', except where it seems to describe a 'racial' grouping. This imprecision and lack of attention to ethnic phenomena is of a piece with his cursory and ambivalent treatment of the relationship of nationalism to the past. Given the focus of his theory, the derivation of nations and nationalism from the consequences of modernity, it is hardly surprising that history and ethnicity are regarded as of secondary importance.[18]

But, as I shall go on to argue, ethnicity, like history, is crucial to an adequate understanding of nationalism. To assimilate ethnicity with nationality begs the question; to equate it with culture, an equally contested, ambiguous and multi-stranded concept, does little to advance our understanding. It also encourages a curious discussion of the strength or weakness of nationalism in terms of the number of 'cultures' (ethnic groups) that fail to 'awake' and strive to become nations ('determined slumberers', in Gellner's words). The fact is that most of these 'cultures' or 'ethnic groupings' are simply externally discerned categories; they have little or no collective self-awareness or sense of community and solidarity. To assume that a localised collection of people who speak similar dialects, observe the same customs and worship in the same liturgy, form an ethnic community and should therefore spawn a nationalism, if nationalism is to be regarded as 'strong', is to miss out vital stages of ethno-genesis, and bypass the search for factors that turn a loose ethnic category into an ethnic association and thence into an ethnic community, let alone a nation (see Handelman 1977; Eriksen 1993).

In those cases where pre-existent cultures were the products of ethnic communities, they often continue to possess a binding, collective quality which cannot be reduced to a series of (counter-entropic) 'traits' or 'shreds and patches'. Ethno-history is no sweetshop in which nationalists may 'pick and mix'; it sets limits to any selective appropriation by providing a distinctive context and pattern of events, personages and processes, and by establishing frameworks, symbolic and institutional, within which further ethnic developments take place. It furnishes a specific but complete heritage which cannot be dismembered and then served up *à la carte*.

The nationalist appeal to the past is therefore not only an exaltation of and summons to the people, but a rediscovery by alienated intelligentsias of an entire ethnic heritage and of a living community of presumed ancestry and history. The rediscovery of the ethnic past furnishes vital memories, values, symbols and myths, without which nationalism would be powerless. But these myths, symbols, values and memories have popular resonance because they are founded on living traditions of the people (or segments thereof) which serve both to unite and to differentiate them from their neighbours. This unity is in turn based on the powerful myth of a presumed common ancestry and shared historical memories. To achieve success, the nationalist presumption must be able to sustain itself in the face of historical enquiry and criticism, either because there is some well attested documentation of early ethnic origins or because the latter are so shrouded in obscurity as to be impervious to disconfirmation and refutation.

What makes these myths, values, symbols and memories so attractive and potent is their invocation of presumed kinship and residence ties to underpin the authenticity of the unique cultural values of the community. In this sense, the ethnic community resembles an extended family, or rather a 'family of families', one which extends over time and space to include many generations and many districts in a specific territory. This sense of extended kinship, of 'kith and kin', attached to a particular 'homeland', underlies the national identities and unity of so many modern nations and endows their members with a vivid sense of kin relatedness and immemorial continuity. These are themes on which I shall enlarge in Part II.

For the moment, we need to grasp the flawed nature of modernist theories such as Gellner's which, for all their perceptive originality, fail to account for the historical depth and spatial reach of the ties that underpin modern nations because they have no theory of ethnicity and its relationship to modern nationalism. The result is to debar their accounts from dealing with questions about which nations and nationalisms were likely to emerge, where and on what basis. While such theories address the questions of why and when nationalism-in-general emerged with considerable conviction, they cannot answer questions about which nations and where, and on what basis these particular nations arose, or which nations and nationalisms are likely to emerge in the future. For answers to those kinds of question, we need to turn elsewhere.

3 Capitalism and nationalism

Two great forces have shaped the modern world, two forces that grew up side by side, spread around the globe, and penetrated every aspect of contemporary life. These are the forces of capitalism and nationalism.

Some of the earliest attempts to provide explanations of nationalism have linked it causally to the rise of capitalism. This is the central thrust of the various socioeconomic variants of classical modernism. The question has always been whether one could convincingly derive the rise and spread of nations and nationalism from the social consequences of capitalism, or more generally from economic motivations and economic change. Here I want to consider some recent models which make these connections and assess the strengths and limitations of such approaches.

The background to these models is, of course, the heritage of classical Marxist interpretations of 'the national question'. Briefly, Marx and especially Engels tended to define modern nations, in the German Romantic tradition, as communities of 'language and natural sympathies', hence as in some sense 'natural', at least in form. In contrast, the national state and national*ism*, the ideological movement, were a peculiar outgrowth of the modern period and especially of the rise of industrial capitalism. For Marx and Engels, the national state was the necessary terrain for the establishment of market capitalism by the bourgeoisie; only a nationally unified territorial state could ensure the free and peaceful movement of the capital, goods and personnel necessary for large-scale production, market exchange and distribution of mass commodities. The creation of linguistically homogeneous nations was therefore a prerequisite of market capitalism, and hence it was inevitable that the further progress of capitalism depended upon the political and cultural development of what Marx called the 'leading nations'. Only in highly developed nations was it possible to envisage the social revolution which would lead to the overthrow of the national bourgeoisie within each nation and the establishment of socialist regimes by the proletariat, a class that was both universal but also the true embodiment of the nation and its culture. Neither Marx nor Engels envisaged the withering away of nations along with the state; on the contrary, they assumed that though there would be global cultural convergence, national forms and cultures would persist, albeit with a socialist content.[1]

As far as more immediate strategies were concerned, Marx and especially Engels tended to divide nationalisms into 'progressive' and 'reactionary', according to whether they were likely to hasten the social revolution and further the socialist development of the 'historic' nations. Engels, in particular, adopted Hegel's theory of 'historyless peoples' which discriminated between the smaller peoples who had no tradition of statehood, and the larger peoples who had possessed a state or political tradition in the past and would therefore be able to build a national state in the future and should be encouraged to do so. For this reason he was especially committed to Poland's independence struggle, and because he felt it would weaken the great bastion of reactionary feudalism, Tsarist Russia.[2]

Their Marxist successors, Lenin, Kautsky, Luxemburg and Bauer, were forced to devote much greater attention to 'the national question', because of the spate of independence struggles in Eastern Europe and the massive national stirrings within the Habsburg empire and the Tsarist empire, 'the prisonhouse of the nationalities'. Several themes were developed in this context, amid heated arguments among the protagonists:

1   the petit-bourgeois nature of nationalism, its locus in an intelligentsia increasingly squeezed between big capital and the great proletarian movements;
2   the use of nationalist ideologies by a triumphant but nervous bourgeoisie to induce 'false consciousness' and thereby divide and divert the masses who threatened their position;
3   the progressive nature of anti-colonial liberation movements, i.e. of nationalisms led by a nascent colonial bourgeoisie against the exploitation of imperialist capitalists;
4   the right of all genuine nations to secede from larger polities, especially semi-feudal empires, until such time as a socialist regime was established in the area.

Though there never was a Marxist consensus about nationalism, these themes have repeatedly surfaced in their writings. Apart from the Austro-Marxists, who sought to recognise the role of culture and community as independent variables in the evolution of nations, the classical Marxists adhered to a largely economistic analysis which either explained or reduced nationalist struggles to the workings of the particular stage of capitalism (early, late, monopoly, imperialist, etc.) held to be responsible for these political developments. As modern components of the political and ideological superstructure, nations and nationalism had, in principle, to be derived from the economic contradictions of capitalism and to be explicable largely, if not wholly, in terms of its class configurations and struggles (see Orridge 1981; Nimni 1994).

Imperialism and uneven development

Postwar socioeconomic models of nationalism have both developed and broken with these Marxist traditions. We see this ambivalence especially in the work of Tom Nairn. Nairn draws on a number of sources for his theory of uneven development and imperialism. Two are derived from the Marxist heritage and have been briefly indicated: Lenin's idea of capitalist imperialism and colonial nationalist liberation movements, and Engels' adaptation of Hegel's theory of historyless peoples. More immediately, however, Nairn makes great use of André Gunder Frank's dependency model and his notions of 'centre and periphery' and 'underdevelopment', though he gives the latter a new direction, and links it to the idea of *'uneven* development', a notion which he takes from Gellner's theory, but attaches the unevenness to capitalism rather than industrialisation.[3]

Nairn starts by placing nationalism within the context of political philosophy. He regards nationalism as the most ideal and subjective of ideological phenomena, and argues that we can only grasp the extraordinary manifestations and gyrations of this most subjective and romantic of phenomena by locating it firmly within the violent workings of modern world political economy which it faithfully mirrors. Nairn concedes that there have been nationalities and ethnic identities before the modern period, but seeks to limit his analysis historically by focusing on the specifically modern and global phenomenon of *nationalism*. To explain why nationalism has spread with such whirlwind force and success across the globe, we need a special theory which derives it from peculiarly modern developments (Nairn 1977: 97–8).

In this context, the key factor is not capitalism *per se*, but the *uneven development* of capitalism. To grasp its effects, we have to adopt the spatial analysis of 'centre' and 'periphery' for the period after 1800. From that date, at least, the world can be divided into capitalist centres in the West, and underdeveloped peripheries outside. On one level, nationalism derives from the unequal encounter between centre and periphery. This inequality derives from the uneven, and often violent and discontinuous, imposition of capitalism by Western bourgeoisies on undeveloped and backward regions of the world, and their exploitation and underdevelopment of successive peripheries in the interests of the further development of the centres. Unlike the metropolitan fantasy of 'an even and progressive development of material civilisation and mass culture' characteristic of the European Enlightenment, imperialist development involves not merely the annexation of overseas territory by force, but the exploitation of the cheap labour and resources of peripheral regions of the world by metropolitan capitalists and states (*ibid.*: 336–7).

On another level, the spread of nationalism can be derived from the class consequences of the uneven diffusion of capitalism. The jagged nature of capitalism's advance across the globe, its tendency to affect successive areas at different times, rates and intensities, necessitates the underdevelopment and exploitation of the peripheries, and the consequent relative helplessness of their elites in the face of the massive superiority of the colonial capitalists in

technology, wealth, arms and skills. The peripheral elites possess no such advantages; they are bound in the 'fetters' of imperialism and are all too conscious of
their helplessness. The only resource left to them is people, masses of people:

> People is all they have got: this is the essence of the underdevelopment
> dilemma itself.
>
> (*ibid.*: 100)

But the elites may be able to turn the tables and achieve development 'in their
own way', if the masses can be mobilised against the exploitation of imperialism.

> This meant the conscious formation of a militant, inter-class community
> rendered strongly (if mythically) aware of its own separate identity vis-a-vis
> the outside forces of domination.
>
> (*ibid.*: 340)

But to 'turn to the people' means speaking their language, taking a kindlier view
of their general 'culture' and

> coming to terms with the enormous and still irreconcilable *diversity* of
> popular and peasant life.
>
> (*ibid.*: 100–1, original emphasis)

This in turn meant adopting the programme of romanticism which extols a
'sentimental culture', one that is 'quite remote from Enlightenment rationalism'
(*ibid.*: 101, 340). Politically, as the most aware section of the native bourgeoisie,

> The new middle-class intelligentsia of nationalism had to invite the masses
> into history; and the invitation-card had to be written in a language they
> understood.
>
> (*ibid.*: 340)

As a result, nationalism is inevitably Janus-headed, facing backward to a mythical past and forward to a future of development in freedom. It is also inevitably
populist as well as romantic. The true nerve centre of political nationalism

> is constituted by a distinctive relationship between the intelligentsia (acting
> for its class) and the people.
>
> (*ibid.*: 101)

The function of this intelligentsia is to construct a national culture out of the
'prehistoric' qualities and 'archaic' naturalness of popular cultures, that is, all
those customs, myths, folklore and symbols which an irrational movement like
romanticism loves to exaggerate. This is what they proceeded to do with such
success in nineteenth-century Europe, starting in Germany and Italy, and what

they continue to do in the recent 'neo-nationalisms' of the West – in Scotland, Catalonia, Quebec, Flanders and elsewhere. Despite some discontinuities with classic nationalisms, the latter share the same basic situation of relative depriva- tion *vis-à-vis* an invasive centre, operating through the oil industry, the multinational companies and the superpowers, and in these cases too their intel- ligentsias seek to construct a militant inter-class community with its own separate identity and myths (*ibid.*: 127–8, 175–81).

Populism and romanticism

Nairn's theory seeks to capture the general mechanism behind the worldwide appeal and spread of nationalism, and he has undoubtedly achieved an original synthesis of spatial and social elements. His basic purpose still derives from the Marxist project of explaining nations and nationalism in terms of the contradic- tions of political economy and the class struggles which they engender, but he has placed this traditional mode of analysis in a new spatial framework which combines elements from dependency models and Gellner's theory. At the same time, he has been mindful of the importance of the cultural content of nation- alism, and the ways in which the intelligentsia seek to mobilise the masses through language, customs and myths.

But does the synthesis work? Can it encompass the rich variety of nation- alisms which Nairn underlines? Will it tell us why, on his own account, the Welsh movement is so romantic and culturally oriented while the equivalent Scots movement is so practical and hardheaded? Will it help us to fathom why some nationalisms are religious, others secular, some are moderate, others aggressive, some are authoritarian and others more democratic?

Nairn might well reply that such refinement is not part of his purpose in furnishing a political economy theory of nationalism. All he has tried to do is to outline the main contours of a global explanation of why political nationalism has become such a powerful and ubiquitous ideological movement in the modern world; it would require other, lower-level theories to account for signifi- cant variations within the field of nationalisms.

At this global level, two main problems require close scrutiny: the characteri- sation of 'nationalism', the dependent variable, and the nature and effectiveness of the explanatory principle, the 'uneven development of capitalism'.

Nairn nowhere defines 'nationalism'. But, as we saw, he characterises it as the creation of a 'militant, inter-class community rendered strongly (if mythically) aware of its own separate destiny *vis-à-vis* the outside forces of domination'. Such a community is forged, mainly by an intelligentsia appealing to, and mobilising, the people; and it is forged in opposition to 'outside forces'. Nationalism supplies a myth: that of the separate destiny of an inter-class community. But how does this sense of a separate destiny emerge? Nairn does not elaborate. There are some observations about pre-existing 'mass sentiments' and peasant ethnic cultures which the intelligentsia must use; but we are offered no theory of ethnicity or history. The sense of separate destiny appears to emerge simply from the confrontation with European imperialism. In practice, this elides two forms of nationalism in Africa and Asia: the civic, territorial form based upon the colonial territory and the colonial experience, which would fit Nairn's model better, and the more ethnic, genealogical form based upon pre-existing popular ethnic communities whose rivalries with other ethnic communities had been sharpened by colonial urbanisation, for which Nairn's analysis is less apposite. For though Nairn recognises that ethnic communities and struggles existed well before the modern period, their role is largely passive: at most, they furnish some materials for the construction of modern nations by intelligentsias. The 'masses' as such play no part in the drama of nationalism.[4]

This important omission stems from another crucial element in Nairn's characterisation of nationalism: the 'populist' element. For Nairn, nationalism's populist character is not the result of a popular movement. It is a movement of the intelligentsia *to* the people, not a movement of the people for themselves. 'The people' remain a *Klasse an Sich*. Now, since the new intelligentsia, in order to construct the nation in Nairn's terms must be united by romanticism, it follows that every nationalism must be 'populist', that is, it must 'appeal to the people' as the repository of everything that romantics value. This blanket, definitional characterisation makes it impossible to distinguish, as Nairn wishes to do in the cases of Scotland and Wales, between nationalisms that were genuinely populist, and those that paid lip-service to the people and remained largely middle-class in inspiration and following, such as early Indian nationalism.[5]

The largely mute and passive role of an undifferentiated 'people' in Nairn's account also derives from a third element in his characterisation of nationalism: the romantic mythical quality of the inter-class community. The myth of the self-aware and self-determining nation, as well as of its class unity, is the product of the romanticism of the intelligentsia, because only romanticism can create a 'national culture' and hence a nationalist movement. There are a number of problems here.

The first is a matter of historical fact. Not all nationalisms were equally romantic, in Nairn's sense of 'idealist and subjectivist'. Yes, they all look back to (or assume) some heroic past, which they doubtless idealise, but the nationalism of the French and American Revolutions, as well as strong currents within Scots and Catalan nationalisms, were (and are) of the more practical, 'sober bourgeois' variety. In fact, several latterday nationalisms, though they contain a romantic element, have become far less idealistic and subjectivist, preferring to base their political claims on social and economic arguments (see Esman 1977; A. D. Smith 1981a: ch. 9).

Nor is it true that only romanticism can create a 'national culture'. This assumes that national cultures are latterday artefacts collected and put together by the intelligentsia from the variety of folk cultures in a given region, because of their idealisation of the 'folk'. In fact, quite a few nationalists have not been particularly concerned with the folk, let alone folk cultures, which are usually local and which a true romantic purist would wish to leave intact. A Nasser, a Sukarno and a Nehru, while eulogising 'the people' in the abstract, was more concerned with trying to create a new public 'high culture' which would unite the diverse ethnic and religious groups within their new states, than with the romanticisation of popular cultures which would be likely to weaken and divide the fragile unity of the state which they had inherited. The fact that they and their successors have had only limited success in forging a united nation says something about the strength of popular ethnic ties that undermine the new 'nation-to-be', but it does not turn all nationalists into romantics.[6]

What this line of reasoning appears to assume is that the German Fichtean version of nationalism which *was* largely romantic, in the sense of idealist and subjectivist, provides the 'true' standard of all nationalisms. But this is to relegate or even deny other forms of nationalism and to judge them all by a single (Western) criterion. While I would concede a 'romantic' element in every nationalism (in that they all seek to measure the present by reference to a heroic past for moral purposes), this does not mean that they are all equally imbued with 'idealism and subjectivism' or that the national culture which accompanies their emergence may not have some 'objective' basis in pre-modern ethnic ties.

Characterising nationalism as a species of romanticism also allows Nairn to treat it as a movement of the periphery. In fact, the earliest nationalisms were firmly metropolitan, as Liah Greenfeld's detailed recent study demonstrates. They emerged in England, then in Britain, in France and in America, even earlier than in Germany (the first periphery?). Shaftesbury, Bolingbroke, Burke, Montesquieu, Rousseau, Sieyes and Jefferson laid the foundations for the secular forms of nationalism in the eighteenth century, some of them even before Herder and well before Fichte, Schlegel and Muller. This means that national sentiment, as well as nationalism, percolated through the educated classes of these national states and began to influence their economic activities and colonial rivalries as much as their politics and culture. The creation of a national culture in these early national states was certainly the work of intellectuals and professionals, but it owed little to romanticism and underdevelopment (Greenfeld 1992; Kemilainen 1964).

'Nationalism-producing' development?

The link between romanticism and backwardness, which goes back at least to Hans Kohn, brings us to the second problem-area: Nairn's explanatory principle of the 'uneven development of capitalism'. The core of his theory is the link between romanticism, backwardness and the periphery. In the centre, the 'West', nationalism is not a major issue (though there are national identities). This is because the centre had no real need of romanticism, as the bourgeoisie possessed the self-confidence that comes with successful social and economic development. Instead, it inflicted nationalism on a periphery which it sought to dominate and exploit. By contrast, that periphery had to adopt nationalism because its underdevelopment, its helplessness, required mythical compensations. These were provided by romanticism with its cult of the people and their culture. As with Kohn's 'Eastern' nationalisms, too, the intelligentsia play a pivotal role in the periphery, where the small bourgeoisie lacks the necessary confidence to beat its own path to self-sustaining growth. Instead, the intelligentsia must provide a mythical sense of separate destiny for a whole community by forging a national culture based on folk elements and mobilising the masses. Hence the strength of idealist and subjectivist components in peripheric nationalisms (see Kohn 1967a, esp. ch. 7; also Kohn 1960).

But many of the sharp dichotomies built into Nairn's analysis cannot be sustained. The romantic movement was, in its eighteenth-century origins, a British (English, Irish, Scots and Welsh) movement, and was developed by both the French and the Germans from the 1770s onwards. The 'periphery' existed as much within regions of England and France (the two cases of bourgeois centres that Nairn singles out) as outside these national states, as Eugen Weber's study of late nineteenth-century France has demonstrated. 'Underdevelopment' characterised Brittany and Wales, but also parts of the north of England, well into the twentieth century, whereas parts of Eastern Europe (Bohemia, Silesia) were relatively developed. Nationalisms have also emerged with great force in 'overdeveloped' regions such as Slovenia, Croatia, Euzkadi and Catalonia, and among peoples who were 'well endowed' relative to their neighbours and/or political centres, such as the Armenians, Greeks and Jews.[7]

To which Nairn might reply that this only goes to demonstrate his basic theorem, the uneven, discontinuous way in which capitalism has spread across the globe, creating conflict between relatively enriched and relatively impoverished regions. Now, few would disagree that industrial capitalism developed in this piecemeal, jagged manner. What they question are the consequences of uneven development for the incidence of nationalism. The trajectory of capitalism's discontinuous spread is not always coterminous with the diffusion of nationalism. Relatively well developed Silesia and Piedmont, for example, did not develop separate nationalist movements, despite some regional sentiment. Relatively underdeveloped regions such as the northeast of England or Crete, southern Italy or southern Egypt, failed to develop a separate nationalism. Given the failure of so many socioeconomic 'regions' to coincide with particular 'ethnic communities', regional economic disparities are unlikely to be translated into nationalist movements. The lines of the economic and the ethnic maps regularly diverge (see Connor 1994: ch. 6).

What this suggests is the relative independence of ethnicity as a variable in the rise and spread of nationalism. It is only in circumstances where regional economic disparities are conjoined and coterminous with particular ethnic communities that there is a likelihood of a nationalist movement emerging in that region. But what does the movement represent? In this case, we are dealing, not with a regional movement of social protest, but with an ethnic nationalism which aims to secure political recognition and perhaps territorial autonomy, even independence, for a self-aware and well developed *ethnie* or ethnic community. In other words, the economic disparities and social deprivations are placed in the service of the wider political purposes of ethnic communities, or of their elites, which the relevant state authorities have suppressed or marginalised. Similarly, the extent to which a movement can organise to press the political claims of an ethnic community, depends in turn on the political context in which it operates and the degree to which state authorities and state ideologies permit some or any political organisations to function (see Webb 1977; A. D. Smith 1981a: ch. 2).

Part of the problem with Nairn's analysis of the relationship between uneven development and nationalism is his oversharp dichotomisation of 'ideal' and 'material' factors, which in reality are so often intertwined. True to the 'economic last instance', Nairn is forced to place culture and ethnicity in the 'ideal' realm and so attempt to 'derive' them from the economic contradictions of global capitalism. The result is a socioeconomic version of modernism which combines explanatory economic reductionism with an expressive, even romantic, characterisation of nationalism, all set within a fixed time-frame determined by the uneven expansion of industrial capitalism. The fact that, as so often in the broad Marxian tradition, ethnicity and uneven ethno-history are never accorded a place alongside class struggle as independent explanatory principles, seriously undermines the chances of constructing a more multi-causal theory, one which can be sensitive to the 'which' and 'where' as well as the 'why' and 'when' of nations and nationalism.

If Nairn has not completely freed his analysis from the Marxist 'fortress' with its constricting view of nationalism, he has at least provided an understanding of one of the fundamental contributing factors to what we may term the 'uneven development of nationalism'. One of the striking facets of nationalism, so often remarked upon, is its explosive unpredictability. In trying to account for each and every explosion in terms of the single factor of capitalism's uneven development, Nairn's arrow has overshot its mark. At the same time, even if there can be no mechanical, one-to-one relationship between the uneven development of global capitalism and that of nationalism, the turbulence generated by both helps to generate further exploitation, underdevelopment and nationalist mobilisations. Nor is the process all one-way. An 'imitative-reactive' nationalism may spur economic growth through the perception of collective *atimia*. Japan is a good example of a 'reactive nationalism' which generated massive economic development which in turn fed the nationalist ambitions of Japan's rulers; but the relationship between nationalism and uneven development was mediated both by the imperial state and Japan's cultural heritage.[8]

All of which suggests that a protean phenomenon like nationalism cannot easily be tied to any particular processes such as relative deprivation and under-development, however powerful, pervasive and global. Other factors in the domains of culture and politics may be even more significant in locating the rise of nations and the spread of nationalism.

The social base of nationalism

One of the central issues raised by Nairn's analysis is the social composition of the ideological movement of nationalism. For many, nationalism is specifically a movement of the intellectuals, or more broadly, the intelligentsia. They occupy a pivotal role in the analyses of Ernest Gellner, Elie Kedourie, J. H. Kautsky, Peter Worsley and Anthony D. Smith and by implication, Benedict Anderson, providing both the leadership and the main following of the movement, as well as being the most zealous consumers of nationalist mythology.[9]

There is considerable truth in this characterisation. Most nationalisms are led by intellectuals and/or professionals. Intellectuals furnish the basic definitions and characterisations of the nation, professionals are the main disseminators of the idea and ideals of the nation, and the intelligentsia are the most avid purveyors and consumers of nationalist myths. One has only to scrutinise the origins and early development of nationalisms in central and eastern Europe, India, China, the Arab Middle East, Nigeria, Ghana, French West Africa and North Africa, to see how intellectuals and professionals have acted as the midwives, if not the parents, of the movement. Even in continents like Latin America, North America and Southeast Asia, 'printmen' and professionals played an important role in the dissemination of national ideals (see Anderson 1991: ch. 4; Argyle 1976; Gella 1976).

In a sense, this is a truism. All modern political and social movements require well educated leaders if they are to make any impact on a world in which secular education, communications and rational bureaucracy have become the hall-marks of modernity. They require the skills of oratory, propaganda, organisation and communications which professionals have made largely their preserve. Besides, the meaning of the term 'intellectual' is not uniform; it takes its char-acter from the traditions and circumstances of each culture area, and we should be careful not to compare cases that are essentially dissimilar (Zubaida 1978; Breuilly 1993: ch. 2).

What is more important is the relationship between the 'intellectuals', however defined, the professionals and the 'people'. This is what Nairn was attempting to characterise and place at the nerve centre of nationalism's success. Miroslav Hroch's analysis of the social composition of nationalist movements in a number of smaller east European countries, takes this suggestion one stage further. Like Peter Worsley before him, Hroch sees a chronological progression from elite to mass involvement in nationalist mobilisation. Only for Hroch, this occurs in three main stages. First, an original small circle of intellectuals redis-covers the national culture and past and formulates the idea of the nation (phase A). There follows the crucial process of dissemination of the idea of the nation by agitator-professionals who politicise cultural nationalism in the growing towns (phase B). Finally the stage of popular involvement in nationalism creates a mass movement (phase C). Hroch applies this schema to the nationalisms of small peoples in the context of processes of urbanisation and industrialisation in Eastern Europe in the latter half of the nineteenth and early twentieth centuries, and shows how regional elites were important elements in the course of nation-alist developments (Worsley 1964; Pearson 1983; Hroch 1985).

But can such a sequence be generalised? And are 'the people' always involved? It is tempting to see nationalism as a river of wave-like movements starting out as a trickle in its cultural heartlands and gaining in power and extent of involvement as it gathers pace. This is one of nationalism's most successful self-images. But it can also be misleading and Eurocentric. The 'trickle' of scholarly circles of ethnic rediscoverers may suddenly break out into a flood, or the political movement of subelites may antedate the cultural revival, while intellectuals (as creators of ideas) may appear later on the scene. This latter scenario can be found in the Eritrean and Baluch struggles for independence, where only later was there any attempt to give cultural substance to an essentially social and political movement of liberation from oppression. Nor can we always count on the movement involving 'the masses'. To some extent this depends on tactical considerations of the leaders. Galvanising the 'people', beyond rhetorical appeals, may jeopardise middle-class interests or it may involve distasteful recourse to religious symbolism and uneasy compromises with traditional elites in order to mobilise strata with subordinate roles and traditional outlooks for the nationalist cause.[10]

Nevertheless, even if the east European pattern is not universal and cultural nationalism sometimes occupies a subordinate role, at least initially, it can still be convincingly argued that for a new nation to achieve lasting popular success and maintain itself in a world of competing nations, intellectuals and professionals have an important, perhaps crucial role to play. Beyond the immediate needs of propaganda, advocacy and communications, the intellectuals and intelligentsia are the only strata with an abiding interest in the very idea of the nation, and alone possess the ability to bring other classes onto the platform of communal solidarity in the cause of autonomy. Only they know how to present the nationalist ideal of autoemancipation through citizenship so that all classes will, in principle, come to understand the benefits of solidarity and participation. Only they can provide the social and cultural links with other strata which are necessary for the ideal of the nation to be translated into a practical programme with a popular following. This is not to deny the importance of other elites or strata like bureaucrats, clergy and officers, who can exert a powerful influence on the cultural horizons and political directions of particular nationalisms. But, whereas such 'leading classes' may vary between and even within movements at different times without endangering the success of the movement, the pivotal role of professionals and intellectuals must remain constant or the movement risks disintegration.

When intellectuals and professionals split into rival nationalist organisations fighting each other, the whole movement is weakened and jeopardised (see Gella 1976; A. D. Smith 1981a: ch. 6; Pinard and Hamilton 1984; and more generally, Gouldner 1979).

Internal colonialism

Some of the same class insights and structural problems can be encountered in a very different variant of socioeconomic modernism. But, with Michael Hechter's reading of the recent revival of ethnic sentiments and nationalist movements in the industrialised West, we move even further away from the original Marxist basis of so much socioeconomic modernism.

Hechter's first and probably his best known formulation arose from his detailed study of the political and economic development of the British Isles from the Tudors until the 1960s. His analysis proceeds at a number of levels. The first is immediate and political, the growing resistance of 'the Celtic fringe' to incorporation by the British state in the 1960s, as evidenced in the growth of power of the Scottish National Party and, to a lesser extent, Plaid Cymru, and the early troubles in Northern Ireland. A second level is theoretical, namely a growing dissatisfaction with the Parsonian functionalist and diffusionist paradigm of development, and the need to replace it with a new framework based on the paradigm of peripheral dependency and underdevelopment. A third level is industrial-global: the possibility of explaining the growth of peripheral protest and resistance in the advanced states of the West as the result of the unequal division of labour within an advancing industrial capitalism (Hechter 1975: ch. 2).

To this end, Hechter traces the relations between 'centre' and 'periphery' within Britain to the expansion of the 'strong' Tudor state in the early sixteenth century. Under Henry VIII and his successors, first Wales and then Ireland were brought firmly within the jurisdiction of the English state, and this process of geopolitical unification was given further impetus by the union of the two Crowns of England and Scotland in 1603, followed a century later by the Act of Union in 1707 which left a single Parliament in London. For Hechter, this process was always unequal: England was variously preponderant or oppressive in political terms (*ibid.*: chs. 3–4).

However, it was only when to political incorporation was added economic exploitation that we may begin to speak of Wales, Ireland and Scotland as being reduced to the status of Britain's 'internal colonies'. This state of affairs emerged with the spread of industrialisation from its English heartlands to the peripheries. Capitalist industrialism created both a new economic dependence of the periphery on the core, and a whole new nexus of social ties as a result of intensified and regular, if unequal, interaction between the peripheries and the centre. Until the advent of industrial capitalism, the colonial situation was latent and obscured; thereafter it became clear and manifest (*ibid.*: ch. 5).

How can the situation of 'internal colonialism' be defined? For Hechter, echoing the dependency theories associated with André Gunder Frank, Robert Blauner and Rodolfo Stavenhagen, it denotes a state of structural dependence. Analogous to relations between the Indian cultural peripheries and the core collectivity in Latin American societies, internal colonies in an industrialised Western Europe possess many of the features found in such overseas colonial situations. Thus:

> Commerce and trade among members of the periphery tend to be monopolised by members of the core. Credit is similarly monopolised. When commercial prospects emerge, bankers, managers, and entrepreneurs tend to be recruited from the core. The peripheral economy is forced into complementary development to the core, and thus becomes dependant on external markets. Generally, this economy rests on a single primary export,

either agricultural or mineral. The movement of peripheral labour is determined largely by forces exogenous to the periphery. Typically there is great
migration and mobility of peripheral workers in response to price fluctuations of exported primary products. Economic dependence is reinforced
through juridical, political, and military measures. There is a relative lack of
services, lower standard of living and higher level of frustration, measured
by such indicators as alcoholism, among members of the peripheral group.
There is national discrimination on the basis of language, religion or other
cultural forms. Thus the aggregate economic differences between core and
periphery are causally linked to their cultural differences.

(*ibid.*: 33–4)

This (internal) colonial situation, as the product of external forces, reveals a
further important difference with the endogenous development found in Europe
and Japan: the development of a 'cultural division of labour'. Thus,

colonial development produces a cultural division of labour: a system of
stratification where objective cultural distinctions are superimposed on class
lines. High status occupations tend to be reserved for those of metropolitan
culture; while those of indigenous culture cluster at the bottom of the stratification system.

(*ibid.*: 30)

For Hechter, cultural distinctions have become increasingly important in an age
of mass literacy and education; but the social conditions of modernity which
encourage individuals to band together as members of ethnic groups are problematic. What is clear is that, in contrast to class relations in the advanced core,
the backward periphery is characterised by status group solidarity. The reason
for this difference is ultimately political.

The persistence of objective cultural distinctiveness in the periphery must
itself be the function of an unequal distribution of resources between core
and peripheral groups.

(*ibid.*: 37)

That unequal distribution of resources is in turn a function of the control exer-
cised by the ethnic core over every aspect of the periphery's social and economic
life, and its refusal to lower the barriers to incorporation and acculturation of the
periphery. In which case, the reverse situation may later develop:

if at some initial point acculturation (sc. of the periphery) did not occur
because the advantaged group would not permit it, at a later time acculturation may be inhibited by the desires of the disadvantaged group for
independence from a situation increasingly regarded as oppressive. This
accounts for the cultural 'rebirths' so characteristic of societies undergoing

nationalistic ferment. It is not that these groups actually uncover evidence of their ancient cultural past as an independent people; most often such culture is created contemporaneously to legitimate demands for the present-day goal of independence, or the achievement of economic equality.

(ibid.: 38–9)

But economic inequalities and cultural differences are not enough to generate ethnic solidarity and ethnic nationalism. What is also required is adequate communication among members of the oppressed group. In the economically backward periphery, occupational stratification is reinforced by residential segregation, and this favours ethnic rather than class solidarity. So the

internal colonialism model predicts, and to some extent explains, the emergence of just such a 'cultural division of labour', and therefore the likelihood of ethnic persistence and ultimately of political secession.

(ibid.: 42–3)

To this structural model, Hechter adds a more ad hoc explanation for the postwar revival of ethnic nationalism in the Celtic periphery of the United Kingdom. Noting the differences between a more unified Ireland, and a more economically and hence politically divided Scotland and Wales, as a result of more intense and focused industrialisation, Hechter argues that all three suffered prolonged economic stagnation as internal colonies as well as cultural stratification. This persisting situation sapped people's faith in the all-British class-based party system so that by the 1960s,

Nationalism has reemerged in the Celtic periphery largely as a reaction to this failure of regional development.

(ibid.: 265)

And even more specifically:

The most recent crystallisation of Celtic nationalism may ultimately be understood as a trenchant critique of the principle of bureaucratic centralism.

(ibid.: 310)

But, ultimately, it is the structural situation of systematic dependance of the periphery that explains the persistence of regional sectionalism, and thereby encourages its members to resist an incorporation and assimilation that had previously been refused them.

Ethno-regionalism

This is a powerful and persuasive thesis. It places the revival of nationalism, and the persistence of ethnic ties, firmly within the transformations of the whole social structure, deducing these outcomes from the situations to which those changes give rise. It correctly predicts the continual resistance of smaller ethnic groups situated at the margins of large states to the pressures of modern state and capitalist penetration. It demonstrates how those very processes of penetration necessarily engender sharp political reactions on the part of the besieged peripheral communities. Moreover, it offers a two-stage historical account, in terms of, first, political conquest, and then economic subordination, to account for the backwardness, exploitation and neglect of the periphery for the development and benefit of the core and its elites.

But how well does the model of 'internal colonialism' fit the many instances of exploited and impoverished regions in the industrialised West? Take the case of Brittany. Here, until the 1980s, we find a relatively neglected region, designated in the 1962 Debré Plan as part of the western *désert* to be turned into 'parklands'. Without proper communications and infrastructure, Brittany showed all the signs of a depressed region and 'internal colony', reinforced by decades of cultural discrimination and disdain by the French core. However, as more and more Bretons compared their plight with other French regions, Brittany in the 1960s began to witness a revival of Breton culture and a renewed Breton political movement, with some violent fringes, to redress the situation; and this in turn helped to change French policy towards redevelopment of the region (Reece 1979; A. D. Smith 1981a: chs. 1, 9).

But, if Hechter's model illuminates the situation in depressed regions like Brittany and Ireland, what of more divided and more affluent regions like Wales and especially Scotland? Do they possess all the features of 'internal colonies'? Hechter is conscious of the difficulty, both at the theoretical and the empirical levels. In a note, he weighs up the question of how many of these features internal colonies must exhibit (*ibid.*: 33, n. 1). As far as Scotland is concerned, he acknowledges that the region does not depend on a single primary product, nor suffer from a lack of services. This leads him to amend his thesis by distinguishing a special 'segmental' division of labour from the more usual 'cultural' division of labour. In a segmental division of labour, ethnic 'members interact wholly within the boundaries of their own group'; and as a result, 'group members monopolise certain niches in the occupational structure'. The point, of course, is that regions like Scotland retained 'considerable institutional autonomy' since the Union, and so cannot be regarded as proletarian nations or depressed internal colonies *tout court* (Hechter and Levi 1979: 263–5).[11]

The introduction of an alternative type of division of labour marks a considerable advance, but it has serious implications for Hechter's original model. By separating the cultural division of labour from the spatial relationships of core and periphery, it makes it possible to analyse the consequences of cultural stratification *within* regions like Wales, with its progressive industrial south and its agricultural north. In fact, these internal cleavages may contribute as much to separatist sentiment as the colonial relationships between a Welsh periphery and an English core.[12]

Even with this amendment, there are other difficulties. First, there is the problem of timing. Why did Scottish and Welsh political nationalism appear only in the late nineteenth century, and full middle-class support only in the 1960s, when industrialisation had appeared much earlier in the nineteenth century? In fact, Hechter's later model abandons an explanation in terms of relative deprivation, which was ambiguous, preferring instead a political argument to explain the timing of ethnic separatism, namely, the nature of state policies (*ibid.*: 270–2).

Second, there is the problem of 'overdeveloped' regions. Ethnic nationalism has surfaced not only in more backward or depressed regions like Brittany and Ireland, but also in more economically advanced areas like Catalonia, the Basque country and Croatia. While the political correlates of internal colonialism fit these cases, it is hard to assimilate them to depressed 'internal colonies' of larger states. Conversely, the failure of some economically backward regions like southern Italy or northeast England to develop a separatist (or any) nationalism, and to channel social discontent into ethnic protest, suggests further limitations in the internal colonialism model (see the essays in Stone 1979; cf. Conversi 1990 and Connor 1994: ch. 6).

But perhaps most important is the failure of the internal colonialism model to do justice to the ethnic basis of separatism. This is clear in the way in which Hechter dismisses 'the evidence of their ancient cultural past', and suggests an instrumentalist reading of the creation of culture to legitimate political aspirations. But this misses the point. Of course, some 'culture' and some 'history' may be created after the event, or simultaneously with it. But the fact that culture provided the basis for exclusion of the periphery by the core over decades and perhaps centuries through the cultural division of labour, tells us that 'culture' and 'history' pertain not just to the creations of 'high culture' and 'reappropriated pasts' by nationalists and others, but to the shared origin myths, experiences and memories of generations of the excluded, the history and culture of 'the people'. The absence of an ethnic separatism in northeast England or southern Italy is a function of the absence, not just of differentiating cultural markers, but of sufficiently separate origin myths, differentiating shared experiences and distinctive historical memories in those regions; memories of Northumbria and of the Kingdom of Naples have faded away, and their more recent experiences and memories are rejected.

But perhaps the basic trouble with the thesis of 'internal colonialism' is its conflation of *region* with *ethnic community* (or *ethnie*). This is plausible where a single *ethnie* occupies a whole and easily identifiable region, as with Bretons in Brittany and Scots in Scotland; less so where they share it with immigrants, as in the Basque country and Catalonia, even less so where advanced ethnic communities like the Armenians, Greeks and Jews have been (or are) scattered across a series of economically developed regions. Again, the thesis is rendered more plausible because of the nationalist demand for 'land'. But a spatial analysis that ends in a kind of territorial reductionism omits the importance of history and culture.

Land is indeed vital to ethnic separatists, but not simply for its economic and political uses. They are equally interested in its cultural and historical dimensions; what they need is a 'usable past' and a 'rooted culture'. Ethnic nationalists are not interested in any land; they only desire the land of their putative ancestors and the sacred places where their heroes and sages walked, fought and taught. It is a historic or ancestral 'homeland' that they desire, one which they believe to be exclusively 'theirs' by virtue of links with events and personages of earlier generations of 'their' people. In other words, the territory in question must be made into an 'ethnoscape', a poetic landscape that is an extension and expression of the character of the ethnic community and which is celebrated as such in verse and song (A. D. Smith 1997a).

This suggests that ethnicity must be treated as an independent factor as much as economic development, if we want to grasp the dynamics of ethnic secession. Neither is reducible to the other. It is only where they are conjoined that we can expect to find movements of ethnic secession. We may go even further. Walker Connor has argued that economic factors play only a contributory or catalytic role in fomenting ethnic separatism. He enumerates a range of historical and contemporary cases which reveal the power of ethnicity independent of economic situation. Thus we find ethnic nationalist movements among economically backward as well as advanced groups, in situations of economic advance and economic decline, and even among economically stagnant groups. There seems to be no easily identifiable pattern to the relationship between economic factors and ethnic nationalism, and on the other side, there is clear evidence of ethnic sentiment and activity emerging independently of other, especially economic, factors (Connor 1994: ch. 6).

Ethno-regional movements, then, are just one of several sub-varieties of ethnic nationalism which emerge from the historic cleavages in the affluent, developed states of the West. Their relationship to economic changes is secondary to the uneven distribution of their ethno-histories and cultures, changes in their geopolitical situation (notably the loss of their empires) and their political treatment by the elites of these states. It follows that the internal colonialism model is of limited applicability and represents a special case within the broader type of politically disadvantaged ethnic communities in national states. For the reasons why we are witnessing the revival of ethnic ties and nationalist movements in complex societies in the latter half of the twentieth century, we must look elsewhere.

Elite strategies of 'rational choice'

This is clearly the problem that has increasingly puzzled Hechter and others: why should people join ethnic and nationalist movements led by elites who are acting on their behalf, when they can so easily avoid doing so in modern societies? As Hechter asks:

If collective action is facilitated when the individual members of a group share common interests, then why does it occur so rarely? How can we explain why some people in the same structural position are free riders (Olson 1965), while others are not?

(Hechter 1988: 268)

This for Hechter is the chief merit of the rational choice approach: while giving due weight to structural constraints, it starts from a methodological individualism that seeks to explain collective outcomes in terms of individual behaviour. It thereby avoids the recourse to explanations of ethnicity and nationalism in terms of historical regression, and explains why individuals act as they do, often against our structural expectations.[13]

> Rational choice considers individual behaviour to be a function of the inter-action of structural constraints and the sovereign preferences of individuals. The structure first determines, to a greater or lesser extent, the constraints under which individuals act. Within these constraints, individuals face various feasible courses of action. The course of action ultimately chosen is selected rationally: . . . When individual preferences are assumed to be known, transitive and temporally stable, behaviour can be predicted in the face of any combination of circumstances.
>
> (*ibid.*: 268)

For Hechter, ethnic groups are, in principle, no different from any other type of group, and therefore demand no special theory. People join ethnic groups or nationalist movements because they think they will receive a net individual benefit by doing so.

> In this regard, ethnic organisations are critical for two basic reasons. First, they are the major source of the private rewards and punishments that motivate the individual's decision to participate in collective action. Second, because the individual's benefit/cost calculation depends in part upon his estimate of the probability of success of any collective action, organisations can play a key role by controlling the information available to their members.
>
> (*ibid.*: 271)

Such organisations are solidarity groups, and ethnic organisations are particu-larly salient examples. They mould the preferences of their members by applying sanctions to deviant individuals (such as free-riders and criminals) and by controlling the information that comes to them from outside the group – as, for example, the Amish communities in Pennsylvania, or the Gypsies in many lands, have done for generations (*ibid.*: 275–6).

Hechter and his colleagues have applied this solidaristic theory of social order to a number of topics. Here I can only consider the two most immediately rele-

vant to the theory of nationalism: secession and nationalist violence. With regard
to secession, Hechter has outlined a systematic, step-by-step account of the
strategies taken and options open to elites on the road to secession, defined as

> a demand for formal withdrawal from a central political authority by a
> member unit or units on the basis of a claim to independent sovereign
> status.
>
> (Hechter 1992, 267)

Secession is to be distinguished from separatism, where there is a drift to fragmentation, and from colonial liberation movements. Secession occurs only in
constituted national host states, where there are regions with populations who
have either common production or common consumption interests, or both.
Such populations may occupy a distinctive economic niche, or possess distinctive
cultural characteristics, like religion or language, particularly where these also
have a corporate character like the millets in the Ottoman empire. Where these
common interests are superimposed, where class and culture coincide, and
where there are intensive communications networks, the sense of a separate
region is likely to emerge.

Hechter is prepared to grant that social movements based on primordial
attachments may, exceptionally, inspire great self-sacrifice. Nevertheless, rational
choice theory, which starts from the preferences of individuals, is more likely to
cover the majority of nationalisms, since it predicts that ethnic and national
groups will closely monitor and sanction their members and control their access
to information, thereby preventing free-riding for what is a collective good,
namely, sovereignty. But, given the great costs of attempted secession, it can only
be private inducements, such as the prospects of jobs, that could tempt ethnic
members, and especially the middle classes who provide its main constituency,
into so risky a course of action (*ibid.*: 273–5).[14]

Even if they are tempted, the position of the host state is critical. Only where
it is perceived to be weak and unable to benefit regional groups, and constitutional reforms and repression have failed, as occurred during the last years of the
Soviet Union, is there a chance of success for secessionists. Even then, the geopolitical situation must be favourable; and in general the state system is opposed to
secession. All this makes

> secession a highly improbable outcome. This analysis reveals why it has
> been so improbable and why it will continue to be improbable in the future.
>
> (*ibid.*: 280)

A similar schema can illuminate even that most intractable of issues, nationalist
violence. Here again we should prefer an analysis based on individual desires for
wealth, status and power, to one based on unknowable value commitments. Now,
to attain these fungible goods, people will be prepared to join groups that
produce these goods and abide by their rules. To prevent free-riding, these

groups will monitor and control their members, and create group solidarity. But where there are several solidary groups in a single territory, there must be an institution to regulate intergroup conflict. That institution is the state, whose functions are to protect productive solidary groups from predators (e.g. criminal gangs) and from ideological oppositional groups (e.g. secessionists) who aim to weaken or dismantle the state. The latter situation may induce violent state repression, and so for members of oppositional groups violence becomes instrumentally rational, in order to resist state repression in the name of the nation. This is where nationalism enters the scene:

> There is ample evidence that nationalist groups employ violence strategically as a means to produce their joint goods, among which sovereignty looms large.
>
> (Hechter 1995: 62)

This is what is occurring in Northern Ireland, where the level of violence has been relatively 'limited'. What this suggests is that

> violence is most likely to break out when a weakly solidaristic nationalist group confronts a strong state apparatus having high domestic and international autonomy. But since such a state will be able to repress secessionists, violence will seldom escalate in this situation. The escalation of violence is most likely to be sustained, therefore, *in the context of a weakened state facing a highly solidary nationalist group.*
>
> (*ibid.*: 64, original emphasis)

Interest and passion

This may well be true, but what, one may ask, has it to do with nationalism? It is perfectly possible, and useful, to specify the conditions in which low and high levels of group violence are likely to occur, but they apply to all kinds of oppositional social movement and every type of belief system. In this regard, there is nothing special about nationalism; just as, for Hechter, there is nothing special about ethnic groups. The problem thereby disappears; and we are left wondering why it is that the nation and nationalism have stirred so much passion and moulded the modern world in their image.

But is this credible? Can we simply subsume nationalist secession under the mantle of 'oppositional movements' and 'solidary groups'? Is the violence of nationalist wars of expansion or resistance identical with the violence of racial hatred, mass communist purges or religious persecutions? Nothing, it seems, is left over for 'beliefs' and 'ideologies'. Is it not just as valid and economical to assume a link between professed beliefs and subsequent actions, and explain the latter, at least in part, in terms of the former? Might not at least some of the actions of nationalists, and those the most intense and impassioned, be explicable through comparative analysis of belief systems and their consequences? In omitting entirely the role of beliefs and ideas, Hechter has altogether elided the problem of why people appeal to the nation. There appears to be no reason why either the state or a solidary group should invoke the name of the nation.

There is a related problem. For Hechter, value explanations are not so much wrong as problematic. Values, he claims, cannot readily be imputed from behaviour; we cannot know if a specific item of consumption behaviour, hungry Hindus refusing to eat beef, for example, is due to fear of sanctions or deeply held beliefs. True, but the methodological difficulty of uncovering a mechanism of explanation does not of itself invalidate a value-driven account. By dismissing values, we are left only with preferences which, of themselves, can never really explain the intensity and passion which give rise to nationalist self-sacrifice. The examples Hechter adduces in Northern Ireland relate only to one kind of nationalist violence, that of armed and trained guerillas who are fighting a war and who naturally make careful calculations in terms of rational life-preserving strategies (Hechter 1995: 62–3).

There is a further omission in rational choice theory: the problem of memory. As we know from the recent wars between Serbs and Croats, memories of previous bloody encounters can play an inordinate role and lead people to commit atrocities which the strategic calculations of battle could never warrant. Similarly, Hitler's war of extermination of every European Jew, even in the last desperate days of the Reich when all manpower and weaponry was needed for the war on two fronts, is not easily explained by the strategic calculations of members of solidary groups. If it can be explained at all, one might more plausibly start from the fanatically held beliefs and values of the Nazi leaders and of their hatreds born, perhaps, of the scars of early memories of imagined wrongs. Such memories need not be so consistently dark; the commemorations of the glorious dead, fallen for their motherlands in battle, stir the living to emulation, enjoining a morality of and for the nation of citizens. It is not clear what functions such mass displays of emotion perform in the rational calculations of preference theory; but that they clearly have individual and collective functions is attested by their ubiquity and by the mass reverence which they so often command (Ignatieff 1998: ch. 2; Gillis 1994).

I do not wish to argue for a specifically 'non-rational', much less an 'emotional' theory of nationalism. Hechter is right to remind us of the need to specify the mechanisms of any explanation that we invoke, and he has performed an important service in demanding more rigorous attention to the logic of such explanations. But explanations, like definitions, can only be as precise and rigorous as the phenomena under consideration permit. The great number of permutations of explanatory factors, the sheer variety of historical cases, above all the elusive complexity of definitional features of concepts of the nation and nationalism, renders the search for certainty in the explanation of ethnic and nationalist phenomena, and the attempt to reduce their variety to a single pattern of preferences, implausible and untenable.

Hechter himself is careful not to make excessive claims for rational choice models. At most, such strategies operate within tightly circumscribed limits. For example, the feasible choices open to elites contemplating secession is largely determined by the possibility of mounting any kind of collective action, and that in turn is dependent upon shared consumption or production interests, and preferably both, together with communications networks. In other words, structural constraints determine a large part of the answer to the question of whether secession is a possibility. There must, first of all, exist a delimited group, defined in economic, territorial and cultural terms, that is, an ethnic group which is separate and distinctive; and the members must be integrated by networks of communications, making the group a self-conscious ethnic community. This does not seem to be so very different a kind of explanation from a good many others, including some perennialist ones, as we shall see later; and it demonstrates the critical importance of these conditions for secession, without invoking rational choice. Indeed, it is only when such conditions exist, and only within the orbit of such conditions, that rational strategies have any meaning.

This is very much what Donald Horowitz has in mind, in his typology of the logic of secession movements. After comparing secession with irredentism, Horowitz identifies the structural and social psychological conditions of the likelihood of bids to secede. Basing himself on a theory of group esteem (to which I shall return), Horowitz analyses the stereotypes of ethnic groups held by the colonial power, and taken over by their ethnic neighbours, in the colonial state. Generally, these stereotypes divide group characteristics into two categories, the one emphasising attributes of 'backwardness' such as ignorance, indolence, ineffiency, submissiveness and pride, the other the attributes of 'advanced' groups such as enterprise, aggression, industry, thrift, ambition and energy. The latter type of group has benefited from advanced educational levels and non-agricultural employment, while backward groups tend to have lower levels of education, income and employment (Horowitz 1985: chs 4–5).

Horowitz then places each type of group in 'regions' that are characterised as advanced or backward, in terms of regional income per capita, and thereby identifies four bases for secession. The most common basis, he argues, is found among backward groups in backward regions, for they have little to lose:

> They conclude rapidly that they have a small stake in preserving the undivided state of which they are a part.
>
> (*ibid.*: 236–40)

This is not just a matter of selfish elite manipulation; it is also a result of genuine and widespread grievances such as the importation of the dominant ethnic group's civil servants into the region. The case is quite different with advanced groups in backward regions. 'Where backward groups are early seceders, advanced groups are late seceders' (*ibid.*: 243). In fact, as population exporters, they tend to secede only as a last resort, as the cases of the Ibo and the Tamils demonstrated; it is their diasporas and the nationwide opportunities open to them, that inhibit secession, until violence persuades them otherwise. The same lure of opportunities inhibits secession among advanced groups in advanced regions, like the Basques, but it is offset by the tendency for such regions to subsidise the other, poorer regions and communities in the national state. Secession is also infrequent among backward groups in advanced regions, mainly because they tend to be numerically weak. They may desire to secede, as did the Lunda in mineral-rich Katanga, driven by fear of immigrants, but their chances of success are limited by powerful neighbours within the region (*ibid.*: 249–59).

For Horowitz, then, structural constraints which include not only economic disparities but group evaluations of themselves and others, are the determinants of secession, rather than individual preferences. One may disagree with Horowitz's empirical predictions (for example, it did not take long for advanced groups in advanced regions such as the Ibo, Latvians and Estonians, or in more backward regions such as the Bangla Deshis, to mount powerful secession movements), but his analysis is surely more illuminating in respect of those structural conditions that Hechter consigns to his initial category of 'structural constraints'. It also reveals how much can be gained by a structural analysis without invoking individual preferences.[15]

Pure instrumentalism, it seems, is a limiting case in this field. It operates successfully only within certain boundaries. It tells us a good deal about the strategies of elites, and makes us remember how much rational calculation exists even within what so many have assumed is *the* subjective phenomenon *par excellence*. There is a rationality to romanticism, a logic to nationalism. But as so often, human motives are mixed, frequently obscure and hard to disentangle. Moreover, just as the individual level of action cannot be read off from collective characteristics, so conversely we cannot deduce the character and features of collectivities like the nation from aggregated individual behaviour. Rational choice theory omits the way in which collectivities, once created through individual experience and action, can operate if not exactly on their own, then at least independently of each individual in every generation. Through institutions, rules, memories, myths, values and symbols, individuals are united into social groups that can perpetuate themselves down the generations, and influence the conduct of their members, not just by means of rewards and sanctions but as a result of socialisation, value example, myth-making, ideology and symbolism. Over and above the analysis of preferences and rational strategies, a general theory in this field would also need to consider these processes and mechanisms, if it was to give a more rounded and convincing account of nations and nationalism.

4   State and nation

In the West, the nation and the state emerged together. From the time of the French and American Revolutions, the 'nation- state' became the predominant, and soon almost the only legitimate form of political organisation, as well as the dominant vehicle of collective identity. Given the West's pioneering role, and its superior power, those areas colonised by the European powers also witnessed the emergence of nations *pari passu* with the colonial states which they established in Africa and Asia. Colonialism has also been the primary source of nationhood in Latin America, where the administrative provinces of the Spanish and Portuguese empires formed the basis, and provided the boundaries, for the subsequent post-colonial states and hence for their nations.

Sources of political modernism

Considerations like these have led many theorists of nationalism to regard the modern, bureaucratic state as the source and framework of modern nations and nationalism, and see political and military forces and institutions as the keys to explaining their emergence. It is this third, political variant of classical modernism that I wish to explore.

The origins of this view are fourfold. To begin with, the Weberian emphasis on relations of domination provided a classical definition of the state as the political organisation where its 'administrative staff successfully upholds a claim to the monopoly of the legitimate use of physical force in the enforcement of its order' within a given territory. A legal-rational kind of legitimation for the modern state requires an administrative and legal order subject to legislation, and claims binding authority over all the citizens and actions taking place within its jurisdiction. For Weber, bureaucracy exemplified the spirit and actions of the modern, rationalised state; hence its intimate association with, and interpenetration of, the state (Weber 1948).[1]

Political explanations of nationalism have also drawn on the Marxist analysis of the growing cleavage between state and civil society in the modern epoch. The levelling of intermediate corporate bodies in the era of capitalism and the growing power and impersonal rationality of the state have left individuals as citizens exposed, and often opposed, to the bourgeois state, just as capitalism has alienated the mass of wage workers and left them at the mercy of the small capitalist class of property owners. Out of this chasm between state and civil society, emerges the historicist vision of the nation and the accompanying nationalist aspirations to reintegrate the civil and the political domains into a single whole (Shaheen 1956).[2]

A third influence contributing to this view is the idea, traceable to Simmel, of endemic conflict between states and societies. The 'societies' of the pre-modern world were varied in form and character, with many kinds of city-state, feudal principality, ethnic community and empire; in the modern world, such 'societies' are nearly always nations and national states. The modern world is one of national competition and warfare; as a result, military factors and militarism assume an increasingly central role in the distribution of resources and the formation of political communities and identities (Simmel 1964; Poggi 1978; cf. A. D. Smith 1981b).

Finally, there is the whole idea of modernity as a revolution in administration and communications, one which requires new kinds of human associations that will be able to operate effectively in such an environment. Here we have the most immediate source of the 'state-to-nation' perspective, since it is in and through the modern state that this revolution has made its most significant impact. Stemming from the work of both Weber and the 'communications' theorists, notably Karl Deutsch, this view sees in the modern state a monitoring and reflexive institution that requires for its success a political community and identity moulded in its image (Deutsch 1963, 1966; Tilly 1975).

The reflexive state

It is a view most clearly exemplified in the work of Anthony Giddens. The rise, nature and consequences of the modern nation-state forms the core of the second volume of his *Contemporary Critique of Historical Materialism*, entitled *The Nation-State and Violence*. Though the state as 'nation-state' bulks large in its pages, the nation and nationalism are given more cursory treatment. Nevertheless, the passages allotted to them allow us to gain a clear idea of Giddens' theoretical position *vis-à-vis* nations and nationalism.

For Giddens, what is at stake is 'a systematic interpretation of the rise of the territorially bounded nation-state and its association with military power' (Giddens 1985: 26). The formation of the nation-state and the nation-state system is 'an expression of the dislocations of modern history', which since the advent of industrial capitalism has witnessed extraordinary change (*ibid.*: 34). Both the nation and nationalism 'are distinctive properties of modern states'; indeed, a nation Giddens defines as

> a collectivity existing within a clearly demarcated territory, which is subject to a unitary administration, reflexively monitored both by the internal state apparatus and those of other states.

> (*ibid.*: 116)

Nationalism, in turn, Giddens regards as primarily a psychological phenomenon:

> the affiliation of individuals to a set of symbols and beliefs emphasising communality among the members of a political order.
>
> (*ibid.*: 116)

But nationalism *per se* is not at the centre of Giddens' concerns. It functions only insofar as it reinforces the territorial cohesion and reflexive qualities of the nation-state. It is the nation-state in its unique administrative, military and territorial properties that commands his attention:

> The nation-state, which exists in a complex of other nation-states, is a set of institutional forms of governance maintaining an administrative monopoly over a territory with demarcated boundaries (borders), its rule being sanctioned by law and direct control of the means of internal and external violence.
>
> (*ibid.*: 121)

In other words, what distinguishes the nation-state from other polities, and nationalism from earlier kinds of group identity, is the rise of stable administration from fixed capital cities over well defined stretches of territory. Before the modern epoch, genealogical myths and religious symbols contributed to the normal exclusionary forms of 'tribal' group identity. In the modern epoch, in contrast, nations were formed through processes of state centralisation and administrative expansion which, through the reflexive ordering of the state system, fixed the borders of a plurality of nations. This leads Giddens to characterise the 'nation-state' as 'a bordered power-container . . . the pre-eminent power-container of the modern era' (*ibid.*: 120).

For Anthony Giddens, as for Eric Hobsbawm and others, nationalism is intimately linked to the modern state. Indeed, it is only insofar as it is linked to the state that Giddens considers it to be sociologically significant. While he regards nationalism as primarily a political movement associated with the nation-state, he recognises its important psychological dimensions, and notes its definite symbolic content in which the 'homeland' is tied to

> a myth of origin, conferring cultural autonomy upon the community which is held to be the bearer of these ideals.
>
> (*ibid.*: 216)

This symbolic content is often grounded on 'historicist' arguments such as those advanced by Herder, and it can lead to more exclusive or to more egalitarian versions of the concept of the nation-state. Similarly, national symbols such as a common language can provide a sense of community and hence some measure of ontological security where traditional moral schemes have been disrupted by the modern state. They can also be linked to populistic leadership figures who gain influence in crises and dislocating situations which often produce anxiety.

More fundamentally, however, nationalism figures in Giddens' theory as

> the cultural sensibility of sovereignty, the concomitant of the co-ordination of administrative power within the bounded nation-state.
>
> (*ibid.*: 219)

Given the vast increase in communications and coordination of activities, we can most usefully regard the nation-state as a 'conceptual community' founded on common language and common symbolic historicity. But only in a few cases where political boundaries coincide with existing language-communities is the relationship between nation-states and nationalism 'a relatively frictionless one'. In most cases the advent of the nation-state stimulates oppositional nationalisms. The origin of these nationalisms is to be sought less in regional economic disparities than in the disruption of traditional modes of behaviour which encourage historicity and the claim to administrative sovereignty. This leads Giddens to conclude that 'all nationalist movements are necessarily political', because nationalism is 'inherently linked to the achievement of administrative autonomy of the modern (sc. reflexive) form' (*ibid.*: 220).

The nation beyond the state

There is no doubt that, historically, the rise of the modern bureaucratic and reflexive state has deeply affected the shape, and to some degree the content, of many nationalisms. This is not only the case in the West; we find it in perhaps its most naked form in the 'state-nations' of Africa and Asia, that is, those post-colonial states striving to become nations on the basis of their ex-colonial territorial boundaries and their administrative format. The inclusive, bounded and homogenising state has been the point of departure, and the mould for many national liberation movements in the period of decolonisation from 1945 to the 1970s. The nation that the leaders of these liberation movements envisaged was equally grounded and defined by a statist ideal inherited from the West and adapted by the immediate post-colonial generation of political leaders.[3]

But there are also problems with state-based explanations. To begin with, not all nationalisms have in practice opted for independent statehood; most Scots and Catalans, for example, have not to date supported their movements and parties which sought outright independence, and have instead settled for a large measure of social, cultural and economic autonomy within their borders. Of course, one could envisage circumstances in which, like the Slovenes and Croats, they too would opt for full sovereignty, but, as the Québécois case reveals, a strong element of 'rational choice', of calculative strategy, enters into any bid for outright independence, as opposed to 'home rule' (see Meadwell 1989; Hechter 1992).

Perhaps more important is the problem of cultural nationalism. It is easy to dismiss the yearnings for cultural regeneration as the contribution of fringe intel-lectuals without much influence on the political course of a given nationalism. But, as John Hutchinson has convincingly shown, cultural nationalism is a force in its own right, and one that exists in a contrapuntal relationship with political nationalism. That is to say, where political nationalism fails or is exhausted, we find cultural nationalists providing new models and tapping different kinds of collective energies, thereby mobilising larger numbers of hitherto unaffected members of the community. Hutchinson documents this extensively in the Irish case, showing for example, how the fall of Parnell in 1891 effectively put an end to the Irish home rule political movement, while at the same time encouraging the cultural nationalists to come forward and propagate their Gaelic ideals and a vision of a new Irish moral community, until such time as a new wave of polit-ical nationalism, drawing on the work of the cultural nationalists, could take up where Parnell had left off. To say, then, that all nationalism is 'necessarily polit-ical' is either true by definition, or severely truncates the nationalist experience (Hutchinson 1987: ch. 4).

A further limitation of state-centred views is their ethnocentric, that is, West European, bias. Historically, Giddens sees the nation-state as a historical phen-omenon which emerged out of European absolutism. Besides overlooking non-European examples of developed absolutism, such as the Japanese Tokugawa Shogunate, this view fails to do justice to the different models of nation-formation outside the West. In Western Europe, it is true, the nation tended to emerge together with, and out of the crucible of, the bureaucratic state, while Western nationalisms, too, can be seen in large part as state-oriented movements, ideological movements for consolidating and enhancing state power (though even here, we may recall that Dutch, Irish, American and even French bourgeois nationalism in the Revolution were oppositional movements directed against the state authorities). But that will hardly help us when we turn to Eastern Europe and parts of Asia. Attempts to modernise the administration of the Romanov, Habsburg and Ottoman empires were certainly a factor in the genesis of ethnic nationalisms within their borders, but the nationalisms they helped to engender, as well as the nations that became the objects of their aspi-rations, were not just 'oppositional'. Their very contours and contents were largely determined by pre-existing ethnic, linguistic and religious heritages, and the 'nations' they aimed to create were in turn based, in varying degrees, upon ties and networks that antedated the imperial reforms and, in some cases, the empires themselves. If the West is generally characterised by a 'state-to-nation' trajectory, that of Eastern Europe and parts of Asia can be more convincingly analysed in terms of a 'nation-to-state' model. Both models, as we shall see, are only crude approximations, but they serve to remind us of the complexities of nation-formation, and the need to exercise caution in generalising from the Western experience (see A. D. Smith 1986b; James 1996: 155–8).[4]

There are two more general criticisms. The first is the problem of definitional reduction. Giddens insists with others that nationalism, and the nation, are really only significant insofar as they are linked to the state, that is, to attaining and maintaining state power; and further that the nation has no independent conceptual status outside of its link with the state. This leaves no room for an independent theory of the nation and nationalism. The nation is subsumed within the concept of the nation-state, and in both theory and practice the emphasis throughout falls on the 'state' component. Carried to its logical conclusion, this would mean that because a Polish 'nation-state' ceased to exist in the Partitions of the late eighteenth century, so did a Polish 'nation'; and that we could only speak once again of a Polish 'nation' when Poland was reconstituted as a 'nation-state' in 1918. By the same logic, Scotland cannot become a 'nation' until the majority of Scottish voters agree with the Scottish National Party's platform and vote for an independent Scottish 'nation-state'. On a theoretical level, to elide the concept of the nation with that of the 'nation-state' precludes consideration of the problem of the nation as community: that is, how the 'nation' has become so important to vast numbers of people across the globe, and why millions have been prepared to lay down their lives for an apparently abstract community of strangers. What the statist formulation omits, then, is the ubiquity of this sense of a community of like-minded people with whom we feel intimate, even though we cannot know most of them, and for whom we are prepared to make real sacrifices (see James 1996: 166–7).

The second criticism concerns Giddens' characterisation of nationalism as a psychological phenomenon, in contrast to the structural nature of the nation-state. In *The Nation-State and Violence*, Giddens drops his earlier suggestion that nationalism feeds upon and reconstitutes an attenuated form of 'primordial sentiments' (in the Geertzian sense) and opts instead for a view derived from Fredrik Barth which emphasises the importance of exclusionary sentiments based on social boundaries between ethnic groups. This kind of argument, which I shall treat more fully later, is open to the charge that it fails to do justice to the unities of social and cultural relations within groups. In fact, Giddens does acknowledge the importance of cultural ties such as language and religion; but he fails to link these with the new kind of 'borders' created by the reflexive nation-state, or see how they can be symbolically reconstituted to form a basis for the modern nation. This is part of the greater failure of modernism: its inability to see how the transformations of modernity revitalise in changed form the social and cultural relations of past epochs. By characterising 'nationalism' as a purely subjective, psychological phenomenon, Giddens reduces its importance to that of a prop for the nation-state, and thereby fails to see how it symbolically defines and infuses with passion the national identities to which the nation as community gives rise. A chasm between the structure of the 'nation-state' and the subjectivity of 'nationalism' is opened up which cannot be bridged except by subordinating the latter totally to the former (A. D. Smith 1986a: ch. 3; James 1996: ch. 7).

This is one example of a more general problem affecting all variants of political modernism. Anthony Giddens clearly recognises the importance of ideology and ethnic symbolism, for he regards them as crucial elements in the formation of the nation-state as a *political community*, or 'power-container'. Yet the concept of the nation embraces far more than the idea of a political community, or vehicle for state power, even one with fixed borders: it refers also to a distinctive culture community, a 'people' in their 'homeland', a historic society and a moral community. The desire for political autonomy in a fixed territory is a vital component of nationalism, but it is very far from exhausting its ideals.

Nations and the inter-state order

The centrality of political institutions was also recognised by Charles Tilly in his work on the formation of national states in Europe. Tilly's focus is the state and its activities, rather than the nation, 'one of the most puzzling and tendentious items in the political lexicon' (Tilly 1975: 6). Yet he also distinguished between those nations that were forged by the economic and military activities of modern states, mainly in Western Europe, and those later nations that were created, as it were, 'by design' by diplomats and statesmen through international treaties following long periods of protracted warfare, as after the Thirty Years or Napoleonic Wars. Though such a distinction implicitly suggests a role for the idea of the nation advanced by statesmen, intellectuals and others, Tilly gives this idea no independent status. For Tilly, it is the modern state that is sociologically paramount, as it is historically prior; the nation is merely a construct, dependant upon the state for its force and meaning, and is treated adjectivally. Certainly, the deliberations of elites – military, political and intellectual – exerted a profound influence on the political map of Europe and overseas, but always within the context of an inter-state system whose members are in a continual state of competition and hence conflict (Tilly 1975: Conclusion).

This inter-state system emerged in a Europe perennially at war, a Europe unable to refashion the Roman empire. Its protected geographical position and multiple groupings, its urban wealth and conflicts between lords and peasants, as well as the military and economic effectiveness of the state form, prevented any one state emerging as hegemonic overlord of the continent. For Charles Tilly, it is, above all, war that 'makes the state', just as it is the state that 'makes war'. War is the engine of state-making, and hence at one remove of national formation. But, after warfare has left the parties exhausted, diplomacy is called in to fashion a new international order of 'national states' in accordance with the balance of power between the leading states, first in Europe and then globally (Tilly 1975: Introduction, Conclusion).[5]

A more recent exposition of the primacy of political institutions can be found in the work of Rogers Brubaker. He argues that the conventional 'substantialist' accounts of nationalism reify the nation and treat it as an enduring collectivity. Far from regarding nations as real communities, which are stable and enduring over time,

> we should focus on nation as a category of practice, nationhood as an institutionalised cultural and political form, and nationness as a contingent event or happening, and refrain from using the analytically dubious notion of 'nations' as substantial, enduring collectivities. A recent book by Julia

Kristeva bears the English title *Nations without Nationalism*; but the analytical task at hand, I submit, is to think about nationalism without nations.

(Brubaker 1996: 21)

Here Brubaker cites the policies and methods by which the Soviet regime institutionalised the territorial and ethnic republics which have taken its place after 1991. Nationalist practices were formed by Soviet political institutions, and, given the occasion, the events of 'nationness' created the successor states. For Soviet institutions comprised a

pervasive system of social classification, an organising 'principle of vision and division' of the social world.

(*ibid.*: 24)

The result of the breakdown of the Soviet system is not a struggle of post-Soviet 'nations', but of 'institutionally constituted national elites' (*ibid.*: 25).

Now it is undeniable that the modern state, like the wider inter-state system, provides a powerful context and constraint on the formation of nations and nationalisms. But to say that it also *constitutes* both interests and actors, in accordance with the postulates of the 'new institutionalism' in sociology, seriously limits the field of theoretical analysis and precludes alternative possibilities. We can, I think, avoid social reification while retaining the idea of nations as real communities (though not necessarily 'enduring', and certainly not 'fixed and given' or 'internally homogeneous'); and we need to do so, because 'nation', besides being a category of practice, an institutionalised form and a contingent event, as Brubaker rightly points out, also refers to a felt and lived community, one which has very real and powerful consequences. It is the social reality of those consequences that has persuaded analysts to treat nations as real (albeit also imagined) communities, alongside other kinds of felt and lived community. (Besides, why should we think that political or other institutions and their practices possess a greater 'reality' than communities? After all, they are all abstractions, but in practice social science cannot do without them. Even rational choice theory operates with 'organisations' and 'corporations' of interest.) The fact is that ethnic communities, conflicts and ethnonational movements were already present in the later Tsarist empire, as well as in the rest of Europe (not to mention in Marxist theorising on the 'national question'), and the Soviet rulers freely adapted, extended and reinforced politically what often already existed sociodemographically and culturally (Bennigsen and Lemercier-Quelquejay 1966). Rogers Brubaker is right to remind us that there, and elsewhere, the 'nation' (like the 'state') is a concept, but to confine its referents to form, practice and event is to strip it of those attributes that give it so much of its potency and appeal. How could we account for the widespread powerful feelings of attachment to mere forms and practices, even when these are backed by the panoply of state institutions and the international system? 'Nationalism' cannot be so readily separated in this fashion from nations-as-communities.

The impact on such nations of the inter-state system is a large topic. It has been explored by sociologists like Stein Rokkan, and by international relations theorists like Hinsley and Mayall. For sociologists, Deutsch's nation-building model needed to be placed in a wider context of international economic, political and cultural linkages. For this purpose, they evolved complex models of the many factors involved – language, religion, trade, administration and regional economies – from which they attempted to show why some communities and regions failed to achieve national status, while others succeeded. In this vein, Andrew Orridge sought to delineate the complex social and historical bases of recent autonomist and secessionist movements in Europe. In a rich and wide-ranging analysis of the many factors at work and of their permutations, he demonstrated the variability of the grounds and content of such movements, revealing thereby the limitations of previous socioeconomic models (Rokkan *et al.* 1972; Orridge 1981, 1982; Tivey 1980).

At a more global and general level, international relations theorists have sought to locate the meaning and impact of nations and nationalism within the context of a pre-existing inter-state system and the role of diplomacy and war. The new state-based world order, first codified at Westphalia in 1648, underlined the naturalness of hierarchy in a world of princely states in which warfare was regarded as a legitimate institution of sovereign states. It was this world that nationalism challenged in the name of the ideals of popular sovereignty and popular culture (see *inter alia* Hinsley 1973; Azar and Burton 1986; Mayall 1990; cf. Posen 1993; Snyder 1993).

For James Mayall, the most systematic modernist theorist of the challenge of nationalism to the international order, nationalism certainly helped to undermine the traditional basis of political legitimacy. At the same time, it widened and deepened the role of warfare. Nationalists themselves were divided about the role of war. Liberal nationalists were men of peace and hoped a world of free states would eliminate this scourge. 'Historicist' nationalists, on the other hand, followed Hegel in regarding warfare as necessary for the survival of the nation and the values it represents. Along with the vast increase in industrial production and the technology of mass destruction, this ideal has encouraged the shift to total warfare in the twentieth century. This has been accompanied by the globalisation of the state system under the impact of nationalism, and the increasing penetration of the state into the everyday lives of its citizens, in the name of the nation (Mayall 1990: 25–34; cf. Navarri in Tivey 1980).

Did the challenge of nationalism succeed in destroying the new world order based on a system of sovereign states? For Mayall,

> an accommodation was reached between the prescriptive principle of sovereignty and the popular principle of national self-determination. The result was the creation of over 100 new states and the development of the first truly global international society the world had known. But the old world did not surrender unconditionally to the new: as in any accommodation, compromise was involved. The principle of national self-determination

which was built into the new system turned out to be much less permissive, or popular, than attention to its philosophical origins and meaning might lead one to expect. Moreover, the global integration of international society on the basis of a principle of popular sovereignty was accompanied by an unprecedented attempt to *freeze* the political map.

(*ibid.*: 35, original emphasis)

This has meant that the inter-state order, resting on the principle of sovereignty, has been unwilling to accommodate new aspirants for national status, unless they are ex-colonial territories. The UN principle of national self-determination was in practice amended to include only states created by the process of decolonisation of empires, and not ethnic secessionist movements seeking their own states by withdrawing from duly constituted national states. Only in rare cases since 1945 have new states been created and accorded international legitimacy, as a result of peaceful agreement between the parties (Singapore) or regional patronage of the seceding nation (Bangla Desh) (*ibid.*: 61–9).

Since 1991, of course, some twenty new states have been created. But this has been mainly the result of the break-up of two empires, the Soviet and the Ethiopian. James Mayall recognises the power of the ethnic resurgence since 1989, but maintains that the inter-state system has shown its customary resilience and remains unwilling to countenance secession or irredentism, except through peaceful agreement, as in the case of Slovakia. This still leaves open the question of the early European recognition of Slovenia, Croatia, Macedonia and Bosnia: were these exceptions to the rule, or do they betoken a deeper change in international emphasis? Given the worldwide and often unpredictable explosions of ethnic conflict and nationalist sentiments, can we be so sanguine about the stability of an international community of sovereign states? Moreover, are not international organisations, in the name of human and minority rights and under the impact of widespread ethnic nationalism, eroding the sovereign powers of individual states? (Mayall 1991, 1992; cf. Preece 1997).

The state and war

The role of war in the creation of ethnic and national communities can, of course, be witnessed in pre-modern epochs. We have only to remember the way in which paired ethnic communities and nations have reinforced a sense of collective identity through mobilisation of men, sustained enmities and protracted warfare, and how memories and myths of battle helped to forge a sense of ethnic or national unity, whether for ancient Greeks after Marathon and Salamis, Romans after Cannae and Zama, the Swiss after Sempach and Morgarten, the French after the siege of Orleans and the English after the Armada. But it is in the modern epoch that warfare has had its most profound impact; and this is largely because, as Michael Howard has so vividly documented, the early modern revolution in warfare had become closely linked causally to the administrative efficiency of the modern state (see Howard 1976; A. D. Smith 1981b).

For Michael Mann, too, military factors are vital in shaping the emergence and course of modern nationalism. Mann, like Tilly and Giddens, is a convinced 'modernist': in the first volume of *The Sources of Social Power*, he argues that though there may have been loose ethnic networks in antiquity and the Middle Ages, they could not, and did not, serve as the basis of polities. Nor could *nations* have emerged prior to the Western democratic revolutions which first brought the masses into the political arena. Nevertheless, Mann is ready to concede that not only military-political, but other factors played some part in the emergence of modern nations and nationalism (Mann 1986: 527–30).[6]

In his second volume, Michael Mann links the emergence of nations and nationalism to that of classes around the end of the eighteenth century. He defines a nation as

> an extensive cross-class community affirming its distinct ethnic identity and history and claiming its own state.
>
> (Mann 1993: 215)

He distinguishes four phases in the rise of nation-states: first, a religous one in sixteenth-century Europe, in which the Protestant Reformation and the Catholic Counter-Reformations both encouraged new networks of discursive literacy in the major vernacular languages, linking family rituals to wider, secular social practices and thereby mobilising a higher degree of 'intensive power' in a limited class. Second, from around 1700, state expansion and commercial capitalism widened the scope of discursive literacy to a broader class through a variety of institutions from contracts and army manuals to coffee house discussions and academies, encouraging a limited sense of 'civil citizenship' among the upper classes (*ibid.*: 216–8).

These two phases brought into being what Mann calls 'proto-nations', whose consciousness was largely elite-based. Real, cross-class nations emerged only in the third phase, towards the end of the eighteenth century, under the pressures of fiscal crises and state militarism. Prior to 1792, the military revolution had profoundly affected geopolitical relations in Europe, producing a series of fiscal crises in several European states. The result was greater conscription, war taxes and regressive war loans, all of which served to politicise the concepts of 'people' and 'nation'. Through the growing demands by propertied classes for representative government and political citizenship, intensive, pre-existing familial networks of ritual and literacy were linked to the extensive power networks of an enlarged and more aggressive state, albeit as yet on a limited scale among the elites. In a centralised Britain and, more radically, in France, the nationalism that emerged from these crises was state-supporting; in confederal Austria and Germany, it was state-subverting, because these polities were organised along provincial lines and had ancient, powerful provincial organisations which controlled taxation. So,

Cross-class nations were propelled forward more by the states' military than by their capitalist crystallisations. Because fiscal-military pressures hit states more directly and more uniformly than commercial or industrial capitalism, nations appeared amid all of them with regional political institutions, not only in the more economically advanced.

(*ibid.*: 226; cf. Mann 1995)

In the post-1792 period, under French revolutionary and Bonapartist military pressure, regimes all across Europe began to penetrate the intensive, familial networks and link them more directly to extensive state and military networks, and on a much broader scale. Of particular importance here was the use made of pre-existing religious and commercial networks of discursive literacy by capitalism and the military state. This was the work of a radical intelligentsia, invoking universal principles which crossed all boundaries – whether of knowledge, social class or social practice. In extreme crises, these ideological principles seemed to be self-fulfilling: they loudly proclaimed an end to privilege and the nation in arms, and the free nation came into being. At these key ideological 'moments', the 'nation-state mobilised greater collective power than old regimes could muster' (*ibid.*: 235).

In Germany and Austria, it is true, the lack of fit between language and political boundaries made the first romantic stirrings of scholarly nationalism curiously 'cultural' and apolitical. But this was not to last. Under the impact of French militarism, national stereotypes were accentuated, whole peoples were pitted against one another, and radical patriot societies, some of them appealing to 'the people' in their local languages, multiplied. In the process, language became a principal means of distinguishing 'us', the local community, from 'them', the conquerors and political rulers; and hence of defining the new 'nation-to-be' in Central Europe (*ibid.*: 238–47).

In the fourth and final phase of nation-formation, industrial capitalism from the later nineteenth century reinforced nations through the agencies of the expanded state. The universal desire for industrial capitalist growth vested the state with ever greater powers of social coordination. The state became increasingly responsible for communications, mass education, health and welfare, even family mores, making states both more representative and 'national', more participant and homogeneous. Of course, this might stir up opposition based on language or religion, subvert the existing state or become the basis for new national states; but the trend to national homogeneity and popular nations of the middle classes, peasants and workers encouraged a more passionate, aggressive nationalism resulting from the tighter links between intensive, emotional spheres and the militarist, capitalist state. Industrialism expanded both civilian and military state networks: these formed the core of aggressive nationalisms. Mann concludes by emphasising the close links forged between state and nation, arguing that:

In the industrial capitalist phase the state-reinforcing nation can be simply represented as three concentric circular bands: the outer one circumscribed by and attached to the total national state, the middle more linked to the inner circle, the statist core.

(*ibid.*: 734)

This is a complex and nuanced modernist account of the rise of nationalism in Europe, which locates it in the historical context of the growth of classes and class conflict in the shadow of the modern, militarised state. Michael Mann can find no single 'ultimate' cause for nations or nationalism, even if capitalism figures prominently in the last two phases. But then, as he intimates, so does the militarist state. Moreover, Mann is careful to warn us that all we can expect is a sketch of the general factors involved in the rise of nations and nationalism, and that thereafter each case must be treated on its own merits in its particular social and historical setting, some European examples of which he accordingly analyses.

A political theory of nationalism?

In apparent contrast, Michael Mann later proposed a starker 'political' theory of nationalism and its excesses. Here, he goes much further in insisting on the primacy of political and military factors. This comes out when he claims that the 'key lies rather in the state'. In the third, or militarist, phase, 'states now loomed over the lives of their subjects, taxing and conscripting them, attempting to mobilise their enthusiasm for its goals'. As people fought back, they demanded political citizenship of the 'people' and the 'nation' (Mann 1995: 47–8).

At this point Mann draws back from single-factor explanations. He is prepared to admit that regional-ethnic, as well as religious components enter into the picture, especially in the early phases of establishing larger spheres of discursive literacy. This is especially clear in 'confederal' structures like the Habsburg, Ottoman and Romanov empires, where 'patriotic' opposition was organised along provincial lines. Yet, he continually returns to 'political' explanations. In respect of state-supporting nationalisms like those of Britain and France, he writes:

> But the clarity of focus on the nation as coterminous with the state cries out for a predominantly political explanation.

(*ibid.*: 48)

And again, in respect of the 'provincial' nationalisms of the Habsburg empire, he observes:

> We cannot predict which few nations successfully emerged on the basis merely of 'ethnicity'. The presence or absence of regional administration offers a much better predictor. This suggests a predominantly political explanation.

(*ibid.*: 50)

Mann is certainly right to underline the growth of the nation within the framework of the state in much of the West. But can such an explanation be supported in the case of Central Europe? How does such an explanation fare in Germany and Italy? Shouldn't we have expected a Prussian and Piedmontese nation to emerge, rather than the 'Germany' and 'Italy' that eventually took their seats in the concert of 'nations'? Why was the fight for democracy and representative government *ipso facto* a movement for a *German* and an *Italian* nation? Mann may be right to say, in partial reply, that nationalism is part of the wider movement for democracy (whatever its subsequent manifestations may have been); but that hardly explains why democratisation is also everywhere nationalist, why it is the *nation* that must be democratised and why democracy must be realised in and through the nation.[7]

Mann is rightly concerned to explain the passionate, often aggressive character of nationalism. He does so by claiming that nationalism originated in protest against the exactions of authoritarian, militarised states which invaded the private spheres of the family, religion and education and linked them to the militarised state. But why should people want to take over an intrusive, often alien, state, and link their private concerns or feel a sense of belonging to a community in the image of a militarised, professional state? Isn't it exactly because the state is so intrusive and alien, and appears so often as a threat to their traditional lifestyle, that people seek to return to some sense of community *against* the state?

Mann sees the nation largely in terms of the state – as its product, either harmoniously or, by way of reaction, in conflict. After all, as Tilly argued, the modern, rationalised state emerged before nations and nationalism; so they can only be understood in a European context of inter-state diplomacy and warfare. This might help to explain why boundaries and the exclusion of those beyond them became an important concern of many nationalists, and why, when the boundary question was unresolved, war appeared to be a normal, even 'natural', option (Tilly 1975: Introduction; see Dunn 1978: ch. 3).

But modern nations and nationalism involve many more elements than a heightened concern for monitored boundaries and the exclusion of 'foreigners'. What is crucial for nationalists is the sense of a 'homeland' and of historic, even sacred territory, not just boundaries. It is not just in the shape, but in the content of what lies within, that we need to seek an explanation. It is the relationship, emotional as well as political, between land and people, history and territory, that provides one of the main motive forces for national mobilisation and subsequent claims to title-deeds. Hence, explanations in terms of inter-state relations and warfare fail to uncover the emotional sources of national sentiment.[8]

In the same way, the nationalists emphasise the uniqueness of a vernacular culture. Mann is sensitive to issues of culture in the context of Germany and Austria and its nationalities, but fails to see that these are general concerns of nationalists everywhere. We need to explain why so many people followed the nationalists in emphasising their distinctive cultures and desiring to belong to 'unique' nations – especially those peoples who did not possess their own state. It is difficult to see how we can derive explanations for these central concerns of modern nationalism from such broad factors as the inter-state order and its constituent militarised states.[9]

One might also question Mann's assertion that failure by national states to institute democracy, especially in what he calls the post-1918 'modernist' phase, resulted in extreme aggressive nationalism, and especially fascism (*ibid.*: 57–63). One could equally argue that the failures of orthodox nationalisms to live up to their promises – economic, cultural and political – opened the way to much more radical 'solutions', which ultimately undermined the very concept of the vertical nation, substituting the idea of horizontal racial castes. The radicals were often non-state personnel: ex-soldiers, lower-class intellectuals and lower clergy, as much as clerks. The state may be the target of their aspirations, but it is not always the source of their discontents (A. D. Smith 1979: ch. 3).

State and society: bridging the gulf?

An attempt to come to grips with some of these problems while upholding the idea of the state as the focus and goal of nationalism is central to the most elaborate and comprehensive 'political' theory of nationalism. John Breuilly is a convinced modernist: he begins by admitting that there may have been something like national consciousness in the late medieval era, but refuses to label this as 'nationalism'. For Breuilly,

> The term 'nationalism' is used to refer to political movements seeking or exercising state power and justifying such actions with nationalist arguments.
>   A nationalist argument is a political doctrine built upon three assertions:
>
> (a) There exists a nation with an explicit and peculiar character.
> (b) The interests and values of this nation take priority over all other interests and values.
> (c) The nation must be as independent as possible. This usually requires the attainment of at least political sovereignty.
>
> (Breuilly 1993: 2)

By limiting the term to a political doctrine, this definition 'avoids the danger of being too vague and all-embracing and, among other things, draws attention to the modernity of nationalism' (*ibid.*: 5).[10]

Breuilly also wants to exclude from his definition those political movements that demand independence on the basis of universal principles like freedom and equality. This leads him to exclude the American colonies' Declaration and War of Independence in 1776. Nationalism demands that such universal principles be married to a concern with a distinct cultural identity, and American leaders before and during the War showed no such concern. At the same time, Breuilly is prepared to concede, à propos the goal of creating a German nation in the Frankfurt Parliament of 1848–9, that, in place of an ethnic criterion, nationalism may base its claims on 'an historical-territorial concept of the nation' (*ibid.*: 6).

Nevertheless, Breuilly is not prepared to accept an extreme voluntarist position: to base national identity purely on individual choice would be to abandon any idea of a culturally specific nation, even in the eyes of nationalists. Nor should nationalist appeals be equated with claims to universal human rights in a given territory, of the kind that many anti-colonialist movements in Africa put forward. In fact, in many of these cases, cultural themes loomed large: modern anti-colonial movements opposed an allegedly superior Western culture to 'accounts of their own, non-western cultures'. These accounts may be very broad, operating at a 'pan-' level: Arab, African, Indian and Chinese. Or they may operate at a 'sub-nationalist' or 'tribalist' level and refer to specific ethnic identities (*ibid.*: 6–7).

John Breuilly is really interested only in politically significant nationalisms, rather than with ideology or ideologies *per se*.

> The focus here is with nationalism as a form of politics, principally opposition politics. The principle of classification will, therefore, be based upon the relationship between the nationalist movement and the state which it either opposes or controls. A nationalist opposition can seek to break away from the present state (separation), to reform it in a nationalist direction (reform), or to unite it with other states (unification).
>
> (*ibid.*: 9)

These distinctions yield six classes of nationalisms, depending on whether separation, reform and unification are from, of and to nation-states or 'non-nation-states' (e.g. empires). Of course, cases like nineteenth-century Polish nationalism were directed against both kinds of state, and aimed to separate from, unify and reform in quick succession. But the differences in their goals and situation dictated very different kinds of nationalist politics within overall Polish nationalism. Hence a political typology is illuminating and 'the *only* starting point for a general understanding of nationalism is to take its form of politics seriously' through comparative historical investigation. Given the variety of social groups brought together by nationalism, and the difficulty of distinguishing clearly between different kinds of nationalist ideology, a political criterion offers the best means of classifying and grasping the nature of nationalism and its impact on the modern world (*ibid.*: 12–14).

Broadly speaking, nationalism is able to seize power in the state because it can generate mass support, bring different social groups together and provide an underlying rationale for their separate social interests. Because it performs the functions of social mobilisation, political coordination and ideological legitimation so effectively, nationalism has spread across the globe, drawn in a variety of social groups and remained a powerful force for the last two centuries. For Breuilly, the role of sub-elites has been crucial, particularly for the important category of oppositional nationalisms in colonial territories. Under this heading,

Breuilly includes middle-level bureaucrats, officers, professionals, traders and intellectuals. In other cases, disaffected and poorer aristocrats or members of the lower clergy provided the vanguard of the nationalist movement, notably in parts of Eastern Europe. At times even the peasants and workers have been drawn into the nationalist cause, though left to themselves manual workers tend to place class solidarity above the nation, as Marx and Engels claimed. However, nationalism has flourished among peasants in certain revolutionary situations in Asia and Africa, just as it has drawn in workers wherever their trade unions have formed the main parties of opposition against the colonial authorities. Workers have also tended to become nationalistic wherever labour competition between workers of different ethnic groups has become acute, as occurred in late nineteenth-century Bohemia. But perhaps the most striking example of working-class adherence to nationalism occurred in the two world wars, though we should remember that, despite the high rate of workers volunteering for battle, it was the leaders of the trade unions in France, Germany and Britain, much more than their rank and file, that acceded to the bourgeois summons to war in 1914 and again in 1939 (*ibid.*: 36–46).[11]

Professionals and intellectuals are often thought to have played a pivotal role in nationalist movements. Given their discursive skills, status interests and occupational needs, professionals have been particularly strong adherents of the nationalist cause. Yet, claims Breuilly, it would be a mistake to see nationalism as the politics of professionals, if only because their positions in the hierarchies of status and power have kept the majority of professionals neutral and apolitical. Similarly with the intellectuals, who are often held to be the central proponents and adherents of nationalism. John Breuilly readily concedes the importance of intellectuals to political movements in general, and is prepared to allow that nationalist ideologies with their claim to speak for the whole nation hold special attractions for those who value both intellectual abstraction and their autonomy from sectional interests. At the same time, such abstraction and autonomy are the hallmarks of all modern ideologies; and intellectuals like others are subject to all kinds of social constraints and must operate within pre-existing political networks. It would be wrong, therefore, to characterise nationalism as the politics of the intellectuals or any other social group. It is to the politics and political contexts of social groups rather than their ideas that we must look to grasp the nature and functions of nationalism (*ibid.*: 48–51).[12]

If nationalism cannot be seen as the politics of intellectuals, does this mean that ideology is unimportant? With certain qualifications, concludes Breuilly,

> ideology can still be regarded as a powerful force which was essential to the work of co-ordination, mobilisation and adding legitimacy to what was carried out by a nationalist movement.
>
> (*ibid.*: 70)

However, the claim to link cultural distinctiveness to the demand for political self-determination had to be related to specific interests, and it worked only in particular sorts of political situations. The fundamental situation was that of modernity. The modern era of capitalism, bureaucracy and secularism saw a growing split between 'state' and 'society', the growth of an absolutist realm of politics on the one hand, and of a private realm of 'civil society' on the other. It was this yawning chasm which various ideologies sought to bridge and to which nationalism offered a pseudo-solution, by holding up a vision of the community defined simultaneously as the cultural and the political 'nation' of theoretically equal citizens. At this point, Breuilly takes Herder's arguments as representative of what he regards as the essentially historicist vision of nationalism. For Herder, language was thought and it only developed within the context of social groups. Thought, therefore, like language, was group-specific and unique; so was every other cultural code – dress, dance, architecture, music – in tandem with the society in which it developed. In its original state of nature, as created by God, each nation is both unique and 'authentic'. The task of the nationalist is clear: to restore his or her community to its natural, authentic state. But this can only be done by realising the cultural nation as a political nation, thereby reintegrating what modernity had sundered. Hence the call for national self-determination, which means reintegrating society with the state, by securing for each unique nation its own territorial state. Only in this way can authenticity be restored and the community, i.e. the nation, realise its distinctive self and its true inner values (*ibid.*: 55–64).

Breuilly regards the historicism of nationalism with deep suspicion insofar as it makes a specious leap from culture to politics by a sleight-of-hand redefinition of the unique cultural nation as the political nation of citizens. At the same time, he concedes that nationalism sets out to tackle a real problem: the split between state and society which modernity opens up. In an important and original passage, he seeks to show how that attempt, although flawed, exerted great power over the masses through the development of a uniquely concrete symbolism. The quality that sets nationalism apart from other ideologies is its unabashed celebration of the community itself.

> Nationalists celebrate themselves rather than some transcendent reality, whether this be located in another world or in a future society, although the celebration also involves a concern with transformation of present reality.
>
> (*ibid.*: 64)

Breuilly illustrates this self-referential quality through the powerful example of the Afrikaner myth of the Great Trek and the Day of the Covenant, recalling the 'deliverance' of the Boer farmers at the battle of Blood River in 1838. The symbolism of liberation and victory was successful in mobilising a sense of Afrikaner destiny (though not immediately of political unity) a century later, when the Ossawatrek was instituted through a re-enactment of the Great Trek. Here, according to Breuilly,

The central message, conveyed through anthems, rallies, speeches and elaborate ceremonials, is of an embattled people. The aim is to return to the heights of the past, though in a transformed fashion.

(*ibid.*: 67–8)

Breuilly ends by conceding, reluctantly, that

the self-reference quality of nationalist propaganda and the theme of the restoration of a glorious past in a transformed future has a special power which it is difficult for other ideological movements to match.

(*ibid.*: 68)[13]

The bulk of John Breuilly's massive study is devoted to historical elucidation of the forms and conditions of nationalisms in each of the six categories (reform, unification and separation nationalisms in nation-states and non-nation-states) both in Europe and in Africa and Asia. He concludes by recapitulating his political modernist theory. The modern absolutist state, at once territorially bounded and globally universal, came to be increasingly challenged and checked by a private domain of 'civil society' based on advancing capitalism, which constituted the growing political community. The idea of a sovereign state and its political community became dominant in Europe in the late eighteenth century and formed the basis of the modern territorial nation. The concept of the nation 'related principally to the institutions of the political community that sustained the monarchy' (*ibid.*: 374). When the opposition to the monarch and the state began to be based on historic or natural rights, the first step towards nationalism was taken. But where political opposition was weak, groups hitherto excluded from political life could be drawn in through an appeal to cultural identity as the basis for a territorial political community. This is the moment when nationalism emerges. So,

The idea of the ruled society which might only be definable in terms of its private character, that is, in terms of its 'culture'; of the sovereign territorial state; of a world made up of such states in competition with one another – these are the essential premises upon which nationalist ideology and nationalist politics build.

(*ibid.*: 375)

For Breuilly, the first real nationalist movements are those of separation or unification, for both kinds of movement aim to make the boundaries of the cultural community coextensive with the political unit. More generally, the development of nationalism was closely bound up with the nature of political modernisation in nineteenth-century Europe and in areas of European settlement and imperial rule overseas. Nationalism should be seen in this specific, political context, not as an intellectual invention to be unmasked, nor as an irrational force erupting in history, much less as the solution propounded by nationalists themselves to a deep human need for identity. It is 'a peculiarly modern form of politics which can only be understood in relation to the way in which the modern state has developed' (*ibid.*: 398–9, 401).

Identity and politics

But can we specify so precisely the nature and limits of nationalism? Breuilly's lucid, tightly-argued case for a political definition of nationalism is bought at considerable cost, of which he is well aware. On several occasions, he reverts to the question of a wider 'identity' sought by nationalists and by people at large, and espoused by rival approaches to nationalism. His arguments for rejecting the idea of nationalism as a language and ideology of cultural identity are twofold. The first is methodological: to try to include the concern with cultural identity is to inflate the definition of nationalism beyond all reason, and to render it vague and imprecise. We should concern ourselves exclusively with nationalism as a form of politics, because only that kind of definition is amenable to historical and social analysis.

But is a commendable concern for precision sufficient reason to reject at least a reference to 'identity' in the definition of the concept, when, on Breuilly's own admission, we can only speak of 'nationalism' at the point where a cultural identity is made the basis for political mobilisation? For Breuilly, nationalism is a species of historicism, premised on cultural diversity and the quest for 'authenticity'. Can we extrude all reference to 'culture' from the definition of a concept whose specificity resides exactly in the relationship it proposes between culture and politics? And if we include 'culture', is it not because culture is supposed, in nationalist ideology, to define a collective identity? Precision and rigour should not be bought at the cost of excluding a concept's key elements and its differentiating characteristics.[14]

There is also a theoretical ground for rejecting a concern with cultural identity as a defining characteristic of nationalism. Breuilly feels that its inclusion would lead us back to the unacceptable primordialism of an irrational need to belong and an atavistic appeal to forces erupting in history. At the same time, he admits at the end that nationalism 'derives much of its power from the half-truths it embodies'. He continues:

> People do yearn for communal membership, do have a strong sense of us and them, of territories as homelands, of belonging to culturally defined and bounded worlds which give their lives meaning. Ultimately, much of this is beyond rational analysis and, I believe, the explanatory powers of the historian.
>
> (*ibid.*: 401)

This might appear to undermine his case for limiting nationalism to a form of politics. But John Breuilly is being perfectly consistent with his premises: exactly because there are ideas and sentiments the historian cannot explain, we must stick to those elements that are amenable to explanation. At the same time, such an 'under-labourer' view of the scholar's task must accept its own limitations; and there will always be those who are tempted to take a different view of what can and cannot be the object of rational analysis. In particular, the interpretive method stemming from Weber's *Verstehende Soziologie* will continue to be used to analyse the subjective motivations of both individuals and communities, without resorting to a primordialist approach.[15]

In fact, there appear to be good reasons for including a reference to cultural identity in the definition of nationalism. One of the goals of nationalism is the attainment and maintenance of cultural identity, that is, a sense of a distinctive cultural heritage and 'personality' for a given named population. Without such a collective identity, there can be, from a nationalist's standpoint, no fully fledged and authentic 'nation'. Of course, this presupposes a more ostensive definition of nationalism than the stipulative one offered by Breuilly; but even he concedes *in his initial definition* of the concept of nationalism that the nation is credited with 'an explicit and peculiar character' in the nationalist doctrine.[16]

A second reason for including a reference to cultural identity is the need to accommodate diferent kinds of nationalism – religious, racial, linguistic and cultural. Indeed, there have been 'pure' cultural nationalists who have either rejected or remained silent about the state and the need to capture state power. Breuilly consistently denies to such ideologies and movements the label 'nationalist'. But not only does this fly in the face of the cultural, religious or linguistic nationalists' own self-description and understanding; it makes it very difficult to do justice to the role of influential cultural nationalists like Yeats, Achad Ha'am or Aurobindo, or of movements for cultural renewal and moral regeneration such as the Irish Gaelic revival or the Finnish literary renaissance (Branch 1985; Hutchinson 1987).

There is also a more empirical objection to Breuilly's restrictive definition of nationalism. Several nationalisms have eschewed the road to outright independence, preferring to attain maximum cultural, social and economic autonomy for their homelands and peoples within a wider, federal sovereign state. The Scots and Catalans, for example, have been given considerable autonomy, including their own legal, educational and cultural institutions, but most Scots and Catalans have opted to date to remain within the United Kingdom and Spain. This may, of course, change, but to deny them the label of 'nationalism' because their oppositional movements have not been bent on capturing state power is to overlook the centrality of national cultural and social regeneration in their movements, an ideal that is common to so many other 'nationalisms'.[17]

Finally, if nationalism is a form of politics, as Breuilly rightly reminds us, it is also a form of culture and society, perhaps even more importantly so. It proposes a form of culture based on 'authentic' and unique experience which aims to regenerate societies by uncovering and releasing their inner rhythms and energies. It does so through the rediscovery, reconstruction and appropriation of the communal past to become the basis of a vision of collective destiny. It offers a kind of collective salvation drama derived from religious models and traditions, but given a new activist social and political form through political action, mobilisation and institutions. Breuilly's reduction of the concept of nationalism to its political forms, while clarifying its political goals and role, omits the crucial dimensions of national cultural and social regeneration which nationalism aims to realise.

Intellectuals and nationalist ideology

Similar problems beset his explanatory paradigm. For John Breuilly, the alienation consequent on the split between the modern state and civil society generates nationalism. Indeed, nationalism is an attempted, though specious, political solution to this very real problem of modernity. Breuilly's emphasis on the pivotal role of the modern rational state provides a welcome corrective to so many sociological accounts that would 'reduce' nationalism to economic, social and psychological levels of analysis, with only the tactics of movements left to a residual political domain. The political level needs to be considered in its own right, and its vaunted autonomy restored. This allows due consideration of the policies of elites, the role of collaborators, and in particular the impact of political institutions in shaping nationalist goals and movements, which Breuilly delineates so acutely in his empirical analyses of particular nationalist movements (see also Brubaker 1996: chs 1–2).

Breuilly is not, however, oblivious to the role of non-political factors. He concedes the importance amd legitimacy of an enquiry into 'standard national cultures' such as Gellner conducts, as well as the impact of ideologies and intelligentsias on *some* nationalisms. If 'national identity' is the object of enquiry, then clearly these cultural and social psychological factors must receive far greater attention. For those interested in nationalism as a political movement, on the other hand, it is the impact of the modern state and its relationship with society that provides the sole crucible of nationalism. But is this proposed division of labour satisfactory? Can we so easily separate the political movement of nationalism from the growth of a sense of national identity? Are they not intimately conjoined, not just on occasion, but in all cases? After all, the fostering of such a sense of national identity is a prime objective of nationalist movements; but can nationalist movements emerge without some sense of national identity among the elites? If nationalism creates 'nations', does it not also create 'national identities', or does it presuppose some sense of national identity among its adherents? (Breuilly 1993: 379–80).[18]

These questions are related to the role of intellectuals and professional intelligentsias in nationalist movements. As Breuilly notes, in one sense, every political movement must have its intellectuals and professionals to promote and help organise it; in another sense, nationalist movements vary as to the extent of involvement of intellectuals and professionals in their ranks. But there is also a specific sense in which intellectuals as well as professionals, notably educators, are crucial to nationalisms: so often, they propose the category of the nation in the first place and endow it with symbolic significance. It is their imagination and understanding that gives the nation its contours and much of its emotional content. Through their images and symbols, they portray and re-present to others the significance and distinctiveness of the nation. Without that imagery and re-presentation, the political movement would be merely an anti- (or pro-) state movement; it would lack the directive guidance that the specific ideal of the nation furnishes (see Argyle 1969, 1976; Anderson 1991: ch. 5).

This in turn means that 'ideology', which Breuilly rightly takes to be essential as a cognitive map in a modern world of abstractions, has a special role in nationalist movements. Not only does it designate such movements, marking them off from other 'ideological movements' like conservatism and socialism; it endows them with those special symbols, images and concepts (for example, 'the people', the 'homeland', authenticity, destiny and autonomy) which give nationalisms their mobilising appeal and direction. Without them, nationalisms would be bereft of that self-reflexive quality which Breuilly, like Giddens, concedes is the source of much of their unique power. Hence the ideology and symbolism of nationalism must be treated as having just as much 'significance' as political institutions and political movements. The ability of nationalism to portray and forge a collective cultural identity is integral to its state-capturing capacity, for it seeks state power in virtue of its unique cultural values.

Nowhere is the power of symbolism and imagery more evident than in the territorial dimensions of nationalism. For Breuilly, territory is treated largely instrumentally, as the necessary arena and format of state power and hence nationalist aspiration. But the urge to possess land which characterises nationalism, is not confined to its political properties: the land is also the land of 'our ancestors', the historic land, and hence desired for its symbolic value as much as for its political empowerment or its economic resources. Like Anderson, Breuilly sees the modern state as the force that shapes the attachment to and identification with a territory, through censuses, maps and plebiscites and all the paraphernalia of centralised bureaucracy and political penetration. But again, while these agencies may define national borders and unify, even homogenise populations within them, they require the symbols, images and concepts of nationalism, the ideology and language, to give life to a bordered territory and attach people to it. The most dramatic case of this is Zionism. But other diaspora nationalisms – Greek, Armenian, Black – have also been nourished by the symbolic power of a historic territory and have only been able to mobilise their peoples by holding out the vision of restoration to 'their' ancestral territory. It has required the imagery and symbolism of nationalism to turn a territory into a homeland (Anderson 1991: ch. 10; cf. Breuilly 1993: ch. 10).[19]

Political modernism and ethnic history

This brings us back to the underlying premise of the political modernists' perspective. Their argument is predicated on the explicit assumption that nationalism can only emerge, and nations can only form, in the modern period and through the agencies of modernity, notably the modern sovereign state. For John

Breuilly, it is the alienation consequent on the split between state and society that fuels nationalism, and such a rift can only occur under modern conditions of state sovereignty, centralisation and capitalism. This is an argument ultimately derived from Marx (and before him Hegel, Schiller and other German idealists), for whom the sovereign modern state levelled all intermediate associations and confronted the citizens as individuals in a capitalist economy. Breuilly is not alone in drawing attention to the specifically political dimensions of the ensuing crisis of alienation felt by so many in this situation. Yet the curious fact is that, as Elie Kedourie clearly sees, it is the intellectuals and professionals who bear the brunt of this alienation, for it is they who most acutely feel their exclusion and isolation from the 'mechanical enginery' of the sovereign bureaucratic state. Not only in Central Europe, but in the European colonies, it was the educated urban classes who, doubly marginalised by the West and their own traditional societies, were unable to climb the bureaucratic ladder and whose education, talents and merits were spurned by an impervious but intrusive colonial state (see Crowder 1968; Kedourie 1971: Introduction).

But even if we accept the intellectuals' and professionals' feelings of alienation as a true reflection of the situation, and as evidence of a gulf between an autonomous state and a burgeoning civil society, why should these feelings turn to nationalism? Why should they find in the culturally defined 'nation' the apparent answer to their discontents? Is it true that nationalism seeks to abolish the distinction between a private domain – civil society – and a public one – the modern state – and is this why intellectuals and professionals have flocked to its banner?

That there have been some forms of fervent nationalism that sought to abolish the distinction between the private and public spheres, is clear enough. But by no means all nationalisms seek to do so. So-called 'civic' examples of nationalism are content to define the nation tacitly in cultural terms while infusing it with a largely civic content and vision. At moments of crisis and danger, the nationalist state often invades the private sphere, even in national states where civic ideals are well established, as occurred in Western countries during the two world wars. But there is also an everyday, banal nationalism where the flag remains 'unwaved', as Michael Billig puts it, but where the assumptions of nationalism are deeply entrenched. In these cases, nationalism as a political movement may be latent, but as ideology and language it has long done its work: national sentiments are widely diffused and the private domain flourishes within the cradle of the nation (Billig 1995).[20]

Breuilly may, of course, exclude such examples from the orbit of his political concept of nationalism, but the fact that situations of danger produce the same nationalist reactions as we find in cases which he would admit as genuine cases of 'nationalism', and that the populations of national states with these civic nationalisms operate on similar nationalist principles and assumptions, makes it difficult to draw a line of exclusion on political grounds. What these cases suggest is that civic nationalisms which accomodate and balance state and society rather than overcoming the one in terms of the other, presuppose a long history of cultural and social ties which are often based on some presumed common ethnic bonds. Even in kingdoms such as England and France where a powerful state shaped the nation, the modern state and its institutions have been forged on the basis of relatively united cultural groups, if not in remote antiquity, then during the period when their states were becoming gradually entrenched. Of course, the state was itself a factor in this process of unification, through its taxes, its wars, its courts and the like. Nevertheless, it benefited from the relative cultural unity of the core community which buttressed its power and which provided its elites (A. D. Smith 1986a: ch. 6).

So, even in the West, where Breuilly's state-centred modernism is best exemplified, an important qualification is necessary: the state developed *pari passu* with the nation, because there already existed unifying myths, memories and symbols of community among a core population which furnished the state elites and inhabited the core historic territory of the state. Even if in a more distant past these populations originated from several ethnic strands, as occurred in England and France, circumstances – including political action – had welded them sufficiently together to endow them with a sense of cultural community which in turn formed the basis of state power and state institutions. This is especially evident in the use of a common administrative language from the late medieval period, but it is also evident in the liturgy and institutions of Catholicism and the relative religious unity of the core cultural community until the mid-sixteenth century, by which time an elite national community was well established (Beaune 1985; Greenfeld 1992: ch. 2; Hastings 1997: chs 1–3).

Outside the West, no such congruence between state institutions and cultural populations existed, except in Poland and Hungary. Here, ethnicity and language provided an alternative basis for mobilising populations in opposition to the state. Granted that, as Breuilly claims, the modernisation of empires, such as Joseph II's reforms in the Habsburg empire or the Tanzimat reforms of the Ottoman empire, provided a stimulus and target for such ethnic oppositional movements; we cannot derive the sources and content of the ensuing *ethnonational* mobilisation from these state forms and institutions. For these, the nationalists had to turn back to a vernacular culture and a putative ancestral past, one which could unite and energise the different interest groups and strata of the designated population. Breuilly, like the other modernists, concedes the significance of such reappropriations of the past, but sees them largely in instrumental terms, as serving current elite needs and interests. The question that always returns to haunt this kind of analysis is why these reappropriations have such widespread popular appeal. It is one to which I shall return.

Conclusion

There is much to commend a modernist political approach in the study of nations and nationalism. For one thing, it highlights the centrality of the mass, citizen nation. Clearly, there are few, if any, parallels for the inclusion of most individuals in a given territory as participant citizens of the state, possessing equal rights and duties; and the ideology of nationalism, insofar as it mobilises the population and legitimates its political role, underpins this crucial political development.

Along with citizenship goes a bordered territory. The nation is a spatially finite category, a nation among nations, each defined in the first place by a set of clearcut and internationally recognised borders. Where in pre-modern times empires and kingdoms were separated from each other by often fluctuating *frontiers*, in the modern era nations are defined through their incorporation in sovereign states demarcated by recognised and regularly policed *borders*, which mark the limits of their jurisdictions, and which are symbolised, as well as realised, by guards, controls and national armies.

Of equal importance is the political modernists' emphasis on the primary role of political elites and political institutions. Of course, bureaucrats play a particularly important role in governmental nationalisms and in the maintenance and renewal of nations. Their vested interests in the state are legitimated as custody of the 'national interest' over and above sectional pressures, and as disinterestedly pursuing the ideals of the nation in opposition to party factions. But political elites also play a vital role in oppositional nationalisms, such as separatism or irredentism. They supply much of the organisation and tactics of struggle, and are often among the first to feel the alienation consequent on exclusion from office by the ruling power. Hence the centrality of this process of bureaucratic exclusion in the genesis of political nationalism in Asia and Africa (see Hodgkin 1956; Crowder 1968; Kedourie 1971).

Finally, political modernists can point with much historical justification to the role of the state as a central element in nationalist ideologies worldwide. So many people have come to regard the attainment of a state as a vital instrument for the protection of the nation and its culture. From the beginning, independent statehood came to be seen as an intrinsic part of every nation's aspirations, and as the sole bearer of the nation's cultural values – in large part because of the spectacular success of the Anglo-French model, and its first imitators in Germany, Italy and the United States.

But by the same token, the state as a necessary instrument of the nation could only attain some of the goals of nationalist ideologies. It proved unable to resolve questions of cultural identity, collective memory and the homeland, of the ethnic past, authenticity and destiny, or even of economic autarchy and national unity. To reduce the scope of nationalism to a cultural argument for independent statehood does scant justice to the range of nationalist concerns and hence their appeal to so many people across the globe.

If the stress on political elites is a strength of the political modernist approach, it is also a limitation. A 'top-down' governmental and elite approach needs to be complemented by a popular perspective 'from below'. If nationalist elites appeal to 'the people', strata within the latter can and do reshape the nationalist ideology in their own image. The most articulate sections of the artisans, clerks, workers and peasants carry through their inherited fund of symbols, memories, myths and traditions, a set of attitudes, perceptions and sentiments that reshape the messages of the nationalist elites. To omit the perceptions and role of non-elite strata is to miss this underlying drive of so many nationalisms and the source of their direction.

Finally, we may note that the modernist emphasis on the role of the territorial state tends to preclude an equally important role for the ethnic origins of nations. This is a large subject to which I shall return. Suffice it to say here that an overt concern with ethnic origins has shaped the ideologies of many non-Western nationalisms; ethnic motifs form an intrinsic element of the historicism of nationalist ideologies, while the model of the ethnic nation has been as potent as the success story of the Anglo-French national state. Here the strength of political modernism is also its weakness. Its exclusive concern with the political modernity of nations and nationalism precludes it from considering the influence of ethnic motifs of origin and the impact of cultural history on the appeal and success of nations and nationalism. As a result, the study of nationalism becomes truncated and shorn of much of its content.

5 Political messianism

On one matter, practically all scholars agree. As an ideology and movement, nationalism is modern. It dates from the late eighteenth or very early nineteenth centuries, and it originated in Western and Central Europe, and the United States. It is, therefore, a product of the discontents of modernity. Just as the world religions constituted a much earlier response to the predicament of humanity in agrarian societies, with their natural disasters and social cataclysms, so the nation and nationalism represent the fundamental response to the crisis of identity so many human beings faced with the onslaught of modernity on the traditions of their ancestors. Nationalism is the natural response of human beings whose social world, with its stable groupings, has collapsed; yearning to belong to a durable community, they turn to the transhistorical nation as the only available replacement for the extended family, neighbourhood and religious community, all of which have been eroded by capitalism and westernisation.

'Political religion'

This was very much the basis of the argument advanced by the theorists of 'political religion' in the 1960s. They saw nationalism in the new states of Africa and Asia as a religion of modernisation, a political version of traditional religion. These modern states, they argued, have a number of requirements; the aggregation of interests, the establishment of strong central authority, the development of economic rationality, the need for flexible institutions for coping with change. But in the new states, the needs of social integration and economic development took on special importance in view of their ethnic heterogeneity and lack of resources. To achieve social integration and development, elites had to mobilise the masses and encourage them to postpone gratification and accept considerable sacrifices. The virtues of patriotism, commitment, hard work, frugality and self-sacrifice had to be inculcated in the newly enfranchised citizens. Nationalism, as a fervent and puritan ideology of mass self-sacrifice, served the purposes of the elites of the new states admirably, for in conditions of national liberation from colonial rule it equated the unitary new nation with the newly independent state, and urged the citizens to labour for the good of the whole nation. In this way, the state, and its one-party or military regime, came to embody the seamless unity of the nation, which was endowed with the characteristics of a faithful church. It became a pure, sinless and seamless community, to be worshipped by the citizenry in the same way as communities of believers had formerly worshipped the deity. Nationalism, in other words, substituted the nation for the deity, the citizen body for the church and the political kingdom for the kingdom of God, but in every other respect replicated the forms and qualities of traditional religions.[1]

In this Durkheimian model, nationalism becomes a form of reflexive collective self-worship, a 'political religion' not just in the sense in which a religion like Islam is sometimes characterised as political, that is, as a way of life which does not distinguish between politics and religion, but as a political surrogate for religion. Nationalism here is really a modern, secular ideology which serves as a 'civil religion', performing the same functions for individuals and groups as did traditional religion, although springing from secular, non-traditional sources. Durkheim himself summed this approach up when, commenting on ideological developments in the French Revolution, he remarked that

> At that time, under the influence of the general enthusiasm, things purely secular in nature were transformed by public opinion into sacred things: these were the Fatherland, Liberty, Reason. A religion tended to become established which had its dogmas, symbols, altars and feasts.
>
> (Durkheim 1915: 214)

For Durkheim, of course, this 'religious' quality, which derives from the etymology of the term, is universal and enduring; it is to be found in different forms in all societies, even in modern, apparently quite secular industrial societies. Traditional worship of God or gods may have been superseded; but the deeper roots of religion, the need for cults to distinguish the sacred from the profane, the need to express the dependance of human beings on a powerful society, will always remain.[2]

This is not the standpoint of the theorists of 'political religion'. They are adherents of an ideological version of modernism. For David Apter, Lucian Pye, Leonard Binder and Manfred Halpern, these relapses into 'political religion' are characteristic of the painful transition to modernity. In order to forge modern nations, elites in the new states resort to what Apter termed 'mobilisation systems', and invent a symbolic mythology and civic religion to persuade the masses to make the necessary sacrifices. Once development has been achieved, and the threshold of modernity crossed, there will be no further need of the political religion of nationalism or of the political mobilisation system built up on its basis (Pye 1962; Apter 1963b; Halpern 1963; Binder 1964; cf. Lerner 1958; Smelser 1962; Eisenstadt 1965).

Marginal youth

This is the starting point for Elie Kedourie's analysis of the spread of nation-alism to colonial societies in the long introduction to his second book, an anthology of writings of nationalists entitled *Nationalism in Asia and Africa*. This is a sequel to his earlier influential *Nationalism*. In that book, Kedourie had argued that nationalism was a doctrine invented in Europe in the early nineteenth century and that it sprang from the philosophical tradition of the Enlighten-ment, notably from Kant's doctrine that the good will can only be the autonomous will. It was the merit of Fichte and other German Romantics like Schlegel, Muller, Schleiermacher, Arndt and Jahn to marry Kant's individualist doctrine to Herder's cultural populism in such a way that autonomy was now predicated of pure linguistic communities, in which, to realise their true freedom, individuals must absorb themselves. To realise its autonomy, the linguistic nation must determine itself and take up its destiny; the individual's self could only be realised in the struggle of his or her nation for self-determination (Kedourie 1960: chs 4–5).

Kedourie went on to sketch a brief social explanation of why this romantic version of nationalism (which he assumed was the only true version of the doctrine) arose in Germany. Aside from Kant's influence, and the example and legend of the French Revolution with its new style of mass politics, the political and social situation in the German-speaking lands, divided as they were into many principalities of varying size and importance, denied to the emerging class of German intellectuals any influence on the direction of affairs. Excluded and alienated from politics, these intellectuals became restless under the impact of Enlightenment rationalism and sought in romantic fantasies a solution to their discontents. They eagerly latched onto the Fichtean nationalist synthesis, espe-cially after the defeat of Prussia by Napoleon in 1806; but they were only the first of many waves of European nationalism spearheaded by alienated young intellectuals for whom the traditions of their fathers had lost all meaning. Young Italy, Young Poland, Young Hungary and the like, children's crusades against the old order, attested to a European *Zeitgeist* of revolutionary messianism that could only end in terroristic nihilism and ethnic hatred, especially in ethnically mixed areas like the Balkans (*ibid.*: ch. 6).

In the Introduction to his second book on nationalism, Kedourie extended his analysis to the colonies of Africa and Asia which had fallen prey to secular European ways and ideologies. Colonies, he argued, had not been established for the export of capital in an age of finance capital, as Hobson, Hilferding and Lenin had claimed; their economic returns were negligible compared to their strategic and psychological benefits. Not only were they territories where immi-grants could find economic opportunities, they also served as imperial outposts against European rivals at a time when the landmass of Europe itself was unable to accommodate territorial expansion. These strategic considerations were abetted by the nineteenth-century imperialist desire for 'glory' in a period of colonial political annexation which for Disraeli and his generation signified the original political meanings of the terms 'imperialism' and 'colonialism' (Kedourie 1971: 4, 8, 10–14).

Now imperialism had a number of unforeseen consequences. To begin with, colonial administration tended to pulverise traditional society and regiment the colony through its bureaucratic measures. This meant that traditional handicrafts and village production suffered; they were no match for the exports of Lancashire industries or the financial speculations of the City. Hence the economic basis of village life, which accounted for the vast mass of the population, collapsed. In addition, the colonial authorities encouraged literacy and secular education on Western lines. Mass literacy undermined traditional religious authority and customary ways, and, along with Western research into the ethnic traditions and cultures of the colonies, prepared the way for alternative conceptions and new leaderships in the African and Asian colonies. From this clash of cultures and confusion of soul, emerged a new class of 'marginal men' who embraced western ideals of independence and self-reliance, yet bore the marks of the strain and discontent of men

> disaffected toward their traditional society, the nucleus and vanguard of a radical and uncompromising opposition and its battering ram pounding down outmoded and obscurantist institutions.
>
> (Kedourie 1971: 27)

Among the many ideas that spread to African and Asian colonies, the most appealing to the marginal men was nationalism, the doctrine that

> holds that humanity is naturally divided into nations, that nations are known by certain characteristics that can be ascertained, and that the only legitimate type of government is national self-government.
>
> (*ibid.*: 28)

As a doctrine, nationalism is utterly alien to the political traditions of Asia and Africa, with their great empires and tribal kingdoms respectively; it is a product of the history of Europe, with its abiding tendency to 'require and enforce uniformity of belief among the members of a body politic' (*ibid.*: 31). From Theodosius in 379 AD through the Crusades and the Wars of Religion right up to Rousseau's 'civil religion', the drive for religious and cultural homogeneity in a polity has reappeared regularly in Europe. This tendency has been reinforced, and given its concrete modern expression, by two additional, if more recent, features of European thought and practice: the elevation of cultural, and especially linguistic, group diversity by the German Romantics, and the profound European preoccupation with history and evolutionary development as the basis for personal and collective identity, which became widespread during the period of the Enlightenment and romanticism (*ibid.*: 34–6).[3]

The cult of the 'dark gods'

What impact did these new European ideas have on Asian and African societies? Kedourie takes as his prototype the early expression of Greek nationalism in the person of Adamantios Korais (1748–1833), the Greek enlightener and native of the Greek Orthodox community of Smyrna. Korais had imbibed Western ideas and languages under the auspices of a Dutch clergyman, and stayed several years during the 1770s in Holland; after returning for a brief sojourn in his homeland, he spent the rest of his life in France. Here, under the influence of the growing radicalism of the French Revolution, Korais began to reinterpret the condition of his native Greece in Western terms, lamenting its decline and expressing (in a lecture of 1803) 'the customary appeal to a glorious past, earnest of a still more glorious future, and warrant for the subversion of present and existing institutions'. In his conclusion, Korais emphasised that modern Greeks are the descendants of the ancient Greeks, and as such must be worthy of them; only by accepting this, would the regeneration of Greece become possible (*ibid.*: 42–3).

For Elie Kedourie, love of the ancient past feeds on hatred of the present. Quoting Yeats' 'More substance in our enmities than our love', Kedourie emphasises the European Enlightenment roots of the non-Western intellectuals' antagonism towards all existing traditional institutions, notably religious ortho-doxies, in the Balkans and in Asia. The same European metamorphosis of beliefs and assumptions invaded the Ottoman Empire, which, from being 'the work of the House of Osman laboring in the triumphant cause of Islam', became 'an achievement of the Turkish, or more generally the Turanian, genius', both 'Turk' and 'Turanian' being nineteenth-century European philolog-ical and historical inventions. In fact, the name 'Turkey' was given to the land of the Turks by the Kemalist regime in the 1920s; there was no name for this idea in the Turkish language. For the foremost Turkish theorist of nationalism, Ziya Gökalp, indeed,

> The country of the Turks is not Turkey, nor yet Turkestan. Their country is a broad and everlasting land – Turan,

a term that could cover Sumerians and Hittites, not to mention Attila, Genghis Khan and Tamerlane, as 'manifestations of the protean genius of Turan'. Later, however, the Turks ceased to be 'Turanians': for Tekin Alp in the 1930s they had become beautiful, tall specimens of the 'Aryan race', in line with the new interest in racial and fascist doctrines (*ibid.*: 48–52).

In Iran, Pakistan, India and Africa, Kedourie finds the identical processes of Europeanisation of thought and the same transvaluation of values. In the past, the Buddha, Confucius, Muhammad and Isaiah were teachers and prophets whose teachings lighted men on their way, a rule of life unvarying and stable, which gave meaning and coherence to the world, a living, self-confident, self-contained tradition; they were not symbols and proofs of national greatness.

(ibid.: 64–5)

Now their role is purely instrumental, to provide an example and harbinger of the 'national' genius; thus Arab nationalism has 'transformed Muhammad from a prophet and lawgiver into a mere harbinger of Arabism'. In order to transform the 'heap of loose sand' which is all that is left of a traditional society pulverised by Europe into something 'solid and powerful', it is necessary to arouse a sense of national identity, appeal to the ethnic past and 'restore' traditional morality as the cement of national solidarity. Indeed, the tendency of nationalism to assimilate traditional religion shows that it is not simply a cognitive doctrine; it is also a 'method of spiral mobilisation, of eliciting, activating, and canalising dormant political energies' *(ibid.*: 70).[4]

Good examples of this political activism are provided by Tilak's instrumental use of the Hindu revival in Marathi festivals such as the worship of the elephant-god Ganesh or the chieftain Shivaji's birthday, or his political reinterpretation of the stoic spiritual teachings of Krishna in the *Bhaghavad-Gita*. For Bipin Chandra Pal, too, popular Hinduism, being partly spiritual and partly social, could easily and naturally furnish the basis for a civic religion of India, through the politicisation of what were originally purely religious ideas. Thus the worship of the dark goddess Kali, with her garland of human heads round her neck, dripping blood, before whom initiates of terrorist societies took their vows, could be made to serve nationalist political ends, simply by substituting a sacrifice of 108 white, rather than black, goats at each new moon – that is, 108 whites *(ibid.*: 70–76; cf. Adenwalla 1961; Kapferer 1988: ch. 3).

If this was the effect of the introduction of nationalist activism on Indian and indeed on all non-European societies, how did it come about that this style of politics and this doctrine became the dominant form of politics outside Europe? Kedourie argues that, although there were well known resistance movements to European incursions in the mid-nineteenth century, such as the Indian Mutiny, the novel pattern of European rule began to attract the new educated classes who had come to accept the superiority of European civilisation. Indeed, they fervently desired to remake their own societies in the likeness of Europe. Unfortunately, they soon found that, despite their Western education and their assimilation into Western ways, they were not accepted on an equal footing with their European counterparts. This was especially true of access to European imperial institutions. Here Kedourie cites the example of European anger at and emasculation of the Ilbert Bill of 1883, which proposed to allow Indian-born magistrates the same rights to try British subjects in India as British-born colleagues, and the ensuing Indian resentment. There was also the influential case of Surendranath Banerjea (1848–1926) who was dismissed from the British civil service for a lesser offence, travelled to London for a fair hearing but was refused reinstatement, and launched in consequence a nationalist lecture campaign, persuaded as he was that 'the personal wrong done to me was an illustration of the impotency of our people' (*ibid.*: 84–5).

Similar slights, frustrations and rejections by the higher echelons of the civil service were experienced by Western-educated Arabs like Edward Atiyah and George Antonius, and they once again revealed the profound gulf between imperial pretensions to impartiality and fairness and imperial practices of racial discrimination. But these illiberal rejections raised a more profound question of identity, of 'What am I?', in the shocked and anguished souls of the marginal men. Their reply was a strident assertion of self in a collective mode unknown to their forbears, and, in revulsion against Europe and its bloody internecine wars, an appeal to the 'dark gods' of ethnic tradition (*ibid.*: 86–9, 91–2).

A millennial opiate

Or was it revulsion? Perhaps, argues Kedourie, the appeal to the dark gods and their rites was really an imitation and adaptation of European ideas, not only the idea that every nation must have a past, preferably heroic and glorious, but also the previously hidden but now manifest European tradition of progress of which the idea that the nation must have a great and splendid future is one variant.

Now the idea that history, in the words of the German enlightener Lessing, is 'a road on which humanity progresses towards perfection' and that 'It will certainly come, the era of a new, everlasting gospel which is the New Covenant', can be traced back, as Lessing himself was aware, to the thirteenth and four-teenth centuries in Europe. The term 'everlasting gospel' figured in the title of a work published in Paris in 1254 by Gerard of Borgo San Donnino, who was in turn inspired by the writings of a Calabrian abbot, Joachim of Fiore (c. 1130–1202). Joachim speculated about the imminent advent of the millennium, basing himself on apocalyptic texts in the Book of Revelations such as:

> Blessed and holy is he that hath part in the first resurrection: on such the second death hath no power, but they shall be priests of God and of Christ, and shall reign with him a thousand years.
>
> (*ibid.*: 94–5, citing Revelations 20: 6)

Joachim speculated that the age of law (the Father) had been followed by the age of grace (the Son) and that this would now give way to an age of love (the Holy Spirit), the 'new heaven and new earth' of the prophecies of St John the Divine. Despite repeated condemnations by church authorities (as well as by rabbis and ulema), such antinomian, millennial heresies reappeared from time to time, wreaking havoc and destruction, as in the terrifying rising of 1534 among the Anabaptists of Münster, or outside Europe in the Taiping rebellion of 1850–61 in southern China.

In all these examples, the political style of millennialism is clear:

The millennial hope is of the inauguration and institution of a totally new order where love reigns and all men are brothers, where all distinctions and divisions, all selfishness and self-regard are abolished. But a society in which the distinction between public and private is annihilated, in which ranks, orders, classes, associations and families are all dissolved into one big family, a society in which all articulations and complexities have disappeared – such a society becomes helpless in the hands of those who prophesy the good tidings of the coming salvation.

(*ibid.*: 97)

Hence the revolutionary aims and style of the politics of millennial nationalism:

All of them [millennialisms] announce the gospel of love and brotherhood, and they must therefore destroy all social and political institutions; they must, as Tseng Kuo-Fan put it, 'depose sovereigns and degrade officials'.

(*ibid.*: 102)

Since the French Revolution, millennialism has re-emerged in secular garb, as the ideal of progress and the quest for absolute liberty which, as Hegel observed, goes hand-in-hand with terror. The idea of progress is a 'secularised and respectable version of the medieval millennium'. Its disreputable political style, *sans-culottisme*, has been placed in the service of a secular politics of the impossible, a frenzied meliorism in which, as Robespierre declared, terror is the emanation of virtue.

Nationalism as it appears and spreads in Europe is one of the many forms of this vision of a purified society in which all things are made new. . . . What gives the doctrine dynamism, what makes it a mainspring of human action is surely this millennial hope that men can somehow put an end to all oppression and injustice.

(*ibid.*: 103–5)

Citing the *Revolutionary Catechism* (1869) of the anarchist Bakunin, written under the influence of the terrorist Nechaev, to reveal the revolutionary political style of the quest for absolute liberty, Kedourie argues that the cult of the dark gods by educated non-Europeans represents the adoption and adaptation of certain revolutionary and terrorist features of the European tradition. The glorification of Kali, goddess of destruction, is the counterpart of Bakunin's regrouping of 'this world of brigands into an invincible and omni-destructive force' and Robespierre's conjunction of virtue and terror. This leads Elie Kedourie to conclude that:

We may say in short that the mainspring of nationalism in Asia and Africa is the same secular millennialism which had its rise and development in Europe and in which society is subjected to the will of a handful of visionaries who, to achieve their vision, must destroy all barriers between private and public.

(*ibid.*: 106)

Kedourie goes on to illustrate his thesis of the politics of the impossible, leading to what the poet Rimbaud called 'the systematic *derangement* of the senses', with examples taken from India, Ghana, Kenya, the Congo and southern Africa.

> Mau Mau, Ethiopianism, the cult of Black messiahs, and the popularity of millenarian varieties of Christianity alike testify to the disturbance and disorientation which contact with Europe brought and which practices and beliefs of this kind promised to assuage and relieve.

(*ibid.*: 127)

From this disorientation and the religious fervour which it breeds, the nationalist movement can fashion a formidable weapon, provided it can be channelled and focused onto a few slogans and symbols. Of these symbols, the national leader is often the most potent, as Kenyatta, Nkrumah and Nehru discovered. For the emotional link between leaders and led, which satisfies the leader's will to power, fosters the 'pathetic fallacy', namely, that

> there is no difference between them and those whom they rule, that their interests, their preoccupations and their aims are exactly identical.

(*ibid.*: 131)

This makes the political tie a 'private, amorous relation, in which the body politic is united by love'; indeed for Michel Aflaq, the ideologue of the Syrian Ba'ath Party, nationalism is love. But government, Kedourie reminds us, is the exercise of power and the governors must be kept apart from the governed; they must not 'feel with the people', for they are not flesh of their flesh. Nationalists, on the other hand, 'feel with the people'. Their despotisms are driven by a tender mercilessness which aims to bring their countrymen back to their true selves, if necessary through terror and death. Hence the celebration of violence by Fanon and the nationalisation of the proletarian struggle by Sultan Galiev, for whom the class struggle becomes a conflict between the white and the coloured races.[5]

In the final analysis, these are all variations on the underlying theme of the virtue of the poor, the guilt of Europe and the innocence of Asia and Africa, salvation through violence and the coming reign of universal love. 'Theory' has indeed become the opium of the masses. But Marx was wrong: opium is no mere soporific.

> As the Old man of the Mountain – whose 'theory' was so potent that legend has transmuted it into *hashish* – could have told him, the drug may also excite its addicts to a frenzy of destruction.

(*ibid.*: 147)

Colonialism and the intellectuals

The idea that nationalism is a product of 'marginal men' or uprooted intellectuals caught between tradition and westernisation is not an original one. It can be found in an early essay by Trevor-Roper, as well as in the works of Thomas Hodgkin, and it owes much to Hans Kohn's characterisation of an organic 'Eastern' nationalism led by tiny coteries of intellectuals in place of a bourgeoisie. But in Elie Kedourie's hands, this thesis is charged with a new emotion and a deeper meaning. Kedourie's makes three claims: first, that the discrepancy between imperial ideals and colonial practices inevitably breeds the discontent of wasted merit among the intellectuals; second, that the ensuing crisis of identity can only be assuaged by a (false because impossible) millennial doctrine of collective political progress; and third, that the violence we so often associate with nationalism is the product of its 'transvaluation of values' and its appeal to mass emotion through the politicisation of ethnic religion. His penetrating exploration and rich illustration of these arguments gives Kedourie's analysis a singular power and originality, and makes it the most compelling statement of ideological modernism (Kohn 1967a: ch. 7; Trevor-Roper 1962; Hodgkin 1956, 1964).

Two considerations frame Kedourie's arguments. The first is that his theoretical claims are limited. Unlike Gellner, Nairn or Hechter, Kedourie rejects the idea that he aims to offer any kind of theory; indeed, he argues that such theoretical understanding is impossible and undesirable. The specificity of history and variety of human responses renders any overall theory pointless and misleading. All we can hope to do is to understand a particular doctrine or movement in its context, as an expression of a particular *Zeitgeist*; all the historian is concerned with are the ways in which specific ideas and practices emerge and are developed in a particular social and cultural milieu. The milieu in which Kedourie locates the birth of nationalism is, first, an early nineteenth-century Central Europe undergoing revolutionary social and political change; and second, a late nineteenth- and twentieth-century Asia and Africa radically transformed by the impact of European colonialism. Common to both is the solvent of cultural westernisation and social modernisation, which undermines traditional communities and breaks the age-old transmission of political habits and ideas (see S. Kedourie 1998).

The second consideration is normative. Kedourie is violently hostile to all expressions of nationalism, as he regards the doctrine as not only intellectually incoherent and erroneous, but also morally pernicious and destructive of all political order. For Kedourie, nationalism is a particularly virulent, because self-destructive, species of the more general Western ideal of progress; its violence stems from its frenzied attempts to realise unattainable ideals in an imperfect world. Worse, nationalists are guilty of the sin of pride. Taking off from the assumptions of their intellectual progenitors, the Cartesian rationalist philosophers from Descartes to Kant, they add a pitiless impiety to their overweening arrogance by seeking moral perfection in an imperfect world. These ruthless but self-deluded would-be gods inevitably wreak havoc on themselves and their peoples, and destroy all hope of peace and a stable international order (see also Dunn 1978: ch. 3; Viroli 1995).

Despite these claims, Kedourie succeeds in offering a general framework for the understanding of nationalism which, at certain points, even manages to evince a degree of sympathy with those who embrace nationalism. That overall framework is the diffusion of ideas under the impact of a discriminatory colonialism. Kedourie sees nationalism as a disease transmitted through travel and reading from its sources in the West; yet he acknowledges that intellectuals may all too easily succumb to the disease because of the unenviable position in which they find themselves. With many an incisive example, Kedourie illustrates their predicament: their fervent embrace of an apparently superior civilisation with its ideals of impersonal merit and impartial justice; their subsequent bitter disappointment on finding themselves excluded both in the metropolis and at home; their tendency to see in their individual rejection the impotency of their people to which racial discrimination in the imperial bureaucracy lends credence; their ensuing self-doubt and identity crisis; and their search for a political solution to their alienation. This tendency to exclude the meritorious Western-educated non-Europeans from the higher echelons of the colonial bureaucracy is well documented, as is the accompanying self-doubt and ambivalence of the intellectuals; indeed, these same intellectuals and professionals can experience similar frustrations in the West itself, for example, in Quebec, where they are in the forefront of Québécois nationalism (Pinard and Hamilton 1984; cf. Wallerstein 1965; Crowder 1968; Gouldner 1979; A. D. Smith 1981a: ch. 6).

But is this diffusionist framework helpful in accounting for the rise of nationalism in Africa and Asia? Diffusionism in itself is always theoretically inadequate; it can never account for the *reception* of ideas that are transmitted from one centre to another. We may accept the Western origins of nationalist ideas, but is that in itself sufficient to explain the emergence, let alone the content, of nationalism in a given colony or state outside Europe? Can we derive the rise of an Arab or Indian nationalist movement from the political self-assertion of a few intellectuals whose discontents have found a political outlet in the idea of an Arab or an Indian nation? Granted that intellectuals are necessary to such movements, at least in their inception, are the latter mere products of their ambivalence and discontent, and is their nationalist thought always merely derivative? (see Chatterjee 1986).

The general picture that Kedourie paints is one in which traditional societies are pulverised and regimented by colonial modernity, leaving the intellectuals as the only social group able to respond to the onslaught. On the other hand, Kedourie admits the persistence of traditional elements, when he analyses the ways in which these intellectuals seek to manipulate the atavistic emotions of the masses and to use or revive their traditional practices. In fact, as we know, colonialism's impact was highly variable. For one thing, it very much depended on the nature and policies of the colonial power. Where the French, for example, tended to assimilate an African or Indo-Chinese elite, leaving the rest of the population uneducated and second-class citizens, the British colonial authorities preferred a policy of 'indirect rule', working with and through traditional but subordinated indigenous authorities. We also have to take into account the variable presence of missionaries and the impact of missionary education in uprooting indigenous beliefs and customs. These are only some of the reasons why many traditional elements – ways of life, customs, beliefs, symbols, myths – persisted in varying degrees in Asia and Africa, even after decades of colonial rule (Crowder 1968; Markovitz 1977; cf. Horowitz 1985).

Now, the important point about colonial rule is that it provided, *in relation to pre-colonial cultures and social structures*, the crucible in which nationalist movements emerged. In other words, the genesis and development of nationalism in, say, Nigeria, Kenya and India must be located, not simply in the diffusion of Western ideas through conspiratorial cells of restless indigenous intellectuals who have returned empty-handed from the West, but in the interests, sentiments and aspirations of a variety of social and cultural groups in colonial India, Kenya and Nigeria. These social and cultural groups are partly formed by the activities of colonial officials, traders and missionaries, but they are also derived from pre-colonial ethnic communities and polities, and from traditional social strata like chieftains and traders, tribal castes and Brahmins, which have taken on a new life in the colonial setting. We cannot understand the specific nature of Indian, Kenyan or Nigerian nationalisms without taking into account the cultures and traditions of these communities and strata. Kedourie indirectly admits this, but sees the process as one-sided, a manipulation of the inert masses by messianic elites; whereas, in fact, the cultural resources and ethnic outlooks of peasants and traders, tribesmen and lower castes, also helped to shape the particular versions of nationalism that emerged in these colonies.[6]

The failure to treat seriously the social and cultural conditions in which nationalism emerges in Africa and Asia stems not only from Kedourie's diffusionism, but also from his psychologism. In fact, his overestimation of the power of ideas is closely linked to his belief in the universal need of human beings to belong to a stable community. It follows that, if such communities are undermined, human beings must immediately look for alternative sources of collective stability. At this point, the nation appears, like some *deus ex machina*, to fill the gap and assuage the pain of their disorientation. A new idea gives birth to a new type of community at the very moment when the old ideas of religion and the traditional forms of community are undermined.

But all this assumes, first, that human beings must belong to stable communities, and second that the nation is indeed a wholly new kind of community and has no links with traditional communities. Now, it may be true that many human beings prefer to live their lives in stable communities, though, given the variety of such groups in the modern world, their collective identities are likely to be multiple and cross-cutting. But it should not be inferred from this that all human beings always prefer stability to change, and tradition to the ability to join or even form their own communities of choice. This is as much a generalisation open to challenge as the nationalist idea that all human beings desire to free themselves from oppression, which Kedourie correctly refutes. Once again, the context is all-important. In some circumstances, human beings may wish to rid themselves of stable but oppressive communities, in others to restore a measure of communal stability even at the cost of curtailing their freedom of choice. In following the conservative tradition of Lord Acton and Michael Oakeshott, Kedourie adopted a rather one-dimensional psychologism that bypasses the social and cultural settings which contribute to the variety of human responses to rapid change in the modern world, and prevents him from seeing how in the contemporary world, many more human beings are experimenting with different forms of social network and cultural community (see Melucci 1989).

Second, even if 'nationalism-in-general' is a modern ideology, it does not follow that nations are themselves wholly novel kinds of community. In fact, as we shall see, this view needs to be seriously qualified. For the moment, it suffices to demonstrate the lack of solid argument or evidence in Kedourie's formulation of the link between the 'need to belong' and the appearance of the nation. Let us concede such a universal need. Why must it fasten on 'the nation'? Why not on 'class', 'city', 'region', indeed 'continent'? Why not just 'the state'? Given these alternatives, we are hardly justified in choosing the nation, simply because of the incubrations of a few German intellectuals and their followers. In other words, Kedourie's idealist and psychologist methodology precludes him from explaining why it was, and is, the *nation* that has won out over all these rivals, and why *nationalism* has become the dominant ideology and culture of our time.

This failure is linked to Elie Kedourie's unique combination of radical socio-historical modernism with a normative anti-modernism. The nation, along with nationalism, is seen as a new-fangled type of community, a construct of disaffected intellectuals, without any precursor or foundation in pre-modern epochs. It is a brutal imposition of the West on innocent cultures and societies. Forced to eat of this tree of knowledge and driven out of their pre-colonial Eden, Africans and Asians have become prey to the lure of the latterday opiate of unattainable perfectibility, which removes them yet further from the ways of life that had served them so well, and bars their return to the warmth and intimacy of family and tradition.

Millennialism and progress

Kedourie traces this modern opiate of messianic secular nationalism to a specific source, medieval Christian and European millennial heresies. The argument proceeds in two ways: by analogy and by filiation. Kedourie seeks to trace first the historical route by which these medieval heresies became by the late eighteenth century the basis for secular nationalism. This route is necessarily obscure, since the heretics were suppressed and often left no records. But Kedourie manages to reconstruct some passages along the way. A view of the last stage is afforded by some paragraphs of Lessing's *Education of the Human Race* (1780) which, in prophetic bursts, proclaims the coming of 'this epoch of perfection' and traces the origin of this 'everlasting gospel' of perfection to 'certain visionaries of the thirteenth and fourteenth centuries'. Of course, as Kedourie readily concedes, this was simply a more lyrical and fervent expression of the enlightened meliorism of the Enlightenment, of which Kedourie quotes an orthodox example from an English theological work of 1773 by William Worthington, which also foresaw a future approximation to 'the innocence and perfection of the paradisiacal state' (Kedourie 1971: 94–7).

Now, we may readily concede some influence on eighteenth-century meliorism from earlier expressions of religious messianism. But it is far more difficult to trace a clear provenance from the medieval apocalyptic millennialism of Joachim of Fiore in the late twelfth century and Gerard of Borgo San Donnino in the thirteenth century to Lessing's outpourings and Mazzini's rhetoric in the eighteenth and nineteenth centuries. In the long intervening period, Kedourie cites only the drama of the Anabaptist rising in Münster under Jan Mathys and Jan of Leyden. Can we seriously trace the origins of German, or indeed any nationalism to the apocalyptic visions of the Franciscan Spirituals, the Brethren of the Free Spirit and the Anabaptists of Münster from the thirteenth to the sixteenth centuries? For Kedourie's filiation thesis to hold, we would need to show that every case of nationalism, at least in Europe, was preceded by a millennial movement with strong chiliastic expectations. It may be possible to show that a few nationalisms were preceded, within a few decades, by a millennial movement – the Taiping Movement in China springs to mind – but there are many more cases where no such chronological succession of millennial and nationalist movements can be discovered. Of course, Kedourie's claim is more limited; merely to have shown a general trend, a thread of heretical ideas, that re-emerged in the late eighteenth century. Yet so many strands went into the making of eighteenth-century meliorism; why give this particular one such importance?[7]

The answer lies in the second, analogical, mode of argument. For Kedourie, nationalism is a species of the revolutionary doctrine of progress, which in turn is a modern analogue of medieval Christian millennialism. Nationalism, therefore, like millennialism, seeks to abolish the distinction between the private and public domains; nationalism, like millennialism, seeks to institute a new morality of absolute purity and brotherhood; nationalism separates its devotees in the movement from the crowd much as millennialism elevates its virtuous elect; and, like millennialism, nationalism renounces earthly pleasures to achieve through struggle its goal of justice on earth. Both are revolutionary rather than reformist doctrines, and both seek a radical break with a corrupt and oppressive past.

Now it is certainly true that nationalism often displays messianic tendencies and seeks the overthrow of particular regimes. But its revolutionary messianism is frequently limited and circumscribed. Nationalists are not seeking to abolish this world and establish the kingdom of God on earth. They are relatively optimistic about this world, but profoundly unhappy with their place in it, or rather their lack of it. Their concerns are relatively local; they aim to rectify a particular anomaly. Admittedly, it is a serious anomaly in their eyes and causes them grievous pain; but it is not one that requires, in Isaiah's words, 'a new heaven and a new earth', only a return to the earth's 'natural state' of autonomous nations. The typical follower of millennial heresies seeks to rid the earth of all corruption; the typical adherent of nationalism seeks only to rid his country of corrupt, because alien, rulers (see Cohn 1957; Burridge 1969).[8]

Nor is it clear that nationalists are intent on destroying all barriers between the private and public domain and instituting a new morality of absolute purity. There have been puritannical nationalisms like the French Jacobin or perhaps the Black 'Nation of Islam' movements, which have enjoined on their followers zeal, self-sacrifice, abstention and self-discipline. But even they have not sought to abolish entirely the private domain. Most nationalisms encourage the puritanical virtues of heroic self-reliance, simplicity, fraternity and discipline in an effort to create the 'new man' and 'new woman', but they also extol family values, prize community and harness religious fervour for their ends. Most nationalisms, once in power, have made use of or re-established status hierarchies and institutions, and have turned their energies to this-worldly projects of 'nation-building'.[9]

Above everything else, nationalisms seek 'auto-emancipation': the self-reliant individual choosing his or her destiny, and the autonomous community determining its own fate without external interference. Nationalism embraces this world, but seeks to reform it in accordance with its own vision of regeneration. This is in stark contrast to the ethos of millennialism, which seeks to escape from and abolish a corrupt world and establish an entirely new order of purity, love and justice. Nationalists may desire purity and proclaim love as their goal, but it is a love that is designed to cement the members of the nation, and a purity that seeks to reappropriate its authentic nature. The love and purity that nationalists seek is this-worldly, a social solidarity, or fraternity, which underpins a world of national states, rendering them peaceful and united.[10]

By concentrating on the most extreme statements and practices of certain nationalists, Kedourie has been able to suggest the close affinity between nationalism and medieval millennialism and tar them both with the brush of antinomianism heterodoxy and chiliastic fanaticism. But most nationalists are none of these things; they are perfectly ordinary bourgeois, lower-middle or working-class men and women seeking an escape from immediate oppression and injustice. Kedourie indeed concedes that this is what animates the great majority of the followers of nationalist movements; but he claims that an elite of fanatical intellectuals uses these quite ordinary grievances of the majority for their own more sinister or wilful ends. This suggests once again the seductive picture of an elite of alienated intellectuals pursuing chimerical dreams, cut off from the everyday needs and aspirations of the vast mass of their compatriots, whom they manipulate through the 'pathetic fallacy' of collective empathy. This in turn presupposes a vast gulf between active elites and inert masses unbridged by any social strata or cultural values and institutions, which we saw was rarely the case even after the advent of colonialism. But this simply compounds the errors of the state-centred versions of political modernism explored in the last chapter, which are then magnified by treating the modern followers of nationalism as analogues of the adherents of millennialism. But, as I have argued elsewhere, the social constituencies of millennialism and nationalism are quite different. Millennialism appealed to the least educated, the poorest, most peripheral and most downtrodden strata, whereas more ambitious, educated, urban classes formed the backbone of most nationalist movements, even when they sought to draw other strata, lower down the social scale, into the movement (A. D. Smith 1979: ch. 2).

It is noteworthy that the French Revolution figures only as a legend and an example in Kedourie's analysis, despite the fact that, already in 1789, let alone 1792, French nationalism was the first fully fledged example of secular nationalism in Europe, and that it directly evoked nationalist responses wherever the Revolutionary and Napoleonic armies penetrated. This means that, both ideologically and socially, the 'progressive' urban bourgeoisie is excluded from the picture, to be replaced by the authoritarian, organic and millennial nationalism of Central and East European intellectuals, as Hans Kohn had already proposed. But it is not only in France that the educated urban classes, including the bourgeoisie, took up the nationalist cause. We find them in the vanguard of the movement in places as far removed from each other as Greece and Tartary, Japan and India, Mexico and the Gold Coast. Nor is the movement they espouse in the least bit apocalyptic or antinomian, even if it often centres on a messianic leader. On the contrary, it is firmly grounded in the realities of the present situation, even when it seeks to change them for the better. In this respect, most nationalisms conform much more closely to what Kedourie calls the British 'Whig doctrine of nationality' of which he approves, than to the 'Continental' unitary doctrine of nationalism, which he so heartily detests (Shafer 1938; Kedourie 1960: ch. 7; Kohn 1967a: ch. 7; Gildea 1994: ch. 3).

So neither at the sociological nor at the ideological level, can nationalism be compared with, or derived from, millennialism, whether of the medieval or of more recent varieties. They belong to different worlds of thought and action, and are divided not just by 'modernity' but, more radically, by the particularism of ethnic history, culture and territory.

The religion of history

Millennialism seeks to abolish the past, and replace it wholly by the future. Nationalism, in contrast, seeks to fashion a future in the image of the past. Not any past, of course; only an authentic past, the genuine past of a people in its homeland. It is this past that must be rediscovered and resurrected to provide a blueprint of the community's destiny; for only through a real understanding of the ethnic past can national regeneration succeed.

Now, for Elie Kedourie, the past is mainly a cultural resource to be politicised so as to mobilise and manipulate the sentiments of the masses. The cult of the 'dark gods' likewise functions as an instrument of mobilisation and activation. In this respect, Kedourie differs from other modernists. They see religion and history as, at best, quarries from which various cultural elements can be appropriated to give legitimacy to, or emotional support for, radical social change.

There is, in this view, something optional about the nationalist attitude to the past. For Kedourie, on the other hand, nationalist mobilisation and manipulation of the masses can only succeed if history and religion are taken seriously and their emotions politicised and harnessed to the national cause. The elites have no option. They are constrained by pre-existing mass cultures and especially religions. To some extent this qualifies Kedourie's modernism. Even if the nation is modern and perhaps 'invented', it does not, cannot, emerge out of nothing. Kedourie may underline the historical novelty of such modern 'nations' as Egypt and Greece, yet he has to concede their basis in the older religious traditions of Islam and Orthodoxy. Instead, he argues that these purely religious traditions have been perverted by being politicised and their values 'transvalued', while the masses have been seduced by millennial promises couched in the language and liturgies of their religious traditions.[11]

This, then, is Kedourie's answer to the problem of 'popular resonance' which all theories of 'elite manipulation' face. How is it that the elites manage to persuade 'the masses' to embrace their ideas and heed their call to action? Through propaganda and control over education, elites have frequently manipulated the masses, often quite successfully in the short term. But the long term success of their endeavours is always in doubt, and so nationalists have often thought it better to build on the traditions and sentiments of the majority, and, as Nairn argued, use those motifs and symbols that have popular resonance. Now, for Kedourie, it is the symbols and rites of traditional religion that resonate with the masses. To mobilise the people, elites must therefore harness the collective emotions roused by traditional religions. That is why they appeal to indigenous beliefs and practices, invoke the dark gods and their rites, and transform purely religious motifs and figures into political and national symbols and heroes – which is all part of the 'ethnicisation' and nationalisation of previously universal and transhistorical religions (Nairn 1977: ch. 2; cf. Brass 1991: ch. 2).

I find this one of the more interesting and convincing parts of Kedourie's thesis. In so many non-Western nationalisms, religion plays and has played a critical role in the life of the vast mass of the population, and as a result the nationalist 'transvaluation' and politicisation of its values has been profoundly significant for the mobilisation of the people and the character of the subsequent nationalism. Of course, Kedourie sometimes exaggerates the contrast between purely religious and purely national motifs and symbols: for many Zionists and Pan-Arabists, Moses and Muhammad have retained their religious significance, while acquiring new political relevance as embodiments of the 'national genius'. Nevertheless, insofar as nationalism is a modern and a secular doctrine – and this is Kedourie's point of departure – its attitude to religious figures like Moses and Muhammad and to religious festivals like Passover is quite different from, and shows scant respect for, the traditional religious understanding (see A. D. Smith 1973c).[12]

But is Kedourie right in seeing in nationalism a purely modern and secular doctrine and movement? For all his assertions, even he thinks this is only part of the story; after all, nationalism is also the secular heir of a religious millennialism.

For a number of other theorists, too, religion continues to be directly relevant to nationalism. Mark Juergensmeyer, for example, distinguishes between the revival of religious nationalisms and the secular statist nationalism of the West. The latter has attempted to reconstitute the nation as a secular and liberal creation of the modern state. This is a project that religious nationalists passionately reject. They denounce the rampant materialism, alienation and corruption of Western society and its secular nationalism, and wish to wrest the nation back from the secular modern state to its 'genuine' spiritual and religious roots. Secular nationalism has failed the people and corroded the nation; it has encouraged greed, vice and corruption; it must be opposed in the name of a higher, purer conception of the nation. Hence it is not nationalism as such, but rather the Western, materialist and secular conceptions of the nation that have proved so disastrous in their consequences. Juergensmeyer sees a new cold war emerging, replacing the old one between the Western and Soviet ideological blocs, with one between a secular, liberal West and a chain of revivalist, even fundamentalist, religious movements stretching from the Protestant revival in America to the Shi'ite revolution in Iran, and from the Sunni revival in Egypt, Saudi Arabia and Pakistan to the Hindu revival in India and the Buddhist renascence in Sri Lanka (Juergensmeyer 1993; cf. Chatterjee 1986).[13]

For Bruce Kapferer, too, there are close links between religion and nationalism. He examines two very different societies and religious settings, Sri Lanka and Australia, showing how in both, nationalism itself takes on the role of a religion whose beliefs and rites address the central ontological problems and supply meaning and purpose to individuals and nations. This religion of the nation may, of course, ally itself with traditional religion and thereby reinforce it. This is what has happened in Sinhalese Sri Lanka: traditional Sinhalese Buddhism has been politicised and its rituals have taken on new and violent meanings in the context of inter-ethnic warfare. The speeches and actions of contemporary Sinhalese leaders are full of allusions and analogies with the Buddhist doctrines and the Buddhist Sinhalese past; ancient wars with Tamils interpret, and are interpreted, in the light of the current Sri Lankan conflict (Kapferer 1988: chs 2–4; Roberts 1993; Subaratnam 1997).

In Australia, in contrast, the religion of the nation replaces traditional religions, Christian or other, while taking over much of their rites and symbols. Thus Kapferer analyses the imagery and symbolism of the Australian War Memorial in Canberra, built to commemorate the egalitarian ideals and self-sacrifice of the ANZAC soldiers in the disastrous Gallipoli campaign of 1915, seeing in it a national shrine which sacralises the secular by using Christian models for the building, the stained glass windows and the rites of ANZAC Day. By emphasising themes of suffering, death, sacrifice and rebirth, a pragmatic, secular Australian nationalism is framed by religious forms, and provides an interesting variant on the 'secular religion' of Western nationalisms (Kapferer 1988: chs 5–6).[14]

In both these cases, as in the religious nationalisms that Juergensmeyer describes, the past plays a vital role, linking the sacred to the secular. It may, of course, be a recent past, as in the Australian case. But it is always about authenticity, continuity, identity, dignity and destiny, the essential themes and motifs of the nationalist drama of salvation for the community as it moves forward through time. The past is as necessary to the nationalist mythology as is the future, and the 'golden age' is as relevant as the nation's glorious destiny. So nationalism must always connect its vision to the nation's past, that is, to the collective memories of the people. The past is not some neutral terrain to be explored and dissected; it is the locus of *exempla virtutis*, of the sacred, of the ancestral homeland, of the golden age, and of communal authenticity and identity. The past embodies the peculiar values and traditions of the community, without which there could be no nation and no national destiny. For nationalism, these are the sacred elements of the national spirit, which must be preserved and revitalised.[15]

In this sense, then, nationalism becomes the 'religion of history', sacralising the authentic past of the community in its ancestral homeland. Elie Kedourie was right to point out the way in which nationalists have used history selectively, viewing it through a special political lens. But this is not to say that the present entirely shapes the past, that immediate preoccupations and current intellectual fashions determine our view of the past. They do, of course, suggest some of the questions we ask of the past. Other questions may be raised by tradition and upbringing. Here the past, reinforced by the panoply of institutions, mores and symbols we have inherited from previous generations, shapes our understanding of the present. The idea that nationalist or other intellectuals can entirely break asunder these bands of the past sits strangely with Kedourie's overall religious conservatism, and suggests that he has greatly overestimated the political role and the autonomy from society of these Europeanised intellectuals.

That the intellectuals are freed from social constraints is, of course, a prerequisite for a psychological and diffusionist theory of 'political religion', one whose mainspring is anomie and alienation. This parallels Liah Greenfeld's emphasis on the alienation and discontent of significant strata, and particularly the *ressentiment* of segments of the upper classes whose status and career prospects are blocked, as occurred with certain orders of the French aristocracy. But Greenfeld does not remove the alienated from social and political constraints, even if, like Kedourie, she does not fully explain the origin and nature of the ideal of the nation to which the thwarted and alienated turn. This means that she ties ideology much more firmly to status group interests, and thereby shows us the variations and parameters of the ideologies espoused. In contrast, Kedourie wants to convince us of the evil that nationalism represents. He does so by showing how restless, alienated intellectuals operating in a social and political vacuum are driven by unbridled nationalist ideology to violence and terror, and how unattainable but godless virtue in an era of revolutionary change leads ineluctably to mass destruction. Concentrating on what Michael Billig calls 'hot' nationalism, Kedourie fails to see how nations and nationalism have become part of the very structure of modern society, and how they have been absorbed and assimilated by the vast majority of the world's populations for whom the colourful rhetoric and slogans of some intellectuals are at best decorative extras, 'icing on the cake'. In other words, nationalist intellectuals are important only to the extent that they articulate and help organise fundamental popular sentiments, perceptions and attitudes which derive as much from pre-existing symbols, memories, myths, values and traditions on which the intellectuals draw for their ideologies of the nation, as from the needs of the modern moment.[16]

Ideology is undoubtedly a key element in the widespread appeal and success of nationalism. It serves to unify and focus the many grievances and aspirations of different social groups within a particular community or state, and to explain to and activate 'the people', wherever circumstances and technologies permit. But these ideologies are not simply the product of intellectuals, nor are most intellectuals, even those who are caught between competing cultures, free-floating and disoriented, nor are most of them able to exercise the kind of influence that Kedourie attributes to them. The same is true of their ideas, which are effective in society to the extent that they mesh with pre-existing popular notions and collective memories. Only then can they mobilise large numbers of people to demonstrate and march, join movements and work for the liberation and unity of their nation. Only then will people put aside their daily cares and overcome their fears for a time to struggle for some improvement in their lot. Only the most extreme conditions breed apocalyptic visions and only minorities are likely to be attracted to their exponents.

But nationalism is a majority movement, not in the purely numerical sense (after all, most people do not join political organisations, at least not for longer periods) but because in every continent the nation has become the norm of political organisation and nationalism has become the main legitimating belief system. It is unlikely that this state of affairs would have obtained if it were simply the product of deranged intellectuals operating in a social vacuum created by modernisation, or that the mass of the people who adhered to their traditional religions and cultures could have been seduced by such visionary fantasies to create a world of nations.

6 Invention and imagination

The year 1983 saw the publication of two seminal books for the study of nationalism. The first, entitled *The Invention of Tradition*, contained a series of essays on a variety of political rituals, and was edited by Eric Hobsbawm and Terence Ranger, with an introductory chapter by Hobsbawm. The second, by Benedict Anderson, under the title *Imagined Communities: Reflections on the Origin and Spread of Nationalism*, put forward some general hypotheses about the development of nationalism in various parts of the world, together with some case studies. Both books stemmed from a Marxist tradition, but sought to move beyond its usual concerns with political economy into the realm of culture by reworking and supplementing them with themes drawn from the analysis of narratives and discourse developed by 'postmodernist' deconstructionism. In both cases, this led to a reading of the nation and nationalism as a central text of modern times, which needed to be unmasked and deconstructed. For both, nations and nationalism are constructs and cultural artefacts; the task of the analyst is to uncover their forms and contents, in order to reveal the needs and interests of those elites and strata which benefit or use their narratives. Hence, in both books a modernist project is overlaid by 'postmodernist' themes and language. The implications of this for the modernist paradigm of nationalism will be explored later.[1]

Inventing nations

Nations as 'invented traditions'

In his introduction to *The Invention of Tradition*, Eric Hobsbawm put forward some general propositions about invented traditions, national traditions and the nation. His message was that we can best understand the nature and appeal of nations by analysing national traditions, and that national traditions are one kind of invented traditions. If we could understand the genesis and function of invented traditions, we would be in a position to explain national traditions and therefore nations. What is an 'invented tradition'? Hobsbawm defines it as follows:

'Invented tradition' is taken to mean a set of practices, normally governed by overtly or tacitly accepted rules and of a ritual or symbolic nature, which seek to inculcate certain values and norms of behaviour by repetition, which automatically implies continuity with the past. In fact, where possible, they normally attempt to establish continuity with a suitable historic past. A striking example is the deliberate choice of a Gothic style for the nineteenth-century rebuilding of the British parliament, and the equally deliberate decision after World War II to rebuild the parliamentary chamber on exactly the same basic plan as before.

(Hobsbawm and Ranger 1983: 1–2)

Hobsbawm regards such references to an historic past as implying a continuity that is largely factitious, and concludes that 'invented traditions' are

responses to novel situations which take the form of reference to old situations, or which establish their own past by quasi-obligatory repetition.

(*ibid.*: 2)

Invented traditions must be clearly distinguished from both custom and convention or routine. Traditions, whether old or new, are invariant; the past to which they refer imposes fixed patterns. Custom is more flexible; it sanctions change up to a point through the sanctity of precedent and continuity.

Custom is what judges do; 'tradition' (in this instance invented tradition) is the wig, robe and other formal paraphernalia and ritualised practices surrounding their substantial action.

(*ibid.*: 2–3)

As for conventions, though they too become invariant, their functions are purely technical, designed to facilitate readily definable practical operations, and they can be changed when practical needs change, as can the rules of a game. Thus soldiers wearing steel helmets is conventional, whereas the hunting pink and hard hats of fox-hunters is a case of tradition.

Hobsbawm does not deny the importance of old traditions adapting to meet new needs, such as those of the Catholic Church or nineteenth-century universities. Nor does he deny that traditions have been 'invented' in past ages. What he claims is that it is the modern age, because it has seen such rapid change, where one would expect to find the 'invention of tradition' occurring most frequently, whether such traditions are invented by a person, such as the Boy Scouts rituals by Baden-Powell, or by a group, such as the Nuremberg rally rituals by the Nazi party. The reason is that

a rapid transformation of society weakens or destroys the social patterns for which 'old' traditions had been designed, producing new ones to which they were not applicable, or when such old traditions and their institutional carriers and promulgators no longer prove sufficiently adaptable and flexible, or are otherwise eliminated.

(*ibid.*: 4–5)

Now every society accumulates large stores of ancient materials to construct invented traditions of a novel type for quite novel purposes. Sometimes new traditions can be grafted onto old ones, and sometimes they can be devised by 'borrowing from the well-supplied warehouses of official ritual, symbolism and moral exhortation'; Hobsbawm gives the example of Swiss nationalism which extended, formalised and ritualised 'existing customary traditional practices' like folksong, physical contests and marksmanship, combining religious with patriotic elements (*ibid.*: 6–7).[2]

Not only did entirely new symbols and devices come into existence with the rise of national states, such as flags and anthems and emblems of the nation, but also

historic continuity had to be invented, for example by creating an ancient past beyond effective historical continuity, either by semi-fiction (Boadicea, Vercingetorix, Arminius the Cheruscan) or by forgery (Ossian, the Czech medieval manuscripts).

(*ibid.*: 7)

Even genuinely ancient traditions, like English Christmas carol folksongs are 'new' in the sense of being revived in new settings for new purposes in the nineteenth century. But movements that revive the past and invent traditions 'can never develop or even preserve a living past'; on the other hand, 'where the old ways are alive, traditions need neither be revived nor invented' (*ibid.*: 7–8).

Modern 'invented traditions' belong to three overlapping types. The first type establishes or symbolises social cohesion or membership of groups, real or artificial communities; the second kind establishes or legitimises institutions, status or relations of authority; while a third type aims to socialise, by inculcating beliefs, value systems and conventions of behaviour. Hobsbawm claims that the first was the dominant type; other functions flowed from identification with a 'community' and its institutions (*ibid.*: 9).

There is an important difference between old and invented practices. The former are specific and strongly binding, whereas the latter are unspecific and vague in the content of the values and obligations of group membership they inculcate – such as 'patriotism', 'loyalty', 'duty' and 'playing the game'. But the practices symbolising these ideals are specific and compulsory, for example, the flag ritual in American schools (*ibid.*: 10–11). For Hobsbawm, the crucial element is the invention of emotionally and symbolically charged signs of group membership, such as flags and anthems. Even though invented traditions occupy a much smaller part of the social space left by the decline of old traditions and customs, especially in the private domain, these neo-traditional practices remain prominent in the public life of citizens, including mass schooling and the institutions and practices of state; and most of them 'are historically novel and largely invented – flags, images, ceremonies and music' (*ibid.*: 12).

In conclusion, Hobsbawm claims that the study of 'invented traditions' is

> highly relevant to that comparatively recent historical innovation, the 'nation', with its associated phenomena: nationalism, the nation-state, national symbols, histories and the rest. All these rest on exercises in social engineering which are often deliberate and always innovative, if only because historical novelty implies innovation. Israeli and Palestinian nationalism or nations must be novel, whatever the historic continuities of Jews or Middle Eastern Muslims, since the very concept of territorial states of the currently standard type in their region was barely thought of a century ago, and hardly became a serious prospect before the end of World War I.
>
> (*ibid.*: 13–14)[3]

We should not be misled by the paradox that nationalists claim their nations are rooted in antiquity and self-evidently natural, when they are in fact quite recent and novel constructs.

> Whatever the historic or other continuities embedded in the modern concept of 'France' and 'the French' – and which nobody would seek to deny – these very concepts must include a constructed or 'invented' component. And just because so much of what subjectively makes up the modern 'nation' consists of such constructs and is associated with appropriate and, in general, fairly recent symbols or suitably tailored discourse (such as 'national history'), the national phenomenon cannot be adequately investigated without careful attention to the 'invention of tradition'.
>
> (*ibid.*: 14)

To give flesh and blood to this programmatic statement, Hobsbawm and the other contributors give us a series of case-studies of the relatively recent invention of the Highland tradition in Scotland, the cultural revival in Wales, the British coronation ceremony, the symbolism of authority in Victorian India, the invention of traditions in colonial Africa, and, in the last chapter by Hobsbawm himself, the efflorescence of mass-produced traditions in late nineteenth-century Europe. In this final chapter, Hobsbawm demonstrates the widespread use of 'invented traditions' of all kinds – Boy Scouts rituals, May Day celebrations, sports competitions like the Olympics, alumni organisations, military parades and national days, jubilees, statuomania, the spate of huge public buildings and monuments, mass school manuals and the like. All these were, to a large extent, state-inspired: they were felt to be socially necessary by state elites intent on controlling rapid social change and managing the influx of enfranchised citizens into the political arena (*ibid.*: 263–8). In France of the Third Republic and Second Empire Germany, the 'invention of tradition' reached its climax during the period before the First World War, with a spate of official and local cere-

monies, a mania for statuary, monuments and public architecture, and the inculcation of national values and ideals in the textbooks of the mass education
system (*ibid.*: 270–9). Some of these new traditions proved ephemeral, others like
the mass ceremonies proved more durable. In any case, concedes Hobsbawm,
only those consciously invented traditions which 'broadcast on a wavelength to
which the public was ready to tune in' succeeded in the long run (*ibid.*: 263).[4]

Two stages of nationalism

In 1990, Hobsbawm amplified his views in his *Nations and Nationalism since 1780*.
This offered a historical analysis of the rise of nations from about 1830 until the
postwar period. Like Gellner, Hobsbawm contended that nations are the product
of nationalism, conceptually and historically, but went on to assert that nationalism's main characteristic and goal, as well as its sole claim to be treated
seriously, is its drive to build a 'nation-state'. Nationalism is a political programme; without the goal of creating a nation-state, nationalism is of little
interest or consequence.

> Nations only exist as functions of a particular kind of territorial state or the
> aspiration to establish one – broadly speaking, the citizen state of the French
> Revolution – but also in the context of a particular stage of technological
> and economic development.
>
> (Hobsbawm 1990: 9–10)

For Hobsbawm, nations are made by nationalists. More than a little artefact,
invention and social engineering enters into the making of nations. Moreover,
national loyalty is only one of many allegiances, which are always shifting with
circumstances.

Hobsbawm distinguishes two types of nationalism and two kinds of analysis
of nations and nationalism. The first type is that of mass, civic and democratic
political nationalism, modelled on the kind of citizen nation created by the
French Revolution; this type flourished in Europe from about 1830–70, notably
in Germany, Italy and Hungary, and it operated a 'threshold principle', namely
that only nations large enough in territory and population to support a large
capitalist market economy were entitled to claim self-determination as sovereign,
independent states. It was swiftly followed by a second type of 'ethno-linguistic'
nationalism, in which smaller groups asserted their right to separate from large
empires and create their own states on the basis of ethnic and/or linguistic ties.
This type of nationalism prevailed in Eastern Europe from 1870–1914, and
resurfaced in the 1970s and 1980s, after the anti-colonial civic political nationalisms in Asia and Africa had spent their force.

Associated with these types, but not entirely, are two kinds of analysis. The
first focuses on official or governmental ideas and institutions, and is 'top-down'
and elite-based. The other is concerned with popular beliefs and sentiments, and
so becomes a community-based view 'from below'. While Hobsbawm considers

nations to be 'constructed essentially from above', he concedes that they must also be analysed from below, in terms of the hopes, fears, longings and interests of ordinary people. In this context Hobsbawm introduces the concept of 'proto-national' bonds to describe either supra-local regional, religious or ethnic communities, or political bonds of select groups linked to pre-modern states. But he regards neither as the ancestor or progenitor of modern nationalism,

> because they had or have no *necessary* relation with the unit of territorial political organisation which is a crucial criterion of what we understand as a 'nation' today.
>
> (*ibid.*: 47)

Hobsbawm regards language as in part a product of state formation and national languages as semi-artificial constructs, only of indirect consequence for modern nationalism. Ethnicity, too, whether in the sense of 'race' or culture, is largely irrelevant to modern nationalism, except where visible differences in physique constitute a means to categorise 'the other' (*ibid.*: 66). Only the memory of having belonged to a lasting political community of some kind had the potential for extension and generalisation to the mass of a country's inhabitants, as in England or France, in Russia or even Serbia with its memories of a medieval kingdom preserved in song and heroic story and 'in the daily liturgy of the Serbian church which had canonised most of its kings' (*ibid.*: 75–6).

For Hobsbawm, the crucial phase of nationalism came in the period 1870–1914, when the mass civic-democratic political type was transformed into an ethnic-linguistic type of nationalism. This new type differed in three ways from the earlier 'Mazzinian phase of nationalism'.

> First, it abandoned the 'threshold principle' which, as we have seen, was so central to nationalism in the Liberal era. Henceforth *any* body of people considering themselves a 'nation' claimed the right to self-determination which, in the last analysis, meant the right to a separate sovereign independent state for their territory. Second, and in consequence of this multiplication of potential 'unhistorical' nations, ethnicity and language became the central, increasingly the decisive or even the only criteria of potential nationhood. Yet there was a third change which affected not so much the nation-state national movements, but national sentiments within the established nation-states: a sharp shift to the political right of nation and flag, for which the term 'nationalism' was actually invented in the last decade(s) of the nineteenth century.
>
> (*ibid.*: 102, original emphasis)

The efflorescence of ethno-linguistic nationalisms was the product of a number of factors: the conflation of 'race', language and nationality during this period; the rise of new classes and the resistance of old classes to modernity; and the unprecedented migrations of peoples in the late nineteenth and early twentieth centuries – all this in the context of the democratisation of politics and the massive new powers of centralised states (*ibid.*: 109–10).

For Hobsbawm, the new linguistic nationalism centred on the vernacular was, 'among other things, a vested interest of the lesser examination-passing classes', especially when it became a medium of secondary-school instruction; and these classes veered to the political right, seeing themselves as embattled and endangered, especially by the 'menace' represented by foreigners like the Jews. This kind of ethnic nationalism, essentially a politics of fear, led to the creation of ethnically homogeneous states and the exclusion and ultimately extermination of minorities (*ibid.*: 111, 121, 133).

The demise of nationalism

The late twentieth century has, for Hobsbawm, witnessed a revival of this fissiparous ethno-linguistic type of nationalism. While not denying the dramatic efflorescence and impact of nationalist or ethnic politics, Hobsbawm argues that 'It is no longer a major vector of historical development'. Rather, these latterday ethno-linguistic nationalisms are the successors, or even the heirs, of the Eastern European small-nationality movements of the late nineteenth century:

> The characteristic nationalist movements of the late twentieth century are essentially negative, or rather divisive. Hence the insistence on 'ethnicity' and linguistic differences, each or both sometimes combined with religion.
>
> (*ibid.*: 164)

Though operating in the name of a model of political modernity, the nation-state, they simultaneously reject modern modes of political organisation, national and supranational.

> Time and again they seem to be reactions of weakness and fear, attempts to erect barricades to keep at bay the forces of the modern world, similar in this respect to the resentment of Prague Germans pressed into a corner by Czech immigration rather than to that of the advancing Czechs.
>
> (*ibid.*: 164)

Massive economic transformations on a global scale, together with huge population movements, disorientate and frighten many people.

> Wherever we live in an urbanised society, we encounter strangers: uprooted men and women who remind us of the fragility, or the drying up of our own families' roots.
>
> (*ibid.*: 167)

But, claims Hobsbawm,

The call of ethnicity or language provides no guidance to the future at all. It is merely a protest against the status quo or, more precisely, against the 'others' who threaten the ethnically defined group.

(*ibid.*: 168)[5]

For nationalism, despite the advantage of its vagueness, excludes all who do not belong to the nation, and is hostile to the real ways of the past or arises on its ruins. It is a reaction to the 'overwhelmingly non-national and non-nationalist principles of state formation in the greater part of the twentieth-century world' (*ibid.*: 173).

The central point is that today, nationalism has lost its state-making and economy-forming functions. In the nineteenth century, nationalism was plainly at the centre of historical development: it carved out states and constituted territorially bounded 'national economies'. But globalisation and the international division of labour has removed these functions, and the revolutions in mass communications and international migration have undermined the possibility of territorially homogeneous nation-states. Nationalism is simply irrelevant to most contemporary economic and social developments, and the basic political conflicts have little to do with nation-states (*ibid.*: 175–6).

This leads to Hobsbawm's conclusion. Nationalism 'is a substitute for lost dreams', a reaction to the disappointment of larger hopes and aspirations. Despite its evident prominence today, nationalism

is historically less important. It is no longer, as it were, a global political programme, as it may be said to have been in the nineteenth and earlier twentieth centuries. It is at most a complicating factor, or a catalyst for other developments.

(*ibid.*: 181)

Nation-states and nations will be seen as retreating before, resisting, adapting to, being absorbed or dislocated by, the new supranational restructuring of the globe. Nations and nationalism will be present in history, but in subordinate, and often rather minor roles.

(*ibid.*: 182)

The progress of late twentieth-century historians in analysing nations and nationalism 'suggests that, as so often, the phenomenon is past its peak'.

And recalling Kedourie's invocation of Hegel's owl of Minerva, Hobsbawm hopefully concludes:

The owl of Minerva which brings wisdom, said Hegel, flies out at dusk. It is a good sign that it is now circling round nations and nationalism.

(*ibid.*: 183)

Ethnic and civic nationalisms?

Of course, Kedourie's conclusion was anything but hopeful. He was asked whether one should oppose or try to placate nationalism, and his reply was that we could only be wise after the event. Hobsbawm, however, sets out to explain nationalism from Marxist premises, from the 'movement of history'. Even if he supplements this basic framework with some 'postmodernist' themes and language, his main concern is to locate nationalism firmly within a specific period of high to late capitalism, a period of industrialisation, urbanisation and democratisation; and within a specific social and geographical milieu – Western and Central, later Eastern, Europe of the mid-to-late nineteenth century. This framework enables Hobsbawm to provide a variety of rich historical characterisations and incisive analyses of various kinds of mainly European nationalism, particularly linguistic movements, and their social composition.

Throughout Hobsbawm seeks to support his thesis of the ultra-modernity of nations by demonstrating their engineered and constructed nature. Far from being primordial or even relatively long-lived, nations are quite recent constructs and artefacts of elites bent on preserving order in the turbulence of late capitalism. There are some interesting similarities here with Kedourie's ideological modernism. Both agree on the nineteenth-century origins of nationalism, though Kedourie is more insistent on its German Romantic provenance. Both stress the artificial nature of nationalist ideology, but Hobsbawm goes further, underlining the contingent and constructed nature of nations. Hobsbawm shares Kedourie's instrumentalist attitude to nationalism and his belief in its uses for elites to tap the emotions of the masses and provide them with social and psychological security; but for Kedourie it is restless intellectuals rather than capitalist power elites who seek to manipulate the masses. Finally, Hobsbawm evinces a contempt and hatred for nationalism no less than Kedourie's, though he is prepared to concede the historical importance of the earlier form of mass civic and political nationalism in the nineteenth century.

On another point, too, there is a curious agreement between two historians whose political views represent the opposite ends of the ideological spectrum. Both put aside, as it were, the impact of the French Revolution on nations and nationalism; or rather, they see its importance in terms of the European reaction to its excesses, and more particularly to Napoleon's ambitions, rather than in its own terms, as the first European example of fully fledged nationalism. For Kedourie, this is because only the organic version of nationalism represents the true doctrine; and the organic version was developed by German, not French intellectuals. For Hobsbawm, despite the early date in the title of his second book, nationalism did not come into its own as a state-making project until 1830, when agitation for German and Italian unification really became a political issue and the first national states created by nationalism (Greece, Belgium, possibly Spain) came into being. In other words, France, like England, was an example of a civic nation (and the Revolution was a legend), but it had emerged long before the age of nationalism.

Now, while it is true that both France and England had emerged several centuries earlier, as indeed had Holland, Sweden, Poland, Russia, Switzerland and Spain, and later 'nation-states' were often created – usually with a bit of geopolitical luck – by nationalists and other elites, this should not mislead us into omitting, or belittling, the role of the French Revolution as a *nationalist* (and not simply a bourgeois) revolution. Already in its first phases, the French revolutionaries disseminated and politicised even earlier ideas of *la nation, la patrie* and *le citoyen*, and chose a new French flag, the tricolor, to replace the old royal standard. In the crisis of war from 1792 they adopted the *levée en masse* and a new anthem, the *Marseillaise*. Likewise, the Estates General became the National Assembly and Convention, new oaths for *la patrie* were sworn on the Champ de Mars, new hymns were sung, new Roman-style heroes and latterday martyrs were adopted and commemorated, the great *journées* acquired a new nationalist liturgy, internal customs and dues were done away with throughout France, regional assemblies and their dialects were abolished and *la belle langue* disseminated, a new calendar was adopted, and all citizens were urged to fight and die for the fatherland. Even the ideas of national mission and destiny, to depose tyrants and liberate the peoples of Europe, were enshrined in the revolutionary French nationalism of the Jacobins (see Kohn 1967b; Herbert 1972; Gildea 1994).[6]

The spectacle of this nationalism in Europe's most populous and civilised nation, and not just Napoleon's dissemination of its ideas and conquests, helped to galvanise the intellectuals in various parts of Europe into formulating their own nationalisms. The period from 1790 to 1820 saw the formation and dissemination of nationalist ideas throughout Europe and the Americas, but Hobsbawm has little to say of this crucial period, perhaps because it saw little in the way of state-making (except in the Americas), and for Hobsbawm, it is its ability to create and underpin large states and markets that alone justifies the historian's interest in nationalism. But this, as we saw with Breuilly, is an unduly restrictive criterion; it omits all the other functions and dimensions of nationalism – social, cultural and psychological – that make it so central to the modern world.[7]

Nor can we distinguish quite so readily the two kinds of nationalism that Hobsbawm uses to characterise the development of nations in Europe. The distinction between an ethnic-linguistic and a civic-political kind of nationalism is well entrenched in the literature; but it is an analytical and a normative one. It does not describe particular nationalisms, nor can it be used to trace the trajectory of nationalism-in-general. For even the most 'civic' and 'political' nationalisms often turn out on closer inspection to be also 'ethnic' and 'linguistic'; this is certainly the case with French nationalism during the Revolution, let alone afterwards, with its appeal to 'nos ancêtres les Gaulois' and a single French people, and its suppression of regional languages in favour of Parisian French. Conversely, Breuilly has pointed to the territorial and civic elements alongside the ethnic ones in German nationalism in 1848, as revealed in speeches and debates of the Frankfurt Parliament. Sometimes these civic and ethnic elements are aligned, as has occurred in Czechoslovakia, Scotland and

Switzerland, at other times they come into conflict, as they did in the Dreyfus Affair in France, or as they are doing in India and Israel today. It is impossible to trace a clear overall pattern of historical development with these concepts (see Poliakov 1974: ch. 1; Breuilly 1993: ch. 4).[8]

Besides, Hobsbawm's use of the term 'ethnic' is unclear. He dismisses a 'genetic' usage (though he returns to it) but cannot accept a cultural usage. This is because he tends to conflate it with language, or confuse it with actual descent, and fails to consider the importance of myths, memories, traditions and symbols of sociocultural groupings – including shared memories of historical events, however selective or idealised, and shared myths and symbols of (presumed) ancestry. This is one reason why Hobsbawm must dismiss all the popular memories and beliefs about kinship, ancestry, origins and golden ages as being either fabricated or irrelevant, or both; and why they must not be allowed to undermine or deflect from his insistence on the ultra-modernity of nations and nationalism, even though he is prepared, in the wake of the break-up of the Soviet Union and Yugoslavia, to acknowledge the continuing force of ethnic ties and sentiments (see Hobsbawm 1996).[9]

'Proto-national' bonds

In fact, what Hobsbawm has given us in modern terminology is the old Hegelian idea of 'historyless peoples', in which only memories of earlier statehood can be extended to the masses and provide the basis for later nationalisms and states. Otherwise, Hobsbawm can accord no role to 'the masses' as subjects of history. They are passive, acted upon, and usually manipulated by elites for political ends, but their cultures and social networks, even where they have a measure of autonomy, have no political relevance. Hence their popular 'proto-national' bonds (a curious term, in view of their radical disconnection with subsequent nations or nationalisms) are, as it were, stillborn; they cannot have any political extension, they cannot provide the basis for a subsequent nation. Only where, as in Russia, there was a popular myth of the holy land and a holy people identified with the kingdom, could such proto-national ties provide the basis for a subsequent nation (Rosdolsky 1964; Hobsbawm 1990: ch. 2; cf. Cherniavsky 1975).

There are a number of objections to this restrictive view. To begin with, many peoples, apart from the Russians (and the Irish and Tyroleans) have entertained vivid ideas of a holy land, and of a chosen kingdom and people. In France, this association was already made in the Frankish kingdom, and disseminated under the Capetians. The Jews retained the most vivid sense of their lost holy land and kingdom of David through all their wanderings, as did the Armenians, Greeks (under Ottoman rule), Amhara, Poles, Czechs and Scots. Why could their 'proto-national' bonds not have provided the basis for subsequent nations? Hobsbawm's explicit assertion that there could have been no connection between medieval German ethno-linguistic and political ties in the Holy Roman Empire and modern German nationalism, or between ancient Jewish political (Davidic, Hasmonean) and cultural bonds, or medieval ones, and modern Zionism, flies in the face of much evidence. Second, why must the 'holy land' be connected to a kingdom or state? The Swiss soon became convinced of their chosen status and the holiness of their mountain and valley confederation; but land and people could form the basis for a subsequent nation without memories of early state-hood. The same is true of the Welsh, who were only briefly united in the thirteenth century; and of the Finns whose lands had been part of the Swedish kingdom for centuries. Third, nations have been formed on the basis of ethnic cultures which had little benefit of popular ideas and sentiments about holy lands, let alone kingdoms. Yet their nationalisms emerged and agitated for inde-pendence, successfully in the end; this was the case with Slovenes, Slovaks and Estonians, who were conquered and apparently absorbed by more powerful neighbours in the early Middle Ages, yet have become separate national states today (see Armstrong 1982; Im Hof 1991; Brock 1976; Williams 1982; Singleton 1985; Raun 1989).

Perhaps more serious is the implication that this passivity of the masses must have its counterpart in the manipulations of the elites, that the emotions of an inert mass are waiting to be aroused and channelled by elites as part of an exer-cise in social engineering. This is a very rationalist view of human conduct. Apart from assuming that the popular strata carry few indigeneous traditions and beliefs, or such as are only local, this view fails to account for the passion and fervour of mass followings for nationalist movements, and the frequent will-ingness on the part of the unlettered and poor to make great sacrifices and even court death to defend their countries and drive out tyrants. One has only to recall the many sacrifices made by the poor masses in countries occupied by the Axis powers during the Second World War – Karens and other hill peoples in Burma, Poles, Czechs and Serbs, French, Dutch and Norwegians – in the name of national liberation.[10]

This view also credits elites with more instrumental rationalism than the record suggests. Of course, there have been many attempts to manipulate the sentiments of the masses, and some have met with success, as in the well known Indian examples of Tilak and Gandhi. But even here the cultural distance between elites and masses was less than this schema suggests; elites were often as much in the grip of nationalist passions, and prepared for idealistic self-sacrifice, as 'the masses' from whom many of them had, after all, emerged. Nationalism did not erase class differences or antagonisms, but it certainly could override them in moments of external danger, and temporarily unify the classes to achieve common goals (Nairn 1977: ch. 2; A. D. Smith 1981b).

What all this suggests is that Hobsbawm has overlooked the possibility that his popular 'proto-national' bonds are, in fact, the very ethnic ties that he dismissed as a basis for nations. But once that equation is accepted, we can begin to see why ethnicity is such a powerful force in the modern world, and why so many nations are, or seek to be, formed on the basis of dominant *ethnies*, or at least attempt to achieve that sense of cultural unity and intimacy that ethnicity provides. For the sense of cultural intimacy is what binds the various classes and strata of an *ethnie*, and can provide, and has so often provided, the basis for forging a modern nation. By ruling this connection out *a priori*, Hobsbawm is unable to give a convincing account of the involvement of 'the masses' in the nation and nationalism.

The nation as construct?

It has become fashionable to characterise the nation as a social construction, an artefact of cultural engineers, and the idea of 'invented traditions' fits well into this perspective. By regarding the nation as a modern construct of elites organising the newly enfranchised masses into new status systems and communities, Hobsbawm aligns himself to a certain extent with 'postmodernist' analyses of political discourses and narratives. This approach raises several questions. What does it mean to say that the nation is a social construct and consists largely of invented traditions? Why do the elites select this particular construct? Why does this type of discourse (of nationalism) resonate with 'the masses'?

For resonate it must, as Hobsbawm recognises, if the idea of the nation – and of this particular nation – is to succeed and retain its efficacy. Hobsbawm provides no clue as to why nationalism has been so successful. He has precluded an account based on pre-existing ethnic ties ('proto-national' bonds). The only other candidate, the nation's functionality for capitalism, is teleological and partial – it cannot explain small-nation ethnic nationalism. Simply to condemn the latter as historically irrelevant (or worse) hardly furthers the cause of explanation.

However, an alternative is provided by one of the contributors to the volume edited by Hobsbawm and Ranger. Prys Morgan, in an essay on the revival of Welsh culture and Welsh nationalism, suggests, *inter alia*, that the revival of the *Eisteddfod* from 1789, though a new departure, was connected to the ancient *eisteddfoddau* which had been held from as far back as 1176 right up to the sixteenth century. Though the official bardic contests had died out by the following century, their traditions remained alive at the popular level into the eighteenth century in the 'tavern' or 'almanack' contests. It was from these local competitions that the Welsh cultural nationalists in London learnt about the traditions of rhyme and metre, and they deliberately incorporated them into their new festivals of Welsh poetry and music (Morgan 1983).

Now, what this and similar examples reveal, is the complex interweaving of relationships between old and new cultural traditions, something that Hobsbawm and Ranger's concept of 'invented traditions' ignores or simplifies. It is certainly true, as Hobsbawm and his associates underline, that modern elites and intellectuals deliberately select and rework old traditions, so that what appears today under the same banner is very different from its ostensible model. At the same time, the selection and reworking takes place within strict limits, and, I would suggest, *must* do so, if the new 'invented' tradition is to be 'on the wavelength to which the public is ready to tune in', in Hobsbawm's phrase. These limits are set by the culture, or cultures, of the public in question – its language, law, music, symbols, memories, myths, traditions and so on. The Welsh *Eisteddfoddau* and the

British coronation ceremony may have been nineteenth-century revivals and rearrangements; but they incorporated several motifs and traditions from previous epochs and earlier ceremonies, and that is, in part, why they resonated with the public. To call them 'invented' traditions does scant justice to the complex ways in which these, and other ceremonies, were reconstructed and reinterpreted. Perhaps part of the trouble lies with the very term 'invention' which, among its meanings, often carries connotations of fabrication and/or creation *ex nihilo* – something that Hobsbawm is at pains to repudiate.[11]

To see nations as composed largely of 'invented traditions' designed to organise and channel the energies of the newly politicised masses, places too much weight on artifice and assigns too large a role to the fabricators. The passion that the nation could evoke, especially in time of danger, the sacrifices it could command from 'the poor and unlettered' as well as the middle classes, cannot be convincingly explained by the propaganda of politicians and intellectuals, or the ritual and pageantry of mass ceremonies – unless, that is, the public was already attuned to both propaganda and ceremonial. It is hard to believe that most people would willingly lay down their lives for an artefact or be duped by propaganda and ritual over a long period, unless that ritual and propaganda expressed and amplified pre-existing popular sentiments which saw the ethnic nation as the family and locality writ large. The problems faced by many new states in Africa and Asia also suggest that the absence of pre-existing state-wide traditions, myths, symbols and memories greatly hampers the process of national integration, and that inventing national traditions does not, and cannot, by itself enable elites to forge a national community out of ethnically heterogenous populations. Where such attempts are being made, they generally proceed on the basis of memories, myths, symbols and traditions of the dominant *ethnie* in the new state (such as the Kikuyu in Kenya or the Burmese in Burma), that is, on the basis of the pre-existing culture of the dominant ethnic community which resonates with the majority of the population.

In arguing against social constructionism and invention as valid categories of explanation, I do not mean to deny the many instances of attempted 'construction' and 'fabrication'. My point is only that, to be successful, these attempts need to base themselves on relevant pre-existing social and cultural networks. Pakistan, both as name and as national state, was quite clearly 'invented', the name by a student in Cambridge, the national state by Jinnah's party. But the idea of a Pakistani state would have had no collective force or meaning, unless the mass of Muslims in northern India had already acquired a vivid sense of common ethnicity based on their shared religion, one which differentiated them from other Indians. In some form, given the strength and geographical concentration of Muslim sentiments in the subcontinent, it was probable that something like Pakistan would have been formed in an age of widespread political nationalism and communal self-assertion (see Kedourie 1971).[12]

Similarly, the Polish national state that came into being in 1918 was neither simply a 'rebirth', nor an 'invention'. The Poland that became an independent state in 1918 was quite different from the polity of the Polish nobles, clergy and gentry which lost its independence in the Partitions of the late eighteenth century. But neither was it an entirely new creation. It was linked in many ways with the earlier Polish state, not least through the shared codes, rituals, memories, myths, values and symbols which bound Poles together during the long nineteenth century of their unfreedom. To some extent, the Poles met Hobsbawm's (and Hegel's) political criterion. Like the Russians, they preserved a sense of themselves as a chosen people with a state of their own in a Catholic land, even though they subsequently lost their kingdom. They had, after all, taken Rousseau's advice to heart and preserved their language, customs and ethnic heritage. So, what the intellectuals and elites had to do was to narrate Polish memories, symbols and myths in Polish verse and music, thereby evoking and heightening the popular ethno-religious sentiments of millions of Poles, and in this way reconstituting and reinterpreting the Polish cultural heritage to meet modern conditions. The element of 'invention', where it exists, is therefore confined to the political form of that reconstitution, and is misleading when it is applied to the sense of cultural identity which is the subject of reinterpretation (see Halecki 1955; Davies 1982; cf. Knoll 1993).

Imagining the nation

Two fatalities

A very different solution to the problem of elite construction and mass response in the formation of nations is provided by Benedict Anderson in his seminal and highly influential *Imagined Communities*. Though springing from the same Marxist heritage, Anderson's approach to nationalism seeks to emphasise just those subjective and cultural dimensions that Hobsbawm's account largely subordinates or treats reductively.

Anderson's initial problem is the inadequacy of Marxist theory in dealing with what Marxists termed 'the national question'. Remarking on the recent (in 1983) and in Marxist terms, theoretically puzzling, wars between the self-styled communist states of Vietnam, Cambodia and China, Anderson argues persuasively that

> the 'end of the era of nationalism', so long prophesied, is not remotely in sight. Indeed, nation-ness is the most universally legitimate value in the political life of our time.
>
> (Anderson 1991: 3)

It is to this persisting 'anomaly', as Marxists view nationalism, that Anderson wishes to address himself; and for this reason, he prefers to regard nations and nationalism as modern cultural artefacts of a particular kind, which arose at the end of the eighteenth century. But, rather than regard 'Nationalism-with-a-big-N' as *an* ideology, he thinks it would make things easier if one treated it as if it belonged with 'kinship' or 'religion' rather than with 'liberalism' or 'fascism'.

(*ibid.*: 5)

In that spirit, Anderson offers his well known definition of the nation: 'it is an imagined political community – and imagined as both inherently limited and sovereign' (*ibid.*: 6).

Anderson goes on to explain that the nation is imagined because its members will never know, meet or even hear of most of their fellow-members, 'yet in the minds of each lives the image of their communion' (*ibid.*: 6). He concedes that all communities larger than villages with face-to-face contact are imagined; so what distinguishes the nation is the *style* in which it is imagined. That is, it is imagined as limited, even if its boundaries are elastic – and therefore as one of a comity of nations. It is imagined as sovereign because, in an age of enlightenment and revolution, nations want freedom and this means possessing a sovereign state. It is imagined as a community, because 'the nation is always conceived as a deep, horizontal comradeship' (*ibid.*: 7).

This brings Anderson to his theoretical point of departure. What he wants to explain is the problem of mass self-sacrifice for the nation, the fact that

> Ultimately it is this fraternity that makes it possible, over the past two centuries, for so many millions of people, not so much to kill, as willingly to die for such limited imaginings.

(*ibid.*: 7)

That is why, says Anderson, we must begin our explanation with the two great fatalities of the human condition: death and Babel. Death brings the threat of oblivion. In a secular age we increasingly look to posterity to keep our memory alive; and the collective memory and solidarity of the nation helps us to overcome the threat of oblivion. Nations are characterised by symbols of commemoration, notably the Tombs of Unknown Soldiers. Without name or known remains, these tombs are filled with 'ghostly *national* imaginings'. What this suggests is that nationalism, like religion, takes death and suffering seriously – in a way that progressive and evolutionary styles of thought like Marxism and liberalism do not. It does so by 'transforming fatality into continuity', by linking the dead and the yet unborn. The nation is particularly suited to this 'secular transformation of fatality into continuity, contingency into meaning' (*ibid.*: 11), since nations

> always loom out of an immemorial past, and, still more important, glide into a limitless future. It is the magic of nationalism to turn chance into destiny.

(*ibid.*: 11–12)

That is why we can really only understand nationalism by aligning it 'with the large cultural systems that preceded it, out of which – as well as against which – it came into being' (*ibid.*: 12).

There is another fatality without which nations and nationalism cannot be understood: Babel, or the diversity of languages. This general condition of 'irre-mediable linguistic diversity' is not to be confused with some nationalist ideologies' insistence on the primordial fatality of *particular* languages. 'Particular languages can die or be wiped out, but there was and is no possibility of man's general linguistic unification'. Yet, like mortality, this linguistic diversity had little political importance 'until capitalism and print created monoglot reading publics'. Only then did the nation, as an imagined political community, come to dominate human thought and social organisation (*ibid.*: 43).

Historical preconditions

How did this come about? If mortality and linguistic pluralism constitute the great underlying fatalities of a diverse humanity in search of posterity, 'three fundamental cultural conceptions, all of great antiquity', had to undergo radical transformations before nations and nationalism could have any plausibility. In fact, all three 'lost their axiomatic grip on men's minds' in the early modern epoch, thereby providing the necessary conditions for the rise of nations and nationalism. They were: sacred script communities, sacred monarchical high centres, and cosmological time (*ibid.*: 36).

The great religious communities of Islam, Christendom and the Middle Kingdom of China saw themselves as overarching and 'cosmically central, through the medium of a sacred language linked to a superterrestrial order of power' (*ibid.*: 13). The ideograms of their sacred languages were treated as emanations of reality, not arbitrary signs; Church Latin, Qur'anic Arabic and Examination Chinese were truth-languages bent on assimilating everyone, and their expert adepts, who mediated between them and the vernacular, also medi-ated between heaven and earth. For all that, the power and 'unselfconscious coherence' of these 'great religiously imagined communities' waned in the late Middle Ages, largely through European explorations of the non-European world and the gradual demotion of the sacred language itself in the sixteenth century (*ibid.*: 16–19).

The second kind of universal cultural conception was monarchy and the dynastic realm, which organised everything around a high centre. These realms expanded both through warfare and sexual politics, which linked them together in a complex political web. But from the seventeenth century, at least in Europe, the 'automatic legitimacy of sacral monarchy' gradually declined, notably after the French Revolution. For, though by 1914 most states remained dynastic, they had replaced the earlier principle of dynastic legitimacy by a national and ulti-mately popular principle (*ibid.*: 19–22).

The final and perhaps most fundamental cultural conception to undergo change was the pre-modern idea of time. In pre-modern ages, men and women had 'no conception of history as an endless chain of cause and effect or of radical separations between past and present' (*ibid.*: 23). Earlier conceptions viewed time as 'a simultaneity of past and future in an instantaneous present', something like Walter Benjamin's 'Messianic time':

> What has come to take the place of the medieval conception of simultaneity-along-time is, to borrow again from Benjamin, an idea of 'homogeneous, empty time', in which simultaneity is, as it were, transverse, cross-time, marked not by prefiguring and fulfilment, but by temporal coincidence, and measured by clock and calendar.
>
> (*ibid.*: 24)

Anderson goes on to illuminate this novel concept of transverse time, with the importance it accords to the word 'meanwhile', through a textual analysis of modern novels from the Philippines, Mexico and Indonesia, all of which portray the solidity of a finite sociological community moving through calendrical time. In the pages of these novels, we are invited to identify with the actions and feelings of their unknown heroes and heroines, which are embedded in realistic yet generalised social landscapes and historical periods, and which are presented in a series of temporally parallel tableaux. The community which the novel represents is an imagined one; yet it is fixed and durable, not only because it comprises a linguistic community which is that of its readers, but also because we are all too familiar with its historical and social landscape of prisons, schools, shops, villages and monasteries. In one such novel, a dinner party is being discussed by hundreds of unnamed people who do not know each other in different quarters of Manila in a particular month, conjuring up the idea of the imagined community of Filipino readers (*ibid.*: 26–7). In another, we see the hero sitting on a long rattam lounge reading a newspaper in deserted Semarang and being moved by a story about the death of a destitute vagrant on the roadside; and we are made to share his emotions, and his anger at the social inequality that caused this poverty. Anderson comments that the phrase 'our young man' used of the unnamed hero, locates the action and people in a specific imagined community, of Indonesians; but also that 'the imagined community is confirmed by the doubleness of our reading about our young man reading' (*ibid.*: 31–2).

This selective fictiveness is just what we experience every day when we read the newspapers, which are nothing more than books on a colossal scale, what Anderson terms 'one-day best-sellers'. For they link together unrelated events worldwide through our imaginations in two ways: by subsuming them under a single calendrical date and by ensuring that they are simultaneously read at specific moments of each day by masses of people who are part of the same print-language community. More than anything else, the newspaper and its market reassures us that 'the imagined world is visibly rooted in everyday life'; and in the longer term it thereby helps to create 'that remarkable confidence of community in anonymity which is the hallmark of modern nations' (*ibid.*: 36).

Print-communities

It was Gutenberg's invention that made possible the idea of a secular, imagined linguistic community, but it was commodity capitalism that made a particular kind of such community, the nation, likely. The masses were, and are, largely monoglot. So the need to expand markets in the mass commodity of the printed book, once the elite Latin market was saturated, gave capitalism a wholly unforeseen and revolutionary vernacularising thrust. This was aided by three factors. First, the sacred tongue, Latin, itself became, in the hands of the antiquarian classical humanists, increasingly Ciceronian, arcane and remote from everyday life and the masses. Second and far more important, Protestantism ably exploited the vernacular market in order to reach the masses in its war against the Papacy and the monarchy; if print-capitalism aided the spread of Protestant ideas, the latter increasingly required familiarity with the Bible on the part of every believer, and hence put a premium on literacy and understanding in the local vernacular. And third, certain dialects, usually those in the political centre, were haphazardly selected by courts and bureaucrats as official vehicles of administration and political centralisation even before the sixteenth century, and were thereby gradually elevated to the status of fixed vernacular languages by means of mass print circulation, challenging the dominance of Latin and its sacred script community (*ibid.*: 39–42).

Yet, claims Anderson, none of these factors alone is a necessary condition for the rise of nations; rather,

> What, in a positive sense, made the new communities imaginable was a half-fortuitous, but explosive, interaction between a system of production and productive relations (capitalism), a technology of communications (print), and the fatality of human linguistic diversity.
>
> (*ibid.*: 42–3)

Anderson is at pains to underline the element of fatality – of both death and linguistic diversity – but also the interaction between these fatalities and the new mode of production and technology (*ibid.*: 43). Capitalism played a crucial role in 'assembling' print-languages, within definite grammatical and syntactical limits, from the immense variety of related local vernaculars or idiolects. Once in being, these print-languages encouraged the growth of national consciousness in a number of ways: by creating fields of communication below Latin and above the local spoken vernaculars; by fixing the language in a standard form and thereby inducing a sense of national antiquity; and finally by creating new languages-of-power in a new cultural hierarchy of dialects and languages. So the stage was set for the global diffusion of the idea of the nation.[13]

In subsequent chapters, Anderson fleshes out this basic structure of explanation by singling out the essential elements of each main cultural and geo-historical type of nationalism. He stresses the way in which the idea of the nation could be 'pirated' by widely different, and sometimes unexpected, hands (*ibid.*: 67). Thus in Latin America and North America, which he claims were the earliest cases of nationalism, creole printmen were important in delineating the ideas of the nation and of republicanism. But equally vital in Latin America were the 'administrative pilgrimages' made by provincial officials of the Spanish empire, whose circuits as officials created a sense of the political separateness of each province as well as a community of like-minded officials (*ibid.*: ch. 4).

In Europe, on the other hand, history and language became crucial. In the wake of the great discoveries, it was the mass-mobilising nationalisms of vernacular intelligentsias intent on providing national histories and modernising print-languages through grammars, dictionaries and the like, that kindled the fires of national consciousness and furnished new models of the nation for pirating across the continent, and outside (*ibid.*: ch. 5). And again, the threat of such popular vernacular mobilisations created an imperial response in the form of 'official nationalisms' on the part of dynastic rulers and their bureaucracies, especially in Eastern Europe and Asia (*ibid.*: ch. 6). Finally, the last wave of 'colonial nationalisms' in Asia and Africa responds to the earlier creole and vernacular forms of nationalism in Europe and the Americas, as well as the official nationalisms, taking something from each, under the impact of a global imperialism (*ibid.*: ch. 7). In each case, the particular agencies and characters of a group of nationalisms differed considerably from those of other groups, but at the same time they bore the marks of their common origin in the conditions that favoured the rise of mass reading-publics joined together by printing and commodity capitalism. Hence, any general theory requires supplementation by a more detailed historical and sociological analysis of circumstances in particular culture areas and periods.

An imagined community?

This is a novel and path-breaking account of nationalism. For all his Marxist provenance, Anderson's great achievement is to provide a postmodernist reading of the nation within a modernist framework. What has attracted most attention is his striking use of the concepts of an imagined political community and print-capitalism, whereas his ideas about the decline of large-scale sacred communities and the emergence of linear time, which lie at the heart of his modernism, have received less recognition. But, as I shall argue, it is a mistake to divorce these concepts from the larger modernist framework, in order to produce a postmodernist reading of Anderson's position. At the same time, the implications of his emphasis on the bond of imagination take us beyond the confines of modernism and look forward to its dissolution.

It could be said that the idea of an imagined political community is the most problematic aspect of Anderson's account. That nations, like other large communities, are imagined is, as Anderson notes, a fairly common notion. What makes it novel is its link with representation. That which is imagined can, and has to be, re-presented, if it is not to remain in the purely private realm of the individual's mental processes. For Anderson, 'imagination' implies 'creation' rather than 'fabrication'; in this vein he speaks of the 'inventions of the imagination', to include both national communities and their modes of representation in plays, novels, scores and newspapers.

There are several problems here. The first is semantic. Terms like 'invention' and 'imagination' can mean different things and are commonly used in just those senses from which Anderson wishes to distance himself: it is so easy to slide from 'imagined' in the sense of 'created' to 'imaginary' in the sense of 'illusory' or 'fabricated', a tendency encouraged by his insistence on regarding the nation as a cultural artefact portrayed/narrated by other cultural artefacts (novels, etc.). The result is to suggest that, once deconstructed, the nation must appear to fragment and dissolve into its individual parts, and that the nation is no more than the sum of its cultural representations. As such, the nation possesses no reality independent of its images and representations. But, such a perspective undermines the sociological reality of the nation, the bonds of allegiance and belonging which so many people feel, and obscures both the institutional political and territorial constitution of nations, and the powerful and popular cultural resources and traditions that underpin so many nations and endow them with a sense of tangible reality.[11]

Second, there is the problem of intellectualism in Anderson's account. Anderson admits that changed consciousness and social change alone cannot account for collective attachments. He recognises the specific 'love' that inheres in the nation (*ibid*.: 141–3). At the same time his emphasis upon a form of individual cognition – imagination – as the key to the rise and spread of nationalism, deflects attention away from collective attachment and sentiment. How can emphasis upon imagination and the imagined community enable us to grasp the power of the nation and nationalism? 'Imagination' certainly helps us to understand how easily the concept of the nation *can* be spread and transplanted; but why *should* it be spread, and why should *it* (the nation) be transplanted? What was it about the nation, and what was it about so many people's circumstances, that made them *feel* bound into 'nations' and assert their 'national' rights? For the nation, as we shall see, is not only known and imagined: it is also deeply felt and acted out.[15]

A third problem is that of voluntaristic individualism. Anderson admits that

> Seen as both an *historical fatality* and as a community imagined through language, the nation presents itself as simultaneously open and closed.
>
> (*ibid*.: 146)

But he claims:

> For it shows that from the start the nation was conceived in language, not in blood, and that one could be 'invited into' the imagined community.
>
> (*ibid*.: 145)

The fact of the matter is that nationalism thinks in terms of historical destinies, while racism dreams of eternal contaminations.

(*ibid*.: 149)[16]

Now, it is quite true that, compared to racism, nationalism has a much more open, historical character. But, as these quotations confirm, the thrust of Anderson's definition of the nation is individualistic and voluntarist, not only because he thinks nations are largely imagined civic communities, but because he singles out language – something that individuals can acquire – as the main criterion of the nation. In his definition, language is not mentioned, only implied; yet the individualistic and voluntarist character of his definition of the nation has no room for other criteria like ethnicity, religion or colour. This means that, provided it is political, finite and sovereign, any imagined community – be it a city-state, a kingdom or even a colonial empire with a single *lingua franca* – can be designated by its members as a nation. For a definition of the nation, this is rather too large a trawl of political communities for comfort.[17]

What, I think, underlies these difficulties is an excessive emphasis on the idea of the nation as a narrative of the imagination, a text to be read and grasped and deconstructed through literary categories and devices. The result is that causal explanations of the character and spread of a specific type of community and movement tend to be overshadowed or relegated. There is much to be gained from cultural analysis, in conveying the nature and feel of particular sociological communities through their literary portrayals. But to describe the nation almost exclusively in these terms is to miss other important elements which define the concept and mark it off from other types of imagined community. National communities do purvey great historical and linguistic narratives, which are vital to their survival and renewal. But they contain much else besides – symbols, myths, values and memories, attachments, customs and traditions, laws, institutions, routines and habits – all of which make up the complex community of the nation.

Print-capitalism and re-presentation

This view of the nation as primarily a text and discourse inevitably suggests a leading causal role for print technology and print-capitalism, one which leaves little room for other modes of cultural representation and omits other vital factors in the rise of nations and the spread of nationalism.

Now the rise of reading publics through the dissemination of print vernaculars undoubtedly had a special importance in various parts of Europe in the nineteenth century, notably in bringing to the fore the various intelligentsias who rediscovered and reconstructed the past or pasts of the nation-to-be. But it would be a mistake to overgeneralise the role of the printed word. Anderson himself is well aware of its secondary role in Latin America, and we can point to many cases in Africa and Asia where literacy, and hence the power of the printed word, was confined to a very small stratum of the designated population. Even in Europe, literacy was often confined to small coteries of intellectuals and upper classes; many more Italians joined and fought in the Risorgimento wars than could read and write (let alone in [Tuscan] Italian). The portrayals of the nation that stirred people into action were oral, audial and visual rather than literary, a matter of symbols, songs, images, reports and rituals. It was the nationalists who, on coming to power, set about educating their populations and turning them into citizens of the nation. Anderson's account captures some of the rhythms of the genesis of nations in Europe; but language and literacy never assumed so central a role outside Europe, being often replaced in public consciousness by religion, about which Anderson has surprisingly little to say.[18]

Outside Europe, in fact, the community of the nation was imagined and portrayed by a variety of media which, with the rise of cheap technologies, percolated to the majority of the designated populations. There were, of course, the traditional media of song, dance, costume, ritual object, artwork; even in Europe Herder had stressed their importance in establishing the cultural authenticity and popular depth of the nation. Unlike print, which for long was confined to elites and some middle strata, these were genuinely popular media, and the works they purveyed were shared by large numbers of people as part of their daily lives. To which we might add: landscapes, monuments, buildings, tomb-styles, the more durable elements of collective cultures, which provided their historical environment. More recently, as Anderson recognises, print has been supplemented, and then overtaken, by radio, cassette, film and television, which can reach vast audiences unknown to the purveyors of pamphlets and novels (*ibid.*: 135).[19]

In other words, while discursive networks provide a key to the role of elites in portraying the nation and disseminating nationalism, other cultural media from music and art to radio and television have penetrated and mobilised the majority of the people, provided always that they 'spoke' to them in a 'language' and culture that they understood, and conveyed messages of myth and symbol, memory and tradition, that resonated with them. By widening the role of cultural media far beyond the relatively limited purview of print and the press, we can also overcome the limitations of an explanation of nations and nationalism in terms of 'print-communities'. For, quite obviously, as Anderson himself recognises, a global map of 'print-communities' does not correspond with one of emergent nations. Too many other factors intervene for so neat a congruence. That is why Anderson supplements an explanation of the rise of nations in Latin America through the work of creole printmen with an analysis of the provincial administrative 'pilgrimages' of creole functionaries. That is why, too, in considering the emergence of such unlikely national states as Indonesia out of its mass of territorial and ethnic groupings, Anderson underscores the importance of colonial state education systems producing literate and bilingual intelligentsias (*ibid.*: 116, 121–30). Indeed, in the second edition of his book, Anderson points to the crucial role of the colonial state, and its census-takers, ethnographers and cartographers, in defining the nations of Southeast Asia from the end of the nineteenth century (*ibid.*: ch. 10).

Yet at the end, Anderson reverts to his original thesis: though language is inclusive, 'Print-language is what invents nationalism, not *a* particular language per se' (*ibid.*: 134). If that is so, then we would expect nations to correspond to the limits of print-languages. But, since this is clearly not the case, we cannot accord a pivotal role to print-language and print-capitalism. It becomes just one among many contributory causes, especially in Europe.

Mass self-sacrifice

I said earlier that the concepts of imagined community and print-capitalism took their meaning from Anderson's modernist historical framework. They can only emerge at specific historical junctures, and only within a determinate sequence which starts with mortality and linguistic diversity, moves on to the long-term decline of sacred monarchies and sacred script-communities and ends in the revolution of linear, 'empty, homogeneous time'. Of course, these processes are long-drawn-out and overlap, but the point for Anderson is that you cannot have one without the other if you want a convincing account of nations and nation- alism, and especially of the attachments that make it possible for so many people to die willingly for the nation. But it is here that we find ourselves in greatest difficulty. We already saw how problematic it becomes to account for mass self- sacrifice through an approach that emphasises imagination and cognition. How do we get from knowing and imagining the nation to feeling it and loving it? Is it because we think the nation is interestless? Anderson rightly points to the way in which the nation is likened to a family, and the family is treated in most of human history as a domain of disinterested love, purity and solidarity. Yet it is not because it is pure and disinterested that the family engenders such powerful attachments. On the contrary: as history too often proves, families have powerful interests, and their members equally fervent attachments bound up with those interests. Similarly with the nation; it is because we know that our interests, indeed our very identities and survival, are bound up with the nation, that we feel such devotion to the nation and are prepared to make such sacrifices for it when it is in danger. Hence the peculiar passion and violence which it elicits from its members, the feeling too that the nation insures us against mortality, or rather against the oblivion that our death so clearly threatens. Nationalism, by its ability to unite the dead, the living and the yet unborn in a single community of fate, and through its vision of the judgment of posterity, provides humanity with a secular version of immortality through absorption into the nation (see Mosse 1994).[20]

The concept of the nation, then, is not only an abstraction and invention, as is so often claimed. It is also felt, and felt passionately, as something very real, a concrete community, in which we may find some assurance of our own identity and even, through our descendants, of our immortality. But transcending death is what the world religions sought in their different ways; so, we may ask, does this not make of nationalism some latterday religion in secular guise? And does not the current revival of religion, and the spate of religious nationalisms today, cast doubt on the validity and utility of the modernist sequence which frames Anderson's post-modernist insights? (see James 1996).

Just as kings and their ministers used nationalism for their own ends well into this century, so priests and prophets have continued to make use of ethnic ties and nationalism, and the passions to which they give rise, to support their own brands of religious politics. It is simply not the case that all the great sacred-script communities declined and thereby made space for the nation. Islam, in states like Pakistan, Malaysia and Iraq, has experienced a massive revival while simultaneously intensifying their national identities and profiles. Something of the same kind has been happening to Jews in Israel, where a vigorous orthodox Judaism is being strengthened while itself reinforcing Israeli nationalism. In other cases, such as Greece, orthodox religion, though subordinated to the state, nevertheless continues to define and underpin the sense of national identity. As we saw, Juergensmeyer's review of religious nationalisms reveals the explosive resilience of this alliance between religion and nationalism, with their combined demands for mass self-sacrifice and their ability to guarantee to their adherents a kind of double insurance for survival through both posterity and the afterlife (Marty and Appleby 1991; Juergensmeyer 1993).

This suggests that the modernist framework employed by Anderson is in need of considerable revision, especially its tendency to over-generalise from the Western experience; and much the same caution applies to Anderson's claim for a revolutionary change in our conceptions of time. After all, linear time, measured by clock and calendar, was well known in antiquity (and not only among the ancient Jews), not to mention the medieval period. We can also find examples of the use of cyclical and cosmological time in modern nationalisms like that of Burma under U Nu. But the real question is: is there any causal connection between the admittedly linear-progressive narratives of nationalism and the growing adoption of linear, chronological time in the West? How could such a link be established? And how important was such a link? (Sarkisyanz 1964; Johnson 1995).

Or was the rise of nationalism rather a result of that democratisation of purposive religion, whereby all adult males were required to hear, if not to read, the Bible with its sacred Old Testament histories and its message of social freedom and justice set in linear time? For Liah Greenfeld, indeed, the return to the Old Testament with its myth of ethnic election marked a crucial phase in the growth of the first nationalism, in early modern England, and therefore of all nationalism – an argument supported by the many peoples, especially in the Protestant tradition, who developed myths of ethnic election and returned to the linear Old Testament ethnic histories. For Michael Walzer, too, the return to biblical Exodus history has shaped the civic-political aspirations of national liberation movements. The implication is that the particular messages and contents of religious and ethnic traditions undermine the validity and detract from the utility of an overall modernist framework. More specifically, modern capitalism encounters in religion another tenacious foe. Only by paying closer attention to these religious myths, symbols and traditions can we hope to understand *which* nations emerged, and where; and why it was the *nation* that triumphed as the norm of social and political organisation (Greenfeld 1992, ch. 1; cf. Walzer 1985).[21]

None of this is to gainsay the achievement of Anderson's twofold synthesis of cultural analysis with a basically Marxist socioeconomic framework, and his postmodernist reading of the concept of the nation with a modernist account of its genesis and diffusion. Yet for all its originality, Anderson's synthesis is only partly successful. The postmodernist reading, and its accompanying cultural analysis, can always be detached from its modernist moorings. In the hands of his followers, this is what has tended to happen. Though print-capitalism has been accorded a respectful hearing, it is the role of imagination, and the idea of the nation as a discourse to be interrogated and deconstructed, that have proved most influential. These are the fruitful concepts that have been taken up and developed by the many theorists in the postmodernist traditions who have drawn their inspiration from a partial reading of Anderson's work.

In a longer perspective, Anderson's role in the modernist theory of nationalism has proved to be double-edged. On the one hand, it has strengthened the modernist paradigm by redirecting the focus of its materialist versions onto the plane of psychology and culture. On the other hand, it has provided, doubtless unintentionally, the means to negate its basic premisses by undermining the ontological status of the nation as a real community grounded in the historical and social life of cultural collectivities. In this way it has bypassed the need to give an overall structural explanation of historical groups of nations, as opposed to specific cultural explanations in different areas and periods. For the many postmodernist writers influenced by his vision, Anderson's methodological legacy has been, not only to replace attempts at causal explanation by literary and textual analyses (something he himself refuses to countenance), but to sacrifice sociological investigation of the origins, spread and effects of nationalism for a more descriptive, and deconstructive, analysis of the characteristics of national projects. Insofar as modernism and the modernist theory of the nation was linked to a fundamentally sociological and historical causal analysis of the origins, spread and effects of nations and nationalism, the introduction of post-modern*ist* readings and methods in such concepts as the 'imagined community' and 'invented tradition' have signalled the dissolution of classical modernism and its replacement by the many smaller, and more limited, 'postmodern' analyses of the nation. To this phase of dissolution I shall return in the last chapter. It is only one of several kinds of response to the crisis of the modernist theory of nations and nationalism which came to a head in the 1980s. The nature of that crisis, and the attempts to replace modernism by more viable paradigms and analyses, form the subject of the second part of my study.

Part II
Critics and alternatives

7 Primordialism and perennialism

The modernist paradigm of nations and nationalism constitutes the most fruitful and comprehensive of the grand narratives in the field. It is also one of the last. It emerged in opposition to the older nationalist, or perennialist, paradigms. But, as in other fields of study in the social sciences, these kinds of all-encompassing explanatory paradigm have been increasingly abandoned in favour of limited models and accounts of particular, usually contemporary, aspects of the study of nations and nationalism. Responding to specific cultural and political problems in specific areas of the world, scholars seek now to account for particular developments, rather than frame a perspective that takes in the whole sequence of processes and full range of phenomena that fall under the rubric of 'nations and nationalism'.

This is not to say that there were no alternative grand narratives, no rival paradigms, in terms of which more or less radical critiques of modernism could be mounted. As we shall see, there have been significant attempts to reveal the flaws and exaggerations in the modernist grand narrative and to provide alternative paradigms of nations and nationalism. Yet despite the validity of many of these criticisms, the proposed alternatives have to date generally failed to attract the support of the majority of scholars in the field. Moreover, the main assumptions of modernism have been so firmly entrenched that even those who seek to 'go beyond' them and, in doing so, undermine and fragment those assumptions, have abandoned all attempts at grand theorising rather than embrace any of the alternatives on offer. The result is that students are faced with an unenviable choice between inadequate or untenable paradigms and a series of limited analytical accounts of specific problems in the field.

In Part II, I seek to explain how this unsatisfactory situation has arisen. In this chapter I shall attempt to show why the alternative 'primordialist' and 'perennialist' paradigms are unacceptable; in the next, why the one alternative that might be acceptable should be viewed largely as an internal critique and expansion of modernism; and in the last chapter, why the more limited, analytical accounts of specific problems do little to advance the overall theory of nations and nationalism. Finally, in the conclusion, I attempt to sketch some of the areas where advances might be made, or where some kind of theoretical convergence could take place.

Primordialism I: inclusive fitness

The oldest paradigm of nations and nationalism, the one against which modernism has always battled, is the nationalist. Or rather, one version of the nationalist ideology, the organic version. Back in 1944, Hans Kohn had made an important distinction between a 'voluntarist' type of nationalism which regarded the nation as a free association of rational human beings entered into voluntarily on an individual basis, and an 'organic' type which viewed the nation as an organism of fixed and indelible character which was stamped on its members at birth and from which they could never free themselves. Kohn thought the first type was characteristic of the Anglo-Saxon world, whereas the second kind of ideology was typical of nationalist movements east of the Rhine (Kohn 1967a).[1]

If we forget Kohn's highly questionable geographical applications and retain only his ideological distinction, we can see that the 'organic' theory first developed by the German Romantics provided an overall account of nations and nationalism which, were it tenable, would make the modernist paradigm irrelevant and superfluous. Organic nationalism holds that the world consists of natural nations, and has always done so; that nations are the bedrock of history and the chief actors in the historical drama; that nations and their characters are organisms that can be easily ascertained by their cultural differentiae; that the members of nations may, and frequently have, lost their national self-consciousness along with their independence; and that the duty of nationalists is to restore that self-consciousness and independence to the 'reawakened' organic nation (see Pearson 1993).[2]

Now, to a modernist, each and every one of these tenets is questionable, if not unacceptable. The world does not consist of 'natural' nations, except thinking makes it so, nor are nations to be likened to evolving organisms; on the contrary, nations and nationality are logically and historically contingent phenomena. Before the modern epoch, nations were largely unknown, and human beings had a multiplicity of collective loyalties; religious communities, cities, empires and kingdoms were the chief collective actors, above the village and district level, and the outlook of most human beings was strictly local. Nor is it easy to define the character and ascertain the cultural differentiae of many nations in the contemporary world, given the multiplicity of overlapping identities in which individuals are enmeshed. In fact, we often witness nationalists disputing among themselves about the 'true' characteristics of their nation. Nor can nationalists explain why the members of particular nations should come to 'forget' their nationality, or why so many should 'slumber' so determinedly for so many centuries and be ready to be 'awakened' at the appointed hour. Might it be that nations have no existence apart from the ideas and goals of nationalism, that we can only verify the existence of the nation *ex post facto* from the activities of the nationalists? Perhaps it is the nationalists themselves who have legitimised their political aspirations and mobilising activities, using the metaphor of 'reawakening' a population who had never for a moment even entertained the idea that they were members of a particular, designated nation (see esp. Gellner 1983: ch. 5).

Now, there is nothing particularly odd about an ideology with such scant regard for logic and historical evidence proving so enduringly influential in so many parts of the world. This is, in fact, part of the data of the problem of nationalism. What is more important about the organic version is its introduction of the concepts of biology and the 'primordial' tie of nationality, albeit in rudimentary form. Both of these ideas have entered into two well known theoretical critiques of modernism. Both can be termed 'primordialist'; one of them is fundamentally biological in character, the other cultural. However, apart from these references to biology and culture, neither of these 'primordialist' critiques has, or seeks to have, anything in common with organic nationalism.

Sociobiology furnishes the basis for the first of these *primordialist* critiques. Broadly speaking, it claims that ethnic groups and nations should be seen as forms of extended kin groups, and that both nations and ethnic groups, along with 'races', must be ultimately derived from individual genetic reproductive drives. For Pierre van den Berghe, the main exponent of a sociobiological approach to ethnicity and nationalism, the modernity of nations is purely formal, a matter of supplementing underlying structures of 'inclusive fitness' with political forms. As he puts it, 'the very concept of the nation is an extension of kin selection', and so nations are to be treated as descent groups in the same manner as ethnic groups. What is important are the ways in which the individual's needs to maximise his or her genetic pool and progeny, favour kin groups and thereby larger genetic pools through extended kin groupings, that is, through 'nepotism' and 'inclusive fitness' (van den Berghe 1978, 1979).

Van den Berghe argues that human sociality is based on three principles: kin selection, reciprocity and coercion. The larger and more complex the society, the more important become reciprocity and coercion. But ethnicity, caste and 'race' 'tend to be ascriptive, defined by common descent, generally hereditary, and often endogamous'. Hence they are based exclusively on kinship and kin selection. Van den Berghe traces such groups from small 'tribes'; linked by ties of kinship, they made 'the tribe in fact a superfamily'. It was only the cultural inventions of unilineal descent and lineage exogamy that permitted the

> extension of that primordial model of social organisation to much larger societies running into tens of thousands of people.
>
> (van den Berghe 1978: 403–4)

For Pierre van den Berghe, ethnic groups were in-breeding superfamilies for most of human history, and signalled that fact by maintaining clear social and territorial boundaries with other ethnic groups. Of course, the common ancestry of 'the people' (the tribe) was always partially fictive, as a result of migration, conquest and interbreeding. But the putative character of some ethnic groups' extended kinship ties is irrelevant.

Just as in the smaller kin units, the kinship was real often enough to become the basis of these powerful sentiments we call nationalism, tribalism, racism and ethnocentrism. The ease and speed with which these sentiments can be mobilised even in modern industrial societies . . . the blind ferocity of the conflicts to which these sentiments can lead, the imperviousness of such sentiments to rational arguments are but a few indications of their continued vitality and primordiality.

What I am suggesting is that ethnocentrism evolved during millions, or at least hundreds of thousands of years, as an extension of kin selection.

(*ibid.*: 404)

For van den Berghe, ethnic sentiments are to be understood as an extended and attenuated form of kin selection. That is why ethnocentrism is the norm, and why

those societies that institutionalised norms of nepotism and ethnocentrism had a strong selective advantage over those that did not (assuming that any such ever existed), because kin selection has been the basic blueprint for animal sociality.

(*ibid.*: 405)

Genetic relatedness, in other words, determines the extent of animal, and human, cooperation, and thereby the degree to which they enhance each other's fitness ('inclusive fitness').

But how do we know who is genetically related, outside our immediate family, and to what degree? If we are programmed to invest only in those who are genetically related to us, how do we recognise 'kin'? What are the quickest and most reliable indicators of probable common ancestry? Any cultural marker which can finely discriminate us from our near neighbours will do: it may be language, religion, customs, dress, hairstyles or manners, or other cultural diacritica. These suggest that people sharing these cultural traits are descended from the same ancestor; and that *myths* of common ancestry are correlated with actual biological ancestry.

Here van den Berghe meets an important objection to his theory. Ethnicity is, in part, defined by myths of common ancestry. But a myth is not a biological reality. Hence the theory is invalid. Yet to be effective, a myth has to be believed; and it

will only be believed if members of an ethnic group are sufficiently alike in physical appearance and culture, and have lived together and intermarried for a sufficient period (at a minimum three or four generations) for the myth to have developed a substantial measure of biological truth. . . . Ethnicity or race cannot be invented or imagined out of nothing. It can be manipulated, used, exploited, stressed, fused or subdivided, but it must correlate with a pre-existing population bound by preferential endogamy and a common historical experience. Ethnicity is *both* primordial *and* instrumental.

(van den Berghe 1995: 360, original emphasis)

Here, it seems, we have the heart of the matter. What van den Berghe has done is to bracket physical appearance with culture, and equate living together and having common myths and historical experiences with preferential endogamy. But some of the best known ethnic descent myths suggest a quite different and more ambiguous interpretation. The Roman myth of common ancestry emphasised their varied origins (Latins, Etruscans, Sabines, etc.) and Rome was a magnet for various cultural populations from a fairly early period. This did not prevent a powerful ancestry *myth* (or two, to be precise) from developing, alongside equally powerful shared historical experiences (the Samnite wars, the Gallic invasions, Pyrrhus, and above all, Hannibal . . .) to give rise to its first literary expressions (see Gruen 1993; Garman 1992). The English, too, developed strong origin myths with references to various descent lines – Briton, Anglo-Saxon, Danish, Norman – and the content of these myths changed considerably over time (MacDougall 1982; Mason 1985). The same is true of the medieval and modern French ancestry myths, with its celebrated contest between Franks and Gauls (not to mention Romans during the Revolution) (Poliakov 1974: ch. 1; Weber 1991: ch.1). If it were really a matter of *actual* biological descent and kin selection, why these mixed references and transformations? In the light of these examples, can we really assert the correspondence of imputed and actual ancestry? Van den Berghe concedes that group definitions were always partly fictive, but believes this to be unimportant. But, as Vernon Reynolds (1980: 311) points out:

Unless his primordial inter-group theory based on sociobiology can explain why the new non-genetic transmission of kinship and group affiliation has to follow the logic of the old genetic one, it breaks down.

Myths of ethnic descent generally contain a kernel of factual truth, but they typically elaborate, exaggerate and idealise that kernel in a one-sided fashion (see Tudor 1972; A. D. Smith 1984a).

Van den Berghe is surely right to remind us that there are limits to ethnic plasticity and malleability. He points out that:

It is impossible to constitute an ethnie on a basis other than a *credible* concept of common descent, and the concept is only credible if it corresponds at least partly to reality.

Ethnicity always involves the cultural *and* genetic boundaries of a *breeding population*, that is, a population bounded by the rule or practice of *endogamy*.

(van den Berghe 1988: 256, original emphasis)

But his genetic and physical inference from cases of ethnic durability cannot account for the considerable variability, wide range and frequent absorptions and dissolutions of instances of ethnic affiliation, and the fact that many *ethnies* have undergone large-scale changes of culture and, in some cases, of demography. This is the case even in such a culturally long-lived example as the Greeks, where undoubted evidence of massive rupture of demographic continuity by the influx of Albanians and Slavs on the Greek mainland from the sixth to eighth centuries AD and of considerable, though not complete, culture change after the conversion to Orthodoxy, call into question the continuity and influence of a common ancient Greek biological and genetic inheritance on modern Greeks (see Just 1989).[3]

More generally, we have to ask how family and clan loyalties of 'inclusive fitness' can be extended to the members of ethnic groups who, running often into the millions, can never know or see their 'ethnic kinsmen', except in imagination and feeling? Without running to the other extreme, and regarding *ethnies* and even more so nations as purely abstract communities of the imagination, how can we *know* that our sentiments of ethnic kinship have a genetic basis, or that family and clan ties can be extended through large-scale nepotism *on the same physical and reproductive basis* to relative strangers because they happen to speak the same language and share the same religion and customs, etc.? This seems to me the central difficulty of any kind of genetic explanation in terms of individual reproductive success. One answer would be to invoke psychoanalytical mechanisms of 'projection' and 'identification'. But even if these mechanisms could be rendered precise, this shifts the basis of ethnic kinship away from the realm of the purely physical and genetic to the domain of the social psychological – something that van den Berghe for one opposes – thereby invoking an alternative structural and/or cultural explanation, without recourse to genes or phenotypes; and so the powerfully felt 'primordiality' of ethnicity and nationality becomes a purely cultural, rather than a biological, phenomenon.[4]

A further problem with sociobiological explanations is their failure to discriminate historically between phenomena of differing degrees of power, inclusiveness and complexity. Nations are elided with ethnic groups, and any differences between them are relegated to the superstructural, i.e. sociopolitical and non-biological realm, making redundant all attempts to provide separate explanations for the rise of nations and nationalism. In the interests of explanatory economy, important differences between historical periods and culture areas are treated as secondary or omitted. If modernists insist on a historical and sociological gulf between the agrarian and capitalist industrial epochs, sociobiological accounts disregard epochal differences altogether in their desire to provide reductionist explanations for a wide range of social and cultural phenomena. The idea that *individual* kin selection in families and clans slowly evolved, over hundreds of thousands of years, by a process of nepotistic extension into ethnocentrism and ethnic groups, is a plausible speculation only insofar as it allows for all the other factors of conquest, migration and intermarriage that van den Berghe admits undermine the separateness and biological 'purity' of extended clan groupings or small-scale *ethnies*. In the end, as societies become more evolved and complex, and as migration and intermarriage undermine group endogamy, individual 'kin selection' becomes an increasingly residual factor, and we must look elsewhere for an understanding of the power and passion of ethnic ties and nationalism. This is the point of departure for the second, cultural version of primordialism.

Primordialism II: cultural givens

For many, the passions aroused by ethnicity and nationalism must be traced back to the 'primordiality' of the 'cultural givens' of human society. In fact, so overpowering and ineffable are ethnic and national ties that we need to return to the cultural 'essence' behind the many forms that ethnicity and nationalism have taken to grasp their continuing hold on so many people to this day.

It was Edward Shils who first identified various kinds of social bond between members of modern societies. In particular, he distinguished between the public, civil ties of the modern state and the primordial ties of family, religious and ethnic groups. Recalling the Durkheimian argument which saw the retention of a kernel of older kinship, moral and religious ties – the similarities of beliefs and consciences in a 'mechanical solidarity' – even within modern, industrial societies with their more individualistic, but at the same time cooperative and complementary division of labour or 'organic solidarity', Shils argued that primordial ties of kinship and religion remained vital even within modern secular societies, as witnessed by their symbols and public ceremonies (Shils 1957).

This theme was taken up by Clifford Geertz who applied the idea to the new states, but often old societies, of Asia and Africa. Here modern states were emerging on colonial territorial and political foundations, but their populations were bound together less by the civil ties of a rational society than by the primordial ties which arose on the basis of language, custom, race, religion and other cultural givens. For Geertz, it was these underlying cultural realities that explained the continuing power of ethnicity, and the sense of overriding commitment and loyalty to the cultural identities that they forged.

Geertz began by distinguishing

> two powerful, thoroughly interdependent, yet distinct and actually opposed motives – the desire to be recognised as responsible agents whose wishes, act, hopes and opinions 'matter', and the desire to build an efficient, dynamic, modern state. The one aim is to be noticed: it is a search for an identity, and a demand that the identity be publicly acknowledged as having import, a social assertion of the self as 'being somebody in the world'. The other aim is practical: it is a demand for progress, for a rising standard of living, more effective political order, greater social justice, and beyond that of 'playing a part in the larger arena of world politics', of 'exercising influence among the nations'.
> (Geertz 1973: 258)

Geertz argues that, though these two motives are intimately related, they are often opposed, and the tension between them is particularly severe and chronic in the new states of Africa and Asia, both because of the growing importance of the sovereign state and because of the 'great extent to which their peoples' sense of self remains bound up in the gross actualities of blood, race, language, locality, religion, or tradition'. People in these multi-ethnic states 'tend to regard the immediate, concrete, and to them inherently meaningful sorting implicit in such "natural" diversity as the substantial content of their individuality' (*ibid.*: 258).

Geertz claims that, considered as societies, the new states are abnormally susceptible to serious disaffection based on primordial attachments. He explained:

> By a primordial attachment is meant one that stems from the 'givens' – or, more precisely, as culture is inevitably involved in such matters, the assumed 'givens' – of social existence: immediate contiguity and kin connection mainly, but beyond them givenness that stems from being born into a particular religious community, speaking a particular language, or even a dialect of a language, and following particular social practices. These congruities of blood, speech, custom, and so on, are seen to have an ineffable, and at times overpowering, coerciveness in and of themselves. One is bound to one's kinsman, one's neighbour, one's fellow believer, ipso facto; as the result not merely of personal affection, practical necessity, common interest, or incurred obligation, but at least in great part by virtue of some unaccountable absolute import attributed to the very tie itself. The general strength of such primordial bonds, and the types of them that are important, differ from person to person, from society to society, and from time to time. But for virtually every person, in every society, at almost all times, some attachments seem to flow more from a sense of natural – some would say spiritual – affinity than from social interaction.
>
> (*ibid.*: 259–60)

I have quoted Clifford Geertz's celebrated essay of 1963 at length, because it has given rise to a fierce debate about the concept of 'primordialism'. Geertz himself does not use this term. Rather he is concerned with the immediate problem of how to explain what came to be known as 'subnationalism' in the new states, and cites in support Ambedkar's frank defence of the sense of primordial ties, of the fellow feeling that they are 'kith and kin', a 'consciousness of kind', but at the same time 'a longing not to belong to any other group' (*ibid.*: 260).[5]

For Geertz, disaffection based on primordial sentiments threatens the very existence of the new states. He lists the main sources of such sentiments:

Assumed blood ties or 'quasi-kinship'; and he explains this:

> 'Quasi' because kin units formed around known biological relationship (extended families, lineages and so on) are too small for even the most tradi-

tion-bound to regard them as having more than limited significance, and the referent is, consequently, to a notion of untraceable but yet sociologically real kinship, as in a tribe.

(*ibid.*: 261–2)

race, which refers to phenotypes rather than any definite sense of common descent;

language, though not necessarily divisive, can give rise to linguism as the basis of primordial conflicts;

region, which can be especially troublesome in geographically heterogenous areas;

religion, a force which can undermine the comprehensive civil sense;

custom, which with life-style often opposes sophisticated groups to what they see as more barbarian populations.

Geertz distinguishes intra-state from inter-state primordial attachments, which encourage respectively separatism and pan- or irredentist movements. Using this distinction, he builds a preliminary classification of ethnic–state relationships, emphasising that their patterns of primordial cleavage and identification 'are not fluid, shapeless and infinitely various, but are definitely demarcated and vary in systematic ways' (*ibid.*: 268). He then goes on to argue that the rise of a modern political consciousness centred on the state actually stimulates primordial senti- ments among the mass of the population:

Thus, it is the very process of the formation of a sovereign, civil state that, among other things, stimulates sentiments of parochialism, communalism, racialism, and so on, because it introduced into society a valuable new prize over which to fight and a frightening new force with which to contend.

(*ibid.*: 270)

This, then, is the 'integrative revolution', and it is clearly a double-edged process. It is particularly noticeable in the new states, where a modern efficient state seeks to unite diverse ethnic groups in a single national territory, but, as Geertz notes in a 1972 addition, it can also be found in Canada, Belgium, Ulster and other 'modern' countries, making the general argument even more germane (*ibid.*: 260–1, note).

The instrumentalist critique

Geertz's arguments, or at any rate a simplified version of them, have come in for a good deal of criticism. In a debate on the formation of political identities in South Asia, specifically Pakistan, Paul Brass in a measured critique highlighted some of the limitations of what he called a 'primordialist' approach. Brass concedes that people form deep emotive attachments which persist into adult life and which may provide a basis for social and political groupings. But he argues that some primordial attachments are variable. Many people are bilingual, change or shift their language, or do not think about their language at all. Religions too are subject to change by reformers, and to conversions and syncretism. Even place of birth and kinship may lose their emotional significance for many people. Massive migration has severed a sense of attachment to their place of birth for many people; besides, place of birth is not usually of political significance, at least until recently. Similarly, the range of genuine kinship relationships is too small to be of political significance.

> Fictive kinship relationships may extend the range of some ethnic groupings rather broadly, but their fictive character presumes their variability by definition.
>
> (Brass 1979: 37)

And, while a belief in shared descent is widespread among ethnic groups, it cannot encompass all culturally defined groups who claim special privileges because of some shared cultural features and who are united by their attachment to them (Brass 1979: 35–7).

There are two further objections to the primordialist position. One is the untenable assumption that recognition of distinct primordial groups 'is sufficient to predict the future development out of them of ethnic communities or nations', an assumption held by the early European ideologists of nationalism. The second, derived from Geertz, is that

> ethnic attachments belong to the non-rational part of the human personality and, as such are potentially destructive of civil society.
>
> (*ibid.*: 38)

But ethnic identities may be felt or adopted for quite rational reasons, for survival or for gain. As for primordial attachments, they have not been shown to be more dangerous to civil order than class conflicts or less amenable to compromise (*ibid.*: 38).

Brass, indeed, makes an important distinction between those ethnic groups that can 'draw upon old and rich cultural heritages with a persisting core' – he cites here the Jews with their core Talmudic tradition transmitted through the rabbinate – and those 'other groups whose core cultures are less easy to identify, but that have nevertheless formed a basis for cohesive and sometimes successful ethnic and nationalist movements' – and here he cites the mushroom growth of ethnic political movements in the United States in recent years (*ibid.*: 38). Brass also claims that knowledge of the substance of a persisting core tradition, say of Orthodox Judaism or of traditional Islam in India,

> may not be of much use in predicting either the development or the form of ethnic movements on behalf of the cultural groups in question.
>
> (*ibid.*: 39)

Nevertheless, it is possible to reconcile the positions of primordialists and instrumentalists simply by recognising 'that cultural groups differ in the strength and richness of their cultural traditions and even more importantly in the strength of traditional institutions and social structures' (*ibid.*: 40).

Brass himself adopts a moderate political 'instrumentalist' approach. Like Thomas Eriksen, he distances himself from the extreme instrumentalists for whom culture is infinitely malleable and elites free to choose whatever aspect of a culture that can serve their political purposes or mobilise the masses. Brass sees various kinds of elites selecting from the range of symbols of the received ethnic cultural traditions those that serve to unite their communities and mobilise them for social and political advantage. He emphasises the advantages accruing to different kinds of elite and counter-elite in symbol selection, but agrees with Francis Robinson in acknowledging the constraints placed upon them by their communities' cultural traditions. The competition of elites and their consequent selections of cultural resources have the effect of politicising the culture and changing the self-definition of the community from that of an ethnic group to one of a nationality competing with others in the political arena. Hence we may infer that it is the competition between elites within a community, and between the elites of different communities, using multiple symbol selection, that mobilises the members of communities and forms them into cohesive nationalities (Brass 1991: ch 2; cf. Eriksen 1993).[6]

If Paul Brass is prepared to concede a modicum of truth to the primordialist position on ethnicity, Jack Eller and Reed Coughlan would prefer to dispense altogether with so unintelligible and unsociological a concept. For them, the concept of primordiality contains three distinct ideas:

1   the 'given', *a priori*, underived nature of primordial attachments, which precedes all social interaction;
2   their ineffable, overpowering, coercive qualities;
3   the emotional, affective nature of primordial sentiments and attachments.

Together, these three ideas place primordial attachments and sentiments outside the realm of socially constructed emotions and bonds (Eller and Coughlan 1993: 187–8).

Eller and Coughlan then set out to demonstrate, by citing a variety of empirical studies, the variable and socially constructed nature of ethnic ties, which are continually being renewed, reinterpreted and renegotiated according to changing circumstances and interests. In particular, they point to the many instances of 'new primordials' which are 'made', not 'given'. They do concede that in some cases of ethnicity 'some old realities and resources were being activated which might arguably be part of a "primordial heritage"'. But in other cases appropriate cultural givens, or 'objective indicators', may be lacking, and they can often be constructed by political entrepreneurs. Eller and Coughlan then go on to criticise the followers of Shils and Geertz who, regardless of their possible intentions, treat primordial attachments as ineffable and therefore unanalysable. But their main objection is to the idea that primordial attachments are exclusively affective, and affective ties are somehow just there, implicit in the ethnic or kin relationship itself, and not born in social interaction.

> This leads to a mystification of emotion, a desocialising of the phenomenon, and in extreme cases can lead to the positing of a biological imperative of bond-formation. In other words, if bonds simply *are*, and if they are to have any source at all, then they must have a genetic source. Sociobiological explanations thus become, curiously, the last bastion of any kind of analytic enterprise, albeit a dead-end one.
>
> (*ibid.*: 192, original emphasis)

But is all this not to seriously misunderstand the import and utility of the concept of the 'primordial' for the study of ethnicity and nationality? Certainly, for Steven Grosby, the concept of primordiality has to do more with *cognition* of certain objects which the emotions that Eller and Coughlan erroneously single out, accompany. Grosby argues that we should return to the sociological tradition that distinguishes between fundamental patterns of human experience, and which recognises a plurality of orientations of human action, with specific beliefs peculiar to each type of orientation; examples would be Weber's types of social action, Parsons' and Shils' pattern variables, and Shils' primordial, personal, sacred and civil ties. Against the current reductionist vogue, this tradition recognises the importance of different kinds of cognition, or belief, which attach to different kinds of object, in this case, beliefs about ancestry and territory (Grosby 1994: 166–7).

For Steven Grosby, human beings perceive certain objects to be in the category of the primordial. This is an act of interpretative cognition. Human beings participate in historically evolving patterns of belief and action, and act in ways that are meaningful to one another. 'The patterns are the legacy of history; they are tradition'.

> Ethnic groups and nationalities exist because there are traditions of belief and action towards primordial objects such as biological features and especially territorial location.
>
> (*ibid.*: 168)

The reason for the significance human beings always attach to primordial objects is that

> the family, the locality, and one's own 'people' bear, transmit, and protect life. That is why human beings have always attributed and continue to attribute sacredness to primordial objects and the attachments they form to them. This is one of the reasons why human beings have sacrificed their

lives and continue to sacrifice their lives for their own family and for their own nation.

(*ibid.*: 169)

Human beings have always stood in awe of these objects and their powers over life, and regarded them as ineffable and coercive. That is why the instrumentalist critique is so fundamentally misguided and its sociological analysis so shallow.

The significance of this fundamental debate for our problem, the explanation of nations and nationalism, is both methodological and theoretical. Despite their protestations to the contrary, there is a reductionist tendency in both polar positions: an attempt to explain ethnicity and nationality as either instruments of rational self-interest, or as collective outgrowths of beliefs about the primordial. For instrumentalists as for primordialists, any distinction between ethnic groups and nations is secondary or irrelevant. Instrumentalists tend to view ethnicity and nationality as sites and resources for collective mobilisation by interest-maximising (and often rationally discriminating) elites; hence their analysis is largely voluntaristic, elite-driven and top-down. Primordialists view ethnicity and nationality as groupings formed on the basis of classifications of self and others in accordance with primordial criteria, i.e. beliefs about life-bearing and life-enhancing objects; hence their analysis tends towards a limited cultural determinism, though ultimately it is based on the slowly changing patterns of popular beliefs and perceptions.

Theoretically, the instrumentalist–primordialist debate appears to pit 'interest' against 'affect', elite strategies of cultural manipulation against the power of underlying cultural cleavages. Certainly, at the extremes of social engineering and organic nationalism, there is no possibility of a plurality of cultural and social orientations or a synthesis of motives. But in between there are a variety of positions on a continuum, which in one way or another recognise what Daniel Bell saw in ethnicity, its unique combination of 'interest' with 'affect' and its consequent superiority to other collectivities as sites of mass mobilisation (Bell 1975; cf. Eriksen 1993: chs 5–6).[7]

In fact, there has been considerable misunderstanding of what might be termed the 'cultural primordialism' of Shils and Geertz. It is quite clear that their views are far removed from the genetic primordialism of the sociobiologists; speaking of 'quasi-kinship', Geertz is careful to underline the 'untraceable but yet sociologically real kinship' of ethnicity, and to stress that real biological kinship units are too small to have political significance. Neither Geertz nor Shils regarded primordial ties as purely matters of emotion; they were careful to circumscribe the domain of primordiality and reveal how it was but one of several sources of beliefs, actions, attachments and sentiments. In fact, Geertz gives a prominent place in his essay to the role of the modern state in actually stimulating beliefs and sentiments of primordiality. Nor did they regard primordiality as inhering in the objects themselves, but only in the perceptions and emotions they engendered. Geertz, in the well known passage cited above, talks about '*assumed* "givens"',

of congruities '*seen* to have an ineffable . . . coerciveness', of 'some unaccount-
able absolute import *attributed* to the very tie itself', of 'a *sense* of natural . . .
affinity' (my emphasis). This is the language of perception and belief, of the
mental and emotional world of the individuals concerned. Geertz is underlining the power of what we might term a 'participants' primordialism'; he is
not saying that the world is constituted by an objective primordial reality, only
that many of us *believe in* primordial objects and feel their power (see Stack
1986: Introduction).

Here lies the vital insight of this kind of 'primordialism'. It lays out starkly the
nature of the data which the problem of ethnicity and nationalism raises. It
draws attention to the powerful perceptions, beliefs and emotions that can
inspire and excite human beings, and rouse them to collective action and self-
sacrifice. It reveals how the participants endow certain objects with primordial
qualities and base some of their actions on such perceptions and beliefs. A
theory of ethnicity and nationalism that fails to address the power of the
resulting ties and their capacity for rousing and guiding mass self-sacrifice, whatever its other merits, is seriously deficient in addressing those elements that so
signally distinguish these phenomena from others. One often has the sense that
instrumentalist and social constructionist models framed for the explanation of
'identity politics' and civic nationalism in the affluent, stable democracies of the
West are totally unsuited to provide convincing accounts of what Michael Billig
terms the 'hot' nationalisms of Eastern Europe, the former Soviet Union, Africa
and Asia. Like sweetwater fish, they cannot survive in the turbulent oceans of
rampant ethnic nationalism. In Bosnia, the Caucasus, India and the Middle
East, a 'blood-and-homeland' primordialism seems more apposite.[8]

But this too would be a mistake. For, while the students of cultural primordiality have highlighted the special dimensions of the problems of ethnicity and
ethnic nationalism, and shown how unamenable they are to the kind of analyses
proposed by the 'instrumentalist' models, their own preferred 'explanation' turns
out to be no more than an interesting tautology. It consists in re-describing at a
higher level of analysis the peculiar features and dimensions of ethnicity and
nationality; and those in very general, if suggestive, terms. It consists in isolating
a particular class of beliefs, attachments and sentiments which differ from others
and showing how ethnicity and nationality exemplify their characteristics.
Though this throws light on their character, it does not thereby *explain* the formation, course and decline of instances of these phenomena.

Moreover, taken seriously, the concept of primordiality precludes the need for
a historical sociology of ethnicity or nationalism, even though some of its adherents are profoundly imbued with a sense of the historical importance of these
phenomena. It accords no separate role for the rise of nations or for the cultures
and ideologies of nationalism, nor does it provide any tools for explaining the
historical development of different forms of ethnic and national attachments.
But, if cultural primordial*ism* is devoid of *explanatory* power, what students of
primordiality have done is to reveal some special features of ethnic and national
phenomena, and especially the powerful popular primordialism of the partici-

pants; and thereby provided the necessary point of departure for more convincing explanations.

Perennialism I: ethnic continuity

The primordialist–instrumentalist debate, which I have only briefly outlined here, is largely concerned with ethnicity and ethnic identity rather than with nations and nationalism. It is, nevertheless, germane to our problem because the competing assumptions of instrumentalists and primordialists have overshadowed and influenced the two main grand narratives of nations and nationalism: modernism and perennialism.[9]

In the past, one could be sure that modernists were also instrumentalists (and vice-versa), while perennialists were always primordialists of one kind or another (and vice-versa). But this simple dualism has given way to more variegated and complex formulations. Not all modernists embrace a robust instrumentalism; and not all perennialists turn out to be primordialists. We can even find an instrumentalist who is a perennialist of sorts; though the converse, a thoroughgoing primordialist who could propound a modernist account of nations and nationalism, is rare. What we find instead are theorists who embrace a perennialist view of ethnicity (with some primordialist overtones), only to adopt a modernist approach to nations and nationalism. Here I shall explore some examples of these combinations.

What is meant here by the term '*perennialism*'? Broadly speaking, it refers to the historical antiquity of the type of social and political organisation known as the 'nation', its immemorial or perennial character. In this view, there is little difference between ethnicity and nationality: nations and ethnic communities are cognate, even identical, phenomena. The perennialist readily accepts the modernity of nationalism as a political movement and ideology, but regards nations either as updated versions of immemorial ethnic communities, or as collective cultural identities that have existed, alongside ethnic communities, in all epochs of human history. On the other hand, the perennialist refuses to see either nations or ethnic groups as 'givens' in nature; they are strictly historical and social, rather than natural, phenomena. *As* perennialists, they could not endorse the central idea of the Abbé Sieyes, for whom nations were *sui generis*, existing in the natural order as part of the substratum of human and social existence. For the perennialist, the ethnic community or nation is a human and social phenomenon like any other. At the same time it is a constant and fundamental feature of human society throughout *recorded* history; and for this reason nations and ethnic communities appear to be immemorial to their members.

This point of view is very clearly exemplified by Joshua Fishman's analysis of ethnicity and language in Eastern Europe. Fishman does not use the language of 'cultural primordialism', though many of his formulations share its spirit. Instead, he wants to reveal the perennial and highly subjective nature of ethnicity by viewing it 'from the inside'. Attacking externalist liberal, Marxist and sociological denigrations and misunderstandings of ethnicity, Fishman briefly traces the history of ethnic belonging from the Greeks and Hebrews, and invokes the spirit of Herder, not only to stress the intimate bond between language and ethnicity, but more fundamentally to reveal the immemorial ubiquity and subjectivity of unmobilised ethnicity as the 'untutored and largely unconscious ethnicity of everyday life'. In this vein, he claims that ethnicity is a matter of 'being', 'doing' and 'knowing'. As far as ethnic 'being' is concerned:

> Ethnicity has always been experienced as a kinship phenomenon, a continuity within the self and within those who share an intergenerational link to common ancestors. Ethnicity is partly experienced as being 'bone of their bone, flesh of their flesh, and blood of their blood'. The human body itself is viewed as an expression of ethnicity and ethnicity is commonly felt to be in the blood, bones and flesh.
>
> (Fishman 1980: 84–5)

Echoing Harold Isaacs' analysis of the bodily substance of ethnic ties, Fishman insists on the need to regard ethnicity as a 'tangible, living reality that makes every human a link in an eternal bond from generation to generation'. Ethnicity has indeed a biological component, but it extends well beyond the biological and bodily, or 'being', dimension. It also involves 'doing'. 'The "doings" of ethnicity preserve, confirm and augment collective identities and the natural order', and include verbal expressions like songs, chants, rituals, sayings and prayers. Unlike 'being', ethnic 'doings' can change the direction of ethnicity; they can reinterpret and redirect the past, provided that the change is 'authentic'. Ethnic 'knowing' too, the wisdom of the collectivity, needs to be authenticated, and expressed in authentic media. Thus ethnic communities undergo change, but their mutability and modernisation must be in 'our own way' and 'true to our own genius', if intimate, deeply rooted belonging – the very meaning of ethnicity – is to be preserved in and through change. Indeed, the same deeply felt need to belong intimately has provided the basis also for modern ethnic nationalisms (*ibid.*: 94; Fishman 1972; cf. Isaacs 1975; Nash 1989).

Though his language resonates with primordial, even quasi-mystic imagery, it is clear that Joshua Fishman does not share the reductionism of sociobiology nor the theoretical interest in primordial beliefs and sentiments of the cultural primordialists. Rather, he is concerned to underline the power, longevity and ubiquity of ethnicity/nationality, to trace its deep roots in both history and the human psyche, and to vindicate the importance of seeing ethnicity empathetically and not to judge it by some externalist criterion of 'objective reality'.[10]

Nevertheless, this kind of analysis raises a number of questions. Who exactly feels the tangible, living reality of ethnicity? Is it ethnic leaders and elites alone or ethnic populations as a whole? If the former, cannot such ethnicity be the site of different, and contested, interpretations? If the latter, how can we verify their beliefs and sentiments, especially in pre-modern epochs? Besides, who authenticates the cultural 'doings' and 'knowings' of the community, and is there only one standard of authenticity? Granted that many people feel a deep need to belong intimately, and therefore the analyst needs to enter into the beliefs and sentiments of ethnic members, how do we explain *from within* the formation and decline of different ethnic communities and nations, the consequences of mass migration and adoption of new ethnic identities, the effects of large-scale inter-marriage on the sense of intimate belonging, and the possibility of mixed heritages and bilingual and dual-ethnic belonging? It seems that Fishman's anal-ysis, in capturing the deeply felt sense of intimate belonging of ethnic communities with vivid memories and well documented histories, fails to address the problems of communities with more ambiguous and less documented pasts, and the situations of so many people who are in transit from one ethnic commu-nity to another or who combine cultural elements of different communities. In other words, the kind of analysis that Fishman embraces may be more suited to the relatively stable ethnic mosaics and hierarchies of pre-modern epochs than to, say, the multiple, cross-cutting identifications and more fluid attachments of modern, Western societies experiencing massive immigration.

Nor is there any attempt in Fishman's kind of analysis to single out a special problem of nations or nationalism. Since nations appear to be equated with ethnic communities, there can be no such special problem, and no periodisation of national phenomena. Nor is there any attempt to disentangle the ideas of 'ethnic continuity' and 'ethnic recurrence' in perennialism. It would appear that ethnicity (and nationhood) continues from generation to generation, as long as there are some people who feel it as a tangible, living reality and retain the sense of intimate belonging. Fishman provides us with no clues about the effects of conquest, colonisation or genocide for particular ethnic communities or ethnicity in general; his appears to be a form of 'continuous perennialism', whereby nations and ethnic communities can be traced back through the generations to their first beginnings, with a corresponding sense of their immemorial character.

Perennialism II: perennial ethnicity, modern nations

A similar ethnic perennialism informs the scholarship of Walker Connor. In a series of powerful and seminal articles, now reprinted in a single volume, Connor argues that the national bond is fundamentally psychological and non-rational. It is not irrational, only 'beyond reason'. Basically, a nation

> is a group of people who feel that they are ancestrally related. It is the largest group that can command a person's loyalty because of felt kinship ties; it is, from this perspective, the fully extended family.
>
> (Connor 1994: 202)

Connor goes on to show how nationalist leaders have grasped and used this point, while scholars have tended to confuse nationalism with patriotism, the nation with the state. He cites a series of nationalist leaders, from Hitler and Mussolini to Mao Tse Tung and Ho Chi Minh, who appealed to blood and kinship to mobilise their fellow-nationals. But, lest he be misunderstood, Connor clearly differentiates his position from that of the sociobiologists:

> The sense of unique descent, of course, need not, and *in nearly all* cases *will not*, accord with factual history. Nearly all nations are the variegated offsprings of numerous ethnic strains. It is not chronological or factual history that is the key to the nation, but sentient or felt history. All that is irreducibly required for the existence of a nation is that the members share an intuitive conviction of the group's separate origin and evolution.
>
> (*ibid*.: 202)

The irreducible ethnopsychological element in nations and nationalism means that rational explanations for these phenomena always miss the point. Economic explanations in terms of modernisation and class conflict or relative deprivation, or political explanations in terms of state power and institutions, or individual-istic rational-choice theories of the strategic manipulations of the intelligentsia, must by their very nature fail to 'reflect the emotional depth of national identity', and the love, hatred and self-sacrifice it inspires. And citing Chateaubriand's statement that 'Men don't allow themselves to be killed for their interests; they allow themselves to be killed for their passions', Connor updates this as: 'people do not voluntarily die for things that are rational' (*ibid*.: 206).

For Connor, there is a clear distinction between patriotism and the much stronger sentiment of nationalism. Patriotism is love of one's state or country and its institutions; nationalism is love of one's nation, the largest felt descent group. This shows us that the nation is a more developed form of the *ethnic group*. For ethnicity too involves a sense of common ancestry, as Weber had already noted when he wrote that

> We shall call ethnic groups those human groups that entertain a subjective belief in their common descent. . . . Ethnic membership (*Gemeinsamkeit*) differs from the kinship group precisely by being a presumed identity.
>
> (Weber 1968: I, 389, cited in Connor 1994: 102)

Connor points out that Weber went on to say that, though the idea of the nation shares this sense of common ancestry with the ethnic group, 'the sentiment of ethnic solidarity does not by itself make a "nation" '. Connor elucidates Weber's analysis and examples as cases of 'prenational peoples, or . . . potential nations'. In these cases a segment of the ethnic group feels a low level of solidarity when confronted with a foreign element; this type of xenophobia consists in knowing ethnically 'what they *are not* before they know what they *are*' (Connor 1994: 102–3, original emphasis). An ethnic group may therefore be readily discerned by outside observers, but until the members are themselves aware of the group's uniqueness, it is merely an ethnic group and not a nation. While an ethnic group *may*, therefore, be other-defined, the nation *must* be self-defined.

(*ibid.*: 103, original emphasis)

Up to this point, Connor presents a perennialist view of ethnicity, with some hints of primordialism. Ethnicity is a non-rational, psychological essence, a sense of ancestral relationship which is presumably immemorial, if not pristine and hence primordial. Connor offers no explanation for the rise of ethnic groups, except in terms of *felt* kinship, which is presumably an extension of real (but small-scale and hence politically insignificant) kinship. But he does offer an explanation of the rise of self-aware nations. In fact, it turns out to be a fairly radical version of modernism. He asks: 'When is the nation?' and answers: when most of the designated population is nationally self-conscious, that is, when the members of ethnic groups become aware of themselves as such. This means that most nations are very recent,

and claims that a particular nation existed prior to the late nineteenth century should be treated cautiously.

(Connor 1990: 100)

After all, national consciousness is a mass, not an elite, phenomenon, and nation-formation is a process, not an occurrence or an event. Though we cannot know exactly what proportion of the population has internalised the national identity and thereby suffices to confer on the ethnic group the title of nation, there are several clues that suggest that, even in the Western democracies, this process has been recent and, even in Europe, incomplete. In support of this contention, Connor cites the lack of self-conscious national identification displayed by immigrants to the United States at the turn of the twentieth century, and Eugène Weber's findings that most of the population of France – the 'peasants' – did not become 'Frenchmen' and 'Frenchwomen' till the First World War, that is, after they had gone through the mass education system and conscript army of the Third Republic. In fact, enfranchisement of most of the population provides a good test of national inclusion and therefore national identity; in which case, even the Western democracies could not claim the title of nation until the early twentieth century, when voting rights were accorded to women and the working classes (*ibid.*: 98–9).[11]

Why is this the case? Basically, over the last two centuries the idea that the right to rule is vested in the *people* has been a potent and ever widening political force, undermining all previous political structures.

Since 1789, the dogma that 'alien rule is illegitimate rule' has been infecting ethnically aware peoples in an ever-broadening pattern.

(Connor 1994: 169)

The result has been a surge of national liberation movements, but it is only from the mid-twentieth century that this wave of nationalism has been extended across the globe and to peripheral hinterlands by the accelerating forces of mass communications and state-sponsored education. Not only, therefore, have Germans, Poles, Italians and Hungarians been stirred into political assertion through ethno-national movements of liberation, but equally have ethnic communities in peripheral areas like the Basques and Bretons, Slovenes and Corsicans. Indeed, what Connor terms 'ethno-nationalism' has swept the globe as a result of the mass communications spreading the message that popular sovereignty is wedded to ethnicity coupled with the 'demonstration effect' of successful ethno-nationalisms. So, though modernisation is a catalyst rather than a cause, and more important for the tempo than the substance of ethno-nationalism, it has greatly aided its diffusion across the globe (*ibid.*: 169–74).

Connor's thought-provoking analysis provides a necessary corrective to all those accounts which have attempted to excise the social psychological and presumed kinship basis of ethnic communities and nationalism. In one particularly incisive essay, Connor reveals the erroneous analysis and misplaced optimism of evolutionary modernisation theory, in the light of renewed worldwide ethnic separatism. In another, he demonstrates the inadequacies of economic explanations and particularly those based on the idea of relative deprivation, in accounting for 'ethno-regional' nationalisms. But his justified critique of Deutschian assimilation theory can lead to an overestimation of the power of ethnic separatism in relation to state sovereignty and a flexible inter-state system. His exclusively social psychological account of ethnicity, too, omits the often rich cultural elements of memory and symbolism, which nationalists subsequently draw upon. While Connor's approach illuminates the ways in which ethnic masses are mobilised in nationalist movements, it is perhaps less useful for analysing the more routine sentiments of national identity in advanced, stable and democratic states, particularly where there is a high degree of immigration and intermarriage.[12]

Connor's modernism with regard to the advent of the nation also poses problems. How are we to measure the extent and diffusion of collective awareness? Connor is all too conscious of the limitations of our sources, particularly for premodern periods and for lower classes. But should we rely on questionnaires and voting patterns to establish the degree of national formation? Can the nation be said to 'exist' only when the majority votes in national elections? This would appear to be too restrictive a criterion. It assumes first that the nation is necessarily a mass phenomenon, second that awareness is tantamount to participation, and third that in democracies, at any rate, participation is measured by voting.

All three assumptions can be contested. While it is true that the '*modern* nation' is a mass phenomenon, this is no more than an interesting tautology, unless of course we claim *a priori* that the only kind of 'nation' is the 'modern nation'. If we do not accept this equation, then, presumably, we would have to concede that in pre-modern epochs there was a type of nation that was more of an elite or a middle-class phenomenon. With regard to the second assumption, people can be aware or be made aware of something without participating in it, for example, the judiciary or the global system of states. We can, moreover, feel a sense of belonging to a community without being able to participate in its political institutions. That is, I suggest, very much what occurred in Europe in the early modern period, if not earlier, as well as in many ethnic communities around the world. As for the third assumption about the franchise, even in democracies people might insist they belonged to a given nation, that they were Frenchmen or Japanese, without having political rights in that nation. They might even volunteer for war service without being able to vote for or against the war. Besides, there are other modes of participation in the nation – education being, perhaps, the most important for mass citizenship, as well as for collective self awareness.

The psychology of ethnic affiliation

A similar combination of perennial ethnicity with political modernism can be found in Donald Horowitz's great study of ethnic group conflict in Africa, Asia and the Caribbean, *Ethnic Groups in Conflict*. He too traces ethnic affiliation to the sense of kinship ties. In the spirit of Weber, he writes:

> Ethnicity is based on a myth of collective ancestry, which usually carries with it traits believed to be innate. Some notion of ascription, however diluted, and affinity deriving from it are inseparable from the concept of ethnicity.
>
> (Horowitz 1985: 52)

Ethnicity is best viewed as a form of greatly extended kinship. The language of ethnicity is the language of kinship; both have an ascriptive character; ethnic ties are pyramided on family ties; and ethnicity meets widespread needs 'for familiarity and community, for family-like ties, for emotional support and reciprocal help, and for mediation and dispute resolution – for all the needs served by kinship, but now on a larger canvas' (*ibid.*: 81).

Citing Fishman, Horowitz argues that the sense of ethnic intimacy and bondedness is based on kinship ties and laden with familial emotion. Ethnicity builds on kinship, even if it extends the range of 'kinsmen' to include neighbours and those who share common cultural traits. It is possible to acquire an ethnic identity by migration, conversion and intermarriage; and ethnic groups vary in the extent to which they are prepared to receive outsiders into the fold. Nevertheless, most people are born into an ethnic group, so that whatever other differences there might be between groups, birth ascription is ultimately the defining element of ethnicity (*ibid.*: 57–60, 77–81).

Of course, group difference and discrimination is near-universal. Horowitz cites Henri Tajfel's experiments in group formation and discrimination on the basis of quite casual differences, to show the willingness of group members to sacrifice economic gain for positive social identity and comparative group advantage. But, unlike other random groups, ethnic groups 'tie their differences to affiliations that are putatively ascriptive and therefore difficult or impossible to change'. In fact, ethnic groups are always comparing themselves with others, and the quest for group worth and collective self-esteem is well nigh universal.

This perennial struggle for relative group worth in comparison with significant others also forms the basis of ethnic conflict today (*ibid*.: 141–3). It is typically expressed in ethnic stereotypes, which categorise groups as economically and culturally 'advanced' or 'backward' in relation to the (ex-) colonial West. These ethnic categorisations, when combined with judgments about the advanced or backward state of the regions in which ethnic groups reside, form the basis for a broad and influential typology of secessionist (and irredentist) movements in polyethnic states (*ibid*.: ch. 6), which I examined in an earlier chapter (see pp. 68–9).[13]

Ethnically plural national states are characteristic of much of contemporary Africa, Asia and the Caribbean. They are the product of the massive changes wrought by the advent of the modern colonial state and capitalist economy. Here Horowitz makes a crucial point. Until the arrival of colonialism, the struggle for relative group esteem was small-scale, localised and sporadic. Today, the huge scale of the territories enfolded by the modern colonial state and the penetration of the modern cash economy has thrown together in constant interaction many previously separate and isolated ethnic groups, and made the struggle for relative group esteem through ethnic comparison much more intense and pervasive, as ethnic communities compete for the prize of power over the modern state (*ibid*.: 66–77; cf. Young 1985).

Unlike Connor and Fishman, Donald Horowitz's focus is on the impact of colonialism and its consequences for the plural ethnic states that it created in Asia, Africa and the Caribbean, and he gives a rich and illuminating account of the ways in which ethnic parties sought to capitalise on the new opportunities opened up by colonialism and to compete in the new political arena of the modern territorial state. At the same time, Horowitz shares their perennialist and functional analysis of ethnicity. Like Fishman and Connor, Horowitz insists on the *presumed* kinship basis of ethnicity, and its vital subjective components, though, curiously, in his analysis of the origins of the plural state, he accords little or no role to pre-colonial ethnic communities and conflicts. His marked interest in the underlying social psychological mechanisms of ethnic identification leads Horowitz to underestimate the power of ethnic cultural traditions and religions in providing resources both for ethnic nationalist competition and for the territorial nationalism of the new state and its dominant ethnic community. At the same time, Horowitz gives us a much more historical, structural, and rationalist account of ethnic conflict in the modern plural national state, and this raises the question of why ethnicity itself might not be amenable to a similar kind of historical and structural, if not instrumental, analysis. While on a general level his analysis of the fictive (or better, presumed) kinship basis of ethnicity and ethno-genesis cannot be bettered, one is left wondering how and why *particular* ethnic communities and identities emerge and decline, and how his analysis relates to the historical fortunes of these groups. It is also not clear how ethnic conflict in the new states is related to the spread of nationalist ideologies and to the formation of *nations* and *national* states.[14]

The immemorial nation?

The analyses of Connor and Horowitz pose a fundamental problem: how can we combine a perennialist account of ethnic ties with a modernist, historical approach to the nation, if it is held that the nation is either a form of, or grew in some way out of the ethnic community? Is not the nation perennial too?

This is the position adopted by John Armstrong and by several historians. For Armstrong, the group identity called the 'nation' is simply a modern equivalent of pre-modern ethnic identity, which has existed all through recorded history. Armstrong argues that throughout history, the distinction between members of the ethnic community and strangers has permeated every language and provided the basis for durable ethnic group boundaries. Following Barth's analysis of social organisation and group boundaries, Armstrong sees the clusters of percep- tions and attitudes that we call 'ethnicity' forming and dissolving in every period of history. Some of these clusters, sustained by various myths and symbols, have endured for centuries, and have provided the bases for the later emergence of 'national' identities. Armstrong distinguishes between ethnicity in pre-modern epochs as a persistent group identity that 'did not ordinarily constitute the over- riding legitimisation of polity formation', and nations in the nationalist era, 'when consciousness of ethnic identity became a predominant force for consti- tuting independent political structures' (Armstrong 1982: 4).

Yet he also regards nations as existing in pre-modern epochs, he speaks of 'the slow emergence of nations in the pre-modern period' (*ibid.*: 7).

And elsewhere he distinguishes between pre-modern nations before the advent of the nationalist era about 1800, and modern nations thereafter, with the latter being formed on the basis of an explicit ideology of nationalism (Armstrong 1992).

But, given his Barthian approach, which sees ethnicity as maintained by social boundaries rather than primordial attachments or presumed kinship ties, how shall we understand Armstrong's perennialism? Does he regard modern nations as continuous with, and in some cases growing out of, older ethnic identities? Or does he see ethnic identities and pre-modern nations as recurrent phenomena in every period of recorded history, emerging and dissolving, with particular modern nations having little or no relationship to pre-modern ethnic identities or nations? In other words, is his a version of perennialism that emphasises *continuity* between modern nations and pre-modern ethnic groups, or one that emphasises *recurrence* of ethnic and national identities, but little or no continuity?

There is evidence in Armstrong's writings for both positions. But I am inclined to think that he adheres more to a 'recurrent' than to a 'continuous' version of perennialism, especially when he sees nationalism as part of a long cycle of ethnic identity. Of course, there are some cases of continuity between modern nations and pre-modern ethnic identities, such as diaspora communities like the Armenians and Jews, or cases like the French and Russians, but for the most part Armstrong seems to stress the ways in which, despite their durable myths and symbols, ethnic identity is subject to long-term emergence, transformation and dissolution, and is therefore a recurrent phenomenon. This would also appear to follow from his largely phenomenological approach, to which I shall return in the next chapter.[15]

In contrast to Armstrong, many historians have been concerned to trace a continuity between particular modern nations and pre-modern ethnic communities. Theirs is a more 'continuous perennialism'. This was certainly the position of an older generation of historian who, under the influence of nationalism, tended to see nations and nationalism everywhere in antiquity and the Middle Ages. But we can also see this kind of 'retrospective nationalism' at work in a number of more recent historical studies. Thus Brandon treated the ancient Zealots in Roman Judea as nationalist guerillas (a term that might be extended to the Hasmonean revolt of the Hasidim under Judas Maccabeus against the Seleucid Antiochus Epiphanes some two centuries earlier); their response to Roman occupation and oppression was of a piece with modern religious nationalisms, as they regarded the land of Israel as God's holy land and the property of His people. In a more circumspect treatment, Doron Mendels also speaks of ancient 'Jewish nationalism' from the Hasmoneans to Bar-Kochba, but qualifies this by equating the idea of nationality in antiquity with ethnicity and separating it from the modern idea of nations and nationalism. In this respect he approaches the distinction made much more forcefully by Moses Finley with regard to the ancient Greeks. There was, argued Finley, no Greek political nation, since the prevalent political unit was the *polis*. On the other hand, there was a a wide cultural network and a broad ethnic identity among the Hellenes (Brandon 1967; Mendels 1992; Finley 1986: ch. 7).[16]

For Steven Grosby, on the other hand, we may use the term 'nation' with caution for the people of ancient Israel, from at least the seventh century BC. Memories of a united kingdom under David and Solomon, the sense of being a trans-tribal people of 'all Israel', the conviction that this people belonged to a designated territory 'from Dan to Beer-sheba', and that it belonged exclusively to them, and finally the belief that the land and people had been sacralised by the covenant with the one God, Yahweh – these were the 'ingredients of nationality' which separated Israel from the many surrounding tribal confederacies, city-states and empires of antiquity. Grosby argues that Israel was not alone in this development; we find it in neighbouring Moab, Edom and probably ancient Egypt, whereas ancient Greece and Mesopotamia remained either city-states or empires because they failed to develop a belief in a single land inhabited by a single people under a single 'god of the land'. Hence, though in the modern epoch nations have become more widespread and numerous, as well as more sharply bordered, and have the benefit of legal citizenship, the idea of the nation was well known in pre-modern epochs, and in the ancient world it had its religiously defined counterparts (Grosby 1991; cf. Wiseman 1973).

Grosby's argument is in line with his emphasis on cultural primordiality, which we discussed earlier, but here he combines this theoretical concern with a careful examination of the Old Testament and other ancient evidence. But is his use of the term 'nation' similar to that of the majority of scholars of modern nations? Does not the substitution of religion for citizenship as a necessary component of the idea of the 'nation' separate his concept entirely from that of the 'modern nation'? Can, and should, we then speak of a 'pre-modern' and a 'modern' kind of nation, and how would they be related? Certainly for modernists like Breuilly or Gellner, Grosby's conception of pre-modern nations has little connection with that of the modern nation defined by citizenship and mass culture and education. But Grosby might well reply that the modernist usage is too restrictive, that it quite arbitrarily excludes members of a single broad category which possesses a number of similar features (named group, defined territory, myths and memories of ancestral peoplehood, cultural (religious) unity), but differ in certain other respects like legal citizenship and mass education. Could we, in fact, be dealing with two kinds of 'nation', or, better, perhaps a continuum from the one polar type to the other, with particular cases being ranged along it? Such a view would have the merit of being able to avoid the rather arbitrary exclusions which plague the field.

Of course, this formulation is necessarily abstract. It misses out the vital element of historical context. Suppose we grant the idea of two kinds of nation, or of a continuum between them; is not the modern type quite different from its predecessors exactly because of the historical context in which it was formed, and from which it derived its quite separate meaning, unknown and indeed unknowable to the ancient or medieval worlds? To bracket together these radically different formations may be simply another case of retrospective nationalism. After all, do not the very meanings of the terms we employ, which are always inadequate to the nuances and complexities of historical development and social life, derive from the changed contexts in which these concepts are used and hence reflect those changes? And were not the changes that inaugurated the modern world massive beyond previous human belief and knowledge?

But this is to beg the question of whether radical changes in some spheres of society and history – technology, communications, economics and demography, for example – necessarily have their counterparts in other spheres like culture, community and collective identity; and whether, if they have, the changes wrought are such as to make it necessary to treat more recent forms of culture, community and identity as utterly different and quite incommensurable with older forms, or whether, *per contra*, certain elements like kinship, memory and symbol, while differing in their particular contents between cases, remain constants of the human condition and are found in every historical context. Certainly, the case of ancient Israel gives us cause to reflect both on the definitional quandary of nationalism, and on the relationship between human communities like the ethnic group or the nation and the historical contexts in which beliefs and attachments to them have been formed.

8　Ethno-symbolism

In the writings of scholars on nations and nationalism, three antinomies are frequently proposed: the 'essence' of the nation as opposed to its constructed quality; the antiquity of the nation versus its purely modern appearance; and the cultural basis of nationalism contrasted with its political aspirations and goals. These antinomies are built into both the theories of scholars and the historical scholarship and political activities of nationalists themselves; and it is well to recall how deeply nationalist formulations (which themselves are quite varied) have influenced the development of historical analysis of nations and nationalism, and through the historians the whole range of theories that we have been exploring.

As far as the historians are concerned, a great debate has raged over the second and third antinomies, the antiquity of nations and the nature of nationalism in the Middle Ages (and indeed in general), a debate that harks back to the conflicting views of Heinrich Treitschke and Ernest Renan over the origins and nature of nations, and of the German and French nations respectively. By the early twentieth century, the lines of division between the 'objectivists' who stressed the role of culture, and more especially language, in the definition and formation of nations, and the 'subjectivists' for whom nations are formed by popular will and political action, were well entrenched in European historiography. One consequence of this debate was that for the 'objectivists', nations and national sentiment could be found as far back as the tenth century, whereas for 'subjectivists' both were products of the eighteenth century (Renan 1882; Tipton 1972; Guenée 1985: 216–20; Guibernau 1996: ch. 1).

'Old, continuous' nations

The debate has its more recent echoes. While most historians would accept that national*ism*, the ideology and movement in general, was a modern phenomenon dating at the earliest to the late eighteenth century, there remain important divisions over the antiquity of nations and the nature of national sentiment. For many historians, national sentiment and nations can already be found as far back as the sixteenth century. Indeed, Liah Greenfeld's massive study presents a wealth of literary evidence of the period to make a cogent case for the first manifestation of national sentiment and the nation in England in the early sixteenth century – in fact, somewhat earlier than Hans Kohn had argued for English nationalism. It is clear from her detailed and wide-ranging account that 'nationalism' signifies 'national sentiment' rather than 'nationalist ideology', although by the early seventeenth century, with its return to Old Testament ideals of chosenness and its development of a Protestant martyrology, English national sentiment had become political in content and turned to outright nationalist ideology couched in religious language. Theoretically, Greenfeld argues that we can only speak of nationalism when significant segments of the population come to identify the 'nation' with the 'people', that is the whole population of the realm, and it was in early sixteenth-century England, she claims, that the fusion took place for the first time, and the totality of the population was defined as the 'nation' (Kohn 1940; Greenfeld 1992: introduction and ch. 1).[1]

The Henrician Reformation is certainly an important moment in the evolution of national sentiment and political ideology in England, but for medieval historians like John Gillingham and Adrian Hastings, it is not clear why it should be preferred to an earlier period like the fourteenth century, when English became prevalent in administration and law, or even late Anglo-Saxon England, when an early nation-state with a common religion, vernacular language, administration and compact territory came into being. While we are unable to find explicit expressions of nationalism in this period, there are clear examples of an English national sentiment, such as the leading ecclesiastical writer, Aelfric, who explained in a letter to a nobleman why he had translated the *Book of Judith* into English:

> It is set down in English in our manner, as an example to you people that you should defend your land against the invading army with weapons.
>
> (cited in Hastings 1997: 42)

Hastings argues, along with some other medieval historians, and against the modernist interpretations of Hobsbawm, Gellner and Anderson, that in England certainly, and less clearly in other West European countries, we can discern the features of nations and strong national feelings (including a similar use of terms like 'nation' to the modern sense) at least from the later medieval period. By the eleventh century, at least,

> England is seen in biblical terms, a nation to be defended as the Israel of the Old Testament was defended. One feels aware of the sense of a people, kingdom and land, something regularly called 'England' though sometimes more grandly 'Britain', holding together local loyalties.
>
> (Hastings 1997: 42; cf. Gillingham 1992)

For Hastings, indeed, the Vulgate version of the Bible, translated into the vernacular and read regularly to the people, proved the decisive factor in the development of a sense of nationhood in the Christian West.

> The Bible, moreover, presented in Israel itself a developed model of what it means to be a nation – a unity of people, language, religion, territory, and government. Perhaps it was an almost terrifyingly monolithic ideal, productive ever after of all sorts of dangerous fantasies, but it was there, an all too obvious exemplar for Bible readers of what every other nation too might be, a mirror for national self-imagining.
>
> (Hastings 1997: 18)

Hastings admits that Protestantism multiplied the effect of the Israelite model through its dissemination of vernacular translations of the Bible, as well as through the *Book of Common Prayer*:

> The impact of the two books on the intensification and re-formation of English consciousness cannot be over-emphasised.
>
> (*ibid.* 1997: 58)

By the late sixteenth and early seventeenth centuries, the many editions of the Bible, but even more the compulsory weekly church services, brought an English Protestantism to almost everyone, heightening and redirecting a long-standing English national sentiment, which came to see the English as a 'peculiar people' engaged in a long struggle for freedom, first from Catholic Spain and then from Catholic France, and as, in Milton's words, a

> Nation chosen before any other, that out of her as out of Sion should be proclaim'd and sounded forth the first tidings and trumpet of Reformation.
> (John Milton: *Areopagitica*, vol. II, cited in Hastings 1997: 57)

By the early eighteenth century a more secularising and politicised version of this Protestant nationalism had become prevalent among the elites, although after the Union with Scotland the sense of 'Englishness' began to be conflated with, though never obscured by, ideas of a Protestant 'British' nation directed against France. Nevertheless, fully fledged *secular* political national*isms*, the first examples of Gellner's 'nationalism-in-general', a vast wave of nationalisms which for Adrian Hastings are 'said to constitute the "Age of Nationalism"' and represent 'a sort of Mark II nationalism', had to wait until the American and French Revolutions, which proclaimed the supremacy of the 'nation', conceived as a willed political union of fellow-feeling and culturally similar 'citizens' (Kohn 1967b; Newman 1987; Colley 1992: ch. 1; Hastings 1997: 28).[2]

The examples of England and France have provided the litmus test of the antiquity of the concept of the nation and the nature of national sentiment, as well as of the historical continuity of particular nations. This is epitomised in the

well known distinction made by Hugh Seton-Watson between the 'old, continuous' nations and the deliberately created, new nations, those that Charles Tilly
called 'nations by design'. For both historians, the distinction related mainly to
the advent of political national*ism*, the ideology and movement. 'Old, continuous
nations' were those that existed before 1789, well before nationalist ideologies
and movements demanded, and provided vehicles for, the creation of nation-
states; 'new nations' were those that nationalists set out to create according to
their ideological blueprints (Seton-Watson 1977: 6–13; cf. Tilly 1975: Introduction and Conclusion).[3]

For Hugh Seton-Watson, the distinction is essentially European. He lists the
nations that evolved gradually, and describes the process by which they were
formed over several centuries:

> The old nations of Europe in 1789 were the English, Scots, French, Dutch,
> Castilians and Portuguese in the west; the Danes and Swedes in the north;
> and the Hungarians, Poles and Russians in the east.
>
> (Seton-Watson 1977: 7)

> The process of formation of national identity and national consciousness
> among the old nations was slow and obscure. It was a spontaneous process,
> not willed by anyone, though there were great events which in certain cases
> clearly accelerated it.
>
> (*ibid.*: 8)

The new nations, on the other hand, were formed over much shorter periods, by
well known leaders using the written word and modern communications.
Language and linguistic politics were the main factors in creating national
consciousness in modern European new nations. Economic and geographical
causes were more important in the formation of overseas nations of European
origin, while state boundaries imposed by imperial governments formed the
matrix of ex-colonial nations in much of Asia and Africa (*ibid.*: 9).

Pre-modern nations?

Seton-Watson's narrative is impressive in its scope and the wealth of historical
evidence he adduces, but it is not without its problems. Seton-Watson himself
concedes the inevitability of some anachronism in singling out elements derived
from the study of new nations in the formation of national consciousness of the
old nations. And he admits to the impossibility of finding a 'scientific definition'
of the nation, claiming that

> a nation exists when a significant number of people in a community
> consider themselves to form a nation, or behave as if they formed one.
>
> (*ibid.*: 5, 11)

This formulation, of course, begs the question not only of the number of people considered to be 'significant', but also of the nature of the 'community' in which they are located. In practice, it is the politically or culturally defined ethnic community that Seton-Watson has in mind, as the rest of his great book demonstrates; where this is absent, as in much of Asia and Africa, the 'nation' to be created is an imposition of European ideas through imperial state institutions.

There is a basic problem with this kind of continuous perennialism. As Susan Reynolds points out, there is the temptation to read back into the formation of the 'old' nations the assumptions of modern nationalism, and in particular the idea that 'nations are objective realities, existing through history'. This tends to promote a teleological emphasis on the 'predestined nation-states'. As Reynolds notes:

> A more fundamental distortion arises from the fact that belief in the objective reality of nations inevitably diverts attention from itself: since the nation exists, belief in it is seen not as a political theory but as a mere recognition of fact. The history of nationalism becomes less a part of the history of political thought than of historical geography, while the starting-point of political development becomes the nation, with its national character or national characteristics. This pre-existing nation is then seen as moving through the attainment of 'national consciousness' to find its own rightful boundaries in the nation-state.
>
> (S. Reynolds 1984: 251, 252–3)

It is from this standpoint that Susan Reynolds takes issue with the teleological framework of historians like Seton-Watson for whom

> The long process by which in Europe sovereign states arose and nations were formed has its origins in the collapse of the Roman empire, the attempts to revive an imperial power, the slow decay of the revival, and the still slower withering away of its mythology.
>
> (Seton-Watson 1977: 15)

According to Reynolds, this kind of perspective prevents us from appreciating the ideas and sentiments of the early (or later) Middle Ages for what they were in themselves, without imposing a retrospective relationship

> between the medieval 'people' and its kingdom on the one hand and the modern 'nation' and its state on the other.
>
> (S. Reynolds 1984: 253)

To avoid confusion, Susan Reynolds proposes to use the adjective 'regnal' in place of 'national', since the medieval kingdom corresponded to a 'people' (*gens, natio, populus*), which was assumed to be a natural, inherited community of tradition, custom, law and descent.

(ibid.: 250)

By about 900, the idea of peoples as communities of custom, descent and government was well entrenched. Soon it became attached to the highest form of medieval government, the kingdom, and was provided with supporting genealogies and myths of origin, which were often traced back to Aeneas or Noah by writers from Isidore of Seville in the seventh century to Fredegar, Orderic Vitalis and Geoffrey of Monmouth, right up to the authors of the Declaration of Arbroath in 1320 (S. Reynolds 1983).[4]

This suggests that, in the medieval West at any rate, a *regnal* consciousness, which married ideas of kinship and custom with royal government, defined the 'peoples' of the area; and, though Reynolds regards the term 'ethnic' as nearly always combining 'connotations of both descent and culture' (and is therefore akin to 'racial'), her own idea of a 'people' (*gens*) as a community having beliefs of common descent, custom and law, associated with the residents of a particular territory, is fairly close to the perennialist's view of recurrent subjective ethnicity – although it is, in her case, clearly differentiated from modern nations and nationalism. For, like Connor and Grosby, Reynolds' analysis focuses on popular ideas, beliefs and perceptions of the participants, rather than on the analyst's view of the referents of those ideas, perceptions and beliefs (*ibid.*: 255, esp. note 8; 256–9).[5]

This still leaves open the question of whether we can speak of a measure of continuity between medieval (or ancient) ethnic or regnal formations and modern nations, in at least some cases. For organic nationalists, of course, the quest for 'our true ancestors' was essential to the cause of the nation. Even voluntarist political nationalists looked for some kind of ideological affinity with an ancient and preferably renowned exemplar, as the French *patriots* harked back to Roman virtue and glory, as well as their 'Gallic ancestors' (Rosenblum 1967: ch. 2; Herbert 1972; Poliakov 1974, ch. 1; cf. Viroli 1995).

But this kind of organic assumption has come in for sharp criticism. Lesley Johnson, who applies the Andersonian view of the nation as an imagined political community to the medieval world, cites a popular example from the introduction to an exhibition catalogue on the Anglo-Saxons, *The Making of England*, where the author argues that 'The Anglo-Saxons . . . were the true ancestors of the English of today.' The search for 'true ancestors' of the nation is part of the nationalist heritage and its concern for cultural authenticity. As such, it tends to assume what has to be proved, and posits a historical continuity which, given the silences and complexities of the historical evidence, is at best problematic (Johnson 1995).[6]

It is, of course, possible to find historical examples where a strong case for some measure of continuity between pre-existing ethnic communities (*ethnies*) and modern nations can be made. This is particularly true of peoples whose identities have been shaped and 'carried' by a scriptural religion, the Armenians and Jews being the outstanding, but by no means the only, examples. At the same time, as John Hutchinson remarks:

> The point here is that one cannot deduce from the prior existence of *ethnie* that they necessarily have any causal status in the formation of modern national societies. To do so without empirical examination is to make uncritical assumptions about continuities between premodern ethnic and modern national identities and to fall into the *post hoc propter hoc* fallacy.
>
> (Hutchinson 1994: 26)

What is needed, then, is more hard evidence of links – social, cultural and political – between medieval regnal or ethnic formations and modern nations. In the nature of things, such evidence is often difficult to obtain, especially if it is stipulated that both ethnicity and nationhood *must* be mass phenomena, and that in the medieval world, the peasants must therefore be aware of their ethnic and regnal ties, if we are to grant the existence of ethnic communities or nations.

But this is exactly what medievalists refuse to countenance. Hastings, for example, argues that

> one cannot say that for a nation to exist it is necessary that everyone within it should want it to exist or have full consciousness that it does exist; only that many people beyond government circles or a small ruling class should consistently believe in it.

> Equally it does not invalidate the existence of a nation in early modern Europe that many of the peasantry had little sense of being part of it. But, of course, if a specific society was overwhelmingly one of peasants and nobles only, then that might indeed be a decisive difficulty.
>
> (Hastings 1997: 26)

As against Connor, Gellner and Hobsbawm, Adrian Hastings cites France as a case of a nation centred on Paris long before most of the peasants could speak French or have some sense of being French, as described by Eugène Weber, and therefore, like England, largely preceding 'its' nationalism (*ibid.*: 26–7). For Hastings, this is a crucial aspect of the 'historiographical schism' between modernists like Hobsbawm, Gellner, Kedourie, Breuilly and Anderson, and their critics, because 'the key issue at the heart of our schism lies in the date of commencement' (sc. of nations and nationalism) (*ibid.*: 9). It is equally, of course, a sociological and political schism, and the vital issue of 'commencement' takes us back to rival definitions of the nation and of nationalism. It is one to which I shall return.

For the moment, I want to focus on the third antinomy, the contrast between the cultural basis and political goals of nationalism, because it throws a different light on both the nature and the antiquity of nations.

Cultural and political nationalism

For Susan Reynolds, the conjunction of *regnum* and 'people' meant that medieval 'regnalism' was always both political and cultural in content. This refutes the common idea that modern nationalism is simply the later politicisation of purely cultural or ethnic sentiments in pre-modern periods, and that the distinctive feature of modern nations is their sovereignty as mass political communities. The Middle Ages were full of loose but politically independent communities or 'peoples', each with its own ruler. It also appears to refute the separation of a purely cultural from an exclusively political type of national (or regnal) senti-ment. In the Middle Ages, at any rate, and perhaps also in antiquity, if Mendels is correct, no such distinction was made (Mendels 1992: ch. 1; Grosby 1991; but cf. E. Hall 1992).

In the modern world, however, such a separation is much more feasible. John Breuilly, as we saw, wished to confine the use of the term 'nationalism' to a purely political movement; and Eric Hobsbawm also argued that nationalism's only interest for the historian lay in its political aspirations, and especially its capacity for state-making (Breuilly 1993. Introduction; Hobsbawm 1990: Introduction).

But, as we saw, such a usage is unduly restrictive. It omits other important dimensions of 'nationalism' such as culture, identity and 'the homeland', and pays little attention to the character of the object of nationalist strivings, the 'nation'. The result is a serious underestimation of the scope and power of nationalism, and of its ethnic roots.

This is the point made by John Hutchinson in his pioneering and thought-provoking analysis of cultural nationalism. Hutchinson does not deny the importance of 'a political nationalism that has as its aim autonomous state insti-tutions'. But he thinks that we cannot overlook the recurrent significance of cultural forms of nationalism; despite their much smaller scale and often tran-sient character, we must accord due weight to 'a cultural nationalism that seeks a moral regeneration of the community' (Hutchinson 1994: 41). In fact, we often find the two kinds of nationalism alternating in strength and influence; as polit-ical nationalism falters and ebbs, cultural nationalists, as it were, pick up the torch and seek to rejuvenate a frustrated and oppressed community.

What exactly is the vision of cultural nationalism and how does it differ from that of political nationalism? The latter's ideal is of

> a civic *polity* of educated citizens united by common laws and mores like the *polis* of classical antiquity.
>
> Their objectives are essentially modernist: to secure a representative state for their community so that it might participate as an equal in the devel-oping cosmopolitan rationalist civilisation.
>
> By contrast, the cultural nationalist perceives the state as an accidental, for the essence of a nation is its distinctive civilisation, which is the product of its unique history, culture and geographical profile.
>
> (Hutchinson 1987: 12–13, original emphasis)

For cultural nationalists, the nation is a primordial expression of the individuality and the creative force of nature. Like families, nations are natural solidarities; they evolve in the manner, so to speak, of organic beings and living personalities. Hence the aim of cultural nationalism is always integrative: it is a

> movement of moral regeneration which seeks to re-unite the different aspects of the nation . . . by returning to the creative life-principle of the nation.
>
> (*ibid.*: 14)

Hence the importance of historians who rediscover the national past and chart its destiny, and of artists who celebrate the heroes of the nation and create out of the collective experience of the people. So the small circles of cultural national-ists form clubs and societies, read poetry, edit journals and engage in rituals, and seek to promote national progress through communal self-help. If popularised by educators and journalists, cultural nationalism can spawn a

> loose network of language societies, dramatic groups, publishing houses, lending libraries, summer schools, agricultural cooperatives and political parties.
>
> (*ibid.*: 16–17)

Under the influence of Herder, this kind of cultural nationalism took root espe-cially in Eastern Europe, for example among the Czechs and Ukrainians of the mid- to late nineteenth century. It could be found both among populations that existed only as ethnic categories, without much self-consciousness, such as the Slovaks, Slovenes and Ukrainians, who had few ethnic memories, distinctive institutions or native elites; and among well defined nations with definite borders, a self-aware population and rich memories, like the Croatians, Czechs, Hungarians and Poles; or among peoples with religious memories and institu-tions like the Greeks, Serbs and Bulgarians (*ibid.*: 17–18, 21–2).[7]

Hutchinson draws three conclusions from his analysis of the dynamics of cultural nationalism. The first is 'the importance of historical memory in the formation of nations'. The second is 'that there are usually competing definitions of the nation', and their competition is resolved by trial and error during interac-tion with other communities. And the third is 'the centrality of cultural symbols to group creation', which are only significant because 'of their power to convey an attachment to a specific historical identity' (*ibid.*: 29–30).

This does not mean that cultural nationalism is a regressive force. It may look back to a presumed glorious past, but it repudiates both traditionalism and modernism. Instead, cultural nationalists should be seen

> as moral innovators who seek by 'reviving' an ethnic historicist vision of the nation to redirect traditionalists and modernists away from conflict and

unite them in the task of constructing an integrated distinctive and autonomous community, capable of competing in the modern world.

(*ibid.*: 34)

Such movements are recurrent. They continually re-emerge in times of crisis even in advanced industrial societies, because they answer to 'a deep-seated conflict between the worlds of religion and science'. Here Hutchinson disputes Hans Kohn's account of the transient nature of cultural nationalism in Eastern Europe as a response to the misalignment of ethnic and political boundaries there and its socioeconomic backwardness. Kohn had argued that once a middle class entered the political arena in Eastern Europe after 1848, cultural nationalism was superseded by a 'rational' political nationalism. But this very common assumption, echoes of which reverberate in today's debate about 'civic' and 'ethnic' nationalism, fails to acknowledge that the

continuing hold of the historic religions suggests that there is no final resolution to this conflict (sc. between religion and science).

(*ibid.*: 40)

It is better, therefore, to see

cultural and political nationalism as competing responses — communitarian and state-oriented — to this problem. They form typically in alternating cycles, each eliciting the other. Their effect . . . is frequently to reinforce rather than to attenuate religious sentiments.

(*ibid.*: 40–1; Hutchinson 1994: ch. 3; cf. Kohn 1967a: ch. 7)[8]

As a sociological historian, Hutchinson underpins this theory with a rich and detailed analysis of the three national-cultural 'revivals' in modern Irish history: that of eighteenth-century intellectuals which culminated in the founding of the Royal Irish Academy in 1785; the romantic archaeological and literary movement of the early nineteenth century under George Petrie which culminated in the Young Ireland movement of Thomas Davis; and finally the much larger Gaelic revival of the 1890s around the Gaelic League and later the journals edited by Moran, Ryan and Arthur Griffith. Hutchinson is at pains to highlight the alternations between failed political nationalism and resurgent cultural movements, and the reasons why the cultural movements appealed to an intelligentsia whose mobility was blocked by professional and occupational restrictions under British rule. For an instrumentalist concerned with ethnic responses to state penetration, an explanation in terms of blocked mobility and frustrated class interests might well suffice. But Hutchinson's analysis is concerned to reveal how the interests and needs of particular classes and strata, caught between religious tradition and modern science, are met by historicist visions which derive from memories and symbols of Ireland's often distant past, and how these rediscoveries could fire the disaffected youth to political action (*ibid.*: chs 4–5).

In his later judicious discussion of the main approaches and debates in the field, Hutchinson distances himself from the modernist positions, while approving of their role in exposing 'the anachronistic Eurocentric and national assumptions of much scholarship about the human past' and 'exploding the primordialist account' of nations and nationalism (Hutchinson 1994: 37). For Hutchinson, Walker Connor's insistence on the either/or nature of collective identities is misplaced. In all ages, most people have had multiple identities and the question we need to ask is: 'do national identities become primary under certain circumstances in pre-modern periods?' (*ibid.*: 12). This means that, *pace* the modernists,

> a politicised ethnicity is neither entirely absent before the eighteenth century nor all-pervasive after it, but may be one of many identities that individuals might simultaneously adopt. There is a reluctance, therefore, to recognise that there may be *recurring* factors in the relationship between populations (e.g. military and cultural conflict) that may embed ethnicity as a political and cultural force in human history.
>
> (*ibid.*: 37, original emphasis)

If this is so, then 'the premodern structure of ethnic groups should have an important bearing on how the modern nation does form'. In other words, leaders and elites do not have the autonomy from previous ethnic traditions and cultures in their projects of nation-building that modernist instrumentalists claim for them. They are constrained by beliefs and ideas about the past and by the cultures of particular communities.[9]

For Hutchinson, then, memories and symbols play an important role in defining the nature and history of the nation, and in securing the attachment of many people to particular nations. He is rightly concerned to vindicate a sepa-rate realm for culture in the formation of nations, and argues convincingly for a distinct politics of cultural nationalism. Hutchinson is more cautious about accepting perennialist notions, perhaps because he is concerned to repudiate any form of primordialism and essentialism; his acceptance of a recurrent ethnicity throughout history is qualified. However, his historical analysis of Ireland and other nations and his emphasis on historical memory and historic religion, suggest a continual interest in the importance of the process of 'reaching back' into the ethnic past and in the revival of older cultural traditions. This implies a rejection of any idea that nations are 'invented'.

Nevertheless, it could be argued that Hutchinson does not go far enough; the movement back, from the present to the (ethnic) past, needs to be supplemented by the movement forward, from the past to the (national) present, even though that method is fraught with problems, something of which Hutchinson is acutely aware. But if we make no attempt to move forward from the past, in an open empirical manner, we risk reading the past only through the eyes of the present, as the product of the needs and preoccupations of present generations and elites. That is as unsatisfactory as to assume the converse, that the past shapes the present, thus leaving no room for rupture and innovation.[10]

Myth-symbol complexes

Reaching back into the past and moving forward from it to the present, implies a concern and a method based on a conception of long-term history. This is the starting-point of John Armstrong's monumental, path-breaking analysis of medieval Middle Eastern and European civilisations and ethnic identities, *Nations before Nationalism*. Its overall aim is to explore 'the emergence of the intense group identification that today we term a "nation"', and its basic assumption is that 'the key to the significance of the phenomena of ethnic identification is persistence rather than genesis of particular patterns'. For this reason,

> A time dimension of many centuries (similar to the *longue durée* emphasised by the *Annales* school of French historiography) is essential for disentangling independent ethnic experiences from the effects of diffusion and mimesis. An extended temporal perspective is especially important as a means of perceiving modern nationalism as part of a cycle of ethnic consciousness. Because the epoch of Absolutism that immediately preceded European nationalism involved, at least for elites, an exceptionally strong rejection of ethnic differentiation, nationalism is often seen as utterly unprecedented. A longer look suggests that widespread intense ethnic identification, although expressed in other forms, is recurrent.
>
> (Armstrong 1982: 4)

Here it is quite clear that, as we saw earlier, the terms 'ethnic' and 'nation' form part of a continuum, and that what matters is not the form they take in different epochs, but the persisting group perceptions and sentiments themselves. Although pre-modern persistent group identities, whether labelled 'ethnic' or 'national', are distinguished from 'nations' after the late eighteenth century, 'where consciousness of ethnic identity became a predominant force for constituting independent political structures', the body of Armstrong's book suggests that he regards ethnicity and nationhood as continuous, even though it is ethnic identities that form the subject of his analysis.[11]

Armstrong's point of departure is ethnic exclusion, the boundary between 'us' and 'them', and the universal comparison with the 'stranger'.

> Terms like '*goyim*', '*barbaroi*' and '*nemtsi*' all imply such perception of the human incompleteness of persons who could not communicate with the in-group, which constituted the only 'real men'.
>
> (*ibid*.: 5)

The universality of ethnic opposition is why John Armstrong finds Fredrik Barth's boundary approach so illuminating. Whereas previous approaches to ethnicity had started from the unique cultural traits of each group, Barth's anthropological model focused on the interactions and perceptions of members of a social group, which was no longer defined by some cultural 'essence', but rather by its self-perceived boundaries. For Barth, ethnicity is a socially bounded type of category, and one that is both ascribed by others and self-ascribed. In Barth's own words:

> A categorical ascription is an ethnic ascription when it classifies a person in terms of his basic, most general identity, presumptively determined by his origin and background. To the extent that actors use ethnic identities to categorise themselves and others for the purposes of interaction, they form ethnic groups in this organisational sense.
>
> (Barth 1969: 14)

If ethnic continuity depends on ascription and the maintenance of a social boundary, then cultural features that signal the boundary may change over time, as may the members' cultural characteristics.

> The critical focus of investigation from this point of view becomes the ethnic boundary that defines the group, not the cultural stuff it encloses.
>
> (Barth 1969: 15)[12]

From Armstrong's point of view, this means that we cannot distinguish 'ethnic' from other types of group in a purely definitional manner.

> The boundary approach clearly implies that ethnicity is a bundle of shifting interactions rather than a nuclear component of social organisation.
>
> (Armstrong 1982: 6)

We must also abandon the idea of every ethnic community occupying an exclusive territory; and this in turn means that ethnicity is part of a continuum of social collectivities, especially classes and religious bodies. Though certain tendencies mark out each of these types of community, over long time periods, each of these may transmute into one of the others. The dividing line between class and ethnicity is sharper, but also harder to define than that between religion and ethnicity. However, lower classes in themselves rarely constitute ethnic collectivities; they lack an elite with the necessary skills in communications and bargaining, and so are unable to maintain a distinct identity within a larger polity (*ibid.*: 6–7).

For John Armstrong, as for Barth, symbols are crucial to the survival of ethnic identification, because they act as 'border guards' distinguishing 'us' from 'them'. But symbols such as words act as signals both to others outside and to members of the group, and so symbolic interaction is always a type of communication, with symbols as the content and communication the means by which they become effective. The content of symbols, such as linguistic 'border guards', is often established generations before they act as cues to group members; that is why 'ethnic symbolic communication is communication over the *longue durée*, between the dead and the living' (*ibid.*: 8).

As important as symbols are legitimising myths. Symbols usually persist because they are incorporated in a mythic structure, and over long periods of time

> the legitimising power of individual mythic structures tend to be enhanced by fusion with other myths in a *mythomoteur* defining identity in relation to a specific polity.
>
> (*ibid.*: 8–9)

The recital of myths can engender an intense awareness among group members of their 'common fate', by which is meant the extent to which an episode

> arouses intense affect by stressing individuals' solidarity against an alien force, that is, by enhancing the salience of boundary perceptions.
>
> (*ibid.*: 9)

A framework of national emergence

Myth, symbol and communication, then, are the three major components in any attempt to analyse the persistence of ethnic identities in pre-modern periods. It is impossible, argues Armstrong, to present a single coherent theory of ethnogenesis, and more broadly, ethnic and national identity, except at a purely abstract and very general level. Instead, we can only isolate recurrent cultural, social, political and economic factors, and try to build up a picture of the patterns of influences which bear on the rise and persistence of such collective cultural identities, proceeding from the broadest and most long-term to the most circumscribed and immediate. Here I can only summarise the main points of Armstrong's argument.

Perhaps the broadest of all factors, but also the most general and hence remote, concerns different ways of life. The most striking thing here is not material attributes, but mental attitudes. Of these, the most important are different kinds of nostalgia, defined as 'a persistent image of a superior way of life in the distant past' (*ibid.*: 16). Two kinds of nostalgia for a lost 'golden age' are historically significant: nomadic attachment for the vast expanses of the desert, typified in the Arab idea of paradise as shady, watered oases with date-palms – despite Islam's urban setting – or the Central Asian ideal of luxuriant pasture with cool mountain conifers. Compare this with the European, and Christian, peasant ideal of secure, tranquil plots of earth, derived from semi-nomadic Jewish roots and the pastoral background of Indo-European peoples such as the Greeks and Romans who sought compact territorial settlements. This contrast between nomadic and sedentary lifestyles and nostalgias found its cultural counterpart in the two main principles of social organisation: the genealogical which was characteristic of the Middle East, and the territorial which was most highly developed in Europe (*ibid.*: ch. 2).

These contrasts tended to be reinforced, with some variations, by the creeds of medieval Christendom and Islam, which provided legitimising myths and symbols for two great civilisations.

> Indeed, their common origins, as well as their geographical proximity, made the Islamic and the Christian civilisations the major negative reference points for one another. In this respect, the two civilisations resembled on a grand scale ethnic groups that commonly define themselves by reference to out-groups.
>
> (*ibid.*: 90)

Armstrong them explores the legacies of different types of city and empire and the effect of their legal systems and especially their universal myths, derived ultimately from Mesopotamian models, for the persistence of ethnic identities. As important to these empires as their economic and military power was their legitimising constitutive political myth, or *mythomoteur*. The growth of capital cities and centralised administrations has been critical to the diffusion of such *mythomoteurs* and the penetration of 'myth-symbol complexes' in wider populations.

This part of the analysis is predicated on Armstrong's belief that politics, notably state formation, was critical in ethnic evolution, though it could never be a sufficient condition, and care must be taken not to ascribe causal roles to earlier institutions that bear superficial resemblances to those familiar in our own time (*ibid.*: 129).

As important for Armstrong are religious organisations. This is especially clear in the archetypal diasporas of the Jews and Armenians, with their relatively decentralised ecclesiastical organisation, which has been as effective in penetrating the population in symbolic communication as the more hierarchical organisations of the established churches or the Islamic courts and ulema. Heretical sects and diasporas also illustrate the way in which ethnoreligious identities were as crucial for preserving ethnic identities as language (*ibid.*: ch. 7).

Indeed, the two main diaspora cases demonstrate how sacral language is separable from everyday vernaculars, and how language itself functions as a marker and symbol of ethnicity, at least within the major 'fault lines' of language groups (Slav, Latin and Germanic). Language as a definer of ethnic boundaries may therefore be regarded as a product of the interplay of other factors.

> In other words, in the long run politics and religion have been the independent variables in the linguistic interaction within each European language family. For somewhat different reasons and with considerably different effects, politics and religion also constituted the principle formative variables in Islam.
>
> (*ibid.*: 282)

In conclusion, Armstrong reiterates his belief in the centrality of myths and symbols in cultural history.

Whatever the ultimate source of the myths, symbols and patterns of communication that constituted ethnic identity, their persistence is impressive.

(*ibid.*: 283)

Armstrong sees ethnic identity as a particular affect phenomenon and a specific value conditioned by the boundary between 'us' and 'them', whereas the great religions have been the major sources of a range of values and value differentiation (*ibid.*: 291). They have also provided much of the myth-symbol content of ethnic identities in Islam and Christendom. Hence Armstrong's typological schema, entitled 'Emergence of national identity', presents a complex matrix of factors influencing the rise of national identity, in which religion and the legitimising myths and *mythomoteurs* it inspires, plays the central role.

Culture and the border

In so bald a summary, it is impossible to do justice to the scope and richness of the historical and sociological materials which John Armstrong presents in his analysis of particular themes and cases, as he compares historical patterns from the medieval Islamic and Christian civilisations. No other work attempts to bring together such a variety of evidence – administrative, legal, military, architectural, religious, linguistic, social and mythological – from which to construct a set of patterns in the slow formation of national identity. Few other works pay such attention to the importance of tracing causal chains over the *longue durée* to disentangle the multiple effects and reciprocal influence of so many factors in the persistence of ethnic identities. In doing so, Armstrong makes a strong case for grounding the emergence of modern national identities on these patterns of ethnic persistence, and especially on the long-term influence of 'myth-symbol complexes'. This represents, by implication, a powerful rebuttal of the more extreme modernist views that reject any connections between modern nations and nationalism and earlier ethnic identities.[13]

This does not mean that Armstrong has given us a complete, alternative 'grand narrative' to that of the modernists. It is indeed doubtful that he would aspire to do so. It is vain, therefore, to look to him for an alternative 'theory' of the kind that Gellner offered, or indeed for a single line of argument through his taxonomy of historical factors. For those in search of *a single* theory, that may be a criticism. For others, it is a virtue, since it sensitises us to the vast range of influences that go into the making and persistence of cultural identities, and thereby puts us on our guard against the temptation to think of ethnicity as something infinitely malleable and 'inventable'.

Nevertheless, in a sense, Armstrong has provided, if not a theory, then a definite perspective from which to judge and research the rise and persistence of both ethnic and national identities. We may regret that he has not sought to detail the differences between pre-modern ethnic and modern national identities or the part played by nationalist ideologies in those differences. This is liable to cause confusion, and to raise questions about the influence of 'retrospective nationalism' and the danger against which Armstrong himself had cautioned, of conflating the effects of earlier collectivities which bear only superficial or very general resemblances to later ones.

There are other, more serious, problems. They spring from John Armstrong's peculiar combination of Barth's transactionalism and the phenomenological approach to social attitudes over the *longue durée*. One problem concerns the difficulty of reconciling a description of ethnic identities as 'affect phenomena', clusters of attitudes and bundles of shifting interactions, with the many examples of ethnic communities that have survived over the centuries, and even millennia. In his concern to recognise the fluctuations of attitudes and sentiments that members of ethnic groups display, Armstrong opts for a phenomenological approach which may be useful in delineating the mixed and changing ethnic identities of the modern West, but is less suited to the much slower rhythms of ethnic identification and communication in pre-modern epochs.

It is clear that other factors must be invoked in the very *definition* of ethnicity if we are to explain such long-term persistence. That definition comes near the end of Armstrong's analysis: it is myths, symbols and patterns of communication that 'constitute' ethnic identity, and it is myths, including *mythomoteurs*, that entrench sets of values and symbols over long time-spans (*ibid.*: 283). But this raises a further problem, this time for the Barthian framework which Armstrong has adopted. In fact, Barth's approach is much more 'transactional' than phenomenological; it focuses on the ways in which transactions between ascriptive categories, far from fragmenting and dissolving them, reinforce the social boundary between them. This element is rather underplayed in Armstrong's own analysis, except in relation to the Crusades and religious heresies. But, more important, Fredrik Barth's own approach suggests that ethnic identities cannot be regarded solely, or even mainly, as bundles of shifting interactions and expressions of affect alone; the ascriptive boundary creates an inter-generational as well as inter-ethnic social organisation of identification, and so is not easily subject to alteration by individuals and their attitudes.[14]

In fact, Armstrong supplies what Barth was at pains to reject: the 'cultural stuff' which the border encloses – in the form of myths, symbols and patterns of communication. The fact that these are often broadly (but not wholly) similar in neighbouring ethnic groups does not mean that the border encloses a black box or that 'culture' lacks potency. On the contrary: the myths, memories, symbols, values and patterns of communication that constitute ethnic identity constitute the distinctive elements of culture which the border encloses. This can be appreciated the moment we focus on the boundary mechanisms and ask: what does the border guard? Why is it that people within the border respond to particular signals and recognise certain myths and memories, while the same myths, symbols and memories leave those outside cold and unmoved? Even more, given the ubiquitous presence of the stranger, why is there so much variation in the scope and intensity of arousal of group members' passions?

Symbols represent to particular human groups distinctive shared experiences and values, while myths explain to them the meanings of those experiences and exemplify and illuminate those values. If myths and symbols fail to resonate with the members of the group, it is because they do not, or no longer, perform these functions; they no longer represent, explain and exemplify. Hence they can no longer unite the members of the group, and they are correspondingly weakened and fragmented. Culture, therefore, the meanings and representations of symbols, myths, memories and values, is not some inventory of traits, or a 'stuff' enclosed by the border; culture is both an inter-generational repository and heritage, or set of traditions, and an active shaping repertoire of meanings and images, embodied in values, myths and symbols that serve to unite a group of people with shared experiences and memories, and differentiate them from outsiders. Such a conception supplements the boundary approach and suggests a fuller method for explaining ethnic persistence (see A. D. Smith 1984b).

'Dual legitimation'

If Armstrong reached forward from the distant past to the age of nationalism, my own work has taken the opposite route: working back from the modern epoch of nation-states and nationalism to the earliest manifestations of collective cultural sentiments.

My starting-point was the ideology and movement of nationalism itself. Given the problems of definition in this field, it was necessary to observe certain methodological procedures. The first was to distinguish the various usages of the term 'nationalism', as

1   doctrines or ideologies,
2   movements,
3   sentiments, and
4   processes of 'nation-building', to which later we could add
5   symbols and languages (of nationalism).

The ideology of nationalism itself could be reduced to its essential propositions, and its main tenets summarised:

1   the world is naturally divided into nations, each of which has its pecu-
    liar character and destiny;
2   the nation is the source of all political power, and loyalty to it overrides
    all other loyalties;
3   if they wish to be free, and to realise themselves, men must identify with
    and belong to a nation;
4   global freedom and peace are functions of the liberation and security of
    all nations;
5   nations can only be liberated and fulfilled in their own sovereign states.

(A. D. Smith 1973a: 10)[15]

Thus we might term these propositions the 'core doctrine' of nationalism. In practice, specific nationalisms have added all kinds of secondary ideas and motifs, peculiar to the history and circumstances of each ethnic community or nation.

Next it was important to distinguish 'nationalism', the movement and ideology, from 'national sentiment', feelings on behalf of the welfare and strength of the nation, because one could have elite national*isms* without nations or widely diffused national sentiments, and vice-versa. Third, we should examine the basic ideals of the self-styled nationalists to establish a baseline for working definitions. This allowed one to define ostensively 'nationalism' as

> *an ideological movement for the attainment and maintenance of self-government and independence on behalf of a group, some of whose members conceive it to constitute an actual or potential 'nation'.*

(A. D. Smith 1983a: 171)

Fourth, the 'independence ideal' of nationalism has a number of ideological correlates, including national integration and fraternity, territorial unification, economic autarchy, national expansion, cultural renewal and the accentuation of cultural individuality, and each of these can be selected as the goal of particular nationalisms at various times and in differing degrees. However, three basic leitmotifs can be found in every kind of nationalism: the ideals of national autonomy, national unity and national identity.

Finally, as a first step towards explanation, we need to distinguish different kinds of nationalist movement, and especially between voluntarist and organic varieties, and between territorially grounded and ethnically based nationalisms. Nevertheless, the three ideals of autonomy, unity and identity are always present in all these sub-types. In my view, they could even be traced in the 'ethnocentric' nationalisms of the ancient world, even though the idea of the nation tended to be submerged in other ideals, as well as in the more outward-looking 'polycentric' nationalisms of the modern world.[16]

This attempt to relate nationalism to ethnocentrism suggested a view of the 'nation', as deriving from the 'ancient social formation of the *ethnie*', where the term 'ethnic' represented those elements of a group's culture that derived from its origins and history. In accordance with its etymology, the 'nation' should therefore be defined as

> *a group of human beings, possessing common and distinctive elements of culture, a unified economic system, citizenship rights for all members, a sentiment of solidarity arising out of common experiences, and occupying a common territory.*

(A. D. Smith 1973a: 18, 26)[17]

With the above important proviso, I accepted the modernity of both nations and nationalism, as befitted a student of Ernest Gellner. However, the initial sketch of the origins of ethnic nationalism which I offered stressed the role of political and religious, rather than social and cultural, factors. It argued that the modern epoch is characterised by the rise of the 'scientific state', a state whose efficacy depends on its ability to harness science and technology for collective purposes. The advent of this type of state challenges the legitimacy of religious explanations, and especially the theodicies which they offer in response to human suffering and evil. This gives rise to situations of 'dual legitimation', in which rival grounds of authority dispute for the allegiance of humanity. Particularly affected by this duality are the modern equivalents of pre-modern clerisies, the intellectuals. Typically, they respond to the painful mental dislocations of the 'dual legitimation' situation in one of three ways. The first is 'neo-traditionalist': adopting modern ways and means to reject the authority of the secular state and reassert traditional divine authority. The second response is 'assimilationist', a kind of messianic leap into the secular future, rejecting divine authority for that of the scientific state. The final response is 'revivalist', an attempt to combine in different ways the two kinds of authority, on the basis that 'God works through the scientific state' and that, when tradition is no longer relevant, human reason and divine providence can bring material progress and spiritual salvation. In this schema, the road to a nationalist solution to the deep crisis of dual legitimation is twofold. First, the messianic assimilationists are disappointed, their mobility is blocked and they are rejected by the (Western) scientific state, so they turn back to their ethnic communities and indigenous values. Second, the religious revivalists despair of abstract reason as the essence of a purified religion, and seek in indigenous culture and ethnic 'history', the specific pasts of their ethnic communities, that 'authentic value' which traditional religion no longer possesses and the secular state by itself can never acquire. From this twofold return to an ethnic past springs the desire to determine the course of the community oneself, without outside interference, and so become a 'nation' (A. D. Smith 1983a: ch. 10; 1973a: 86–95).

To this general schema, *The Ethnic Revival* (1981) attempted to add a more rounded picture of the rise of romantic historicism of which nationalism was the political outgrowth, and a fuller account of the reasons why the intellectuals, and more especially the intelligentsia, turned to nationalism as a cure for their status discontents. Basically, the continual overproduction of high-skill professionals by the scientific state and the rigidities of their line bureaucracies, coupled with the contrast between the imperialist rhetoric of impersonal merit and frequent cultural discrimination, meant that highly educated men and women were being turned away from the centres of wealth and power in increasing numbers, and were thereby made available for mobilisation by historicist intellectuals seized by their community's plight (A. D. Smith 1981a: chs 5–6). If we add the tendency for neo-romantic nationalism, of the kind that flourished in Western Europe's 'ethnic revival' of the 1960s and 1970s, to surface as the result of a bureaucratic cycle of centralisation, alienation and fragmentation, followed by a renewed cycle of centralisation and state penetration, the inevitability of the nation and nationalism in an era of bureaucratic modernity becomes assured (A. D. Smith 1979: ch. 7).

However, by the early 1980s, I came to feel that, while this analysis of alienated and deracinated indigenous intelligentsias radicalised by alien bureaucratic states helped to explain part of the phenomenon of nationalism, it signally failed to account for the broader social picture or explain the configurations of nations and the incidence and intensity of nationalisms. Its rather intellectualist analysis of the elites' movement towards nationalism, from abstract 'reason' to ethnic 'history', hardly explained the passion with which they and their followers embraced indigenous 'history' and culture. Moreover, emphasis on intellectuals and elites obscured the broad, often cross-class nature of the movement and the national attachments of middle and lower strata. Such a 'top-down' modernism failed to do justice to the constraints on elite action and the limits on intellectual 'construction' set by popular ideas and culture. Finally, by using the same term 'nationalism' for both, I had overlooked the real ideological differences between ancient religious motifs and modern political ideologies, while obscuring the possible links between ancient and modern social formations. 'Ethnocentric nationalism' did not mark out a type peculiar to pre-modern epochs, and it assumed an ideological similarity across the ages which could not be supported by historical evidence. The problem, and its resolution, lay elsewhere.[18]

Ethnies and ethno-symbolism

In effect, what was needed was an historical sociology of nations and nationalism. In terms of ideologies, the specific concepts and movements of national*ism* could be fairly securely dated to the later eighteenth century, even if there were earlier religious nationalisms in England and Holland. But in terms of national structures, sentiments and symbolism, the picture was much more complicated. It was possible to trace examples of all three, in sufficient and well documented quantities, back to at least the late medieval period in a number of European nations from England and France to Poland and Russia. Here was evidence of *some measure* of *national continuity*. But more important, it was possible to find examples of social formations in pre-modern periods, even in antiquity, that for some decades or even centuries approximated to an inclusive definition of the concept of the 'nation', notably among the ancient Jews and Armenians, but also to some extent among the ancient Egyptians, and perhaps the medieval Japanese and Koreans. In other words, the concept of the 'nation' was perennial, insofar as *recurrent instances* of this formation could be found in various periods of history and in different continents. Here, then, one could speak of *national recurrence* (see Greenfeld 1992: chs 1–3; A. D. Smith 1994; cf. Lang 1980; Lehmann 1982).

Though hardly sufficient to undermine the modernist paradigm, these examples seemed to cast doubt on Gellner's insistence on the impossibility of nations in pre-modern periods. But there was a further problem. Throughout history and in several continents, there was considerable evidence, not just of 'objective' cultural (linguistic, religious, etc.) differences and categories, but of 'subjective' ethnic identities and ethnic communities, many of them locked into paired antagonisms. Again, one could point to both *ethnic continuity* and *ethnic recurrence*. Greeks, Armenians, Jews, Persians, Chinese and Japanese could be cited as examples of ethnic continuity, since, despite massive cultural changes over the centuries, certain key identifying components – name, language, customs, religious community and territorial association – were broadly maintained and reproduced for millennia. In other cases, such as the peoples of Ethiopia, the Fertile Crescent, northern India and the Balkans, ethnicity has been more of a recurrent phenomenon. That is to say, these regions have seen a succession of often well defined and well documented ethnic communities, with different groups forming, flourishing and being dissolved, usually through conquest, absorption or fragmentation (see Wiseman 1973; Ullendorff 1973; A. D. Smith 1981b, 1986a: chs 2–5).

In the light of these considerations, the focus of my analysis began to shift from nationalisms to nations, and from nations to ethnic communities. The study of *ethnies* (the French term for 'ethnic communities') became central to the understanding of why and where particular nations are formed, and why nationalisms, though formally alike, possess such distinctive features and contents. The focus of this analysis was the role of myths, memories, values, traditions and symbols. Already in *The Ethnic Revival*, I singled out

> the myth of a common and unique origin in time and place that is essential for the sense of ethnic community, since it marks the foundation point of the group's history, and hence its individuality.
>
> (A. D. Smith 1981a: 66)

Symbols, too – emblems, hymns, festivals, habitats, customs, linguistic codes, sacred places and the like – were powerful differentiators and reminders of the unique culture and fate of the ethnic community. So were shared memories of key events and epochs in the history of the community: memories of liberation, migration, the golden age (or ages), of victories and defeats, of heroes and saints and sages. So, in *The Ethnic Origins of Nations* (1986), ethnic communities (*ethnies*) were defined as

> *named human populations with shared ancestry myths, histories and cultures, having an association with a specific territory, and a sense of solidarity.*
>
> (A. D. Smith 1986a: 32)

and their main components – collective name, myth of ancestry, historical memories, shared cultural elements, association with a homeland, and (partial) collective sentiments – were explored (*ibid.*: 22–32).[19]

In the ancient and medieval worlds, ethnicity played a much larger role than modernists, who rightly rejected the conflation of earlier collective cultural identities with modern nations and nationalisms, were willing to concede. There were ethnic minorities, diaspora communities, frontier *ethnies*, ethnic amphictyonies and even ethnic states, states dominated by particular ethnic communities such as ancient Egypt or early medieval Japan. In particular, the role of ethnic cores of empires such as the Assyrian had to be distinguished from that of peripheral *ethnies*, and the chances of survival of each assessed. The problem of ethnic survival seemed particularly important for later nationalisms: the ability to call on a rich and well documented 'ethno-history' was to prove a major cultural resource for nationalists, and myths of origins, ethnic election and sacred territories, as well as memories of heroes and golden ages, were crucial to the formulation of a many-stranded ethno-history. All this points to the importance of social memory; as the example of the relationship between modern and ancient Greeks shows,

> *ethnies* are constituted, not by lines of physical descent, but by the sense of continuity, shared memory and collective destiny, i.e. by lines of cultural affinity embodied in myths, memories, symbols and values retained by a given cultural unit of population.
>
> (A. D. Smith 1991: 29; cf. A. D. Smith 1992a)

This also reveals the distance between my 'historical ethno-symbolic' type of analysis and any version of primordialism. It is the sense of cultural affinities, rather than physical kinship ties, embodied in a *myth* of descent, shared historical memories and ethnic symbolism, that defines the structure of ethnic communities; and the same is true for any nations created on the basis of cultural affinity.[20]

In line with Armstrong's perspective, but without his specific phenomenological analysis, I came to see clusters of myths, symbols, memories, values and traditions, emerging from the shared experiences of several generations of cohabiting populations, as the defining cultural elements from which ethnic groups emerged. On the other hand, their crystallisation as self-aware *communities*, as opposed to other-defined ethnic *categories*, was the product of external factors such as folk cultures resulting from shared work and residence patterns; group mobilisation in periodic inter-state warfare producing memories and myths of defeat and victory; and especially the impact of organised religions with scriptures, sacred languages and communal priesthoods. From time to time, outside attacks on the homelands or customs of the community could inspire a heightened ethnicism, and a determined ethnic resistance, as occurred among some Greeks at the time of the Persian invasions or among some Jews under the hellenisation policies of the Seleucid monarch Antiochus Epiphanes IV. But on the whole, ethnicity in pre-modern periods was not normally the basis of alternative polity formation, except where it combined with religion (A. D. Smith 1986a: 32–41).[21]

As John Armstrong points out, this was to alter significantly in the modern world. Here the modernists make an important point. It was the revolutionary nature of the economic, administrative and cultural transformations of seventeenth- and eighteenth-century Europe that brought culture and ethnic identity to the fore as a basis for polity formation. But the origins of such a transformation can, in some cases, be traced even further back than the growth of vernacular printed literature stemming from Gutenberg and Luther's Bible. A recent study of elite Scottish identity found that the crucial moment came in the reflective aftermath of Bannockburn and the Wars with England, with the rise of a distinctive ethno-history in historical and literary writings of the late fourteenth and fifteenth centuries. The same is true of the early formation of Swiss national identity. Its foundations in the Rütli Oath and Tell exploits were first recorded in *The White Book of Sarnen* (c. 1470) and subsequent writings. In these and other cases, we can trace the beginnings of an elite nationalism, and of the coalescence and gradual transformation of ethnic communities into early nations (Webster 1997; Im Hof 1991).[22]

Origins and types of nation

How then is this transformation effected? Basically, there are two routes in the formation of nations, and they depend on the kind of ethnic community that served as their point of departure.
Of the two kinds of pre-modern *ethnie*,

> The first is lateral and extensive, the second is vertical and intensive. In the first, we find communities that rarely penetrate deep in the social scale, but extend in ragged and imprecise fashion in space. Typically, 'lateral' *ethnie* are aristocratic, though usually clerical and scribal strata are included, along with some of the wealthier urban merchants. Equally typically, 'vertical' *ethnie* are urban-based, priestly, trading and artisan in their composition, with their ruling strata often thrown up from the wealthy and powerful factions in the towns; alternatively, they are loose coalitions of tribesmen under their clan chiefs, united for battle and later amalgamating, or coexisting with a dominant if primitive state and its monarch. In either case, the bond that unites them is of a more intensive and exclusive kind than among the lateral, aristocratic *ethnie*; hence its often marked religious, even missionary, quality.
>
> (A. D. Smith 1986a: 77–8)

The first route to nationhood, that of *bureaucratic incorporation*, involves the transformation of a loose, aristocratic *ethnie* into a territorial nation. The upper-class members of most lateral *ethnies* had no interest in imbuing their middle classes, let alone their subject lower classes, with their own ethnic culture. But, perhaps because of the failure to recreate the (Holy) Roman empire in Western Europe, the ensuing competition between the various monarchs and courts of France, England and Spain forced them to mobilise their urban middle classes, if only to extract their wealth, in order to wage war and display their pomp, as Henry VIII and Francis I did so conspicuously on the Field of the Cloth of Gold. Inadvertently at first, they drew their middle classes into an increasingly accented, territorialised and politicised 'national' culture, i.e. one that, from being a preserve of the court, the aristocracy and the clergy, became a culture of 'the people', at first identified with the urban middle classes, but some centuries later with the mass of working men and, later, women. The result has been a more 'civic' type of national identity, fuelled by a largely territorial nationalism, although assimilating ethnic and cultural elements are usually to be found in even the most ardent civic nationalisms, such as the republican nationalism in France (A. D. Smith 1995a: ch. 4; cf. Corrigan and Sayer 1985).

In these cases, it was the bureaucratic state itself which forged the nation, gradually penetrating to outlying regions from the ethnic core and down the social scale. The second route to nationhood we may term one of *vernacular mobilisation*. Here a demotic *ethnie* is transformed largely under the aegis of an indigenous intelligentsia into an ethnic nation. In Central and Eastern Europe, and later in the Middle and Far East, and parts of Africa, native intellectuals and professionals rediscovered and reappropriated a selective ethno-history out of the pre-existing myths, symbols and traditions to be found in the historical record and in the living memories of 'the people', the mainly rural lower strata. This latterday return to an 'ethnic past' (or pasts) is a corollary of the nationalist quest for 'authenticity'. Only that which can be shown to be 'genuine' and 'ours' can form the basis for a national identity, and that in turn requires a cultivation of indigenous history and vernacular languages and cultures, and the *vernacular mobilisation* of 'the people' in and through their own history and culture. The result is a type of nation founded on 'ethnic' conceptions, and fuelled by a genealogical nationalism; although even here, the nation, as in Germany or Greece, is simultaneously defined in territorial and political terms and minorities are, albeit more precariously, admitted (A. D. Smith 1989; cf. Kitromilides 1989; Brubaker 1992).

There is, in fact, a third route in the formation of nations which consist largely of immigrant fragments of other *ethnies*, particularly those from overseas. In the United States, Canada and Australia, colonist-immigrants have pioneered a providentialist frontier nationalism; and once large waves of culturally different immigrants were admitted, this has encouraged a 'plural' conception of the nation, which accepts, and even celebrates, ethnic and cultural diversity within an overarching political, legal and linguistic national identity (A. D. Smith 1995a: ch. 4; cf. Hutchinson 1994: ch. 6).

Of course, none of these routes ensures the automatic attainment of nation-hood. To begin with, it depends on the degree to which the great modern revolutions of market capitalism, the bureaucratic state and secular, mass educa-tion have penetrated given areas and communities, either directly, as in the West, or through the mediation of imperialism and colonialism (A. D. Smith 1986a: 130–4). Nor should we forget the role of historical accident in specific cases of nation-formation. More generally, human agency, individual and collective, has been vital in the process of uniting *ethnies* and transforming them into nations. Kings, ministers, generals, merchants, priests, missionaries, lawyers, artists, intel-lectuals, educators, journalists and many others have contributed to the formation of particular nations, now more consciously and deliberately, now unintentionally. Among these groups, modern nationalist leaders and their followers have often played a disproportionate role; as 'political archaeologists' they have furnished blueprints of the 'nation-to-be' by rediscovering an 'authentic' popular ethno-history and providing convincing narratives of historical continuity with a heroic, and preferably glorious, ethnic past. By their quest for heroic legends and poetic landscapes, the nationalists aim to provide cognitive 'maps' and public 'moralities' for the members of their nation-to-be (A. D. Smith 1986a: ch. 8; A. D. Smith 1995b; cf. Just 1989).

If nationalism is modern and shapes nations in the image of its *weltanschauung*, then nations too are the creations of modernity. But this is only half the story. Specific nations are also the product of older, often pre-modern ethnic ties and ethno-histories. Not all nations, of course. There are 'nations-in-the-making' (Tanzania, Eritrea, Libya) that are relatively recent and do not appear to be rooted in a longer ethnic past. One may ask how firmly based and secure are these colonial creations; certainly, the recent experience of other African 'state-nations' does not give grounds for optimism. But the real point is that the first and most influential examples of the concept of the 'nation' did have such pre-modern grounding, as have a great many others, and they provided the basic models, civic and ethnic, for later examples, even if the stages of attaining nationhood have been telescoped and even inverted.

The nation, then, as concept and ideal formation, is historically firmly embedded; and so, in varying degrees, are its most influential and successful exemplars. In our day, the nation has become the norm of social and political organisation, and nationalism the most ubiquitous of ideologies. Attempts to construct supra-national unions have to date failed to attract the passions and loyalties commanded by nations; even a European 'identity'

> has looked pale and shifting beside the entrenched cultures and heritages that make up its rich mosaic.
>
> If 'nationalism is love', to quote Michel Aflaq, a passion that demands overwhelming commitment, the abstraction of 'Europe' competes on unequal terms with the tangibility and 'rootedness' of each nation.
>
> (A. D. Smith 1995a: 131)

As for the predictions of a global culture, they fail to take into account the rootedness of cultures in time and place, and the ways in which identity depends on memory. A truly non-imperial 'global culture', timeless, placeless, technical and affectively neutral, must be memory-less and hence identity-less; or fall into a postmodern pastiche of existing national cultures and so disintegrate into its component parts. To date, we cannot discern a serious rival to the nation for the affections and loyalties of most human beings (A. D. Smith 1990; 1995a: ch. 1).

Ethno-symbolism considered

On one level, this account is an empirical tautology, in that my definitions of the nation and of the *ethnie* are closely aligned. It is, then, not difficult to show nations being based on, and being created out of, pre-existing *ethnies*. At least, some nations. There is, of course, no necessity about this transformation; otherwise, national*ism* and nationalists would be superfluous. But they are not. Hence, we are dealing with something more than an interesting empirical tautology. It is exactly those features of nations that *ethnies* lack – a clearly delimited territory or 'homeland', a public culture, economic unity and legal rights and duties for everyone – that make nations ultimately quite different from *ethnies*, despite the fact that both possess such features as an identifying name, myths of common origins and shared historical memories. These differences need to be kept in mind when considering the ways in which, as Hastings so clearly shows, nations transcend ethnic communities, and can in principle include more than one culture-community (Hastings 1997: 25–31).

A more serious objection is that levelled at the versions of perennialism I considered in the last chapter, namely that ethno-symbolism is guilty of 'retrospective nationalism', of projecting back onto earlier social formations the features peculiar to nations and nationalisms. But this is to confuse a concern with *la longue durée* with perennialism. Armstrong may use the terminology of 'nation' for pre-modern *ethnies*, but he clearly differentiates modern nations from these earlier ethnic identities. Hutchinson reserves the term 'nation' for the modern period and, like myself, he clearly separates off a modern nationalism from pre-modern ethnic sentiments. The differences in historical context are too great to permit such retrospective generalisation. The 'family analogy' in nationalism which Connor, for example, rightly emphasises is not central to the concerns of ethno-symbolists; kinship affords too narrow a social base for larger *ethnies*, let alone nations. Rather, it is a question of tracing in the historical record the often discontinuous formation of national identities back to their pre-existing cultural foundations and ethnic ties – which is a matter for empirical investigation rather than *a priori* theorising.

A more recent criticism of my position, brought by John Breuilly, is that it assumes too close a connection between pre-modern ethnic identities and modern nations and neglects the necessary role of institutions as historical carriers of national or ethnic identities. Pre-modern ethnic identities, he argues, are essentially local and apolitical.

> The problem with identity established outside institutions, especially those institutions which can bind together people across wide social and geographical spaces, is that it is necessarily fragmentary, discontinuous and elusive.
>
> (Breuilly 1996: 151)

In contrast to such kinship-based ethnic identities, only those carried by institutions like dynasties or churches could have their 'myth-symbol' complexes codified and reproduced. However, dynasties were actually threatened by modern national identities and churches were universalist. Only when their universal mission had failed did they accomodate to ethnic identities and furnish rallying-points for later movements of national autonomy. On the whole, claims Breuilly, the *discontinuities* of ethnic sentiments with 'modern national identity' are more striking. This is as true of the invention of myths, such as the epic of Ossian, as of the codification of written languages and their institutional uses in law, the polity and the economy. As long as language is simply a repository of national culture, myth and memory, it has significance only for a few self-selected cultural elites; only when it is used for legal, economic, political and educational purposes, does it have real political significance. Breuilly concludes:

> Pre-modern ethnic identity has little in the way of institutional embodiment beyond the local level. Almost all the major institutions which construct, preserve and transmit national identities, and which connect those identities to interests, are modern: parliaments, popular literature, courts, schools, labour markets, et cetera. . . . National identity is essentially modern, and any useful approach to the subject must begin from this premiss.
>
> (*ibid.*: 154)

That institutions are important as carriers and preservers of collective cultural identities is indisputable; if nothing else, Armstrong's monumental work demonstrates their crucial role in pre-modern epochs. But I would argue that Breuilly's understanding of such 'institutions' is narrowly modernist. It is quite true that many people in pre-modern epochs were not included in 'institutions' to the extent that they are in the modern state and its organs. But significant numbers of people in several pre-modern societies were included, going back to ancient Egypt and Sumer: in schools, for instance, in legal institutions, in temples and monasteries, sometimes even in representative political institutions, not to mention extended aristocratic families like the Alcmaeonids or the Metelli. But perhaps more important was their inclusion in linguistic codes and in popular literature, in rituals and celebrations, in trade fairs and markets, and in ethnic territories or 'homelands', not to mention the corvée and army service. Certainly, not all these 'institutions' reinforced a straightforward sense of ethnic identity, but many did. Breuilly himself concedes that

> ethnic identity does have some meaning in past times and that it can impose limits upon claims made in modern nationalism.
>
> (*ibid.*: 150)

I would add there are many more cases of vivid ethnic identities in pre-modern periods than he allows, and some of them do have 'political significance', such as the ethnic states of hellenistic antiquity (see Tcherikover 1970; Wiseman 1973; Mendels 1992).

The question that John Breuilly, like Eric Hobsbawm, raises is whether even widespread ethnic identities can have any connection with modern nationalism. By stressing only its modern features, Breuilly necessarily widens the gap between the modern nation and pre-modern ethnicity. But the historical evidence is often contradictory; it can point to clear links with modern nationalisms, and not just because latterday nationalists sincerely believed in and needed a usable ethnic past. The basic point is the one I raised in connection with Hobsbawm's account: the 'inventions' of modern nationalists must resonate with large numbers of the designated 'co-nationals', otherwise the project will fail. If they are not perceived as 'authentic', in the sense of having meaning and resonance with 'the people' to whom they are addressed, they will fail to mobilise them for political action. Better, then, to 'rediscover' and reappropriate an ethnic past or pasts that mean something to the people in question, and so reconstruct anew an existing ethnic identity, even where it appears shadowy and ill documented.

Clearly, Breuilly has raised an important issue when he challenges ethno-symbolists to provide the historical links with the past ethnic identities and communities which they postulate as the basis for the formation of subsequent nations. There is clearly much work to be done here. But it requires a broader conception of the channels through which such identities are transmitted and transformed, and of the links which bind them to modern nations. Only then will we be able to gauge the depth of the ties that bind the members of nations and the passions which such ties can arouse. In this task, we should not dismiss the evidence provided by the intense nationalist concern with the 'heroic legends' of antiquity, and with the 'poetic spaces' of the homeland. They point us in directions which reveal the religious foundations of nationalism and the often sacred status of its concerns (see Hooson 1994; A. D. Smith 1997a, 1997b).

9   Beyond Modernism?

In his 1986 lectures entitled *Polyethnicity and National Unity in World History*, the great world historian William H. McNeill argued that nations and nationalism are phenomena peculiar to a particular period of history, the age of Western modernity, and that just as in pre-modern ages nations and nationalism were unknown, so in the future we shall witness the demise of the nation and the withering away of nationalism. It was only in a short, but vividly documented period of modern European history, from about 1789 to 1945, that the ideal of national unity held sway, and the nation-state became accepted as the political norm. Before and after, the norm was not national unity, but polyethnic hierarchy.

Polyethnicity, past and future

For McNeill, only barbarism is monoethnic. The moment we reach the stage of civilisation, polyethnicity becomes the norm. The reasons are relatively straightforward. Civilisation is largely metropolitan, so centres of wealth and power require many kinds of skilled labour, and attract envious outsiders. Military, demographic and economic reasons support the polyethnic character of urban civilisation. After the 'cavalry revolution' of the early first millennium BC, we find a common pattern of conquest of civilised societies by nomadic tribesmen. Frequent epidemics among concentrated urban populations also encouraged urban polyethnicity, since depleted centres continually need to be replenished by rural populations to meet labour needs. Finally, long-distance trade gave rise to far-flung, alien merchant communities, often with their own portable religions. The overall result was that pre-modern civilisations with labour specialisation were necessarily culturally pluralist and soon bred ethnic hierarchies of skill; only those populations and polities far removed from the centres of civilisation like Japan, and perhaps England, Denmark and Sweden, could retain their ethnic homogeneity (McNeill 1986: ch. 1).

It was only after about 1700 that the ideal of independence for ethnically homogeneous populations, or nations, emerged. This was the result of a confluence of four factors. The first, and least important, was the influence of classical humanism, and hence the models of civic solidarity found in classical city-states like Athens, Sparta and republican Rome, which captured the imaginations of humanist intellectuals. More important was the growth of reading publics, versed in standardised forms of vernacular languages, which formed the elite basis of future nations. To this we must add the rapid growth of population in Western Europe, which allowed depleted cities to be replenished by ethnically homogeneous migrants from the countryside, and in the process fuelled revolutionary discontent among superfluous labour. Finally, and perhaps most important, was the new emphasis on modern infantry drill, which from this period became increasingly allied to state power, and by encouraging military participation on a large scale, also induced a new sense of civic solidarity and fraternity. McNeill argues that all these factors 'came together in western Europe at the close of the eighteenth century to give birth to modern nationalism', first in France and then throughout Europe. Although ethnic pluralism remained the social norm even in Western Europe, no state could henceforth afford to be without a 'national identity', for the unitary nation state and 'the myth of national brotherhood and ethnic unity' justified self-sacrifice in national wars, sustained public peace domestically and strengthened the state and the hand of government in everyday life (*ibid.*: 51, 56).

All this came apart after 1945. Two world wars revealed the immense costs of nation-states and nationalism. Revulsion against Nazi barbarism and the huge military sacrifices, was followed by a realisation that no nation-state could prosecute such a total war alone. They had to coordinate their efforts, and in the process draft in thousands of ethnically heterogenous soldiers and labourers, free or enslaved. This set the precedent for the flow of *Gastarbeiter* from alien cultures and lands; with higher birth rates and access to mass communications, these ethnic enclaves were able to perpetuate themselves on Western soil. In addition, the emergence of vast transnational companies and the internationalisation of military command structures have severely curtailed the autarchy of even the richest and most powerful nation-states. All this has undermined the power and the unity of 'nation-states', and presages the pluralisation of nations. For McNeill, once again, 'Polyethnic hierarchy is on the rise, everywhere'. Nations and nationalism are transitory phenomena, reversions to a barbarian ideal of ethnic purity which is crumbling before our eyes because of the urgent need for adequate supplies of alien skilled labour. Only a moment in the much-read histories of the classical city-states made it appear otherwise (*ibid.*: 82).

In fact, for NcNeill as for many others, this short aberrant period of national unity is really only a matter of ideology; the social reality was always that of polyethnic hierarchy, even in the nation-states of Western Europe. One is left wondering how the nationalist mirage was created, and why so few people saw through it.

But the point I want to concentrate on here is McNeill's prognosis of a return to polyethnic hierarchy at the cost of national unity, that is, through the breakdown of the nation-state and nationalism. McNeill appears to assume that the nation-state and its nationalism is the antithesis of polyethnic hierarchy, although in practice, as he himself demonstrates, they are coextensive, if not symbiotic.

But this is to forget the 'onion character' of ethnicity, its capacity for forging 'concentric circles' of identity and loyalty, the wider circle encompassing the narrower. This is not the same as the much-spoken-of 'multiple identities'. The latter often create competition and rivalry for people's loyalties; class, region, religion, gender, ethnicity all create identities and loyalties that may cut across each other. Whereas ethnicity can operate at several levels, the wider identity and community encompassing the narrower, so that a person may be equally and harmoniously a member of a clan, an ethnic group, a national state, even a pan-national federation: a member of a tartan clan, a Scot, a Briton and a European.[1]

If this was the case in the 'age of nationalism', according to McNeill, might it not continue to operate, even within the more continental and global contexts of the next century? This is just as plausible a scenario as the imminent breakdown of the nation-state into its constituent ethnic parts. In other words, it is too easy to assume a zero-sum relationship between ethnicity and nationalism, the *ethnie* and the nation. Such a relationship needs to be tested empirically in each case, and the conditions for the relationship specified.

The post-national agenda

McNeill's tripartite periodisation of history – pre-modern polyethnic hierarchy, modern national unity and postmodern polyethnicity – provides the historical setting for the main themes of discussion and research on nations and nationalism in the last decade. These themes include:

1   the impact of current population movements on the prospects of the national state, and especially the fragmentation of national identity and the rise of multiculturalism;
2   the impact of feminist analysis and issues of gender on the nature of national projects, identities and communities, and the role of gendered symbolism and women's collective self-assertion;
3   the predominantly normative and political debate on the consequences for citizenship and liberty of civic and ethnic types of nationalism, and their relations with liberal democracy;
4   and the impact of globalisation trends, and of 'postmodern' supranational projects, on national sovereignty and national identity.[2]

With the exception of gender issues, each of these themes is prefigured and encompassed by McNeill's world-historical framework. Even the changed role of women and the impact of gender divisions can be viewed, on this reading, as the final extension of a 'post-national' citizenship to the largest and most underprivileged, because hitherto invisible, 'minority', as a result of the pressing needs for skilled labour in civilised polyethnic societies. Immigration and hybridisation; processes of globalisation and supra-nationalism; and the transition to a looser, civic form of liberal nationalism; all these issues and debates can be seen to form elements in that trend to re-establish polyethnic hierarchies portrayed by McNeill.

Here I can only touch on the most salient of these issues, and try to show that, while they ostensibly turn their backs, not only on modernism, but on all large-scale narratives and higher-level theorising, these discussions and debates, and the research they have spawned, constitute in reality one part (the last epoch) of that larger framework which McNeill's analysis exemplifies. Theirs is an analysis which attempts to go beyond the modernist paradigm of nations and nationalism, and reveal its necessary supersession alongside the decomposition of its objects of reference, that is, the nation and nationalism. Yet in going beyond modernism they do not mean to challenge its assumption of the modernity of nations and nationalism. The 'postmodernist turn' does not seek to overturn the modernist paradigm, as does perennialism; nor does it seek to revise the modernist analysis 'from within', by revealing the debts of the modern nation to pre-modern ethnic ties, in the manner of the ethno-symbolists. Rather, it seeks to extend the range of modernism to what it sees as a 'postmodern' phase of social development. But in doing so it subtly undermines and problematises some of the basic assumptions of modernism, notably its belief in the sociological reality of nations, and the power of nationalist ideologies.

The underlying leitmotif of the most recent phase of theorising in the field of ethnicity and nationalism, which we may very loosely call 'postmodern', is that of cultural and political fragmentation coupled, in varying degrees, with economic globalisation. Let me try to sketch this leitmotif in each of the themes listed above.

Fragmentation and hybrid identities

Of course, Anderson's analysis of the literary tropes and devices which sustain the narratives of 'nation-ness' foreshadowed the uses of deconstructionist techniques in the analysis of ethnic and national phenomena. For many his example has served as the inspiration, and point of departure, for their own more radical application of these techniques. For Homi Bhabha, for example, the very idea of a 'national identity' has become problematic. That idea had first emerged in the totalising project of the Enlightenment which sought to incorporate all being, including the Other. Hence the nationalist narratives of the national self (which was, in fact, always constructed and defined by the Other, the significant outsider) always claimed to incorporate the Other and purported to create total cultural homogeneity. But such a claim is fictitious. Cultural difference is irreducible, and it reveals the hybrid quality and ambivalence of national identity in every state (Bhabha 1990).

For Bhabha, national identities are composed of narratives of 'the people', and they operate under a 'doubled' and 'split' signifier – split between past and present, the self and the other, and above all between pedagogical and performative narratives. This superimposed dualism fragments the nation. The received versions of national identity inculcated by the nationalists are always challenged and decomposed into their component cultural parts by the alternative narratives based on the actions and performances of members of the designated community. In the manner of Simmel, Homi Bhabha directs our attention to the impact of the stranger and the outsider in defining the national identity of the host group. Only here the host is an imperialist national community, acting as magnet to the ex-colonised. The great influx of ex-colonials, immigrants, *Gastarbeiter* and asylum-seekers has eroded the bases of traditional narratives and images of a homogeneous national identity, revealing their fragmented and hybrid character. Today, every collective cultural identity has become plural. Housed in 'anxious states', national identities have become precarious and hybridised, as they face in different directions. Composed of cultural elements from the ex-colonial periphery, which are neither able nor willing to be incorporated and assimilated, national identities have fragmented and lost their erstwhile hold on people (*ibid.*: ch. 16).

A similar emphasis on the importance of the cultural fragment, and the irreducibility of its experience and testimony, can be found in the work of Partha Chatterjee. In general, he is concerned with the relationship between the hegemonic nationalist discourses of the West which for Benedict Anderson provide 'modular' forms for pirating by nationalist elites in Asia and Africa, and the indigenous nationalisms created by those non-Western elites. In his earlier work Chatterjee had demonstrated how, typically, the nationalist discourses of Asia and Africa both derived from Western models and at the same time opposed a 'material' outer world dominated by the West and the colonial state, to an inner, 'spiritual' domain which was the preserve of the national culture being created by indigenous elites since the mid-nineteenth century (Chatterjee 1986). In *The Nation and Its Fragments* (1993) Chatterjee shows, through a richly detailed analysis of nationalism in Bengal, how in such institutions as language, drama and the novel, art, religion, schooling and the family, a new, creative 'inner domain of national culture' was fashioned by nationalist Indian elites which is simultaneously modern and non-Western, using both Western and indigenous (Sanskrit) models. At the same time, this dominant Indian nationalist discourse is influenced by those of the many marginalised groups outside the mainstream of politics, the 'fragments of the nation' which in this case include Bengalis, women, peasants and outcastes, even when their alternative images of the nation were bypassed or suppressed, and their aspirations 'normalised' by an incorporating Indian nationalism. The interesting point here is that such nationalist culture creation precedes the political challenge to the West, and the ensuing nationalist conflict, a point also made by John Peel in his analysis of the 'cultural work' of Yoruba ethnogenesis in the same period. The encounter with the Other is certainly crucial, but the forms and contents of the Indian, Middle Eastern or African nationalism which that encounter triggers are also derived from other, non-Western sources within the traditional cultures of the community (albeit greatly modified) (Chatterjee 1993: chs 1, 5; Peel 1989).

Such readings still leave intact the cultural differences which fragment the nation. But here too some radical postmodernist theorising has decentred and decomposed ethnicity. For Stuart Hall, Etienne Balibar and others, ethnicity must be viewed as a plastic and malleable social construction, deriving its meanings from the particular situations of those who invoke it and the relations of power between individuals and groups. Not only is it one among many competing identities, it derives its meanings from its articulation with other kinds of identity, notably class and gender. Shifting, permeable and 'situational', ethnicity has no essence or centre, no underlying features or common denominator. For Etienne Balibar, there is only a discourse of 'fictive ethnicity'. Thus:

> No nation possesses an ethnic base naturally, but as social formations are nationalised, the populations included within them, divided up among them or dominated by them are ethnicised – that is, represented in the past or in the future *as if* they formed a natural community, possessing of itself an identity of origins, culture and interests which transcend individuals and social conditions.
>
> (Balibar and Wallerstein 1991: 96, original emphasis)

Ethnicity itself is produced through two routes, those of the language community and the race, both of which create the idea of predestined, autonomous communities.

In similar vein, Stuart Hall views a sense of ethnicity as the expression of a hegemonic national identity, as in the concept of 'Englishness'. But Hall also sees the new 'identity politics' of representation in the West as constructing a new 'positive conception of the ethnicity of the margins, of the periphery'. This kind of voluntary ethnicity involves a

> new cultural politics which engages rather than suppresses *difference* and which depends, in part, on the cultural construction of new ethnic identities.
>
> (S. Hall 1992: 257)

Once again, the hegemony of a dominant discourse of national (and racial) identity is challenged by alternative discourses of peripheral ethnicity, newly constructed out of popular experiences, and predicated on the celebration of diversity. This is the premise, and justification, of the politics of multiculturalism, to which I shall return.

In sensitising us to the more complex and multifaceted nature of contemporary national identities in the West, and in revealing the differences between the older received traditions of the nation and the much more varied, and contested, understandings of national community among and within the many cultural groups that comprise most modern national states, this kind of postmodern analysis has done much to illuminate the latest phase of national formation, especially in the West. There is little doubt that modern Western nations have become 'frayed at the edges', and that their members have had to rethink former assumptions about national community and identity in the light of much larger movements of population. It is also true that different groups in both Western and non-Western societies such as India have had quite different visions and interpretations of the 'nation'. At the same time, we should not underestimate the continuing hold of a sense of national identity among the majority of the population in Western states, nor the desire of many members of immigrant communities to become part of a reshaped nation, while retaining their ethnic and religious cultures, perhaps increasingly in the form of a 'symbolic ethnicity'. Nor should we overestimate the degree to which most Western nations either were or felt themselves to be homogeneous in earlier periods. To do so is to set up a false 'before-and-after' dichotomy. National unity was never so assured in the past, even when it was sought by nationalists, nor today are fragmentation and voluntary ethnicity so marked. For most people, even in the West, there remain clear boundaries in determining their ethnic identities and national allegiances, even when they may dissent from them or their power-holders. They can change their national allegiances, though often with difficulty, and perhaps modify their ethnic identities, usually through their children, for example in mixed marriages. But this enhanced individual latitude in the West does not allow people to 'pick and mix' or consume at will among ethnic identities; their choices remain restricted by ethnic history and political geography. As Michael Billig put it:

> One can eat Chinese tomorrow and Turkish the day after; one can even dress in Chinese and Turkish styles. But *being* Chinese or Turkish are not commercially available options.
>
> (Billig 1995: 139, original emphasis)

For most people, 'voluntary ethnicity' is not an option, even in democratic societies, if only because other ethnic communities are unlikely to accept such a radical boundary change; an example is the failure of Mauritian Muslims in the 1970s and 1980s to become accepted as of Arab rather than Indian descent (Gans 1979; Eriksen 1993: 72; Billig 1995: ch. 6).[3]

Gender and nation

The second major theme which overlaps with that of fragmentation is the mutual impact of gender and nation. Early feminist analyses did not seek to address the issues of ethnicity and nationalism, but from the mid-1980s there has been a growing literature in this area. Gender theorists complain, rightly in my view, of the failure of theories of nationalism to adddress either the role of women in national projects or the impact of gender cleavages on our understanding of nations and nationalism.

Of course, modernists might claim that their theories are universal and there is no need for a separate account of the role of women and gender in nationalism. But, if the very nature of nations and nationalism (or national projects) is gendered, then a separate, or at least, a different kind of theory is required, one which takes this key attribute of the *explanandum* into account – particularly from those who regard nationalism as linked to ethnicity and ethnicity to kinship, or from ethno-symbolists for whom ethno-history and 'myth-symbol' complexes are central to the development of nations.

To date, the question of the relations between issues of gender and nationalism has been pursued at a number of levels, and with very different assumptions and methodologies. These are lucidly set out in a masterly survey of the main works in the field to date by Sylvia Walby.[4]

The role of women in nationalism

The first such level is empirical: the varying role of women in nations and nationalist projects, and the differential impact of such projects on women and their prospects. Here, Walby cites Kumari Jayawardena's seminal study which demonstrated that women's movements were active in many non-Western nationalisms, and were an integral part of national resistance movements; they were, according to Jayawardena,

> acted out against a backdrop of nationalist struggles aiming at achieving political independence, asserting a national identity, and modernising society.
>
> (Jayawardena 1986: 3)

Jayawardena nevertheless emphasised the separate demands and roles of feminist movements alongside, or within, the nationalist movements; they might even be at variance with its goals or interpretations, as Haleh Afshar stresses in her analysis of women's struggles in Iran (Afshar 1989).

Conversely, nationalist movements view the question of women's emancipation in quite a different light. Walby points out how in the older nations of the West, the formation of nations was long drawn out and women's emancipation came very late in their 'rounds of restructuring'; whereas in the new states of Africa and Asia, women were accorded full citizenship rights with independence.

> Indeed the granting of full citizenship to all was one of the ways in which previously dominated colonies could make a claim to a nationhood.
>
> (Walby 1992: 91)

But, as Deniz Kandiyoti points out in a scholarly study of the Turkish emancipation movement, it was only on their own terms that nationalists accorded women full rights. In the Turkish case, their emancipation as equals flowed, in the eyes of the influential Turkish social theorist Ziya Gökalp, from ancient Turkish egalitarian mores. Kandiyoti perceptively concludes:

> Thus, there appears to be one persistent concern which finally unites nationalist and Islamist discourses on women in Turkey: the necessity to establish that the behaviour and position of women, however defined, are

congruent with the 'true' identity of the collectivity and constitute no threat
to it.

(Kandiyoti 1989: 143; cf. Kandiyoti 1991)

Female symbolism of the nation

Deniz Kandiyoti here touches on a second level of analysis, the ideological and
symbolic uses of women. Symbolism and ideology are two of the main dimensions along which Floya Anthias and Nira Yuval-Davis, in their pioneering
volume, locate women within ethnic and national processes. They regard women
as central to the creation and reproduction of ethnic and national projects, and
list five major dimensions of their activity and presence. Women, they argue,
should be seen as:

a) as biological reproducers of members of ethnic collectivities;
b) as reproducers of the boundaries of ethnic/national groups;
c) as participating centrally in the ideological reproduction of the collectivity and as transmitters of its culture;
d) as signifiers of ethnic/national differences as a focus and symbol in
ideological discourses used in the construction, reproduction and transformation of ethnic/national categories;
e) as participants in national, economic, political and military struggles.

(Yuval-Davis and Anthias 1989: 7)

In a later thought-provoking and systematic survey of the field, Nira Yuval-Davis
goes on to apply a deconstructionist analysis to the relationships between gender
and nation, and includes the ideological and symbolic modes of locating women
(c and d above) as vital components of cultural reproduction. Culture or 'cultural
stuff', she argues, rather than being fixed and homogeneous, should be seen as

a rich resource, usually full of internal contradictions, which is used selectively by different social agents in various social projects within specific
power relations and political discourse in and outside the collectivity.

(Yuval-Davis 1997: 43)

As a result, hegemonic symbols and cultures are generally strongest in the centre
of the polity and always evoke resistance, particularly at the periphery.
Hegemonic nationalist symbols and narratives proclaim the need for men to
defend both the 'Motherland' and the nation's women who symbolise and
express its 'purity'. They call on men to sacrifice themselves for their women and
children, so that they may be eulogised by their women in the manner of
Plutarch's Spartan women, whom Rousseau so admired.[5]

Yuval-Davis points out that women 'are often constructed as the symbolic
bearers of the collectivity's identity and honour':

A figure of a woman, often a mother, symbolises in many cultures the spirit of the collectivity, whether it is Mother Russia, Mother Ireland or Mother India. In the French Revolution its symbol was 'La Patrie', a figure of a woman giving birth to a baby; and in Cyprus, a crying woman refugee on roadside posters was the embodiment of the pain and anger of the Greek Cypriot collectivity after the Turkish invasion.

(Yuval-Davis 1997: 45)

This is in line with the central nationalist construction of the 'home'. In the home gender relations become constitutive of the 'essence' of cultures, which in turn are to be seen as intergenerational ways of life that include such facets as family relations, ways of cooking and eating, domestic labour, play and bedtime stories (*ibid.*: 43).

Nationalism as a male phenomenon

Yet another level of analysis of gender–nation relationships concerns the nature of nations and nationalisms as largely masculine organisations and projects. For Cynthia Enloe, indeed,

nationalism has typically sprung from masculinised memory, masculinised humiliation and masculinised hope.

(Enloe 1989: 44)

And this is also the burden of Jean Bethke Elshtain's analysis of masculine patri-otic self-sacrifice. Such considerations lead Sylvia Walby to argue that men and women are differentially involved in the nation and nationalism. Perhaps, she reasons, this is why many women, for example those in the Green and anti-nuclear movements, often display more international commitments and less militarism; alternatively, their greater pacifism and internationalism may make women less involved with the nation and nationalism than men (Elshtain 1993; Walby 1992: 92–3).

Against this view, we have seen plenty of evidence of women's political and even military involvement in national liberation struggles, even if the reasons are as much instrumental as expressive. This suggests that there are times, at least, when the national struggle supersedes or subsumes all other struggles, including those of class and gender. This does not mean that 'nationalism' as a discourse is not oriented primarily to the needs of men and for this reason possesses a 'masculine' symbolic content. In an age of revolutionary nationalism, after all, such neo-classic images as David's painting of the *Oath of the Horatii* (1784), West's *The Death of Wolfe* (1770) and Fuseli's *Oath of the Rütli* (1779) focus explic-itly on the traditional masculine attributes of energy, force and duty.[6]

How do we explain the basic male character of this nationalism? George Mosse draws on his earlier path-breaking analyses of the choreography of mass nationalism to reveal how its rise and development, particularly in Central

Europe, was conditioned by the Western bourgeois family morality with its concern for 'respectability', moral character and physical (Greek) beauty. This produced a sharp differentiation, not only in gender roles but also in gendered attributes and stereotypes, already evident in the anti-revolutionary German-speaking regions, which identified the French forces as 'loose-living', in opposition to the respectable, masculine German morality, which nationalists like Ernst Moritz Arndt embraced. As the nineteenth century progressed, the integral nationalist search for a specific masculine morality, 'Aryan' male beauty and a respectable and distinctive 'national character' merged with racist fascism's cult of male activism and aggressive virility (Mosse 1985, 1995; cf. Leoussi 1997).

More recently, Glenda Sluga, in a penetrating historical investigation, traced the gendered nature of both nations and nationalist ideologies further back to their origins in the French Revolution, where by 1793 'the legislators of the new French Republic had defined popular national sovereignty in terms of its masculine citizenry'. In the name of social order, women were returned to the private sphere as patriot wives and mothers of citizens, as Rousseau had recommended. Drawing on the work of Joan Landes, Sluga shows how the division between public and private spheres, stemming from the scrutiny of boundaries initiated by the Enlightenment, not only excluded women from the Revolution's invocation of universal rights, but ensured the entirely masculine character of the nation-state. Like Rousseau, Fichte, Michelet and Mazzini all emphasised the different roles of the sexes in national education, the supportive, nurturing function of women and the heroic, military role of men:

> Mazzini, like Michelet and Fichte, drew on the image of the patriarchal family (with the father at its head) as a natural unit to shore up the legitimacy of the fraternal nation-state and determine its preference for the male citizen as the active and military patriot.
>
> (Sluga 1998: 9, 24; see also Landes 1988)

Feminism and identity politics

Finally, there is the normative level of analysis: the ways in which feminists should address 'identity politics' and the politics of multiculturalism. For Nira Yuval-Davis the problem with 'identity politics' is that it tends to harden ethnic and gender boundaries, and homogenise and naturalise categories and group differences (Yuval-Davis 1997: 119). Similarly with multiculturalism. Here too the dangers of reifying and essentialising cultures ignore power differences between and within minorities, overemphasise the differences between cultures and privilege as 'authentic' the voices of the most unwesternised 'community representatives'. This can have particularly detrimental effects for women in terms of encouraging minority male control over their behaviour. Even allowing for the 'counter-narratives' which emerge from the nation's margins and 'hybrids', there is always the danger that homogeneity and essentialism are attributed to the homogeneous collectivities from which the 'hybrids' have emerged, thus replacing the mythical image of society as a 'melting pot' with the mythical image of society as a 'mixed salad'.

(Yuval-Davis 1997: 59; cf. Kymlicka 1995)

Given the differential positioning of minorities and of women among and within them, there can be no simple approach to a 'feminist agenda'. For Yuval-Davis, feminists can only construct identities across difference by a 'transversal politics' which starts from different cultural roots and aims to 'shift' and move towards those from other cultures whose values and goals are compatible with one's own (*ibid.*: 130).

From this all too brief summary of some of its major themes, it is clear that the 'gender-nation' field is rich in potential for analysing the character and effects of nations and nationalism. How far it is useful to deconstruct its concepts and issues in terms of various 'narratives' and 'discourses', and whether we need to describe them as hegemonic (or otherwise) 'constructs', is open to question. Certainly, employing this kind of postmodernist approach sensitises us to the great complexity of women's positions in ethnic and national projects, and vice-versa, but it does so at a cost: a clear shift away from the task of causal explanation. It is noteworthy that, for all their analytical insights, only a few of the works discussed above (specifically, those that opt for a historical modernist approach) are concerned with the origins and formation of nations and the role of gender relations therein, or with why nations and nationalism have become so ubiquitous, or indeed, except in passing, with the issue of why nations and nationalisms evoke such passions among so many people (including so many women) across the globe. This suggests that 'nation-gender' theories have considerable work to do if they are to provide a more comprehensive causal analysis of the ways in which the complex interrelations of gender and nation contribute to the formation of nations and the spread and intensity of nationalism.

Liberalism and civic or ethnic nationalism

Yuval-Davis' espousal of 'transversal politics' makes sense only in a more liberal democracy where the form of nationalism is inclusive, participant and relatively open in character. This is the type of nationalism which the 'nation-building' theorists had in mind, and it is this 'civic' version of nationalism that has been taken up by some liberals and social democrats, in opposition to its antithesis, 'ethnic' nationalism.

There is a burgeoning literature on the relationship between liberalism and/or social democracy and this form of nationalism, but most of it is philosophical and normative, and so lies outside the scope of my enquiry. I should only like to mention the debate provoked by David Miller's lucid defence of a civic version of the doctrine of nationality (his preferred term to 'nationalism'). Miller starts by discussing the idea of national identity or the nation, and lists five distinguishing marks of a nation as a community:

it is (1) constituted by shared belief and mutual commitment; (2) extended in history; (3) active in character; (4) connected to a particular territory; (5) marked off from other communities by its distinct public culture.

(O'Leary 1996a: 414; see Miller 1993: 6–8, and Miller 1995: ch. 1)

For Miller, nations can be defended on three grounds. First, they are valid sources of personal identity. Second, they are ethical communities, and as members we owe special obligations to our compatriots. Finally, nations have a valid claim to be self-determining, so as to allow their members to decide matters for themselves. Despite our commitment to ethical universalism, Miller argues, in practise we are ethical particularists, and the nation affords a larger and better basis for performing duties and achieving social justice. Moreover, the nation offers a better arena for achieving liberal and social democratic goals than radical multiculturalism, which cannot restrain the rich and strong and only encourages fragmentation. Nationality is also superior to citizenship and a purely abstract 'constitutional patriotism' of the type favoured by Jurgen Habermas, since it connects political principles and practice to a sense of shared history and culture, and a sense of place and time (Miller 1995: chs 2–3; O'Leary 1996a: 419–20).

One of the difficulties in Miller's approach, as Brendan O'Leary points out, is that he qualifies the claim to national self-determination in ways that tend to favour the powers-that-be, and is especially critical of the claims of ethnic communities in polyethnic nations. In effect, Miller comes down, as do so many others, in favour of a civic form of nationalism which is ultimately dependant on the state and its liberal practices. Yet Miller is also careful to distinguish nations from states. What then of all those ethnic groups that aspire to the status of nationality and desire to determine their own destinies? How shall we judge the claims of separatists and irredentists? (O'Leary 1996b: 445–7; cf. Beitz 1979).[7]

Recognition of the political power of ethnicity has inspired a number of cognate debates, mainly in political science, notably about the ways of managing or eliminating ethnic differences and conflict. As McGarry and O'Leary demonstrate, these methods range from the extremes of partition, population transfer and genocide to assimilation, consociationalism and federation, and they reveal much about the consequences of nationalism in a world of mainly polyethnic states. Three topics have provoked particular controversy. The first is the merits (and features) of the 'consociational democracy' model associated with the work of Arend Lijphart, and its relationship to both class conflict and liberalism. The second is the meanings and political uses of concepts of 'ethnic democracy' and/or 'herrenvolk democracy' to characterise exclusive dominant-*ethnie* democracy in polyethnic states, and the differences of such regimes from liberal democracies. The third theme, the vicissitudes of ethnic minority rights and their relations with states and the inter-state system, has only recently been linked to questions about the nation and nationalism. However, in most of the literature these issues have a strong normative (and legal) content and have only been tangentially related to issues of national identity and nationalism. On the whole, therefore, they lie outside the scope of this survey (Lijphart 1977; McGarry and O'Leary 1993).[8]

The debate about the civic or ethnic character of nationalism, on the other hand, is directly related to our concerns. It has, as one might expect, received much attention from analysts of immigrant societies like Canada and Australia. Raymond Breton's analysis of the evolution of English-speaking Canada, for example, emphasises a long-term shift from 'ethnic' to 'civic' nationalism. Even in Quebec, he can trace a similar, albeit slower development: as a result of immigration, both the French language and Catholicism have become increasingly detached from their Québécois ethno-cultural base, and

> membership cannot be defined in terms of ethnic attributes, but in terms of citizenship. As in English Canada, the collective identity has to be redefined in such a way as to incorporate the people of non-French origins who are legally members of the polity.
>
> (Breton 1988: 99–102)

In reality, few modern national states possess only one form of nationalism. Nevertheless, we *can* usefully distinguish between 'ethnic', 'civic' and 'plural' types of nation and nationalism; and these analytical distinctions may help to explain, for example, different traditions of state immigration policies. Thus Rogers Brubaker has shown how the territorial conception of belonging which formed the French tradition gave rise to a civic policy that naturalised immigrants on the basis of prolonged residence in France (*ius soli*); whereas the German conception of ethnic belonging entailed a genealogical policy (*ius sanguinis*) that till recently denied German citizenship to migrants and *Gastarbeiter*, however long their residence on German soil, while at the same time according immediate rights of citizenship to dispossessed ethnic Germans from the East. Similarly, Daniele Conversi has contrasted the pattern of cultural values among Basques and Catalans, revealing how Sabino Arana's influence has incorporated the Basque concern with purity of blood and exclusive rights, whereas the Catalan tradition of linguistic and cultural nationalism has encouraged a more open, assimilationist and inclusive Catalan nationalism, one that is far more respectful to immigrants (Brubaker 1992; Conversi 1997).

Yet in practice, these types frequently overlap, and a given national state will often display ethnic as well as civic components in its form of nationalism, sometimes in a historical layering, or its nationalism may move some way from one type to another and back. Moreover, each type, as I have argued, has its peculiar problems. If the ethnic-genealogical type tends towards exclusivity (though not necessarily), the civic-territorial type stemming from the French Revolution is often impatient of ethnic difference; it tends towards radical assimilation, some might call it 'ethnocide', of cultural differences and minorities. As for the 'plural' type of nationalism found mainly in immigrant societies like Canada and Australia, its celebration of cultural diversity risks a loss of political cohesion and tends towards a national instability which could in turn provoke reactive nationalisms (and in extreme cases like Quebec, secession movements) (A. D. Smith 1995a: ch. 4).[9]

For these reasons, those scholars who, in the tradition of Hans Kohn and John Plamenatz, oppose a 'good' civic to a 'bad' ethnic nationalism, overlook the problems associated with each type and in particular rewrite the civic version to accomodate the new politics of multiculturalism. Not only does this conflate, unhistorically, the civic and the plural types of nationalism; it fails to see how closely intertwined all three conceptions of the nation tend in practice to be, and how easy it is to move from one version to another as circumstances dictate. Nationalism will not be easily tamed and categorised to fit the prescriptions of moral and political philosophers (Kohn 1967a: ch. 7; Plamenatz 1976; Ignatieff 1993; Kristeva 1993).

Nor can we easily accept the prescriptions of those who, like Habermas, would replace nationalism by a form of 'constitutional patriotism' that would make the political institutions and the constitution the focus of collective loyalties. Perhaps the most plausible of these prescriptions is that provided by Maurizio Viroli, who argues for a break with nationalism and a return to a modernised form of democratic republicanism. After a rich survey of the republican and nationalist traditions (nationalism here being exclusively of the German 'ethno-cultural' variety), Viroli argues that a territorially and historically grounded republicanism would replace nationalist exclusivity with a truly democratic and civic loyalty appropriate to the modern era. But, we may ask, is such a proposition feasible in large-scale industrial societies? If it were, why is it that nationalism rather than republicanism has swept the globe and drawn so many peoples and areas into its orbit? Besides, as we saw, there is no proof that republicanism might not turn out to be just as exclusive as (ethnic) nationalism; was not Athens after the citizenship law of 451 BC, were not Sparta and republican Rome, or many of the medieval Italian city-states, just as exclusive and rigorous? (Viroli 1995).[10]

It is a welcome sign that there has been a renewed interest in the ethics of nationalism, after so many decades when nationalism was equated with fascism and was felt to be morally untouchable. But as long as ethnic nationalism – still the most popular and frequent of the versions adopted by elites and peoples around the world – continues to occupy a pariah status, and like the head of Medusa, turns the philosophic mind to stone, a large part of the subject, and that the most vexed and explosive, will remain unaddressed and unanalysed.

Nationalism and globalisation

Can we envisage a time, not only when ethnic nationalism has run its course, but when nation-states, national identities and nationalism-in-general will have been superseded by a cosmopolitan culture and supranational governance? This, the last major theme in the literature that attempts to move beyond modernism, foresees the inevitable supersession of nation-states and nationalism by broader supranational, or global, organisations and identities in a 'postmodern' era.

The general belief in supersession has three main components which are often conflated: first, the imminent demise of the 'nation-state', second, the supersession of nationalism, and third, the transcendence of ethnicity. Each of these trends, it is argued, is gathering pace, as nation-states, nationalism and ethnicity are being more or less gradually replaced by supra-national (for example, European) and/or global identities and associations.

With the exception of Hobsbawm, most modernists have in fact been reticent about the fate of the national state and the prospects of nationalism. It has been left to so-called 'postmodernists' to proclaim the demise of the 'nation-state' through an overwhelming combination of political dependence, economic globalisation, mass communications and cultural hybridisation. Thus for Stephen Castles and his colleagues, the nation-state 'is increasingly irrelevant on both the economic and cultural levels', as a result of global economic interdependence and cultural homogenisation. In a multicultural state like Australia, attempts to return to primordial themes of nationalism are likely to fail because of a lack of heroic myths and the impact of migrants and their cultures (Castles *et al.* 1988: 140–4).[11]

But even if this is the case, are immigrant societies like Australia typical? Are the forces of globalisation and mass communications producing a similarly 'non-national nation' elsewhere? Or, indeed, a move altogether away from no longer viable national states and nationalisms, to allow greater space for the 'tribe' and the 'stranger', as Zygmunt Baumann argues? Can we consign nationalism to the 'great museum' of tourist history, as Donald Horne's amusing guide would have it? (Baumann 1992; Horne 1984).

This is very much the argument, and hope, of those who embrace the notions of 'supra-nationalism' and 'global culture'. They point, not only to the fragmentation of national identities discussed above, but to the loss of economic sovereignty and the growing political dependence of all national states. There is, indeed, considerable evidence to support this contention – provided, of course, that we assume that there was a time when the 'nation-state' was largely autonomous in both spheres, something which, as even McNeill concedes, is at best doubtful; one has only to consider the many smaller states like Luxembourg, Nepal or Guatemala that were indeed sovereign states, but could hardly be said to have been ever autonomous. More important, in the post-1945 era, the political and economic dependence of most states has been accompanied by a huge expansion of internal state power and penetration in the social and cultural spheres, notably in such fields as mass education, the cultural media, health and social welfare. This expansion has been legitimated by nationalist ideologies and has done much to offset and 'compensate' the 'nation-state' for its external dependance (A. D. Smith 1995a: ch. 4; Billig 1995: 141).[12]

Similar problems arise with the claim that mass communications and electronic technology are creating a global consumerist culture that is making national cultures increasingly permeable, similar and even obsolete. As some scholars have argued, the idea of a 'global culture' can be seen as another form of (consumer) imperialism operating through the prism of the cultural media;

though it presents itself as universal, it bears the imprint of its origins and flows from a single source, the United States. Alternatively, global culture is presented as a playfully eclectic and 'depthless' pastiche, attuned to the 'pastiche personality' of the affectually attenuated, decentred ego inhabiting 'an electronic, global world'. Here global culture appears as an entirely new technical construction, what Lyotard called 'a self-sufficient electronic circuit', at once timeless, placeless and memory-less, contradicting all our ideas of cultures which embody the distinctive historical roots, myths and memories, and the specific lifestyles, of ethnic communities and nations (Billig 1995: ch. 6; cf. Tomlinson 1991: ch. 3; A. D. Smith 1995a: ch. 1).[13]

Besides, as Philip Schlesinger demonstrated, the electronic cultural media and information technology on which much of the cultural globalisation thesis rests, are more variable in their effects on different classes, regions and ethnic communities than this argument allows. Paradoxically, too, the electronic media serve to reinforce old ethnic identities or encourage the (re-)creation of new ones. This is also the burden of Anthony Richmond's analysis of the ways in which the latest technological revolution is replacing industrial by 'service societies'. In these 'post-industrial' societies, new modes of electronic mass communications are encouraging the resurgence of ethnic communities using these dense networks of linguistic and cultural communications (Schlesinger 1987; 1991: Part III; Richmond 1984).

From a more interactionist standpoint, Alberto Melucci also suggests that, with the crisis and decline of the nation-state, the revival of ethnicity in modern societies is to be expected, although for quite different reasons to those proposed by McNeill. In an age of voluntary networks of social interaction based on individual needs and activities, ethno-national organisation provides an important channel for individual identification and solidarity 'because it responds to a collective need which assumes particular importance in complex societies'. Ethno-national movements are actively political, but they are also pre-eminently cultural:

> As other criteria of group membership (such as class) weaken or recede, ethnic identity also responds to a need for identity of an eminently symbolic nature. It gives roots, based on a language, a culture and an ancient history, to demands that transcend the specific condition of the ethnic group.
>
> (Melucci 1989: 89–92)

This suggests, not the transcendence of ethnicity but the revitalisation of ethnic ties by the very processes of globalisation that are presumed to be rendering them obsolete, in much the same way, and perhaps for similar reasons, as the resurgence of strong religious identities among ethnic communities in multi-faith and multicultural societies like Britain and the United States, or in ethnically and religiously divided societies like Nigeria and India. As Giddens would argue, the global and the local feed each other (see Igwara 1995; Jacobsen 1997; Deol 1996).[14]

Recent international events seem to have lent some credence to this view of a global ethnic resurgence. We have witnessed a remarkable spate of ethnic secession movements since the end of the Cold War. Yet, despite the recurrent power of ethnic nationalism, the norms of international society remain basically the same, and they have long been hostile to any attempt to change the political map by force or challenge the sovereignty of individual states through separatism or irredentism. The international community will only condone secession in special circumstances, where it is the result of mutual and peaceful agreement (as in Singapore) or where there is a strong regional patron favouring secession, as India did in the bid for secession of Bangla Desh from Pakistan. The recent creation of some twenty new ethnic states is largely the consequence of exceptional events – the break-up of the Soviet and Ethiopian empires – though this will not entirely account for the secession of Slovakia, Slovenia, Croatia, Bosnia and Macedonia. For James Mayall, as we saw earlier, the inter-state system has proved largely resilient to the challenge mounted by nationalism since the French Revolution, insisting on the primacy of the principle of state sovereignty over that of national self-determination, despite the Wilsonian attempt to incorporate the latter into the fabric of international society. Mayall endorses the realist view of most theorists of international relations, yet he also demonstrates how territorial nationalism has underpinned state power and, by extension, a community of national states requiring popular legitimacy (Mayall 1991, 1992; see also Chapter 4 above).[15]

National identity and supra-nationalism

But, if we cannot yet expect a leap from ethno-national identity to global cosmopolitanism, are we not at least witnessing a less dramatic, but still unprecedented, shift of loyalties from nations and national states to 'supra-national' continental regionalisms that can accommodate sub-national ethnic identities and cultural differences?

Evidence for this more limited and realistic position comes mainly from studies of European political and cultural integration. Once again, the literature is already too vast to summarise here. One theme is the growth of a European citizenship transcending or complementing the existing national citizenships. Thus *Gastarbeiter* and asylum-seekers are able to obtain most of the social, economic and even political rights of citizens in the form of 'human rights', without being granted formal citizenship of the host country to which they have migrated or fled, even if the organisation of those human rights remains national and therefore specific to each host national state. For this reason, scholars like Yacemin Soysal argue that we can see the emergence of a 'post-national' type of citizenship in Europe alongside the existing national model, though how widespread and potent such a model has become is open to question in view of the continuing hold of both national state and ethnic allegiances, the resurgence of ethnic nationalism in Eastern Europe and the racial nationalist backlashes in the West (Soysal 1994, 1996; cf. Mitchell and Russell 1996; Delanty 1995: ch. 10; Husbands 1991).[16]

Another theme is the possibility of creating a European cultural 'identity' alongside or overarching existing national identities through the centralised use of the cultural media, planned student exchanges and labour mobility, the invention and dissemination of pan-European myths, memories and symbols, and the selection, reinterpretation and popularisation of pan-European history (see Duroselle 1990; cf. A. D. Smith 1992b). However, as Philip Schlesinger and others have shown, the creation of a European 'identity' has become a cultural battlefield. Given the continuing strength of existing national identities within Europe, as well as Europe's uncertain boundaries and many cleavages, Schlesinger concludes:

> It is difficult to conceive of engineering a collective [sc. European] identity. . . . The production of an overarching collective identity can only seriously be conceived as the outcome of long-standing social and political practice.
>
> (Schlesinger 1992: 16–17)

No wonder that confusion surrounds the 'European' cultural dimensions of the project of European integration, and that there are different models of the ultimate rationale for 'Europe', many of which take the nation as well as the national state as their reference points. Michael Billig points to the continuing importance of boundaries for 'Europe', both in respect to trade and defence, and to the prevention of immigration.

> Thus, Europe will be imagined as a totality, either as a homeland itself or as a homeland of homelands. Either way, the ideological traditions of nationhood, including its boundary-consciousness, are not transcended.
>
> (Billig 1995: 142)

How then can we envisage the creation of a European 'identity'? Quoting Raymond Aron's opinion in the 1960s that 'the old nations will live in the hearts of men, and love of the European nation is not yet born – assuming that it ever will be', Montserrat Guibernau argues that the construction of Europe will require the development of a 'European national consciousness':

> The engineers of the new Europe will have to look at 'common European trends' and design a myth of origin, rewrite history, invent traditions, rituals and symbols that will create a new identity. But, even more important, they will have to discover a common goal, a project capable of mobilising the energy of European citizens.
>
> (Guibernau 1996: 114)

But this means that some form of nationalism will have to be invoked, raising problems, not only of a 'democratic deficit', but of ethnic and even racial exclusion against immigrants. 'Europe' will have to be forged from above after the German (*Zollverein*) or the United States (federal) models, with all the problems of popular resonance which we discussed *vis-à-vis* Hobsbawm's thesis. At the same time, the new European cultural identity would have to compete with and incorporate strongly entrenched *national* identities, and therefore raise the external cultural (as well as economic) barrier. If the prospect of an ethnic 'fortress Europa' is unattractive, so is the assimilatory potential of a civic model, which in any case may fail to command the affections and loyalties of most of Europe's citizens who remain locked into a historically embedded mosaic of ethno-cultural nations (see Pieterse 1995; A. D. Smith 1995a: ch. 5).[17]

Beyond modernism?

Does all this suggest that we have moved beyond the nationalist epoch, in tandem with the shift away from modernism? Is a 'postmodern' epoch *ipso facto* a 'post-national' one, and are both reflected in 'postmodernist' styles of analysis?

The suspicion that 'objective' referents and empirical trends are, in some sense, a reflection of a particular style of analysis suggests a measure of caution in accepting the last part of McNeill's tripartite periodisation. Perhaps the reality we see here is the reflection of the kind of mirror 'held up to nature'; the evidence of 'fragmentation' may be as much a product of the deconstructive modes of analysis employed as of any empirical trends. Just as a perennialist paradigm looks for and finds continuity and rootedness, so the various postmodernist modes of analysis seek out and discover contestation, flux and fragmentation. And, of course, one can find plenty of evidence for both.

Looked at strictly from the standpoint of a theory of, or at least a fruitful perspective on, nations and nationalism, neither approach appears very helpful. Both have important things to tell us about aspects of the field of ethnic and national phenomena; and surely even from the brief survey I have conducted, it is clear that the themes of fragmentation and globalisation of the loosely labelled 'postmodern/post-national' approaches are rich in suggestion and insight into *contemporary* problems of ethnicity and nationalism. But here lies the rub. Except for some of the feminist accounts, there is a lack of historical depth to so many of the analyses under this broad heading, in a field that above all demands such depth, and for phenomena that are so historically embedded. It is as if the analysts had entered the drama in the third act (in terms of William McNeill's periodisation), taking for granted some version of modernism's script for the two previous acts. But which version, and why modernism? After all, both McNeill and the cultural fragmentation school of postmodernists stress the hard bedrock of 'cultural difference'. That suggests a joining of hands with perennialism over the heads of the modernists. Yes, the nation, the nation-state and all its works may be modern, contested, multi-stranded and fluid; but, in surpassing it and them, contemporary societies have rediscovered the power of fundamental cultural differences. Is this not, as Nira Yuval-Davis pointed out, just another form of 'essentialism', perhaps even of primordialism? (Yuval-Davis 1997: 59).

It is not only in their lack of historical depth that most of the recent analyses appear partial and 'fragmentary'. Again, with the exception of some feminist analyses, they propose no general explanation of nations and nationalism, and make no attempt to uncover the mechanisms by which they were formed, developed and spread. This is, in many cases, a consequence of postmodernism's anti-foundationalism and decentred analysis. But it is also evident in discussions of globalisation and Europeanisation, and of the civic or ethnic types of nationalism, which adhere to the usual canons of subject-centred and causal analysis. They too tend to take the phenomena of ethnicity and nationalism, and their cultural and political significance, as historical givens, even when they recast them as discursive narratives and deconstruct their meanings. But they offer no general explanation for their presence, variations and significance, no understanding of which nations emerged and where, why there are nations and nationalisms at all, and why they evoke so much passion.

This lack of theorising may have something to do with the deep ambivalence or, in the case of nationalism, downright hostility to these phenomena on the part of most of the analysts. This is not without its interest in that unpoliticised ethnicity, by itself, often evokes some sympathy, as 'cultural difference'; and, on the other side, a purely civic form of nationalism is commended by some analysts. It is the fatal combination of ethnicity and nationalism, as 'ethno-nationalism', that, in the tradition of Elie Kedourie, provokes the greatest fear and condemnation. But, as many of these analysts realise, it is precisely this combination that, whether it is tacit and 'unflagged', as in parts of the West, or explicit and explosive, as in Eastern Europe and parts of Africa and Asia, most requires to be addressed and explained. The fact that it is so deeply ingrained and routinised ('enhabited', in Michael Billig's term) in the West, also requires explanation. To see it as a de-ethnicised, civic form of nationalism is, I would suggest, not only a historical and analytical, but also a policy, error, and to that extent, misleading and unhelpful (see Billig 1995: 42–3).

Common to most of these analyses, with the exception of McNeill's brief account and a few of the historical gender analyses, is a turning away from any 'grand narrative' like modernism or perennialism at the very moment when ethno-nationalism is resurgent and when the national state and national identity have once again become central to arguments about the direction of politics and society. Without an explicit theory of the character, formation and diffusion of nations and nationalism, such arguments will lack depth and validity. In the absence of a new encompassing grand narrative, all the partial 'little narratives' will have to lean on, and tacitly take their meaning from one or other version of the existing grand narratives. That can be good neither for systematic social understanding nor for political and social policy. Of course, research can be conducted on only a small part of the overall canvas; but equally its meaning and significance can only be clarified in terms of that wider framework or canvas. If that framework is tacitly assumed in the research without it being subjected to scrutiny, then the results of that research will be called into question along with its research programme. In these circumstances it is more helpful to relate the research directly to one or other version of the major paradigms, or fashion a new one that can justify the particular research programme.

In my view, most of the analyses I have all too briefly considered in this chapter assume one or other version of the modernist paradigm, which they then seek to 'go beyond' in time-period as well as in the 'phase' of development of the phenomena themselves. It is doubtful whether, in their theoretical understanding, deconstructionist analyses go much beyond the ways in which modernists like Gellner or Anderson or Hobsbawm characterised and understood the nation and nationalism. But whereas these modernists (including some 'gender-nation' theorists) provide us with full and rounded historical, political and sociological accounts of nations and nationalism, postmodernist and allied analyses, in their desire to demonstrate the fluid, fragmented and constructed qualities of these phenomena, repudiate the need for such overall accounts or simply assume them as given. In doing so, they illuminate a corner of the broader canvas only to leave the rest of it in untraversed darkness. From the standpoint of a theory of nations and nationalism, this development can only represent a retreat from the advances made by modernism.

This is not to say that analyses that focus on the postmodern character and phase of nationalism have not made important empirical contributions to our understanding, only that their empirical discoveries have not been matched by similar broad theoretical advances. Some of these findings, notably those of the 'gender-nation' perspectives, which have drawn on concepts from other fields, can be fruitfully integrated with, while modifying, one or other of the existing paradigms and thereby enrich our understanding of the wider phenomena of ethnicity, nations and nationalism. Whether it will be possible to create a new overarching paradigm, or whether it will be enough to integrate gender concepts with existing (but modified) paradigms in the field, remains to be seen. But, in general, until the analyses of 'fragmentation' and 'post-modernity' make their assumptions explicit within a broader sociological and historical framework, they will be unable to advance the theory of nations and nationalism and elucidate the many problems in this field.

Conclusion
Problems, paradigms and prospects

So where does the theory of nations and nationalism stand today?

Problems

Many years ago, Max Weber warned of the difficulties facing the attempt to construct a 'sociological typology' of 'community sentiments of solidarity', and his warning applies equally to a general theory of nations and nationalism. The problems that our survey has revealed include:

1   The failure to reach a consensus on the delimitation of the field, in particular, the disagreement between those who wish to treat problems of nations and nationalism as quite separate and distinct from issues of ethnicity, and those who regard ethnic and national phenomena as comprising different aspects of a single theoretical and empirical field, a distinction that corresponds to that between the modernist and the perennialist (and primordialist) paradigms.

2   The notorious terminological difficulties in the field, and the failure to reach even a preliminary agreement on the definitions of key concepts. It is also clear that scholars have quite different approaches to the question of definitions, and in particular whether the concept of the 'nation' can only apply where a majority of the designated population is included (and participates) in the nation.

3   The problems of definitions arise, in part, from the deep divisions between basic paradigms and methodological approaches in the field. Once again, there is no agreement about the fundamental theoretical objectives, let alone substantive elements, of explanations, for example: whether explanations should be causal, whether they ought to be framed in purely individualistic terms, how far they should be reductionist, and so on.

4   From these broad differences spring the many divergent research programmes and interests in the field. Coupled with the swiftly evolving politics of ethnicity and nationalism, it is hardly surprising if research should be carried out on a wide range of topics and problems within the vast terrain of ethnic and national phenomena; and that it is often quite

difficult to relate various research concerns to each other to form a more composite picture of progress in the field.

5   Finally, there is the problem of different value-orientations to issues of ethnicity and nationalism. From these spring often quite opposed ideological positions *vis-à-vis* ethnic and national phenomena, which in turn help to determine different research problems and interests – as, for example, with the current interests in civic nationalism, hybridised identity and globalisation.

There is a further difficulty: the problem of defining the relevant questions in the field. Very often, we are dealing with theories, models and approaches which are equally plausible and valid, even if they appear to be based on opposed premises, because they seek answers to quite different questions. The most obvious distinction here is between accounts of the causes and of the consequences of nationalism. But equally, as we have seen, various theories and perspectives may be concerned with quite different objects of explanation, for example, ethnic identity and community as opposed to nations and/or nationalism, or politically significant nationalisms as opposed to national identity. This means that, in an important sense, we cannot easily assess the relative merits of rival theories and models; and that their vaunted rivalry is more apparent than real, given the very different questions they seek to answer and hence the varied dimensions on which they focus. In the place of genuine theoretical dialogue, we often find monologues that intersect.

In fact, none of the theories begins to cover the full range of even the most general questions one might ask of phenomena in this field. These would include questions about the origins and formation of *ethnies*, the conditions of ethnocentrism, the basis of ethnic community, as well as the nature and significance of ethnic identity; the origins and formation of nations, the nature and significance of national identity, the social, cultural and political bases of nations and the modernity or otherwise of nations; the (gendered, class and cultural) character of nationalist ideologies and movements, their role in forging nations and national identities, and the contribution of nationalist intellectuals and others; and finally, the consequences for society and culture of a world of national states, the geopolitical impact of nations and nationalism, and the chances of creating an orderly community of states.

Paradigms

Given these difficulties and problems, one might be forgiven for thinking the task of evolving a theory of nations and nationalism both undesirable and impossible. Yet such a conclusion would be unwarranted and overly pessimistic. A general theory is desirable for both intellectual and sociopolitical reasons: to understand and explain ever larger segments of the field of ethnic and national phenomena, and grasp the mechanisms and linkages between various aspects, dimensions and processes in this ramified field, both for their own sake and because of the considerable impact of ethnic and national phenomena on other fields of human existence, notably international politics and global security. Given the interrelations between phenomena in this field, a general theory would enable us to understand lower-level, more specific phenomena or aspects, and thereby reveal the possibilities of and constraints upon policy-making.

But is such a theory possible? Is there any likelihood of explaining the great variety of phenomena, and addressing the many and varied questions and dimensions, in and through a single theory? In the light of the preceding critical survey of approaches, the answer at present can only be negative. The field is so riven by basic disagreements and so divided by rival approaches, each of which addresses only one or other aspect of this vast field, that a unified approach must seem quite unrealistic and any general theory merely utopian.

Nevertheless, even if we are as yet far from any theoretical convergence, we can still point to a number of significant contributions which have advanced our knowledge of the field. Compared to the relatively crude models of the 1950s and early 1960s, these contributions reveal a much greater level of sophistication and understanding of the complexities of the field. Unlike the earlier approaches and models which focused either on the ideologies of nationalism *per se* or on the sociodemographic correlates of 'nation-building', the contributions of the last three decades have paid much greater attention to the *subjective* dimensions of collective cultural identities – the impact of language and mass culture, the strategies of political and intellectual elites, the properties of discursive networks and ritualised activities, and the influence of ethnic symbol, myth and memory. These advances have greatly enlarged our understanding of ethnic and national phenomena. Here, surely, are grounds for limited optimism.

In fact, each of the major paradigms in the field has generated research contributions that have enhanced our grasp of the dynamics of nations and nationalism. Let me give a few examples.

Primordialists attempt to understand the passion and self-sacrifice characteristic of nations and nationalism by deriving them from 'primordial' attributes of basic social and cultural phenomena like language, religion, territory, and especially kinship. Primordialist approaches, whether of the cultural or the sociobiological varieties, have sensitised us to the intimate links between ethnicity and kinship, and ethnicity and territory, and have revealed the ways in which they can generate powerful sentiments of collective belonging. This is evident, not only in the work of van den Berghe and Geertz, but also in Grosby's research on ancient Israel.

Perennialism views nations over the *longue durée* and attempts to grasp their role as long-term components of historical development – whether they are seen as temporally continuous or recurrent in history. Perennialists tend to derive modern nations from fundamental ethnic ties, rather than from the processes of modernisation. Perennialist approaches, like those of Fishman, Armstrong, Seton-Watson and, in respect of ethnicity, Connor and Horowitz, have contributed greatly to our understanding of the functions of language and ethnic ties, and the power of myths of origin and familial metaphors, in rousing popular support for nationalism. Here they serve as valuable correctives to the more extreme modernist interpretations and remind us of continuities and recurrences of ethnic phenomena.

Ethno-symbolism aims to uncover the symbolic legacy of ethnic identities for particular nations, and to show how modern nationalisms and nations rediscover and reinterpret the symbols, myths, memories, values and traditions of their ethno-histories, as they face the problems of modernity. Here too the attempts by Armstrong, Hutchinson and myself to trace the role of myths, symbols, values and memories in generating ethnic and national attachments and forging cultural and social networks, have added to our appreciation of the subjective and historical dimensions of nations and nationalism. This is matched by a parallel concern with investigating the ways in which nationalists have rediscovered and used the ethnosymbolic repertoire for national ends, in particular the myths and memories of ethnic election, sacred territory, collective destiny and the golden age.

Modernists seek to derive both nations and nationalism from the novel processes of modernisation, and to show how states, nations and nationalisms, and notably their elites, have mobilised and united populations in novel ways to cope with modern conditions and modern political imperatives. Modernist approaches like those of Anderson and Hobsbawm have been particularly illuminating in uncovering the role of discursive networks of communication and of ritualised activities and symbolism in forging national communities. Scholars such as Mann, Breuilly, Tilly and Giddens have done much to demonstrate the formative role of the state, warfare and bureaucracy, while the often decisive role of political elites and their strategies has been explored by scholars like Brass and Hechter. This is paralleled by the work on the intelligentsia's seminal role by Hroch, Nairn and others, who have developed the powerful insights and wide-ranging analyses of Gellner and Kedourie.

Postmodern analyses have revealed the fragmentation of contemporary national identities, and suggest the advent of a new 'post-national' order of identity politics and global culture. Analyses of such postmodern themes as fragmentation, feminism and globalisation can be seen as continuations of components of the modernist paradigm. Some of them, notably those of Bhabha, Chatterjee and Yuval-Davis, have embraced a 'postmodern*ist*' deconstructionism, whereas others – for example, those of Mosse, Schlesinger, Kandiyoti, Brubaker and Billig – are intent on exploring novel postmodern dimensions. Though they may eschew a more general theory of nationalism, they embody significant advances in our understanding of the dynamics of identity in plural Western societies.

These five perspectives reveal, I think, a certain order and coherence in what at first sight appears to be an inchoate and indeterminate field of phenomena. While some research interests and problems may still fall outside their scope, most of the issues of central concern to scholars in the field can be encompassed, and grasped, in terms of one or other of these major paradigms. They in turn allow us to gauge the main contributions and advances in the field, revealing a field with a high level and wide range of research activity, and one in which several new theoretical advances have been made in recent decades. While most have been monologues, there have also been some important theoretical debates such as those between primordialists and instrumentalists, and between modernists and perennialists; and compared to the position in the 1960s, when so few scholars had entered the field, the theoretical study of nations, nationalism and ethnicity has matured considerably in scope, depth and sophistication.

Prospects

We are left with a not unfamiliar paradox. On the one hand, there is little sign of any theoretical convergence in the field, let alone a unified theory or agreed paradigm. The study of nations and nationalism is rent by deep schisms. On the other hand, a host of significant theoretical and empirical advances and contributions have widened our horizons and deepened our understanding of issues in the field. For all that, the analysis of nationalism remains elusive. So many basic questions continue unanswered, so few scholars are prepared to agree even on first principles. Given the rate at which new ideas and findings are thrown up, our bafflement is likely to increase. Though we may see a measure of consolidation, as the field becomes a subject for teaching and courses proliferate, the theoretical assumptions, research interests and value-orientations of scholars remain too divergent to ensure that greater coherence can be introduced into the analysis of ethnicity and nationalism. For the present, all we can hope for is the generation of new ideas which will illuminate one or other corner of the broad canvas, especially as so many scholars have abandoned the larger narratives and operate with tacit paradigms according to their particular interests. Hopefully, in some years, scholars will return to the major paradigms and seek some resolution of outstanding problems. Certainly, progress in the field depends as much on systematic attempts to answer questions and deal with debates thrown up by the major paradigms as it does on generating new ideas and research.

Does this mean that there is no prospect of bridging the gulf between the various paradigms, and especially that between perennialists and modernists? Such a conclusion would, again, be unduly pessimistic. I can see two ways in which we could envisage some kind of accommodation, if not agreement, between not just medieval (and ancient) and modern historians, but also between perennialist and modernist social scientists.

The first is on the level of theory. We can envisage scenarios of at least partial theoretical convergence, in which the concerns and assumptions of some of the paradigms might be fruitfully combined. But this can only be achieved by accepting the close links between ethnicity and nations and nationalism and the perennialist historians' argument that *some* nations and their particular nationalisms have existed well before the advent of modernity (however defined). This in turn means that we must decouple nations and specific nationalisms from 'modernisation'. At the same time, the modernists are surely right to insist on the modernity of *many* nations, as well as of 'nationalism-in-general' (the ideology and theory). The conditions of modernity clearly favour the replication of nations, national states and nationalisms in all parts of the globe. This would also allow us to accept the ethno-symbolist contention that most nations are formed on the basis of pre-existing ethnic ties and sentiments, even if in time they go well beyond them, and that their nationalisms necessarily use those ethnic symbols, memories, myths and traditions which most resonate with the majority of the designated 'people' whom they wish to mobilise. This kind of combined approach might also help us to explain some of the characteristic postmodern concerns with globalisation, ethnic fragmentation, and the revitalisation of ethnic ties, while also suggesting deep historical grounds for the sense of immemoriality and continuity which underpins the profound attachments of so many people to their *ethnies* and nations.

Second, we can also seek some accommodation of paradigm assumptions at the level of research. Here I have in mind a research programme that would encourage historians and social scientists to compare the various forms of key institutional and cultural dimensions of nations and nationalism, with a view to discovering how their recent and 'modern' forms differ from earlier, 'premodern' ones. As a first step, we might envisage comparisons along six main institutional dimensions, namely:

1 **The state**. A comparison of forms of polities from early kingship and city-state forms to the most recent polyethnic democratic national states would help to reveal how far the sentiments of loyalty associated with each resembled, or differed, from each other; and how far each was able to mobilise different strata and forge unity within the polity. In particular, this project should throw light on how far 'citizenship' and citizens' rights constituted a necessary component of any view of the nation and its nationalism.

2 **Territory**. Here too we might compare ancient, medieval and modern forms of territorial attachments, and the nature of boundaries of both communities and polities in each period and continent. It would also be necessary to explore the more elusive issues of how landscapes and sacred sites contributed to the generation of ideas of 'homeland' and national territory, as well as the related questions of ethnoscapes, 'natural frontiers' and national borders.

3   **Language**. In the light of the importance attached to language by various theories of nationalism, this project would need to compare the ways in which languages and scripts contributed to ethnic and national feelings in different periods of history; and especially to what extent, and when, various vernacularising movements and language revivals, as well as their associated literatures, contributed to the rise of ethnic attachments and national sentiments.

4   **Religion**. Given the resurgence of religious nationalisms, it becomes even more important to determine how far earlier forms of ethnic sentiment and later forms of nationalism were similarly imbued with religious beliefs and sentiments. Here we would need to undertake comparative studies of the impact of the belief-systems of the various world religions, and notably of their ideas of ethnic election, to see how far they were able to mobilise people and influence modern, even secular, nationalisms. We would also need to discover to what extent scriptures, liturgies, clergies and shrines were successful in propagating these beliefs and sentiments in various ethnic cultures and in successive periods of history.

5   **History**. In view of the centrality of 'history' and history-writing in the creation of national communities, we need to compare the various forms of historical consciousness and historiography in different cultures and periods, in order to determine how far modern modes differ from earlier forms and how far, in each period, a sense of history was vital to the creation and maintenance of ethnic communities and nations. Such a project would concentrate especially on the various kinds of 'ethno-history' and the significance of different images of communal 'golden ages'.

6   **Rites and ceremonies**. This project would explore the role of public ceremonies, festivals, symbols and rituals in the creation and maintenance of collective identity and solidarity in different cultures and historical periods. Given the centrality of foundation and origin myths, the place of ancestral monuments and remembrance ceremonies, especially those that commemorate the 'glorious dead' and fallen heroes in both pre-modern and modern societies, needs particular attention.

A combination of perspectives and paradigms, and a set of research programmes along these lines, does not seek to mask the deep theoretical divisions which have been highlighted throughout this survey. Nor is it meant to suggest that we can somehow 'transcend' the very real problems which the paradigm debates have thrown up. The problems will not go away, nor will the divisions disappear. But what the above sketches suggest is that the paradigm divisions are not set in stone, that scholars do in fact cross the divide, and that we can envisage fruitful permutations and research programmes which may produce further advances in our understanding of ethnicity and nationalism. Here, too, we have grounds for guarded optimism.

What we can be sure of is that, just as the old red lines of nationalism erupt once again across the globe, and just as the field of ethnic and national phenomena is becoming a magnet for scholarship and research everywhere, so the need to explain and understand the many issues that it throws up becomes all the more urgent. This means that we cannot evade the task of theory-construction. If the former grand narratives of nations and nationalism no longer command respect, the imperatives of the times in which we live urge us to fashion new explanations more attuned to our perceptions and to the problems that we face.

Notes

Introduction

1 For a critique of such group realism and essentialism, from the standpoint of the 'new institutionalism' in sociology, see Brubaker (1996: ch. 1). Brubaker argues that the conventional 'substantialist' view reifies nations and treats them as real communities and as 'substantial, enduring collectivities'. We should avoid reifying the concept of the 'nation' and rather 'think about nationalism without nations'. For a brief discussion of this view, see Chapter 4.

2 This kind of individualistic 'recipe' analysis was applied, in a rather psychologistic manner, to national development by Daniel Lerner (1958) and, in a much more sociologically sophisticated way, by W. Smith (1965) and Ronald Dore (1969). I have discussed this approach in A. D. Smith (1983a: ch. 5).

3 Brubaker rightly calls our attention to the developments in social theory that have challenged the conventional 'realist' understanding of the nation: these include the flourishing of 'network theory', the theories of rational action, the rise of 'constructivist' theoretical stances, and finally an emergent postmodernist sensibility that emphasises 'the fragmentary, the ephemeral, and the erosion of fixed forms and clear boundaries' (Brubaker 1996: 19). In fact, not all these developments point in the same direction; see my discussions of the rational choice model in Chapter 3, of 'constructivist' theory in Chapter 6, and of 'postmodernist' approaches in Chapter 9.

4 Unfortunately, we lack adequate, up-to-date bibliographies of the field, at least in the English language. The earlier one by Koppel Pinson (1935) was superseded by the more ambitious one by Karl Deutsch (1956); this was supplemented by short annotated bibliographies by Stein Rokkan and his colleagues (1972) and by A. D. Smith (1973a). Brief bibliographies may also be found in the Readers on *Nationalism* and *Ethnicity* edited by John Hutchinson and Anthony D. Smith (Hutchinson and A. D. Smith 1994, 1996).

5 For this emphasis on the shaping of the (ethnic) past by the present and by contemporary preoccupations and interests, see Tonkin *et al.* (1989: Introduction). For a critique which sees this approach as embodying a 'blocking presentism', see the essay on Yoruba ethnogenesis by Peel (1989) in the same volume.

1 The rise of classical modernism

1 J. Michelet: *Historical View of the French Revolution*, tr. C. Cocks, London: S. Bell & Sons, 1890: III, chs 10–12, 382–403, cited in Kohn (1955: 97–102). For Michelet, see Kohn (1961); and on the Abbe Siéyès, Cobban (1957).

2 On Herder and Moser, see Barnard (1965) and Berlin (1976); see also the argument in Viroli (1995: ch. 4). For Mill's views, see Mill (1872). On the early development of

nationalist thought, see the detailed study of Kemilainen (1964) and the concise survey by Llobera (1994: ch. 7).

3 For the racist schemas of nationalism, see Poliakov (1974) and A. D. Smith (1979: chs 3–4). Marxism's Hegelian legacy and especially its influence on Engels is explored in Rosdolsky (1964); cf. also Davis (1967: chs 1–3).

4 See Bauer (1924) and the long extract in English in Balakrishnan (1996: 39–77). For the Austro-Marxists, see Talmon (1980: Part III, ch. 7) and Nimni (1994).

5 I know of no study of these dilemmas in the thought of the founding fathers or leading exponents of nationalism. But see Baron (1960) and A. D. Smith (1979: ch. 5). On Mazzini, see Mack Smith (1994).

6 For example, in Stalin's well known essay of 1912 (Stalin 1936). On early Marxist assumptions about nationalism, see Fisera and Minnerup (1978); for latterday Marxist assumptions, see the discussion of Tom Nairn's account by Eric Hobsbawm (1977).

7 For functionalist developments of crowd behaviour models, see Kornhauser (1959) and Smelser (1962); cf. my critique in A. D. Smith (1983a: ch. 3). For debts to the later Freud, Simmel and Mead, see Grodzins (1956), Doob (1964) and Barbu (1967).

8 We can trace this influence especially on what I call theorists of state-centred modernism like Giddens, Breuilly and Mann, whom I discuss in Chapter 4.

9 See also the analyses of Hertz (1944) and Shafer (1955). For a critique of Kohn's schema, see Hutchinson (1987: ch. 1); for critiques of the typologies of Kohn, Hayes and Snyder and others: see A. D. Smith (1983a: ch. 8).

10 For the French Revolution and nationalism, see Shafer (1938), Cobban (1969), Kohn (1967b) and O'Brien (1988b). For the view that nationalism emerged in the sixteenth century, see Marcu (1976) and the critique in Breuilly (1993: 3–5). For the question of the European sources of nationalism in Asia and Africa, see Hodgkin (1964) and Kedourie (1971), and the critical discussion in Chatterjee (1986).

11 See, for example, Walek-Czernecki (1929), Handelsman (1929), Levi (1965) and Brandon (1967). See also the debates in Tipton (1972) and the critique of Hugh Seton-Watson (1965 and 1977) by Susan Reynolds (1984) discussed in Chapter 8.

12 This is especially true of Gellner's theory, for example, 'nationalism is not the awakening of an old, latent, dormant force. . . . Nations as a natural, God-given way of classifying men . . . are a myth' (1983: 48–9). On the 'naturalisation' of nationalist constructions of the nation, see Penrose (1995) and Brubaker (1996: ch. 1). On primordialism, see Chapter 7.

13 For the concept of 'state-nation', see Zartmann (1964) who derives it from the African experience of territorial nationalisms; cf. A. D. Smith (1983b: chs 1–3).

14 The sources of this model are to be found in the work of Karl Deutsch (1966, 1st edn 1953), Daniel Lerner (1958) and Karl Deutsch and William Foltz (1963). See also, *inter alia*, Pye (1962), Apter (1963a), Binder (1964), Almond and Pye (1965), Bellah (1965) and Eisenstadt (1965, 1968). For a critique of their functionalist assumptions, see A. D. Smith (1983a: ch. 3; 1973b).

15 I have analysed these early modernist perspectives and theories up to 1970 in A. D. Smith (1983a: chs 1–6).

2 The culture of industrialism

1 See also Gellner's lecture of 1982 (reprinted in 1987: ch. 2). For critiques of this early formulation, see Kedourie (1971: 19–20, 132); A. D. Smith (1983a: ch. 6).

2 Gellner adds that, although other modern developments, from the Reformation to colonialism, have contributed to its spread, nationalism is basically a product of industrial social organisation, exactly because cultural homogeneity is imposed by the requirements of an industrial society, with the result that every modern state must be legitimated in terms of the national principle (Gellner 1983: 40–3).

3 It is probably the experiences of the Czech migrations into German-speaking Bohemian areas in the Habsburg empire that Gellner has in mind in his depiction of Ruritanians in Megalomania; just as it was the experience of the *bidonvilles* of Morocco which he encountered during his research on the Berbers that inspired an important part of his earlier formulation.

4 Here, of course, Gellner has in mind the archetypal diaspora communities of the Armenians and the Jews, who despite being polyglot and flexible economic middlemen, found that their scriptural religion placed an insuperable barrier, a 'moral chasm', between them and the host society; cf. Armstrong (1976) and Zenner (1991).

5 Gellner uses the term 'proletariat', not in the traditional Marxist sense of wage-earning manual labourers, but more inclusively of all peasants and villagers physically and mentally uprooted by modernisation.

6 See my critique of the historical links between nationalist movements and industrialism, in A. D. Smith (1983a: ch. 6); see also Nettl and Robertson (1968: part I).

7 For general critiques of evolutionary modernisation theories and their applications to contemporary social and political change, see Geiger (1967), Gusfield (1967), Dore (1969), Nisbet (1969) and A. D. Smith (1973b).

8 In his last debate on the subject at Warwick, Gellner (1996) cited the Estonians as an example of a purely modern 'high' culture, which appeared *ex nihilo* in the nineteenth century. The question remains: why did the Estonians not adopt the high cultures of their German overlords or their Russian neighbours rather than modernise their own 'low' culture? See A. D. Smith (1996b). In his posthumously published *Nationalism*, Gellner (1997) amplified his view of the purely modern origins of nations. On the development of an Estonian national consciousness, see Raun (1987: 23–4, 32–3, 53–6, 62–7, 74–80). For Gellner's application of his theory to Eastern European nationalisms, see Gellner (1994: esp. ch. 2).

9 For the problem of ethnic volunteering in the First World War, see the discussion in Breuilly (1993: ch. 2).

10 On the French Third Republic and Lavisse, see Citron (1988); also more generally, Ozouf (1982). For the case of Japan, see Lehmann (1982); for Turkey, Berkes (1964) and Kushner (1976), and for Nigeria, Igwara (1993).

11 On Rousseau's views of the nation and patriotism, see Cohler (1970) and Viroli (1995: ch. 3). For Fichte's nationalism, see Reiss (1955) and the critique in Kedourie (1960). On Gökalp, see Lewis (1968: ch. 10) and Kedourie (1971: Introduction). For Ben-Zion Dinur, see Dinur (1969).

12 It was Walker Connor who first drew attention to the ethnically plural nature of ninety per cent of the world's states in the context of a radical critique of the model of 'nation-building', in a celebrated article entitled 'Nation-building or nation-destroying?' (Connor 1972; reprinted in Connor 1994: ch. 2). See also my discussion of territorial and ethnic nationalisms in A. D. Smith (1991: chs 5–6). All nationalisms strive for the unity of the nation, but not all of them conceive such unity in terms of ethnic purity or cultural homogeneity. It is this variability in the nature of the explanandum, the concept of the nation, that makes it so difficult to apply a single general theory globally.

13 The problems of maintaining or reconstructing a national identity in multicultural societies have occupied the attention of theorists of 'postmodernity' concerned with cultural difference in western liberal democracies. I touch on some of these issues in Chapter 9 below. See, for example, Miller (1995: ch. 4) and Tamir (1993), and on the politics of multiculturalism, Kymlicka (1995).

14 On the Czechs and their nationalism, see Zacek (1969), Seton-Watson (1977: 149–57), Agnew (1993) and Pynsent (1994: chs 2, 4). On the Finns and the rise of Finnish nationalism, see Branch (1985: Introduction), Singleton (1989) and Tagil (1995: part III). On the Ukrainian, see Portal (1969) and, for their growing sense of

difference from Great Russians, see Saunders (1993). On the Slovaks and the rise of Slovak nationalism, see Brock (1976), Paul (1985) and Pynsent (1994: ch. 2).

15 For this general view, see Tonkin *et al.* (1989: Introduction); but cf. A. D. Smith (1997b). For images of national *exempla virtutis*, see Rosenblum (1967: ch. 2).

16 On Tilak's nationalist use of the Hindu religion and episodes from the past, see Adenwalla (1961) and Kedourie (1971: 70–4). For the recent development of Hindu nationalism in India, see van der Veer (1994).

17 On this 'blocking presentism', see Peel (1989); for a more general critique, see A. D. Smith (1988, 1997b).

18 For discussions of 'ethnicity', see Tonkin *et al.* (1989) and Eriksen (1993). For the relationship of *ethnies* to nations, see Chapters 7 and 8.

3 Capitalism and nationalism

1 There is a large literature on the Marxist approaches to nationalism; see for example, Shaheen (1956), Davis (1967), Fisera and Minnerup (1978) and Connor (1984).

2 On the question of historyless peoples, see Rosdolsky (1964) and Cummins (1980).

3 For this idea of 'uneven development' in Gellner's early formulation, see Gellner (1964: ch. 7). For Frank's ideas, see Frank (1969) and for critiques, see Laclau (1971), Warren (1980) and, more directly related to nationalism, Orridge (1981).

4 For a general discussion of Nairn's analysis, see James (1996: ch. 6). For the two kinds of nationalism, see A. D. Smith (1991: chs 5–6).

5 See Nairn (1977: ch. 5). On early Indian nationalism, see McCulley (1966), Seal (1968) and Chatterjee (1986). On populism, see Gellner and Ionescu (1970); for romantic metaphors of nationalism, see Pearson (1993), and for national romantic movements, see Porter and Teich (1988). Nairn's emphasis on populist nationalism is criticised from a Marxist standpoint by Hobsbawm (1977).

6 On the 'nation-to-be', see Rotberg (1967). The nationalism of the French revolution eulogised 'the people', but in a pre-romantic, neo-classicist, manner; see Minogue (1967) and Kohn (1967b). On the relationship between neo-classicist and romantic elements, see A. D. Smith (1976).

7 For these criticisms, see the essays in Stone (1979). On late nineteenth-century France, see E. Weber (1979). On the rise of nationalism among 'overdeveloped' peoples, see Horowitz (1985: ch. 6) and Gellner (1983: 101–9).

8 This is the thesis propounded by Rostow (1960), but it can hardly be generalised. On the relationship of cultural nationalism to economic growth in Japan, see Yoshino (1992). On the concept of *atimia*: see Nettl and Robertson (1968: Part I).

9 This was a favoured theme in the late 1950s and 1960s: the era of decolonisation in Africa and Asia was associated both by colonial rulers and their opponents with the activities of intellectuals and, more generally, intelligentsia who were held responsible for the prevalent socialist nationalisms of so many 'Third World' states. See especially Hodgkin (1956), Coleman (1958), Shils (1960), Seton-Watson (1960), J. H. Kautsky (1962), Worsley (1964), Binder (1964), as well as the theories of Gellner (1964), Kedourie (1960, 1971) and A. D. Smith (1983a: ch. 10; 1979: chs 4–5, 7; 1981a: chs 5–6). The effect of singling out the intellectuals was to obscure the role of other strata and of the relationship between elites and mass of the population.

10 For some patterns of relationships between secular nationalists, traditional elites and the mass of the population, see D. Smith (1974) and Brass (1991). For the Eritrean case, see Cliffe (1989); for the Baluch struggle, see the penetrating essay by S. Harrison, 'Ethnicity and the political stalemate in Pakistan', in Banuazizi and Weiner (1986: 267–98, esp. 271–7); and, more generally, Brown (1989).

11 As part of the bargain in the negotiations for Union in 1707, the Scottish elites agreed to give up their own Parliament, but retained their autonomy in education,

local government, the legal system and ecclesiastical organisation; see Hanham (1969) and Webb (1977).

12 See, for example, the analyses of Quebec by McRoberts (1979) and of Hungarians in Transylvania under the Habsburg empire, by Verdery (1979).

13 Here I am only concerned with the application of 'rational-choice' theory to nation-alism, not with the general debate about its validity and utility; but see Olson (1965) and Hechter (1987).

14 Hechter considers the costs of secession to be widely known and understood. On the middle classes as the main constituency of a secessionist nationalism, see Hroch (1985) and Breuilly (1993: ch. 2). For a detailed empirical confirmation from Quebec, see Pinard and Hamilton (1984).

15 For a discussion of Horowitz's general theory, see Chapter 7. For other analyses of secession movements which give greater weight to geopolitical factors, as well as inter-national attitudes and legal norms, see Beitz (1979: Part II), Wiberg (1983), Mayall (1990: ch. 4) and Heraclides (1991).

4 State and nation

1 There is a large literature on bureaucracy and the state, but little on its relationship to the nation and nationalism. But see, apart from the theorists discussed in this chapter, Bendix (1996; 1st edn 1964), Poggi (1978) and Tivey (1980). For some case studies, see Corrigan and Sayer (1985), Brass (1985) and Brubaker (1996: ch. 2).

2 Again, there is a large literature on Marxist analyses of the state, but little that links it closely with nations or nationalism; but see Alavi (1972), Markovitz (1977), Saul (1979) and Amin (1981); also Poggi (1978).

3 On the colonial and post-colonial state in Africa, see Montagne (1952), Zartmann (1964), A. D. Smith (1983b: ch. 2) and Neuberger (1986).

4 Besides these typical West European and East European models, there are at least two others: the colonial state-to-nation model in Africa and parts of Asia, which is not the same as the indigeneous state-to-nation Western model, being a product of foreign rule; and the immigrant pioneer model, whereby an ethnic fragment creates a state and then seeks to incorporate other immigrant ethnic fragments, as in the United States, Canada and Australia; see Laczko (1994) and Castles *et al.* (1988).

5 For the impact of nationalism on the inter-state order and vice-versa, see Hinsley (1973) and Azar and Burton (1986). Posen (1993) and Snyder (1993) stress the security needs of states and communities as vital elements in the rise of nationalism.

6 Mann cites the case of 'Sumer' (Mann 1986: 90–3) as a federal 'people' whose 'professional scribes wrote in a common script, learned their trade with the help of identical word lists, and asserted they were indeed one people, the Sumerians'. He warns against adopting the claims of nineteenth century ethnography that 'the Sumerians were united by ethnicity, by membership in a common gene pool' (*ibid.*: 92). This seems to confuse ethnic culture with biology, and fails to give sufficient weight to subjective factors, such as Sumerian beliefs about their collective identity. Yet, Mann concedes, the Sumerians may have been an 'ethnic community' and had 'a weak but nonetheless real sense of collective identity, buttressed by language, foun-dation myths, and invented genealogies' (*ibid.*: 92). In general, except for ancient Egypt, pre-modern ethnic communities were 'small and tribal', like the Jews, while larger social units (empires or tribal confederacies) 'were too stratified for communi-ties to cross class barriers' (*ibid.*: 159). (The exceptions in the ancient world appear to have been the Assyrians, who developed what Mann regards as an upper-class form of 'nationalism', and the Greeks who had three concentric cultural networks, to the *polis*, Hellas and humanity.) Otherwise, Mann accepts Gellner's thesis that there was no possibility of a cross-class cultural unity within a particular territory, and hence of

nations and nationalism, before the onset of modernity (Mann 1993: 215–6; cf. Hall 1985).

7 On German nationalism and unification, see Droz (1967: 147–52) and Hughes (1988); on Italian unification, see Beales (1971) and Riall (1994); and on German and Italian unification, see Alter (1989: ch. 3) and Breuilly (1993: 96–115).

8 On nationalism and territory, see Anderson (1991: ch. 10), the essays in Hooson (1994) and A. D. Smith (1996a) and (1997a).

9 For the intimate connection between vernacular language and ethnicity, especially in Eastern Europe, see Fishman (1972, 1980) and Petrovich (1980). Examples of the close connection between such vernacular mobilisation and nationalism, see Branch (1985) on Finland and the *Kalevala*, Kitromilides (1979, 1989) on Greek language and nationalism, and Conversi (1990, 1997) on Basque and Catalan nationalism. See also the analysis of the role of vernacular and oral communications in spreading the Sikh ethno-nationalist demand for Kalistan by Deol (1996). For late medieval England, Christianity and the vernacular, see Hastings (1997: ch. 2).

10 Breuilly counterposes his set of nationalist propositions to those I outlined (in A. D. Smith 1983a: ch. 1; 1973a: section I), explicitly rejecting my assumption of the universality and polycentrism of modern nationalism.

11 For other studies of the social composition of nationalist movements, see Hroch (1985) and A. D. Smith (1983a: ch. 6).

12 John Breuilly is right to oppose the characterisation of nationalism as the politics of the intellectuals (which clearly belittles its power and resonance). At the same time, he underestimates and mistakes the reasons why nationalism holds special attractions for intellectuals. This, I think, resides less in its intellectual abstractions than its appeal to the aesthetic imagination. It is the nation's aesthetic and poetic properties (as Breuilly himself concedes a propos the importance of Afrikaner ceremonies and rituals), as well as the moral and didactic dimensions of nationalism, that hold such strong attractions for artists, writers, poets, historians, broadcasters and educators. This is well analysed and illustrated in the work of George Mosse (1964, 1976, 1994).

13 On Afrikaner myths of election and migration, see Thompson (1985) and Cauthen (1997); for myths and nationhood generally, see Hosking and Schöpflin (1997).

14 For a similar argument, brought against the Marxist developmentalists, see Orridge (1981) who emphasises the large number of dimensions and issues included in the concept of 'nationalism'.

15 Weber, of course, complemented the 'empathetic' approach with a 'causally adequate' analysis; see Freund (1970) and Giddens (1971); and see Chapter 3 (on Hechter).

16 On the question of method in defining the concept of the 'nation', see A. D. Smith (1983a: ch. 7); Connor (1978); Greenfeld (1992: ch. 1); Hastings (1997: ch. 1); and also Calhoun (1997: Introduction and ch. 1).

17 On these nationalisms and their culture values, see Conversi (1997) and Brand (1978). Other cases include Wales, Brittany and perhaps Quebec; see Mayo (1974), Williams (1977) and McRoberts (1979).

18 See Chapter 2 for my response to Gellner's version of the nationalism-to-nation argument. For a recognition that we cannot separate the analysis of 'national identity' from that of 'nationalism', see Billig (1995).

19 On these diaspora nationalisms, see Sheffer (1986) and A. D. Smith (1995c); more generally on diasporas, see Armstrong (1976) and Cohen (1997).

20 I exclude here the Nazi example which Breuilly himself highlights, as it includes other racial, and non-nationalist, ideological dimensions and motifs; see A. D. Smith (1979: ch. 3).

5 Political messianism

1 On the functionalist perspective on politics and religion, see especially Apter (1963b) and Eisenstadt (1968). For a critique, see A. D. Smith (1983a: ch. 3).

2 On Durkheim and nationalism, see Mitchell (1931). See also A. D. Smith (1983b) and Guibernau (1996: 26–31).

3 For Kedourie, nationalism is a purely secular and modern, as well as invented, ideology. It is also a doctrine that requires cultural homogeneity, and as such appeals to the intellectuals whose status depends on linguistic and cultural attainments and recognition. Kedourie also points out that literacy and rationalist education were specifically European preoccupations and attainments, and that scholarly European research into overseas peoples and territories, coupled with the spread of literacy, encouraged the discovery and classification of non-Europeans as ethnic groups and nations, and the rise of 'marginal men' (Kedourie 1971: 27).

4 For some examples of nationalism's tendency to assimilate traditional religion, see Binder (1964), A. D. Smith (1973c) and D. Smith (1974). But see the more general analysis of Juergensmeyer (1993) who argues the reverse: the attempt by a revived traditional religion to take the nation into its domain against the secular state.

5 Kedourie (1971) also analyses the religio-political ideals and activities of Nkrumah, Ghandi, Dedan Kimathi, Simon Kimbangu, André Matswa, John Chilembwe, Kenyatta, Sukarno and Marcus Garvey, among others, all of whom embraced an extremism that was characteristic of the 'marginal men'; see also Kedourie (1966).

6 For an account of the reception of nationalist ideas in sub-Saharan Africa which takes the local milieux into account, see Markovitz (1977: ch. 3), and for India, see Chatterjee (1986 and 1993).

7 There is, for example, no millennial movement in Egypt (rather than the Sudan) preceding the rise of Egyptian nationalism in the 1880s or in Turkey preceding the emergence of a Turkish nationalism in the 1900s. We look in vain for an Indian millennialism preceding the rise of Indian nationalism in the 1880s or any millennial movements preceding the rise of French or German nationalisms; see A. D. Smith (1979: ch. 2).

8 Of course, Kedourie is right in one respect: 'local anomalies' are legion and their global manifestations attest a wider vision of nationalism whereby the 'true nature' of the world must be revealed. It is this 'naturalising' quality of nationalism that makes it so radical. Kedourie (1992) analyses the transition to such radical politics in the Middle East.

9 These are, of course, seen as predominantly male virtues (with women serving in the role of mothers of warriors), on which see Nira Yuval-Davis (1997) and Sluga (1998) and my brief discussion in Chapter 9. For self-sacrificing, stoic nationalisms, see Herbert (1972) and Draper (1970); and Elshtain (1993).

10 The title of Pinsker's classic proto-Zionist pamphlet was *AutoEmancipation* (1882). *Fraternité* (this did not include *sororité*) demanded self-denial and self-sacrifice – on whose visual representation, see Rosenblum (1967: ch. 2), Honour (1968: ch. 3) and Detroit (1975).

11 It is also not clear whether Kedourie believes *ethnies* to antedate nationalism and the rise of nations. At times he appears to suggest that there is some kind of pre-existing ethnic community whose (religious) past can be used and perverted, as by modern nationalist Turks, Greeks and Jews.

12 On the contrasts and similarities between religious and nationalist attitudes and practices, see the early work of von der Mehden (1963); cf. also Brass (1974) and (1991). Kedourie's view is not a case of simple instrumentalism. For him, the shift from religion to nationalism is part of a profound, if catastrophic, revolution, signalling the end of a tolerant, pluralist world and its replacement by a harsh, homogenising and

subversive world. This is no aberration, nor is it simply a conspiracy. The damage goes much deeper and the danger is much greater.

13 One may doubt Juergensmeyer's method, which leans heavily on interviews with official spokespersons (and in some cases, only a few such representatives), and question his conclusion of an overall opposition between the secular West and religious nationalism, given the absence of any sign of unity between the different forms of religious (including fundamentalist) nationalisms, on which see Marty and Appleby (1991). But Juergensmeyer is surely right to emphasise the continuing importance of religion and religious community in many lands, and the ways in which religious beliefs and sentiments underlie many nationalisms.

14 Kapferer's analysis is rich in meaning and suggestion for the relations between religious traditions and nationalism, but one wonders whether the ANZAC example which he so perceptively analyses retains its hold for most Australians today and whether, in consequence of being an increasingly multicultural immigrant society, it can sustain a sense of nationhood; see Castles *et al.* (1988).

15 For fuller discussions of these themes, see A. D. Smith (1996a) and the essays in Hosking and Schöpflin (1997).

16 The causal weight of *ressentiment* for nationalism is open to question, but Greenfeld (1992) offers a rich and wide-ranging analysis which draws together a variety of other causal factors in each of her historical case-studies.

6 Invention and imagination

1 The literature on postmodernism is vast, but though postmodernists have much to say about social identities, feminism and post-colonialism, they have not devoted so much attention to nationalism. But see Bhabha (1990: ch. 16) and Chatterjee (1993), briefly discussed in Chapter 9; also some of the essays in Ringrose and Lerner (1993) and in Eley and Suny (1996). It is impossible in such a short survey as this to do justice to this burgeoning literature. On the theme of 'nationalism and postmodernity', see the brief overview in Smart (1993: 139–45).

2 Hobsbawm cites the study of Swiss cultural and social development by Rudolf Braun: *Sozialer and kultureller Wandel in einem landlichen Industriegebiet im 19. und 20. Jarhundert*, ch. 6 (Erlenbach-Zurich 1965). But equally germane is the enquiry into Swiss foundation myths by Kreis (1991); cf. Kohn (1957).

3 Note that Hobsbawm here shifts the emphasis from the 'nation' and nationalism to the 'nation-state', since he regards the concept of 'nation' as irrelevant unless it is linked to the territorial state. But the real question is how far the Israeli and Palestinian 'nations' are novel, without the state; see Kimmerling and Migdal (1994) and Shimoni (1995: ch. 1).

4 This goes some way to meeting the key point made by his critics, though Hobsbawm is only interested in the spate of production of 'invented traditions', rather than their reception. On French memorials and monuments, see the volumes edited by Pierre Nora (1984, 1986) (vols I, *La République*, and II, *La Nation*). For German nineteenth-century commemorations and ceremonies, see Mosse (1976). For the deliberate creation of a Zionist culture and art, combining Jewish traditions with secular, Enlightenment ideals, by and for the Western Jewish middle classes, see Berkovitz (1996).

5 Here Hobsbawm follows Barth's (1969) analysis of ethnicity as a social boundary phenomenon of exclusion.

6 It is, of course, only by insisting on the primacy of the German Romantic and organic version of nationalism that the seminal role of French nationalism in the Revolution can be overlooked. For pre-Revolutionary ideas about the nation in France, see Palmer (1940), Godechot (1965) and Baker (1990: ch. 2). For the importance of linguistic politics during the Revolution, see Kohn (1967b) and Lartichaux

(1977). See also Leith (1965) and Crow (1985: ch. 7) on artistic propaganda and representations before and during the Revolution.

7 On the nationalisms in this period in the West, see Kohn (1967b) and Seton-Watson (1977: ch. 3); and for Latin America, see Phelan (1960), Humphreys and Lynch (1965), Brading (1985) and Anderson (1991: ch. 4).

8 For the normative and analytical debate about 'civic' and ethnic' nationalisms, see Chapter 9. For the two kinds of nationalism in France, see Kedward (1965) and Gildea (1994).

9 Eric Hobsbawm's discussion of 'ethnicity' veers between culture and 'race' (*ibid*.: 63–7), and his discussion of ethnic community in non-European plural states (*ibid*.: 153–62), together with his note on the term *ethnie* (*ibid*.: 160, note 24), aim to show how far removed ethnic conflicts are from what Marxists referred to as 'the national question' and from nationalism. The idea that some *ethnies* may provide bases (as cultural network, social institution and popular myth, memory and belief-system) for the formation of nations and national states is, for Hobsbawm, as still-born as his 'proto-nations'. This does not prevent him from recognising the need for ethnic belonging and the persistence of ethnic conflicts since the events of 1989–92.

A similar instrumentalism, this time employing Freud's theory of the 'narcissism of minor differences', is invoked by Michael Ignatieff (1998: ch. 2) to explain why the 'neutral facts about a people', the '"minor differences" – indifferent in themselves', are transformed by nationalism into major differences; and so why minor ethnic differences between Serbs and Croats became hardened into the battle lines of Serbo-Croat ethnic hatred. Again, this assumes that both ethnicity and nationalism are largely fictive narratives, constructed to bestow or withold power and privilege on some to the exclusion of others (*ibid*.: 38–9, 50–3, 56–7). At the same time, Ignatieff assumes the reality of ethnic groups, concedes the history of ethnic differences and even antagonisms in the Balkans, and the frequency with which nationalism answers to genuine needs (*ibid*.: 39, 44, 59). To which we may add that Tito's Yugoslavia institutionalised the major ethnic communities in six republics, giving political and economic expression to their ethnic myths and memories.

10 There is also the fact of the well known mass self-sacrifices of the First World War, on which see Gillis (1994) and Winter (1995).

11 Yet the context of his use of the term 'invention' does call to mind a powerful instrument for deconstructing and denigrating both nations and nationalisms.

12 The formation of Pakistan is the subject of a seminal debate on 'primordial' versus 'instrumental' accounts of ethnicity and nationalism by Paul Brass and Francis Robinson in Taylor and Yapp (1979); and see Brass (1991). See Chapter 7 for further discussion.

13 Deutsch and the communications theorists had singled out the importance of the mass media in creating 'publics' available for political participation and action. But Anderson's analysis goes beyond the rather crude determinism implicit in the earlier approach, in linking these 'objective' technological, economic and political processes with discursive networks and subjective factors.

14 In contrast to the modernist belief in the powerful sociological reality of nations (though not that of their own myth and self-image) to be found in the work of Ernest Gellner or Tom Nairn, Anderson denies such reality to the nation outside the representations of its members and portraitists. But, in that case, on what basis can we explain the evident fact (which Anderson underlines) of the continuing hold, and indeed renewal, of nations and their nationalisms? See the critique in Hastings (1997: ch. 1) and the discussion of Brubaker in Chapter 4.

15 'Intellectualism' here is not only a question of the human faculty (of imagination), but also of the particular medium (the printed word) as opposed to other kinds of media. For the idea of the nation as felt and acted out, see my brief discussion of Fishman (1980) in Chapter 7.

16 On racism and nationalism generally, see Poliakov (1974), A. D. Smith (1979: chs 3–4) and Balibar and Wallerstein (1991: ch. 6). For some case-studies which reveal their complex interrelations, see Geiss (1974), MacDougall (1982), Thompson (1985) and Mosse (1994, 1995).

17 See the critique by Gellner (1983: ch. 5) of such subjectivist and voluntarist definitions.

18 Massimo d'Azeglio, former Prime Minister of Piedmont, is said to have remarked after the unification of Italy: 'We have made Italy: now we must make Italians' (cited in Seton-Watson 1977: 107). On the growth of a sense of *italianita* among the middle classes in Italy, see Riall (1994: ch. 5). On the political importance of an oral culture in sub-Saharan Africa, see Mazrui (1985). It is perhaps surprising that Benedict Anderson underplays the role of religion outside (and within) Europe, given his recognition of its critical importance in relation to death and the desire for immortality. In making an over-sharp dichotomy between 'religion' and its successor, 'nationalism', Anderson seems to accept the traditional Marxist 'supersession of religion' schema.

19 On Herder's 'cultural populism', see Berlin (1976). The role of the mass media, particularly television, is discussed in Schlesinger (1991); and see Deol (1996).

20 See Chapter 7 below for Walker Connor's ideas about the hold of kinship sentiments and the political role of familial analogy. For the 'appeal to posterity' in neo-classical representations of nations and national heroes, see Honour (1968: ch. 3).

21 On the myth of ethnic election, which appears among a variety of peoples from Armenians, Jews and Greeks to Russians, Poles, Swiss, French, English, Scots, Welsh, Irish, Afrikaners, Americans and Mexicans, as well as among non-Christian peoples like the Persians, Arabs, Chinese, Japanese and Sinhalese, see Cherniavsky (1975), Armstrong (1982: ch. 7), A. D. Smith (1992a) and Akenson (1992).

7 Primordialism and perennialism

1 Kohn (1967a) differentiated within the 'Western' type of nationalism a 'collectivist' French version from the 'individualistic' Anglo-Saxon version of the nation. Both versions, however, viewed the nation as a rational association of free citizens.

2 For the sources of 'organic' nationalism among German Romantics, see Reiss (1955) and Barnard (1965); and for a powerful critique, Kedourie (1960).

3 Similar problems can be found in other cases of 'long-lived peoples' – Egyptians, Armenians, Chinese, Japanese and Jews. On the question of Egyptian continuity, see Gershoni and Jankowski (1987: ch. 6); and on Armenian ethno-history, see Lang (1980). On Jewish continuities, see Seltzer (1980) and Zerubavel (1995). For Japan and its culture, see Lehmann (1982) and Yoshino (1992).

4 This is the solution preferred by Horowitz (1985), whose approach I outline below.

5 Geertz refers here to B. R. Ambedkar: *Thoughts on Linguistic States*, Delhi (ca. 1955, 11). On subnationalism in Africa, see Olorunsola (1972), and in Europe, Petersen (1975).

6 Francis Robinson argued that the growth of Muslim sentiment in northwest India, and the concentration, collective memories and cultural resources of the Muslims in the United Provinces, acted as important constraints on the freedom of action of Muslim elites in India. But Robinson goes further, claiming that 'Islamic ideas and values . . . both provide a large part of the framework of norms and desirable ends within which the UP Muslim elite take their rational political decisions, and on occasion act as a motivating force', because of the central Islamic tradition of community, the *umma* (Robinson 1979: 78–82).

7 For an overview of some 'primordialist' positions, see Stack (1986: Introduction). For 'instrumentalist' views, see *inter alia* Bonacich (1973), Cohen (1974), Okamura (1981) and Banton (1983, 1994), Eriksen (1993) and most of the essays in Wilmsen and McAllister (1996). A range of views is presented in Glazer and Moynihan (1975), who

adopt an intermediate position themselves. See also Epstein (1978) who focuses on the creative, subjective aspects of ethnicity. For attempts to synthesise the rival positions, see McKay (1982) and Scott (1990).

8 For Edwin Wilmsen (in Wilmsden and McAllister 1996: 3) 'Primordialist ethnic claims are nothing more than claims to ownership of the past and rights to its use for present purposes'. This is very different, but perhaps not incompatible with, the understanding of a theorist like Grosby (1995), whose analysis of the significance of national territory as an object of primordial beliefs rests on its widely perceived life-enhancing qualities for those who reside on it and who are, in part, collectively constituted by those beliefs. See also Chapter 9.

9 For these terms, see Brass (1991), A. D. Smith (1984b, 1995b), as well as McKay (1982) and Scott (1990).

10 This is also the project of Manning Nash (1989), for whom the most common ethnic boundary markers are kinship, commensality and a common cult. These form 'a *single recursive metaphor*. This metaphor of blood, substance, deity symbolise the existence of the group while at the same time they constitute the group. . . . This trinity of boundary markers and mechanisms is the deep or basic structure of ethnic group differentiation' (*ibid.*: 111). Nash is wary of the concept of 'primordial ties' as applied to ethnicity: the building blocks of ethnicity (the body, language, shared history, religion, territory) may be relatively unchanging, but 'primordial ties' are 'like any other set of bonds, forged in the process of historical time, subject to shifts in meaning, ambiguities of reference, political manipulation, and vicissitudes of honour and obloquy'. This means that history, politics and other circumstances vary the kind of building blocks and the nature of the boundaries in each case (*ibid.*: 4–6).

11 E. Weber (1979) is a study of the incorporation of the great majority of the population into the French national state through the mass, compulsory education system, the conscript army after the defeat by Prussia, and the creation of a centralised communications network linking all the French provinces. Connor cites the slow stages of extension of the franchise in Britain, culminating only in 1918 with the enfranchisement of women and the remaining 20 per cent of men; at the same time, a highly elitist view of the French nation obtained in French politics until 1848.

12 On which see Doob (1964) and Billig (1995). For a very different view of the power and resilience of the inter-state order, see Mayall (1990); and see Chapter 9.

13 See Chapter 3 for Horowitz's analysis of the causes of secession and irredentism. On the differences between these types of ethnic movement, see Horowitz (1992).

14 It is not clear whether Horowitz regards nationalism as a mainly state-centred ideology and movement, or whether we can speak of 'ethno-nations' in the new states of Asia and Africa. For a different account, see D. Brown (1994).

15 The title of his book and an article (Armstrong 1992) may imply a leaning towards 'continuous' perennialism, but a later article (Armstrong 1997) supports the view that Armstrong is interested in the *recurrence* of the nation.

16 On national sentiment in the Middle Ages, see Tipton (1972), Guenée (1985) and Hastings (1997). For antiquity, see Levi (1965), Tcherikover (1970) and Alty (1982).

8 Ethno-symbolism

1 Another historian who dates the rise of nationalism to the sixteenth century is Marcu (1976). But most historians regard the late eighteenth century as the watershed which ushers in the ideology of 'national*ism*'.

2 This might be construed as an argument for the precedence of England, but a similar evolution, in which the state used religious (Catholic) and linguistic homogenisation to forge an (upper- and middle-class) nation, took place in France from at least the

fifteenth century; see Beaune (1985). But cf. Palmer (1940) and Godechot (1965) on the relative modernity of secular French national*ism*.

Hastings (1997: ch. 3) also argues for the early formation of the Scots, Irish and Welsh nations, the first on a mainly territorial basis, the others on an ethnic basis, with clear expressions of national*ism* consequent on Anglo-Norman invasions from the twelfth century.

3 But for Tilly it is political and economic activities, notably war-making by the state and the rise of the bourgeoisie, rather than ideas or symbols that shape both the older national states and the nations by design.

4 A good example is afforded by the chroniclers of fourteenth- and fifteenth-century Scotland, on which see Webster (1997: ch. 5); cf. also the Swiss chroniclers in the fifteenth and sixteenth centuries, on which see Im Hof (1991).

5 In eschewing any notion of primordialism, Reynolds also differs from the analysis of Guenée (1985); cf. also the debates in Tipton (1972), and the very different analyses in Bartlett (1994: ch. 8) and the selective continuous perennialism in Hastings (1997).

6 For this catalogue, see Webster and Backhouse (1991). The historical introduction by Nicholas Brooks opens with these words:

> The Anglo-Saxons, whose artistic, technological and cultural achievements in the seventh, eighth and ninth centuries are diplayed in this exhibition, were the true ancestors of the English of today. At the time the works were produced, there were several rival Anglo-Saxon kingdoms, each of which had its own dynasty, its own aristocracy and its own separate traditions and loyalties. Spoken English already showed wide regional variations of dialect. None the less the Anglo-Saxons had a sense that they were one people.
>
> *(ibid.: 9)*

Guidebooks and museum catalogues also tend to emphasise the continuities of the present with a national past. But for an argument that very rough territorial and cultural continuities can be found in Western Europe, in Hispania, Francia and Germania, for example, see Llobera (1994) and Hastings (1997: ch. 4) and for Spain, Barton (1993).

7 For cultural nationalism's elevation of peasant cultures in Eastern Europe, see Hofer (1980). See also Argyle (1976), Kitromilides (1979) and Hroch (1985).

8 Here Hutchinson's analysis has affinities with those of Kapferer (1988), Juergensmeyer (1993) and van der Veer (1994). See also Petrovich (1980) and the essays in Ramet (1989), which document the continuing power of religious ties, and in some cases religious institutions, in many East European and former Soviet republics. On religion and nationalism, see O'Brien (1988a) and Hastings (1997: ch. 8).

9 Hutchinson is in sympathy with the position taken by Francis Robinson in his debate with Paul Brass on the origins of Pakistan and the role of religion in shaping elite political actions; see Taylor and Yapp (1979). Hutchinson also, by implication, shares the conviction of John Armstrong that pre-modern ethnic ties have a shaping influence on nations, while otherwise adhering to the modernist position that nations are both recent and qualitatively 'modern'. See also Hutchinson (1992).

10 Hutchinson's stress on culture emphasises the links between modern nations and pre-modern ethnic ties, as does his stress on *la longue durée*. In that sense, he does not share the view of Tonkin *et al.* (1989: Introduction) who see the past as inevitably shaped by the interests, needs and preoccupations of the present, but is closer to Josep Llobera's (1994) argument that pre-modern (medieval) cultural and territorial structures form the long-term foundations for modern European nations. Llobera (1996) also emphasises the role of shared memories in shaping modern nations, like Catalonia.

11 As opposed to his title, and a later essay (Armstrong 1992), which emphasise the pre-modernity of nations; cf.Hastings (1997: ch. 1, note 10).

12 For an analysis of Barth's 'transactional' model of ethnic group boundaries, see Jenkins (1988).

13 Though a later essay (Armstrong 1995) stresses some areas of convergence with the predominantly modernist analyses of participants in the Prague conference, on which see Periwal (1995: esp. 34–43).

14 Barth's emphasis on relatively fixed ascription is the burden of Wallman's (1988) critique of his model.

15 Not all nationalists embrace the fifth tenet. Cultural nationalists tend to be wary of the state, and hence of 'a state of one's own'. Moreover, some nationalisms (for example, in Wales and Catalonia, though perhaps no longer in Scotland) are content to pursue 'home rule', where the nation has internal social, cultural and economic autonomy, but chooses to remain part of a wider federal state which has control over defence and foreign policy.

16 For critical analyses of Kohn's distinction, see A. D. Smith (1983a: ch. 8) and Hutchinson (1987: ch. 1). The term 'ethnocentric' signified here a rather weak, solip-sistic and diffuse sense of nationalism without clear political goals, and it was conflated with a 'tradition–modernity' dichotomy and an associated chronology. Clearly, this confuses a series of analytically separate variables. What this glossed over was the absence of a clearcut ideology of nationalism (an operational theory of 'nationalism-in-general') in the ancient or medieval worlds, one which provides a set of concepts and ideas and a symbolic language ready for use and adaptation world-wide, such as we witness today.

17 This was an earlier and vaguer definition of the concept of the 'nation', which omitted the features of the proper name and the 'mass, public' nature of the common culture, and spoke generally about sentiments of solidarity and common experiences, as the only subjective element.

18 A number of separate issues helped to reorient my position, including a study of the impact of war on ethnicity and nations; a conference on 'legitimation by descent'; the impact of Walker Connor's articles, which pointed to the key role of ethnicity and myths of ancestry; and the rise of religious nationalisms in the 1980s, which compelled a critical reconsideration of the issue of 'secular nationalism'.

19 There was a corresponding change in my definition of the 'nation' as *a named human population sharing an historic territory, common myths and historical memories, a mass, public culture, a common economy and common legal rights and duties for all members* (A. D. Smith 1991: 14). Compared with the earlier definition (see note 17 above) this revised version sharpens the constituent elements, and seeks to balance the more 'subjective' with the more 'objective' components (for example, it speaks now of an 'historic' territory rather than just a 'common' one). This follows, in my opinion, from the method of defining the concept of the nation as an ideal-type drawn, as closely as possible, from the various concepts and ideas of the nation held by self-styled nation-alists (see A. D. Smith 1983a: ch. 7).

20 In this, I share the position on uneven cultural resources of Brass (1991) and Hutchinson (1994). Some of these resources – ethno-history and the 'golden age', sacred territory, myths of origin and ethnic election – are enumerated in A. D. Smith (1996a). For the different kinds of pre-modern ethnic communities, see A. D. Smith (1986a: chs 2–5); for the role of ethnic myths, see Hosking and Schöpflin (1997).

21 See Tcherikover (1970) on attempted Seleucid hellenisation of Judea and the Maccabean reaction; for Greek ethnic and linguistic divisions, see Alty (1982). For an attempt to apply the 'ethno-symbolic' approach to the problem of national identity in antiquity and the Middle Ages, see A. D. Smith (1994); on particular nationalisms in the Middle Ages, see Hastings (1997: chs 2–4).

22 For some other examples of an early elite nationalism, see the studies of France by Beaune (1985), of Anglo-Saxon England by Howe (1989) and Hastings (1997: ch. 2), and of Poland by Knoll (1993). It is a moot point how far, despite their early politicisation, we can or should regard these upper- and middle-class sentiments of collective cultural identity as cases of ethnicity tied to statehood or of a *national* identity or of particularist national*ism* (we can hardly speak of 'national*ism*' as a generalised ideological movement until the eighteenth century).

9   Beyond modernism?

1 For Coleman's concept of 'concentric circles of loyalty' see Coleman (1958: Appendix); cf. Yuval-Davis (1997).
2 McNeill does not use the term 'postmodern', but his scheme links up with many of its assumptions. Nor does he share any of the 'postmodern*ist*' assumptions.
3 I am well aware of the deeply contested nature of basic approaches to 'ethnicity'; see, among many others, the essays in Glazer and Moynihan (1975), de Vos and Romanucci-Rossi (1975), Rex and Mason (1988), Wilmsen and McAllister (1996), and the readings in Hutchinson and Smith (1996).
        To enter into this debate would necessitate a much more extensive discussion and deflect us from the main purpose of this book, to assess explanatory theories of nations and nationalism. I might just add that the problems of the study of ethnicity are exacerbated by a failure to keep the individual and collective levels of analysis distinct, and a tendency to read off characteristics of one level from those of the other; on which, see Scheuch (1966).
4 Walby's essay (1992) predated the recent work of Yuval-Davis and others; it is reprinted in Balakrishnan (1996).
5 See Elshtain (1993). For other studies concentrating on this symbolic aspect of the field, see, for example, South Bank Centre (1989) and Ades (1989: esp. chs 7, 9).
6 See Brookner (1980: ch. 7) on David's *Oath of the Horatii* and Abrams (1986: ch. 8) on West's *Death of Wolfe*; for other *exempla*, see A. D. Smith (1993). Of course, this is only one side of the matter: stereotypical female attributes of nationalism are also portrayed by romantic artists, for example, the nation as a woman in combat or mourning, as by Rudé, Delacroix or Ingres (see South Bank Centre 1989), or women engaged in 'male' activities, such as Joan of Arc (Warner 1983).
7 The symposium on Miller's book and his reply can be found in O'Leary (1996a and b).
8 There is an extensive literature on each of these subjects, though most of it only touches on the issues of concern here. See, *inter alia*, Lustick (1979), Smooha (1990), Smooha and Hanf (1992), Baron (1985) and Preece (1997).
9 On the issue of the definition of nationalism by analysts and (or versus) the ethnic or civic concepts of the participants, see the debate between Dominique Schnapper and myself, in Schnapper (1997).
10 For these restrictions in ancient Greek and medieval Italian city-states, see Ehrenburg (1960) and Waley (1969).
11 This, of course, has become a political issue and is hotly contested by some Australians, including some scholars (for example, the historian Geoffrey Blainey); cf. also the rather different analysis in Kapferer (1988).
12 Here I have only alluded to an extensive debate on the crisis and/or decline of the 'nation-state' (see Tivey 1980). But most of this debate centres on the functions, and sovereignty, of the state, and says little about the transformation of the nation or national identity, which needs separate treatment; see Horsman and Marshall (1994), and, for a brief discussion, A. D. Smith (1996a).
13 For a fuller discussion of the issues of globalisation in relation to nationalism, see Featherstone (1990) and Tomlinson (1991: ch. 3).

14 For George Schöpflin (1995), it is rather the nature and extent of modernisation and its political expressions that are significant for the re-emergence of ethnicity and ethnic nationalism in Europe. But the weakness of democracy in the eastern half of the continent makes the appeal of ethnic nationalism much more attractive than in the West, where there is greater commitment to democratic modernity and civic institutions.

15 Another large and relatively under-explored subject is the growing contribution of international relations theorists to the study of ethnicity and nationalism. Apart from the early classics by Cobban (1969; 1st edn 1945) and Carr (1945), this includes the studies by Hinsley (1973), Beitz (1979), Bucheit (1981), Lewis (1983), Azar and Burton (1986), Buchanan (1991), Ringrose and Lerner (1993) and M. Brown (1993), notably on the geopolitical conditions of success for ethnic secession movements.

16 Immigration and nationalism is another large and growing field of analysis (see for example Soysal 1994), as is the study of refugees and ethnonationalist conflicts (see Newland 1993). Equally important is the study of genocide and nationalism, on which see *inter alia* Kuper (1981), Chalk and Jonassohn (1990), Fein (1993) and, in the colonial context, the penetrating analysis in Palmer (1998). A 'world of nations' is equally one of diasporas, and the analysis of diaspora communities has increasingly been related to nationalist and Pan movements; see Geiss (1974), Armstrong (1976), Landau (1981) and especially the essays by Jacob Landau, Walker Connor and Milton Esman in Sheffer (1986); also Cohen (1997). Though all these studies have implications for our understanding of nations and nationalisms, few of them have made (or sought to make) a contribution to the *theory* of nations and nationalism – as opposed to furthering our knowledge of its contemporary *manifestations* and *consequences*.

17 For a wide range of views and analyses of the issues of European integration, see Gowan and Anderson (1996).

Bibliography

Abrams, Anne U. (1986) *The Valiant Hero: Benjamin West and Grand-Style History Painting*, Washington DC: Smithsonian Institution Press.

Acton, Lord (1948) 'Nationality' (1862) in *Essays on Freedom and Power*, Glencoe IL: The Free Press.

Adenwalla, Minoo (1961) 'Hindu concepts and the *Gita* in early Indian nationalism', in R. A. Sakai (ed.) *Studies on Asia*, Lincoln NE: University of Nebraska Press, 16–23.

Ades, Dawn (1989) *Art in Latin America: The Modern Era, 1820–1980*, London: South Bank Centre, Hayward Gallery.

Afshar, Haleh (1989) 'Women and reproduction in Iran', in N. Yuval-Davis, and F. Anthias (eds) *Woman-Nation-State*, London: Sage, 110–25.

Agnew, Hugh (1993) 'The emergence of Czech national consciousness: a conceptual approach', *Ethnic Groups*, 10, 1–3, 175–86.

Akenson, Donald (1992) *God's Peoples: Covenant and Land in South Africa, Israel and Ulster*, Ithaca NY: Cornell University Press.

Alavi, Hamza (1972) 'The state in post-colonial societies – Pakistan and Bangla Desh', *New Left Review*, 74, 59–81.

Almond, Gabriel and Pye, Lucian (eds) (1965) *Comparative Political Culture*, Princeton NJ: Princeton University Press.

Alter, Peter (1989) *Nationalism*, London: Edward Arnold.

Alty, J. H. M. (1982) 'Dorians and Ionians', *Journal of Hellenic Studies* 102, 1–14.

Amin, Samir (1981) *Class and Nation*, London: Heinemann.

Anderson, Benedict (1991) [1983] *Imagined Communities: Reflections on the Origins and Spread of Nationalism*, 2nd edn, London: Verso.

Apter, David (1963a) *Ghana in Transition*, rev. edn, New York: Athenaeum.

——(1963b) 'Political religion in the new nations', in Clifford Geertz (ed.) *Old Societies and New States*, New York: Free Press.

Argyle, W. J. (1969) 'European nationalism and African tribalism', in P. H. Gulliver (ed.) *Tradition and Transition in East Africa*, London: Pall Mall Press, 41–57.

——(1976) 'Size and scale as factors in the development of nationalism', in A. D. Smith (ed.) *Nationalist Movements*, London: Macmillan, 31–53.

Armstrong, John (1976) 'Mobilised and proletarian diasporas', *American Political Science Review*, 70, 393–408.

——(1982) *Nations before Nationalism*, Chapel Hill NC: University of North Carolina Press.

——(1992) 'The autonomy of ethnic identity: historic cleavages and nationality relations in the USSR', in Alexander Motyl (ed.) *Thinking Theoretically about Soviet Nationalities*, New York: Columbia University Press, 23–44.

——(1995) 'Towards a theory of nationalism: consensus and dissensus', in Sukumar Periwal (ed.) *Notions of Nationalism*, Budapest: Central European University Press, 34–43.

——(1997) 'Religious nationalism and collective violence', *Nations and Nationalism*, 3, 4, 597–606.

Avineri, Shlomo (1968) *The Social and Political Thought of Karl Marx*, Cambridge: Cambridge University Press.

Azar, Edward and Burton, John (eds) (1986) *The Theory and Practice of International Conflict Resolution*, Brighton: Wheatsheaf.

Baker, Keith M. (1990) *Inventing the French Revolution: Essays on French Political Culture in the Eighteenth Century*, Cambridge: Cambridge University Press.

Balakrishnan, Gopal (ed.) (1996) *Mapping the Nation*, London and New York: Verso.

Balibar, Etienne and Wallerstein, Immanuel (1991) *Race, Nation, Class*, London: Verso.

Banton, Michael (1983) *Racial and Ethnic Competition*, Cambridge: Cambridge University Press.

——(1994) 'Modelling ethnic and national relations', *Ethnic and Racial Studies* 17, 1, 1–19.

Banuazizi, Ali and Weiner, Myron (eds) (1986) *The State, Religion and Ethnic Politics: Afghanistan, Iran and Pakistan*, Syracuse NY: Syracuse University Press.

Barbu, Zevedei (1967) 'Nationalism as a source of aggression', in CIBA, *Conflict*, London: CIBA Foundation.

Barnard, Frederick (1965) *Herder's Social and Political Thought: From Enlightenment to Nationalism*, Oxford: Clarendon Press.

Baron, Salo (1960) *Modern Nationalism and Religion*, New York: Meridian Books.

——(1985) *Ethnic Minority Rights: Some Older and Newer Trends*, Oxford Centre for Postgraduate Hebrew Studies.

Barth, Fredrik (ed.) (1969) *Ethnic Groups and Boundaries*, Boston: Little, Brown.

Bartlett, Robert (1994) *The Making of Europe*, Harmondsworth: Penguin.

Barton, Simon (1993) 'The roots of the national question in Spain', in M. Teich and R Porter (eds) *The National Question in Europe in Historical Perspective*, Cambridge: Cambridge University Press, 106–27.

Bauer, Otto (1924) [1900] *Die Sozialdemokratie und die Nationalitatenfrage*, 2nd edn, Vienna: Volksbuchhandlung.

Baumann, Zygmunt (1992) 'Soil, blood and identity', *Sociological Review*, 40, 675–701.

Beales, Derek (ed.) (1971) *The Risorgimento and the Unification of Italy*, London: Allen & Unwin.

Beaune, Colette (1985) *Naissance de la nation France*, Paris: Editions Gallimard.

Beetham, David (1974) *Max Weber and the Theory of Modern Politics*, London: Allen & Unwin.

Beitz, Charles (1979) *Political Theory and International Relations*, Princeton NJ: Princeton University Press.

Bell, Daniel (1975) 'Ethnicity and Social Change', in Nathan Glazer and Daniel Moynihan (eds) *Ethnicity: Theory and Experience*, Cambridge MA: Harvard Univerisity Press.

Bellah, Robert (ed.) (1965) *Religion and Progress in Modern Asia*, New York: Free Press.

Bendix, Reinhard (1996) [1964] *Nation-Building and Citizenship*, enlarged edn, New Brunswick NJ: Transaction Publishers.

Bennigsen, Alexandre and Lemercier-Quelquejay, Chantal (1966) *Islam in the Soviet Union*, London: Pall Mall Press.

Berkes, Niyazi (1964) *The Development of Secularism in Turkey*, Montreal: McGill University Press.

Berkovitz, Michael (1996) *Zionist Culture and West European Jewry before the First World War*, Chapel Hill NC and London: University of North Carolina Press.

Berlin, Isaiah (1976) *Vico and Herder*, London: Hogarth Press.

Bhabha, Homi (ed.) (1990) *Nation and Narration*, London and New York: Routledge.

Billig, M. (1995) *Banal Nationalism*, London: Sage.

Binder, Leonard (1964) *The Ideological Revolution in the Middle East*, New York: John Wiley.

Bonacich, Edna (1973) 'A theory of middlemen minorities', *American Sociological Review*, 38, 583–94.

Brading, David (1985) *The Origins of Mexican Nationalism*, Cambridge: Centre for Latin American Studies, University of Cambridge.

Branch, Michael (ed.) (1985) *Kalevala, The Land of Heroes*, trans. W. F. Kirby, London: The Athlone Press and New Hampshire: Dover.

Brand, Jack (1978) *The Scottish National Movement*, London: Routledge and Kegan Paul.

Brandon, S. G. F. (1967) *Jesus and the Zealots*, Manchester: Manchester University Press.

Brass, Paul (1974) *Language, Religion and Politics in North India*, Cambridge: Cambridge University Press.

——(1979) 'Elite groups, symbol manipulation and ethnic identity among the Muslims of South Asia', in David Taylor and Malcolm Yapp (eds) *Political Identity in South Asia*, Dublin: Curzon Press, 35–77.

——(ed.) (1985) *Ethnic Groups and the State*, London: Croom Helm.

——(1991) *Ethnicity and Nationalism*, London: Sage.

Breton, Raymond (1988) 'From ethnic to civic nationalism: English Canada and Quebec', *Ethnic and Racial Studies*, 11, 1, 85–102.

Breuilly, John (1993) [1982] *Nationalism and the State*, 2nd edn, Manchester: Manchester University Press.

——(1996) 'Approaches to nationalism', in Gopal Balakrishnan, (ed.) *Mapping the Nation*, London and New York: Verso, 146–74.

Brock, Peter (1976) *The Slovak National Awakening*, Toronto: Toronto University Press.

Brookner, Anita (1980) *Jacques-Louis David*, London: Chatto and Windus.

Brown, David (1989) 'Ethnic Revival: Perspectives on state and society', *Third World Quarterly*, 11, 4, 1–17.

——(1994) *The State and Ethnic Politics in Southeast Asia*, London and New York: Routledge.

Brown, Michael (ed.) (1993) *Ethnic Conflict and International Security*, Princeton NJ: Princeton University Press.

Brubaker, Rogers (1992) *Citizenship and Nationhood in France and Germany*, Cambridge MA: Harvard University Press.

——(1996) *Nationalism Reframed: Nationhood and the National Question in the New Europe*, Cambridge: Cambridge University Press.

Buchanan, A. (1991) *Secession, The Morality of Political Divorce from Fort Sumter to Lithuania and Quebec*, Boulder CO: Westview.

Bucheit, Lee (1981) *Secession, The Legitimacy of Self-determination*, New Haven CT: Yale University Press.

Burridge, K. (1969) *New Heaven, New Earth*, Oxford: Blackwell.

Calhoun, Craig (1997) *Nationalism*, Buckingham: Open University Press.

Carr, Edward (1945) *Nationalism and After*, London: Macmillan.

Castles, Stephen, Cope, Bill, Kalantzis, Mary and Morrissey, Michael (1988) *Mistaken Identity: Multiculturalism and the Demise of Nationalism in Australia*, Sydney: Pluto Press.

Cauthen, Bruce (1997) 'The myth of divine election and Afrikaner ethnogenesis', in Geoffrey Hosking and George Schöpflin (eds) *Myths and Nationhood*, London: Macmillan, 107–31.

Chalk, Frank and Jonassohn, Kurt (eds) (1990) *The History and Sociology of Genocide*, New Haven CT and London: Yale University Press.

Chatterjee, Partha (1986) *Nationalist Thought and the Colonial World: A Derivative Discourse*, London: Zed Books.

——(1993) *The Nation and Its Fragments*, Cambridge: Cambridge University Press.

Cherniavsky, Michael (1975) 'Russia', in Orest Ranum (ed.) *National Consciousness, History and Political Culture in Early Modern Europe*, Baltimore MD: Johns Hopkins University Press, 118–43.

Citron, Suzanne (1988) *Le Mythe National*, Paris: Presses Ouvriers.

Cliffe, Lionel (1989) 'Forging a nation: the Eritrean experience', *Third World Quarterly*, 11, 4, 131–47.

Cobban, Alfred (1957) *A History of Modern France*, vol. 1, Harmondsworth: Penguin.

——(1969) [1945] *The Nation-State and National Self-Determination*, rev edn, London: Collins.

Cohen, Abner (ed.) (1974) *Urban Ethnicity*, London: Tavistock.

Cohen, Robin (1997) *Global Diasporas: An Introduction*, London: UCL Press.

Cobler, Anne (1970) *Rousseau and Nationalism*, New York: Basic Books.

Cohn, Norman (1957) *The Pursuit of the Millennium*, London: Secker and Warburg.

Coleman, James (1958) *Nigeria: Background to Nationalism*, Berkeley CA and Los Angeles CA: University of California Press.

Colley, Linda (1992) *Britons: Forging the Nation, 1707–1837*, New Haven CT and London: Yale University Press.

Connor, Walker (1972) 'Nation-building or nation-destroying?', *World Politics*, XXIV, 3, 319–55.

——(1978) 'A nation is a nation, is a state, is an ethnic group, is a . . . ', *Ethnic and Racial Studies*, I, 4, 378–400.

——(1984) *The National Question in Marxist-Leninist Theory and Strategy*, Princeton NJ: Princeton University Press.

——(1990) 'When is a nation?', *Ethnic and Racial Studies*, 13, 1, 92–103.

——(1994) *Ethno-Nationalism: The Quest for Understanding*, Princeton NJ: Princeton University Press.

Conversi, Daniele (1990) 'Language or race? The choice of core values in the development of Catalan and Basque nationalism', *Ethnic and Racial Studies*, 13, 1, 50–70.

——(1997) *The Basques, the Catalans and Spain: Alternative Routes to Nationalist Mobilisation*, London: C. Hurst & Co.

Corrigan, Philip and Sayer, Derek (1985) *The Great Arch: English State Formation as Cultural Regulation*, Oxford: Blackwell.

Crow, Thomas (1985) *Painters and Public Life*, New Haven CT and London: Yale University Press.

Crowder, Michael (1968) *West Africa under Colonial Rule*, London: Hutchinson.

Cummins, Ian (1980) *Marx, Engels and National Movements*, London: Croom Helm.

Davies, Norman (1982) *God's Playground: A History of Poland*, 2 vols, Oxford: Clarendon Press.

Davis, Horace (1967) *Nationalism and Socialism: Marxist and Labor Theories of Nationalism*, New York: Monthly Review Press.

Delanty, Gerard (1995) *Inventing Europe: Idea, Identity, Reality*, Basingstoke: Macmillan.

Deol, Harnik (1996) 'Religion and nationalism in India: the case of the Punjab, 1960–95', unpublished Ph.D. thesis, University of London.

Detroit (1975) *French Painting: The Age of Revolution*, Detroit MI: Wayne State University Press.

Deutsch, Karl (1956) *An Interdisciplinary Bibliography on Nationalism, 1935–53*, Cambridge MA: MIT Press.

——(1963) *The Nerves of Government*, New York: Free Press.

——(1966) [1953] *Nationalism and Social Communication*, 2nd edn, New York: MIT Press.

Deutsch, Karl and Foltz, William (eds) (1963) *Nation-Building*, New York: Atherton Press.

Dinur, Ben-Zion (1969) *Israel and the Diaspora*, Philadelphia PA: Jewish Publication Society of America.

Doob, Leonard (1964) *Patriotism and Nationalism: Their Psychological Foundations*, New Haven CT: Yale University Press.

Dore, Ronald (1969) *On the Possibility and Desirability of a Theory of Modernisation*, Communications Series no. 38, Lewes: Institute of Development Studies, University of Sussex.

Draper, Theodore (1970) *The Rediscovery of Black Nationalism*, London: Secker and Warburg.

Droz, Jacques (1967) *Europe between Revolutions, 1815–48*, London and Glasgow: Collins.

Dunn, John (1978) *Western Political Theory in the Face of the Future*, Cambridge: Cambridge University Press.

Durkheim, Emile (1915) *The Elementary Forms of the Religious Life*, trans. J. Swain, London: Allen & Unwin.

——(1964) *The Division of Labour in Society*, trans. G. Simpson, New York: Free Press of Glencoe.

Duroselle, Jean-Baptiste (1990) *Europe, A History of Its Peoples*, trans. Richard Mayne, London: Penguin Books.

Edwards, John (1985) *Language, Society and Identity*, Oxford: Blackwell.

Ehrenburg, Victor (1960) *The Greek State*, Oxford: Blackwell.

Eisenstadt, Shmuel (1965) *Modernisation: Protest and Change*, Englewood Cliffs NJ: Prentice-Hall.

——(ed.) (1968) *The Protestant Ethic and Modernisation*, New York: Basic Books.

Eley, Geoffrey and Suny, Ronald (eds) (1996) *Becoming National*, New York and London: Oxford University Press.

Eller, Jack and Coughlan, Reed (1993) 'The poverty of primordialism: the demystification of ethnic attachments', *Ethnic and Racial Studies*, 16, 2, 183–202.

Elshtain, Jean Bethke (1993) 'Sovereignty, identity, sacrifice', in Marjorie Ringrose and Adam Lerner (eds) *Reimagining the Nation*, Buckingham: Open University Press, 159–75.

Enloe, Cynthia (1989) *Bananas, Beaches, Bases: Making Feminist Sense of International Politics*, London: Pandora.

Epstein, A. L. (1978) *Ethos and Identity*, London: Tavistock.

Eriksen, Thomas H. (1993) *Ethnicity and Nationalism*, London and Boulder CO: Pluto Press.

Esman, Milton (ed.) (1977) *Ethnic Conflict in the Western World*, Ithaca NY: Cornell University Press.

Featherstone, Michael (ed.) (1990) *Global Culture: Nationalism, Globalisation and Modernity*, London, Newbury Park CA and Delhi: Sage.

Fein, Helen (1993) *Genocide, A Sociological Perspective*, London: Sage.

Finley, Moses (1986) *The Use and Abuse of History*, London: Hogarth Press.

Fisera, Vladimir and Minnerup, Gunter (1978) 'Marx, Engels and the national question', in Eric Cahm and Vladimir Fisera (eds) *Nationalism and Socialism*, 3 vols, vol. I, Nottingham: Spokesman, 7–19.

Fishman, Joshua (1972) *Language and Nationalism: Two Integrative Essays*, Rowley MA: Newbury House.

——(1980) 'Social theory and ethnography: neglected perspectives on language and ethnicity in Eastern Europe', in Peter Sugar (ed.) *Ethnic Diversity and Conflict in Eastern Europe*, Santa Barbara CA: ABC-Clio, 69–99.

Fishman, Joshua, Ferguson, C. and Das Gupta, J. (eds) (1968) *Language Problems of Developing Nations*, New York: John Wiley.

Frank, André Gunder (1969) *Latin America: Underdevelopment or Revolution?*, New York: Monthly Review Press.

Freund, Julian (1970) *The Sociology of Max Weber*, London: Allen Lane, The Penguin Press.

Gans, Herbert (1979) 'Symbolic ethnicity', *Ethnic and Racial Studies*, 2, 1, 1–20.

Garman, Sebastian (1992) 'Foundation myths and political identity: Ancient Rome and Saxon England compared', unpublished Ph.D. thesis, University of London.

Geertz, Clifford (ed.) (1963) *Old Societies and New States*, New York: Free Press

——(1973) *The Interpretation of Cultures*, London: Fontana.

Geiger, T. (1967) *The Conflicted Relationship*, New York: McGraw-Hill.

Geiss, Immanuel (1974) *The Pan-African Movement*, London: Methuen.

Gella, Alexander (ed.) (1976) *The Intelligentsia and the Intellectuals*, Beverley Hills CA: Sage.

Gellner, Ernest (1964) *Thought and Change*, London: Weidenfeld and Nicolson.

——(1973) 'Scale and nation', *Philosophy of the Social Sciences*, 3, 1–17

——(1982) 'Nationalism and the two forms of cohesion in complex societies', *Proceedings of the British Academy*, 68, 165–87, London: Oxford University Press.

——(1983) *Nations and Nationalism*, Oxford: Blackwell.

——(1987) *Culture, Identity and Politics*, Cambridge: Cambridge University Press.

——(1994) *Encounters with Nationalism*, Oxford: Blackwell.

——(1996) 'Do nations have navels?', *Nations and Nationalism*, 2, 3, 366–70.

——(1997) *Nationalism*, London: Weidenfeld and Nicolson.

Gellner, Ernest and Ionescu, Gita (eds) (1970) *Populism, Its Meanings and National Characteristics*, London: Weidenfeld and Nicolson.

Gershoni, Israel and Jankowski, Mark (1987) *Egypt, Islam and the Arabs: The Search for Egyptian Nationhood, 1900–1930*, New York and Oxford: Oxford University Press.

Giddens, Anthony (1971) *Capitalism and Modern Social Theory*, Cambridge: Cambridge University Press.

——(1981) *A Contemporary Critique of Historical Materialism*, vol I, London: Macmillan.

——(1985) *The Nation-State and Violence*, Cambridge: Polity Press.

——(1991) *The Consequences of Modernity*, Cambridge: Polity Press.

Gildea, Robert (1994) *The Past in French History*, New Haven CT and London: Yale University Press.

Gillingham, John (1992) 'The beginnings of English imperialism', *Journal of Historical Sociology*, 5, 392–409.

Gillis, John R. (ed.) (1994) *Commemorations: The Politics of National Identity*, Princeton NJ: Princeton University Press.

Glazer, Nathan and Moynihan, Daniel (eds) (1975) *Ethnicity: Theory and Experience*, Cambridge MA: Harvard University Press.

Godechot, Jacques (1965) *France and the Atlantic Revolution of the Eighteenth Century, 1770–99*, New York: Free Press.

Gouldner, Alvin (1979) *The Rise of the Intellectuals and the Future of the New Class*, London: Macmillan.

Gowan, Peter and Anderson, Perry (eds) (1996) *The Question of Europe*, London and New York: Verso.

Greenfeld, Liah (1992) *Nationalism: Five Roads to Modernity*, Cambridge MA: Harvard University Press.

Grodzins, Morton (1956) *The Loyal and the Disloyal: The Social Boundaries of Patriotism and Treason*, Cleveland OH and New York: Meridian Books.

Grosby, Steven (1991) 'Religion and nationality in antiquity', *European Journal of Sociology*, XXXII, 229–65.

——(1994) 'The verdict of history: the inexpungeable tie of primordiality – a reply to Eller and Coughlan', *Ethnic and Racial Studies*, 17, 1, 164–71.

——(1995) 'Territoriality: the transcendental, primordial feature of modern societies', *Nations and Nationalism*, 1, 2, 143–62.

Gruen, Erich (1993) *Culture and National Identity in Republican Rome*, London: Duckworth.

Guenée, Bernard (1985) [1971] *States and Rulers in later medieval Europe* (French original 1971) trans. Juliet Vale, Oxford: Blackwell.

Guibernau, Montserrat (1996) *Nationalisms: The Nation-State and Nationalism in the Twentieth Century*, Cambridge: Polity Press.

Guibernau, Montserrat and Rex, John (eds) (1997) *The Ethnicity Reader: Nationalism, Multiculturalism and Migration*, Cambridge: Polity Press.

Gusfield, J. (1967) 'Tradition and modernity: misplaced polarities in the study of social change', *American Journal of Sociology*, 72, 351–62.

Halecki, Oscar (1955) *A History of Poland*, rev. edn, London: Dent.

Hall, Edith (1992) *Inventing the Barbarian: Greek Self-definition through Tragedy*, Oxford: Clarendon Press.

Hall, John (1985) *Powers and Liberties: The Causes and Consequences of the Rise of the West*, Oxford: Blackwell.

Hall, Stuart (1992) 'The new ethnicities', in J. Donald and A. Rattansi (eds) *Race, Culture and Difference*, London: Sage.

Halpern, Manfred (1963) *The Politics of Social Change in the Middle East and North Africa*, Princeton NJ: Princeton University Press.

Handelman, Don (1977) 'The organisation of ethnicity', *Ethnic Groups*, I, 187–200.

Handelsman, M. (1929) 'Le rôle de la nationalité dans l'histoire du moyen age', *Bulletin of the International Committee of the Historical Sciences*, 2, 2, 235–46.

Hanham, H. J. (1969) *Scottish Nationalism*, London: Faber.

Hastings, Adrian (1997) *The Construction of Nationhood: Ethnicity, Religion and Nationalism*, Cambridge: Cambridge University Press.

Hayes, Carlton (1931) *The Historical Evolution of Modern Nationalism*, New York: Smith.

Hechter, Michael (1975) *Internal Colonialism: The Celtic Fringe in British National Development, 1536–1966*, London: Routledge and Kegan Paul.

——(1987) *Principles of Group Solidarity*, Berkeley CA: University of California Press.

——(1988) 'Rational choice theory and the study of ethnic and race relations', in John Rex and David Mason (eds) *Theories of Ethnic and Race Relations*, Cambridge: Cambridge University Press, 264–79.

——(1992) 'The dynamics of secession', *Acta Sociologica*, 35, 267–83.

——(1995) 'Explaining nationalist violence', *Nations and Nationalism*, 1, 1, 53–68.

Hechter, Michael and Levi, Margaret (1979) 'The comparative analysis of ethno-regional movements', *Ethnic and Racial Studies*, 2, 3, 260–74.

Heraclides, Alexis (1991) *The Self-determination of Minorities in International Politics*, London: Frank Cass.

Herbert, Robert (1972) *David, Voltaire, Brutus and the French Revolution*, London: Allen Lane.

Hertz, Frederick (1944) *Nationality in History and Politics*, London: Routledge and Kegan Paul.

Hinsley, F. H. (1973) *Nationalism and the International System*, London: Hodder and Stoughton.

Hobsbawm, Eric (1977) 'Some reflections on *The Break-Up of Britain*', *New Left Review*, 105, 3–23.

——(1990) *Nations and Nationalism since 1780*, Cambridge: Cambridge University Press.

——(1996) 'Ethnicity and nationalism in Europe today', in Gopal Balakrishnan (ed.) *Mapping the Nation*, London and New York: Verso, 255–66.

Hobsbawm, Eric and Ranger, Terence (eds) (1983) *The Invention of Tradition*, Cambridge: Cambridge University Press.

Hodgkin, Thomas (1956) *Nationalism in Colonial Africa*, London: Muller.

——(1964) 'The relevance of "western" ideas in the derivation of African nationalism', in J. R. Pennock (ed.) *Self-Government in Modernising Societies*, Englewood Cliffs NJ: Prentice-Hall.

Hofer, Tamas (1980) 'The ethnic model of peasant cultures: a contribution to the ethnic symbol building on linguistic foundations by Eastern European peoples', in Peter Sugar (ed.) *Ethnic Diversity and Conflict in Eastern Europe*, Santa Barbara CA: ABC-Clio, 101–45.

Honour, Hugh (1968) *Neo-Classicism*, Harmondsworth: Penguin.

Hooson, David (ed.) (1994) *Geography and National Identity*, Cambridge MA and Oxford: Blackwell.

Horne, Donald (1984) *The Great Museum*, Sydney: Pluto Press.

Horowitz, Donald (1985) *Ethnic Groups in Conflict*, Berkeley CA and Los Angeles CA: University of California Press.

——(1992) 'Irredentas and secessions: adjacent phenomena, neglected connections', in Anthony D. Smith (ed.) *Ethnicity and Nationalism: International Studies in Sociology and Social Anthropology*, volume LX, Leiden: Brill, 118–30.

Horsman, Matthew and Marshall, Andrew (1994) *After the Nation-State*, London: Harper Collins.

Hosking, Geoffrey and Schöpflin, George (eds) (1997) *Myths and Nationhood*, London: Routledge.

Howard, Michael (1976) *War in European History*, London: Oxford University Press.

Howe, Nicholas (1989) *Migration and Mythmaking in Anglo-Saxon England*, New Haven CT and London: Yale University Press.

Hroch, Miroslav (1985) *Social Preconditions of National Revival in Europe*, Cambridge: Cambridge University Press.

——(1993) 'From national movement to the fully-formed nation: the nation-building process in Europe', *New Left Review*, 198, 3–20.

Hughes, Michael (1988) *Nationalism and Society: Germany, 1800–1945*, London: Edward Arnold.

Humphreys, R. A. and Lynch, J. (eds) (1965) *The Origins of the Latin American Revolutions, 1808–26*, New York: Knopf.

Husbands, Christopher (1991) 'The support for the *Front National*: analyses and findings', *Ethnic and Racial Studies*, 14, 3, 382–416.

Hutchinson, John (1987) *The Dynamics of Cultural Nationalism: The Gaelic Revival and the Creation of the Irish Nation State*, London: Allen & Unwin.

——(1992) 'Moral innovators and the politics of regeneration: the distinctive role of cultural nationalists in nation-building', in Anthony D. Smith (ed.) *Ethnicity and Nationalism: International Studies in Sociology and Social Anthropology*, volume LX, Leiden: Brill, 101–17.

——(1994) *Modern Nationalism*, London: Fontana.

Hutchinson, John and Smith, Anthony D. (eds) (1994) *Nationalism*, Oxford and New York: Oxford University Press.

——(eds) (1996) *Ethnicity*, Oxford and New York: Oxford University Press.

Ignatieff, Michael (1993) *Blood and Belonging: Journeys into the New Nationalisms*, London: Chatto and Windus.

——(1998) *The Warrior's Honour: Ethnic War and the Modern Consciousness*, London: Chatto & Windus.

Igwara, Obi (1993) 'State and nation building in Nigeria', unpublished Ph.D. thesis, University of London.

——(1995) 'Holy Nigerian nationalisms and apocalyptic visions of the nation', *Nations and Nationalism*, 1, 3, 327–55.

Im Hof, Ulrich (1991) *Mythos Schweiz: Identität-Nation-Geschichte, 1291–1991*, Zurich: Neue Verlag Zürcher Zeitung.

Isaacs, Harold (1975) *The Idols of the Tribe*, New York: Harper Collins.

Jacobsen, Jessica (1997) 'Perceptions of Britishness', *Nations and Nationalism*, 3, 2, 181–99.

James, Paul (1996) *Nation Formation: Towards a Theory of Abstract Community*, London and Delhi: Sage.

Jayawardena, Kumari (1986) *Feminism and Nationalism in the Third World*, London and Atlantic Highlands NJ: Zed Books.

Jenkins, Richard (1988) 'Social-anthropological models of inter-ethnic relations', in John Rex and David Mason (eds) *Theories of Ethnic and Race Relations*, Cambridge: Cambridge University Press, 170–86.

Johnson, Lesley (1995) 'Imagining communities: medieval and modern', in Simon Forde, Lesley Johnson and Alan Murray (eds) *Concepts of National Identity in the Middle Ages*, Leeds: School of English, University of Leeds, 1–19.

Jones, Sian (1997) *The Archaeology of Ethnicity: Constructing Identities in the Past and the Present*, London and New York: Routledge.

Juergensmeyer, Mark (1993) *The New Cold War? Religious Nationalism confronts the Secular State*, Berkeley CA and Los Angeles CA: University of California Press.

Just, Roger (1989) 'The triumph of the *ethnos*', in Elisabeth Tonkin, Maryon McDonald and Malcolm Chapman (eds) *History and Ethnicity*, London and New York: Routledge, 71–88.

Kamenka, Eugene (ed.) (1976) *Nationalism: The Nature and Evolution of an Idea*, London: Edward Arnold.

Kandiyoti, Deniz (1989) 'Women and the Turkish state', in Nira Yuval-Davis and Floya Anthias (eds) *Woman-Nation-State*, London: Sage, 126–49.

——(1991) 'Identity and its discontents: women and the nation', *Millennium, Journal of International Studies*, 20, 3, 429–44.

Kapferer, Bruce (1988) *Legends of People, Myths of State: Violence, Intolerance and Political Culture in Sri Lanka and Australia*, Washington DC and London: Smithsonian Institution.

Kautsky, John H. (ed.) (1962) *Political Change in Underdeveloped Countries*, New York: Wiley.

Keane, John (1995) 'Nations, nationalism and European citizens', in Sukumar Periwal (ed.) *Notions of Nationalism*, Budapest: Central European University Press, 182–207.

Kedourie, Elie (1960) *Nationalism*, London: Hutchinson.

——(1966) *Afghani and Abduh*, London and New York: Frank Cass.

——(ed.) (1971) *Nationalism in Asia and Africa*, London: Weidenfeld and Nicolson.

——(1992) *Politics in the Middle East*, Oxford: Oxford University Press.

Kedourie, Sylvia (ed.) (1998) *Elie Kedourie CBE, FBA, 1926–92: History, Philosophy, Politics*, London and Portland OR: Frank Cass.

Kedward, Roderick (ed.) (1965) *The Dreyfus Affair*, London: Longman.

Kemilainen, Aïra (1964) *Nationalism: Problems Concerning the Word, the Concept and Classification*, Yvaskyla: Kustantajat Publishers.

Kimmerling, Baruch and Migdal, Joel (1994) *Palestinians, The Making of a People*, Cambridge MA: Harvard University Press.

Kitromilides, Paschalis (1979) 'The dialectic of intolerance. ideological dimensions of ethnic conflict', *Journal of the Hellenic Diaspora*, VI, 4, 5–30.

——(1989) ' "Imagined communities" and the origins of the national question in the Balkans', *European History Quarterly*, 19, 2, 149–92.

Knoll, Paul (1993) 'National consciousness in medieval Poland', *Ethnic Groups*, 10, 1–3, 65–84.

Kohn, Hans (1940) 'The origins of English nationalism', *Journal of the History of Ideas*, I, 69–94.

——(1955) *Nationalism, Its Meaning and History*, New York: Van Nostrand.

——(1957) *Nationalism and Liberty, The Swiss Example*, London: Macmillan.

——(1960) *Pan-Slavism*, 2nd edn, New York: Vintage Books.

——(1961) *Prophets and Peoples*, New York: Collier.

——(1967a) [1944] *The Idea of Nationalism*, 2nd edn, New York: Collier-Macmillan.

——(1967b) *Prelude to Nation-States: The French and German Experience, 1789–1815*, New York: Van Nostrand.

Kornhauser, William (1959) *The Politics of Mass Society*, London: Routledge and Kegan Paul.

Kreis, Jacob (1991) *Der Mythos von 1291: Zür Enstehung des Schweizerischen Nationalfeiertags*, Basel: Friedrich Reinhardt Verlag.

Kristeva, Julia (1993) *Nations without Nationalism*, New York: Columbia University Press.

Kuper, Leo (1981) *Genocide*, Harmondsworth: Penguin.

Kushner, David (1976) *The Rise of Turkish Nationalism*, London: Frank Cass.

Kymlicka, William (1995) *Multicultural Citizenship: A Liberal Theory of Minority Rights*, Oxford: Clarendon Press.

Laclau, Ernesto (1971) 'Imperialism in Latin America', *New Left Review*, 67, 19–38.

Laczko, Leslie (1994) 'Canada's pluralism in comparative perspective', *Ethnic and Racial Studies*, 17, 1, 20–41.

Landau, Jacob (1981) *Pan-Turkism in Turkey*, London: C. Hurst & Co.

Landes, Joan (1988) *Women in the Public Sphere in the Age of the French Revolution*, Ithaca NY: Cornell University Press.

Lang, David (1980) *Armenia: Cradle of Civilisation*, London: Allen & Unwin.

Lartichaux, J-Y. (1977) 'Linguistic politics in the French Revolution', *Diogenes*, 97, 65–84.

Lehmann, Jean-Pierre (1982) *The Roots of Modern Japan*, London and Basingstoke: Macmillan.

Leith, James (1965) *The Idea of Art as Propaganda in France, 1750–99*, Toronto: University of Toronto Press.

Leoussi, Athena (1997) 'Nationalism and racial Hellenism in nineteenth-century England and France', *Ethnic and Racial Studies*, 20, 1, 42–68.

Lerner, Daniel (1958) *The Passing of Traditional Society*, New York: Free Press.

Levi, Mario Attilio (1965) *Political Power in the Ancient World*, trans. J. Costello, London: Weidenfeld and Nicolson.

Lewis, Bernard (1968) *The Emergence of Modern Turkey*, London: Oxford University Press.

Lewis, Ioann (ed.) (1983) *Nationalism and Self-Determination in the Horn of Africa*, London: Ithaca Press.

Lijphart, Arend (1977) *Democracy in Plural Societies: A Comparative Exploration*, New Haven CT and London: Yale University Press.

Llobera, Josep (1994) *The God of Modernity*, Oxford: Berg.

——(1996) *The Role of Historical Memory in (ethno-)Nation-Building*, London: Goldsmiths College.

Lustick, Ian (1979) 'Deeply divided societies: consociationalism versus control', *World Politics*, XXXI, 3, 325–44.

McCulley, B. T. (1966) *English Education and the Origins of Indian Nationalism*, Gloucester MA: Smith.

MacDougall, Hugh (1982) *Racial Myth in English History: Trojans, Teutons and Anglo-Saxons*, Montreal: Harvest House, and Hanover NH: University Press of New England.

McGarry, John and O'Leary, Brendan (eds) (1993) *The Politics of Ethnic Conflict Regulation: Case Studies of Protracted Ethnic Conflicts*, London and New York: Routledge.

Mack Smith, Denis (1994) *Mazzini*, New Haven CT and London: Yale University Press.

McKay, James (1982) 'An exploratory synthesis of primordial and mobilisationist approaches to ethnic phenomena', *Ethnic and Racial Studies*, 5, 4, 395–420.

McNeill, William (1986) *Polyethnicity and National Unity in World History*, Toronto: University of Toronto Press.

McRoberts, Kenneth (1979) 'International colonialism: the case of Quebec', *Ethnic and Racial Studies*, 2, 3, 293–318.

Mann, Michael (1986) *The Sources of Social Power*, Volume I, Cambridge: Cambridge University Press.

——(1993) *The Sources of Social Power*, Volume II, Cambridge: Cambridge University Press.

——(1995) 'A political theory of nationalism and its excesses', in Sukumar Periwal (ed.) *Notions of Nationalism*, Budapest: Central European University Press, 44–64.

Marcu, E. D. (1976) *Sixteenth-Century Nationalism*, New York: Abaris Books.

Markovitz, I. L. (1977) *Power and Class in Africa*, Englewood Cliffs NJ: Prentice-Hall.

Marty, Martin and Appleby, R. Scott (eds) (1991) *Fundamentalisms Observed*, Chicago IL and London: University of Chicago Press.

Marwick, Arthur (1974) *War and Social Change in the Twentieth Century*, London: Methuen.

Mason, R. A. (1985) 'Scotching the Brut: the early history of Britain', *History Today*, 35, January, 26–31.

Mayall, James (1990) *Nationalism and International Society*, Cambridge: Cambridge University Press.

——(1991) 'Non-intervention, self-determination and the "new world order"', *International Affairs*, 67, 3, 421–9.

——(1992) 'Nationalism and international security after the Cold War', *Survival*, 34, Spring, 19–35.

Mayo, Patricia (1974) *The Roots of Identity: Three National Movements in Contemporary European Politics*, London: Allen Lane.

Mazrui, Ali (1985) 'African archives and oral tradition', *The Courier*, February, 13–15, Paris: UNESCO.

Meadwell, Hudson (1989) 'Cultural and instrumental approaches to ethnic nationalism', *Ethnic and Racial Studies*, 12, 3, 309–28.

Mehden, Fred von der (1963) *Religion and Nationalism in Southeast Asia*, Madison WI, Milwaukee WI and London: University of Wisconsin Press.

Melucci, Alberto (1989) *Nomads of the Present: Social Movements and Individual Needs in Contemporary Society*, London: Hutchinson Radius.

Mendels, Doron (1992) *The Rise and Fall of Jewish Nationalism*, New York: Doubleday.

Michelet, Jules (1890) *Historical View of the French Revolution*, trans. C. Cocks, London: S. Bell and Sons.

Mill, John Stuart (1872) *Considerations on Representative Government*, London.

Miller, David (1993) 'In defence of nationality', *Journal of Applied Philosophy*, 10, 1, 3–16.

——(1995) *On Nationality*, Oxford: Oxford University Press.

Milton, John (1959) *Areopagitica*, vol. II, New Haven CT: Yale University Press, 552.

Minogue, Kenneth (1967) *Nationalism*, London: Batsford.

Mitchell, Marion (1931) 'Emile Durkheim and the philosophy of nationalism', *Political Science Quarterly*, 46, 87–106.

Mitchell, Mark and Russell, Dave (1996) 'Immigration, citizenship and the nation-state in the new Europe', in Brian Jenkins and Spyros Sofos (eds) *Nation and Identity in Contemporary Europe*, London and New York: Routledge.

Montagne, Robert (1952) 'The "modern state" in Africa and Asia', *The Cambridge Journal*, 5, 583–602.

Morgan, Prys (1983) 'From a death to a view: the hunt for the Welsh past in the Romantic period', in Eric Hobsbawm and Terence Ranger (eds) *The Invention of Tradition*, Cambridge: Cambridge University Press, 43–100.

Mosse, George (1964) *The Crisis of German Ideology*, New York: Grosset and Dunlap.

——(1976) 'Mass politics and the political liturgy of nationalism', in Eugene Kamenka (ed.) *Nationalism: The Nature and Evolution of an Idea*, London: Edward Arnold, 39–54.

——(1985) *Nationalism and Sexuality: Middle Class Norms and Sexual Morality in Modern Europe*, Madison WI: University of Wisconsin Press.

——(1994) *Confronting the Nation: Jewish and Western Nationalism*, Hanover and London: Brandeis University Press.

——(1995) 'Racism and nationalism', *Nations and Nationalism*, I, 2, 163–73.

Nairn, Tom (1977) *The Break-up of Britain: Crisis and Neo-Nationalism*, London: New Left Books.

Nash, Manning (1989) *The Cauldron of Ethnicity in the Modern World*, Chicago IL and London: University of Chicago Press.

Nettl, J. P. and Robertson, Roland (1968) *International Systems and the Modernisation of Societies*, London: Faber.

Neuberger, Benjamin (1986) *National Self-determination in Post-Colonial Africa*, Boulder CO: Lynne Rienner.

Newland, Kathleen (1993) 'Ethnic conflict and refugees', *Survival*, 35, 1, 81–101.

Newman, Gerald (1987) *The Rise of English Nationalism: A Cultural History, 1740–1830*, London: Weidenfeld and Nicolson.

Nimni, Ephraim (1994) *Marxism and Nationalism: Theoretical Origins of a Political Crisis*, 2nd edn, London: Pluto Press.

Nisbet, Robert (1965) *The Sociological Tradition*, London: Heinemann.

——(1969) *Social Change and History*, London and New York: Oxford University Press.

Nora, Pierre (ed.) (1984) *Les Lieux de Mémoire*, Vol. I: *La République*, Paris: Gallimard.

——(ed.) (1986) *Les Lieux de Mémoire*, Vol. II: *La Nation*, Paris: Gallimard.

O'Brien, Conor Cruse (1988a) *God-Land: Reflections on Religion and Nationalism*, Cambridge MA: Harvard University Press.

——(1988b) 'Nationalism and the French Revolution', in G. Best (ed.) *The Permanent Revolution: The French Revolution and Its Legacy, 1789–1989*, London: Fontana, 17–48.

Okamura, J. (1981) 'Situational ethnicity', *Ethnic and Racial Studies*, 4, 4, 452–65.

O'Leary, Brendan (ed.) (1996a) 'Symposium on David Miller's *On Nationality*', *Nations and Nationalism*, 2, 3, 409–51.

——(1996b) 'Insufficiently liberal and insufficiently nationalist', in Brendan O'Leary (ed.) 'Symposium on David Miller's *On Nationality*, *Nations and Nationalism*, 2, 3, 444–51.

Olorunsola, Victor (ed.) (1972) *The Politics of Cultural Nationalism in Sub-Saharan Africa*, New York: Anchor Books.

Olson, Mancur (1965) *The Logic of Collective Action*, Cambridge MA: Harvard University Press.

Orridge, Andrew (1981) 'Uneven development and nationalism, I and II', *Political Studies*, XXIX, 1 and 2, 10–15, 181–90.

——(1982) 'Separatist and autonomist nationalisms: the structure of regional loyalties in the modern state', in Colin Williams (ed.) *National Separatism*, Cardiff: University of Wales Press, 43–74.

Ozouf, Mona (1982) *L'Ecole, L'Eglise et la République, 1871–1914*, Paris: Editions Cana/Jean Offredo.

Palmer, Alison (1998) *Colonial Genocide*, Bathurst NSW: Crawford House Publishing.

Palmer, R. R. (1940) 'The national idea in France before the Revolution', *Journal of the History of Ideas*, I, 95–111.

Paul, David (1985) 'Slovak nationalism and the Hungarian state', in Paul Brass (ed.) *Ethnic Groups and the State*, London: Croom Helm, 115–59.

Pearson, Raymond (1983) *National Minorities in Eastern Europe, 1848–1945*, London: Macmillan.

——(1993) 'Fact, fantasy, fraud: perceptions and projections of national revival', *Ethnic Groups*, 10, 1–3, 43–64.

Peel, John (1989) 'The cultural work of Yoruba ethno-genesis', in Elisabeth Tonkin, Maryon McDonald and Malcolm Chapman (eds) *History and Ethnicity*, London and New York: Routledge, 198–215.

Penrose, Jan (1995) 'Essential constructions? The "cultural bases" of nationalist movements', *Nations and Nationalism*, I, 3, 391–417.

Periwal, Sukumar (ed.) (1995) *Notions of Nationalism*, Budapest: Central European University Press.

Petersen, William (1975) 'On the sub-nations of Europe', in Nathan Glazer and Daniel Moynihan (eds) *Ethnicity: Theory and Experience*, Cambridge MA: Harvard University Press, 177–208.

Petrovich, Michael (1980) 'Religion and ethnicity in Eastern Europe', in Peter Sugar (ed.) *Ethnic Diversity and Conflict in Eastern Europe*, Santa Barbara CA: ABC-Clio, 373–417.

Phelan, John L. (1960) 'Neo-Aztecism in the eighteenth century and the genesis of Mexican nationalism', in Stanley Diamond (ed.) *Culture in History: Essays in Honor of Paul Radid*, New York: Columbia University Press, 760–70.

Pieterse, Jan Nederveen (1995) 'Europe among other things: closure, culture, identity', in K. von Benda-Beckmann and M. Verkuyten (eds) *Nationalism, Ethnicity and Cultural Identity in Europe*, Utrecht: ERCOMER, 71–88.

Pinard, Maurice and Hamilton, Richard (1984) 'The class bases of the Quebec independence movement: conjectures and evidence', *Ethnic and Racial Studies*, 7, 1, 19–54.

Pinsker, Leo (1932) [1882] *AutoEmancipation*, trans. D. S. Blandheim, ed. A. S. Super, London.

Pinson, Koppel (1935) *A Bibliographical Introduction to Nationalism*, New York: Columbia University Press.

Plamenatz, John (1976) 'Two types of nationalism', in Eugene Kamenka (ed.) *Nationalism: The Nature and Evolution of an Idea*, London: Edward Arnold, 22–36.

Poggi, Gianfranco (1978) *The Development of the Modern State*, London: Hutchinson.

Poliakov, Leon (1974) *The Aryan Myth*, New York: Basic Books.

Portal, Roger (1969) *The Slavs: A Cultural Historical Survey of the Slavonic Peoples*, trans. Patrick Evans, London: Weidenfeld and Nicolson.

Porter, Roy and Teich, Mikulas (eds) (1988) *Romanticism in National Context*, Cambridge: Cambridge University Press.

Posen, Barry (1993) 'The security dilemma and ethnic conflict', *Survival*, 35, 1, 27–47.

Preece, Jennifer Jackson (1997) 'Minority rights in Europe from Westphalia to Helsinki', *Review of International Studies*, 23, 75–92.

Pye, Lucian (1962) *Politics, Personality and Nation-Building: Burma's Search for Identity*, New Haven CT and London: Yale University Press.

Pynsent, Robert (1994) *Questions of Identity: Czech and Slovak Ideas of Nationality and Personality*, Budapest, London and New York: Central European University Press.

Ramet, Pedro (ed.) (1989) *Religion and Nationalism in Soviet and East European Politics*, Durham NC and London: Duke University Press.

Ranum, Orest (ed.) (1975) *National Consciousness, History and Political Culture in Early Modern Europe*, Baltimore MD: Johns Hopkins University Press.

Raun, Toivo (1987) *Estonia and the Estonians*, Stanford CA: Hoover Press Institution.

Reece, J. (1979) 'Internal colonialism: the case of Brittany', *Ethnic and Racial Studies*, 2, 3, 275–92.

Reiss, H. S. (ed.) (1955) *The Political Thought of the German Romantics, 1793–1815*, Oxford: Blackwell.

Renan, Ernest (1882) *Qu'est-ce qu'une Nation?*, Paris: Calmann-Lévy.

Rex, John and Mason, David (eds) (1988) *Theories of Ethnic and Race Relations*, Cambridge: Cambridge University Press.

Reynolds, Susan (1983) 'Medieval *origines gentium* and the community of the realm', *History*, 68, 375–90.

——(1984) *Kingdoms and Communities in Western Europe, 900–1300*, Oxford: Clarendon Press.

Reynolds, Vernon (1980) 'Sociobiology and the idea of primordial discrimination', *Ethnic and Racial Studies*, 3, 3, 303–15.

Riall, Lucy (1994) *The Italian Risorgimento*, London and New York: Routledge.

Richmond, Anthony (1984) 'Ethnic nationalism and post-industrialism', *Ethnic and Racial Studies*, 7, 1, 4–18.

Riekmann, Sonja Puntscher (1997) 'The myth of European unity', in Geoffrey Hosking and George Schöpflin (eds) *Myths and Nationhood*, London: Macmillan, 60–71.

Ringrose, Marjorie and Lerner, Adam (eds) (1993) *Reimagining the Nation*, Buckingham: Open University Press.

Roberts, Michael (1993) 'Nationalism, the past and the present: the case of Sri Lanka', *Ethnic and Racial Studies*, 16, 1, 133–66.

Robinson, Francis (1979) 'Islam and Muslim separation', in David Taylor and Malcolm Yapp (eds) *Political Identity in South Asia*, Dublin: Curzon Press, 78–112.

Rokkan, Stein, Saelen, K. and Warmbrunn, J. (1972) 'Nation-Building', *Current Sociology*, 19, 3, The Hague: Mouton.

Rosdolsky, R. (1964) 'Friedrich Engels und das Problem der "Geschichtslosen Völker"', *Archiv für Sozialgeschichte*, 4, 87–282.

Rosenblum, Robert (1967) *Transformations in Late Eighteenth Century Art*, Princeton NJ: Princeton University Press.

Rostow, W. W. (1960) *The Stages of Economic Growth*, Cambridge: Cambridge University Press.

Rotberg, Robert (1967) 'African nationalism: concept or confusion?', *Journal of Modern African Studies*, 4, 1, 33–46.

Sakai, R. A. (ed.) (1961) *Studies on Asia*, Lincoln NE: University of Nebraska Press.

Sarkisyanz, Emmanuel (1964) *Buddhist Backgrounds of the Burmese Revolution*, The Hague: Martinus Nijhoff.

Saul, John (1979) *State and Revolution in East Africa*, London: Heinemann.

Saunders, David (1993) 'What makes a nation a nation? Ukrainians since 1600', *Ethnic Groups*, 10, 1–3, 101–24.

Scheuch, Erwin (1966) 'Cross-national comparisons with aggregate data', in Richard Merritt and Stein Rokkan (eds) *Comparing Nations: The Use of Quantitative Data in Cross-National Research*, New Haven CT: Yale University Press.

Schlesinger, Philip (1987) 'On national identity: some conceptions and misconceptions criticised', *Social Science Information*, 26, 2, 219–64.

——(1991) *Media, State and Nation: Political Violence and Collective Identities*, London: Sage.

——(1992) 'Europe – a new cultural battlefield?', *Innovation*, 5, 1, 11–23.

Schnapper, Dominique (1997) 'Beyond the opposition: "civic" nation versus "ethnic" nation', *ASEN Bulletin*, 12, Winter, 4–8.

Schöpflin, George (1995) 'Nationalism and ethnicity in Europe, East and West', in Charles Kupchan (ed.) *Nationalism and Nationalities in the New Europe*, Ithaca NY and London: Cornell University Press.

Scott, George Jnr (1990) 'A resynthesis of primordial and circumstantialist approaches to ethnic group solidarity: towards an explanatory model', *Ethnic and Racial Studies*, 13, 2, 148–71.

Seal, Anil (1968) *The Emergence of Indian Nationalism*, Cambridge: Cambridge University Press.

Seltzer, Robert (1980) *Jewish People, Jewish Thought*, New York: Macmillan.

Seton-Watson, Hugh (1960) *Neither War, Nor Peace*, London: Methuen.

——(1965) *Nationalism, Old and New*, Sydney: Sydney University Press.

——(1977) *Nations and States*, London: Methuen.

Shafer, Boyd (1938) 'Bourgeois nationalism in the Pamphlets on the eve of the Revolution', *Journal of Modern History*, 10, 31–50.

——(1955) *Nationalism: Myth and Reality*, New York: Harcourt, Brace.

Shaheen, S. (1956) *The Communist Theory of Self determination*, The Hague: Van Hoeve.

Sheffer, Gabriel (ed.) (1986) *Modern Diasporas and International Politics*, London: Croom Helm.

Shils, Edward (1957) 'Primordial, personal, sacred and civil ties', *British Journal of Sociology*, 7, 13–45.

——(1960) 'The intellectuals in the political development of the new states', *World Politics*, XII, 3, 329–68.

——(1995) 'Nation, nationality, nationalism and civil society', *Nations and Nationalism*, 1, 1, 93–118.

Shimoni, Gideon (1995) *The Zionist Ideology*, Hanover and London: Brandeis University Press.

Simmel, George (1964) *The Sociology of George Simmel*, ed. Kurt Wolff, New York: Free Press.

Singleton, Fred (1985) *A Short History of the Yugoslav Peoples*, Cambridge: Cambridge University Press.

——(1989) *A Short History of Finland*, Cambridge: Cambridge University Press.

Sluga, Glenda (1998) 'Identity, gender and the history of European nations and nationalisms', *Nations and Nationalism*, 4, 1, 87–111.

Smart, Barry (1993) *Postmodernity*, London and New York: Routledge.

Smelser, Neil (1962) *Theory of Collective Behaviour*, London: Routledge and Kegan Paul.

Smith, Anthony D. (1973a) '*Nationalism*, a trend report and annotated bibliography', *Current Sociology*, 21, 3, The Hague: Mouton.

——(1973b) *The Concept of Social Change*, Boston MA and London: Routledge and Kegan Paul.

——(1973c) 'Nationalism and religion: the role of reform movements in the genesis of Arab and Jewish nationalisms', *Archives de Sociologie des Religions*, 9, 35–55.

——(ed.) (1976) *Nationalist Movements*, London: Macmillan.

——(1979) *Nationalism in the Twentieth Century*, Oxford: Martin Robertson.

——(1981a) *The Ethnic Revival in the Modern World*, Cambridge: Cambridge University Press.

——(1981b) 'War and ethnicity: the role of warfare in the formation, self-images and cohesion of ethnic communities', *Ethnic and Racial Studies*, 4, 4, 375–97.

——(1983a) [1971] *Theories of Nationalism*, 2nd edn, London: Duckworth, and New York: Holmes and Meier.

——(1983b) 'Nationalism and classical social theory', *British Journal of Sociology*, XXXIV, 1, 19–38.

——(1984a) 'National identity and myths of ethnic descent', *Research in Social Movements, Conflict and Change*, 7, 95–130.

——(1984b) 'Ethnic persistence and national transformation', *British Journal of Sociology*, XXXV, 4, 452–61.

——(1986a) *The Ethnic Origins of Nations*, Oxford: Blackwell.

——(1986b) 'State-making and nation-building', in John Hall (ed.) *States in History*, Oxford: Blackwell, 228–63.

——(1988) 'The myth of the "modern nation" and the myths of nations', *Ethnic and Racial Studies*, 11, 1, 1–26.

——(1989) 'The origins of nations', *Ethnic and Racial Studies*, 12, 3, 340–67.

——(1990) 'Towards a Global Culture?', in Michael Featherstone (ed.) *Global Culture: Nationalism, Globalisation and Modernity*, London, Newbury Park CA and Delhi: Sage, 171–91.

——(1991) *National Identity*, Harmondsworth: Penguin.

——(1992a) 'Chosen peoples: why ethnic groups survive', *Ethnic and Racial Studies*, 15, 3, 436–56.

——(ed.) (1992b) *Ethnicity and Nationalism: International Studies in Sociology and Social Anthropology*, volume LX, Leiden: Brill.

——(1992c) 'Nationalism and the historians', in A. D. Smith (ed.) *Ethnicity and Nationalism: International Studies in Sociology and Social Anthropology*, volume LX, Leiden: Brill, 58–80.

——(1992d) 'National identity and the idea of European unity', *International Affairs*, 68, 1, 55–76.

——(1993) 'Art and nationalism in Europe', in J. C. H. Blom *et al.* (eds) *De Onmacht van het Grote: Cultuur in Europa*, Amsterdam: Amsterdam University Press, 64–80.

——(1994) 'The problem of national identity: ancient, medieval and modern?', *Ethnic and Racial Studies*, 17, 3, 375–99.

——(1995a) *Nations and Nationalism in a Global Era*, Cambridge: Polity Press.

——(1995b) 'Gastronomy or geology? The role of nationalism in the reconstruction of nations', *Nations and Nationalism*, 1, 1, 3–23.

——(1995c) 'Zionism and diaspora nationalism', *Israel Affairs*, 2, 2, 1–19.

——(1996a) 'The resurgence of nationalism? Myth and memory in the renewal of nations', *British Journal of Sociology*, XLVII, 4, 575–98.

——(1996b) 'Memory and modernity: reflections on Ernest Gellner's theory of nationalism', *Nations and Nationalism*, 2, 3, 371–88.

——(1997a) 'Nations and ethnoscapes', *Oxford International Review*, 8, 2, 11–18.

——(1997b) 'The Golden Age and national renewal', in Geoffrey Hosking and George Schöpflin (eds) *Myths and Nationhood*, London: Macmillan, 36–59.

Smith, Donald (ed.) (1974) *Religion and Political Modernisation*, New Haven CT: Yale University Press.

Smith, Wilfred (1965) *Modernisation of a Traditional Society*, London: Asia Publishing House.

Smooha, Sammy (1990) 'Minority status in an ethnic democracy: the status of the Arab minority in Israel', *Ethnic and Racial Studies*, 13, 3, 389–413.

Smooha, Sammy and Hanf, Theodor (1992) 'The diverse modes of conflict regulation in deeply divided societies', in A. D. Smith (ed.) *Ethnicity and Nationalism: International Studies in Sociology and Social Anthropology*, volume LX, Leiden: Brill, 26–47.

Snyder, Jack (1993) 'Nationalism and the crisis of the post-Soviet state', *Survival*, 35, 1, 5–26.

Snyder, Louis (1954) *The Meaning of Nationalism*, New Brunswick: Rutgers University Press.

South Bank Centre (1989) *La France: Images of Woman and Ideas of Nation, 1789–1989*, London: South Bank Centre.

Soysal, Yasemin (1994) *Limits of Citizenship: Migrants and Post-national Membership in Europe*, Chicago IL: University of Chicago Press.

——(1996) 'Changing citizenship in Europe: remarks on post-national membership and the national state', in David Cesarani and Mary Fulbrook (eds) *Citizenship, Nationality and Migration in Europe*, London and New York: Routledge.

Spillman, Lyn (1997) *Nation and Commemoration: Creating National Identities in the United States and Australia*, Cambridge: Cambridge University Press.

Stack, J. F. (ed.) (1986) *The Primordial Challenge: Ethnicity in the Contemporary World*, New York: Greenwood Press.

Stalin, Joseph (1936) *Marxism and the National and Colonial Question*, London: Lawrence and Wishart.

Stone, John (ed.) (1979) 'Internal colonialism', *Ethnic and Racial Studies*, 2, 3.

Subaratnam, Lakshmanan (1997) 'Motifs, metaphors and mythomoteurs: some reflections on medieval South Asian ethnicity', *Nations and Nationalism*, 3, 3, 397–426.

Sugar, Peter (ed.) (1980) *Ethnic Diversity and Conflict in Eastern Europe*, Santa Barbara CA: ABC Clio.

Tagil, Sven (ed.) (1995) *Ethnicity and Nation Building in the Nordic World*, London: Hurst & Co.

Talmon, Jacob (1980) *The Myth of the Nation and the Vision of Revolution*, London: Secker and Warburg.

Tamir, Yael (1993) *Liberal Nationalism*, Princeton NJ: Princeton University Press.

Taylor, David and Yapp, Malcolm (eds) (1979) *Political Identity in South Asia*, Dublin: Curzon Press.

Tcherikover, Victor (1970) *Hellenistic Civilisation and the Jews*, New York: Athenaeum.

Thaden, E. C. (1964) *Conservative Nationalism in Nineteenth-Century Russia*, Seattle WA: University of Washington Press.

Thompson, Leonard (1985) *The Political Mythology of Apartheid*, New Haven CT and London: Yale University Press.

Tilly, Charles (ed.) (1975) *The Formation of National States in Western Europe*, Princeton NJ: Princeton University Press.

Tipton, Leon (ed.) (1972) *Nationalism in the Middle Ages*, New York: Holt, Rinehart and Winston.

Tivey, Leonard (ed.) (1980) *The Nation-State*, Oxford: Martin Robertson.

Tomlinson, John (1991) *Cultural Imperialism: A Critical Introduction*, London: Pinter.

Tonkin, Elisabeth, McDonald, Maryon and Chapman, Malcolm (eds) (1989) *History and Ethnicity*, London and New York: Routledge.

Trevor-Roper, Hugh (1962) *Jewish and Other Nationalisms*, London: Weidenfeld and Nicolson.

Tudor, Henry (1972) *Political Myth*, London: Pall Mall Press.

Ullendorff, Edward (1973) *The Ethiopians: An Introduction to the Country and People*, 3rd edn, London: Oxford University Press.

van den Berghe, Pierre (1978) 'Race and ethnicity: a sociobiological perspective', *Ethnic and Racial Studies*, 1, 4, 401–11.

——(1979) *The Ethnic Phenomenon*, New York: Elsevier.

——(1988) 'Ethnicity and the sociobiology debate', in John Rex and David Mason (eds) *Theories of Ethnic and Race Relations*, Cambridge: Cambridge University Press, 246–63.

——(1995) 'Does race matter?', *Nations and Nationalism* I, 3, 357–68.

van der Veer, Peter (1994) *Religious Nationalism: Hindus and Muslims in India*, Berkeley CA: University of California Press.

Verdery, Katherine (1979) 'Internal colonialism in Austro-Hungary', *Ethnic and Racial Studies*, 2, 3, 378–99.

Viroli, Maurizio (1995) *For Love of Country: An Essay on Nationalism and Patriotism*, Oxford: Clarendon Press.

Vos, George de and Romanucci-Rossi, Lola (eds) (1975) *Ethnic Identity: Cultural Continuities and Change*, Chicago IL: University of Chicago Press.

Walby, Sylvia (1992) 'Woman and nation', in A. D. Smith (ed.) *Ethnicity and Nationalism: International Studies in Sociology and Social Anthropology*, volume LX, Leiden: Brill, 81–100; reprinted in Gopal Balakrishnan (ed.) (1996) *Mapping the Nation*, London and New York: Verso, 235–54.

Walek-Czernecki, M. T. (1929) 'Le rôle de la nationalité dans l'histoire de l'antiquité', *Bulletin of the International Committee of the Historical Sciences*, 2, 2, 305–20.

Waley, Daniel (1969) *The Italian City-Republics*, London: Weidenfeld and Nicolson.

Wallerstein, Immanuel (1965) 'Elites in French-speaking West Africa', *Journal of Modern African Studies*, 3, 1–33.

Wallman, Sandra (1988) 'Ethnicity and the boundary process in context', in John Rex and David Mason (eds) *Theories of Ethnic and Race Relations*, Cambridge: Cambridge University Press, 226–45.

Walzer, Michael (1985) *Exodus and Revolution*, New York: Basic Books.

Warner, Marina (1983) *Joan of Arc*, Harmondsworth: Penguin.

Warren, Bill (1980) *Imperialism, Pioneer of Capitalism*, New York: Monthly Review Press.

Webb, Keith (1977) *The Growth of Nationalism in Scotland*, Harmondsworth: Penguin.

Weber, Eugène (1979) *Peasants into Frenchmen: The Modernisation of Rural France, 1870–1914*, London: Chatto and Windus.

——(1991) *My France: Politics, Culture, Myth*, Cambridge MA: Harvard University Press.

Weber, Max (1948) *From Max Weber: Essays in Sociology*, eds Hans Gerth and C. Wright Mills, London: Routledge and Kegan Paul.

——(1968) *Economy and Society*, 3 vols, New York: Bedminster Press.

Webster, Bruce (1997) *Medieval Scotland: The Making of an Identity*, Basingstoke: The Macmillan Press.

Webster, Leslie and Backhouse, Jane (eds) (1991) *The Making of England: Anglo-Saxon Art and Culture, AD 600–900*, London: British Museum Press.

Wiberg, Hakan (1983) 'Self-determination as an international issue', in Ioann Lewis (ed.) *Nationalism and Self-Determination in the Horn of Africa*, London: Ithaca Press, 43–65.

Williams, Colin (1977) 'Non-violence and the development of the Welsh Language Society, 1962–74', *Welsh Historical Review*, 8, 26–55.

——(ed.) (1982) *National Separatism*, Cardiff: University of Wales Press.

Wilmsen, Edwin and McAllister, Patrick (eds) (1996) *The Politics of Difference: Ethnic Premises in a World of Power*, Chicago IL and London: University of Chicago Press.

Winter, Jay (1995) *Sites of Memory, Sites of Mourning: The Great War in European Cultural History*, Cambridge: Cambridge University Press.

Wiseman, D. J. (ed.) (1973) *Peoples of the Old Testament*, Oxford: Clarendon Press.

Worsley, Peter (1964) *The Third World*, London: Weidenfeld and Nicolson.

Yoshino, Kosaku (1992) *Cultural Nationalism in Contemporary Japan*, London and New York: Routledge.

Young, Crawford (1985) 'Ethnicity and the colonial and post- colonial state', in Paul Brass (ed.) *Ethnic Groups and the State*, London: Croom Helm, 57–93.

Yuval-Davis, Nira (1993) 'Gender and nation', *Ethnic and Racial Studies*, 16, 4, 621–32.

——(1997) *Gender and Nation*, London: Sage.

Yuval-Davis, Nira and Anthias, Floya (eds) (1989) *Woman-Nation-State*, London: Sage.

Zacek, Joseph (1969) 'Nationalism in Czechoslovakia', in Peter Sugar and Ivo Lederer (eds) *Nationalism in Eastern Europe*, Seattle WA and London: University of Washington Press, 166–206.

Zartmann, William (1964) *Government and Politics in Northern Africa*, New York: Praeger.

Zenner, Walter (1991) *Minorities in the Middle: A Cross-Cultural Analysis*, Albany NY: State University of New York Press.

Zernatto, Guido (1944) 'Nation: the history of a word', *Review of Politics*, 6, 351 66.

Zerubavel, Yael (1995) *Recovered Roots: Collective Memory and the Making of Israeli National Tradition*, Chicago IL and London: University of Chicago Press.

Zubaida, Sami (1978) 'Theories of nationalism', in G. Littlejohn, B. Smart, J. Wakeford and N. Yuval-Davis (eds) *Power and the State*, London: Croom Helm.

Index

Page references given in **bold** indicate a significant section on a particular subject in the text.